COLLECTOR'S REFERENCE AND VALUE GUIDE

KEITH LAUER & JULIE ROBINSON

COLLECTOR BOOKS
A Division of Schroeder Publishing Co., Inc.

Cover design by Beth Summers
Book design by Karen Smith
Photography by J.P. Robinson unless otherwise noted

Collector Books
P.O. Box 3009
Paducah, Kentucky 42002-3009

Contents

About the Authors

Keith Warren Lauer, the curator of the National Plastic Center and Museum of Leominster, is a native of Marietta, Ohio.

During WWII Lauer served as a combat infantryman with the 9th Infantry Division in Europe. After his combat service, he resumed his college education and in 1947 he graduated from Marietta College with a B.S. in business administration.

Following his graduation, Keith became associated with the Barker-Davis Machine Co., Inc. of Leominster, Massachusetts. That business had long been associated with the plastics industry beginning in the era of natural plastics. Lauer was employed there for 39 years. During that time he became an owner and president of the company.

Following his semi-retirement he pursued his interest in the history of the plastics industry and its artifacts. He entered local politics and served as a city council member for 14 years.

Lauer is a member of the American Plastics History Association, the Plastics Historical Society (England), the Plastics Pioneers Association, and the Antique Comb Collectors Club International. He is an emeritus member of the Society of Plastics Engineers, and a past president of the S.P.E. Pioneer Valley Section. Lauer also served the Leominster Historical Society as its president.

He resides in Leominster and is the father of a son and two daughters.

Julie Pelletier Robinson lives in Davidsville, Pennsylvania with her husband George and three of their four children. A native of Fayette, Maine, and long-time collector of antiques, in 1991 she enrolled at the Institute for the Study of Antiques and Collectibles in Emmaus, Pennsylvania. As a student, a required research paper began her involvement with celluloid.

Julie is a member of the the American Plastics History Association and the Pennsylvania State Antiques Association. A freelance writer/photographer with a primary focus on nineteenth century antiques, and natural, semi-synthetic and synthetic plastics, Julie frequently lectures on the subject of celluloid and the natural materials which it imitated.

Introduction

By Keith W. Lauer

Celluloid, not to be confused with cellulite, is truly the "grand-daddy of all plastics." Celluloid is the material of many desirable collections, unlike cellulite.

Celluloid was the patented name of cellulose nitrate, the first semi-synthetic plastic, and the name celluloid has evolved through popular use into the generic term for cellulose nitrate. The term celluloid shall be used in this work to identify this classic material which was commercially produced for over one hundred years, beginning in 1870.

Guide books for collectors have been recently printed for many types of plastics in general including celluloid, but this is the first attempt to produce an historically accurate account of the early American pyroxylin plastics industry and the collectible articles produced by the manufacturers thereof.

This work is an attempt to offer information in word and graphics that will help others share in the satisfaction of collecting and preserving some of the approximately 25,000 different products that have been made of celluloid since its development.

Information is provided about identification sources, developmental history, and preservation of celluloid items. The fullest satisfaction cannot be attained merely by accumulation of celluloid collectibles. Only by an understanding of the history, properties, preservation, uses, and variety of celluloid items can they be fully appreciated.

Collecting celluloid is a challenge, and the thrill of discovery is bound to come to the serious collector as he or she comes across the material in a form which is unknown and unexpected by the collector. Collectors will marvel that items of celluloid have endured so long in view of its flammability, abuse in children's play activity, and its fragility when produced in thin sections, as in blow-molded items.

This author has made his observations on celluloid from his location in Leominster, Massachusetts. Leominster is the pioneer plastic city with a background in the production of items made of horn, hooves, ivory, and tortoise shell, continuing through celluloid and into the modern synthetic materials. Leominster also has had four men of the community named to the Plastics Hall of Fame, which is housed in the recently opened National Plastics Center and Museum.

By Julie P. Robinson

I first became interested in researching celluloid in 1991 after receiving several small advertising premiums from my mother-in-law, Evelyn Robinson. The pieces had belonged to her parents during the early part of the twentieth century and held special sentimental significance. I sought to locate information on my small collection of early plastic goods and knew just where to find it.

At the time, I was a student at the Institute for the Study of Antiques and Collectibles in Emmaus, Pennsylvania. The tremendous research library at the Institute houses thousands of books on antiques and collectibles. To my disappointment, I discovered there were none written exclusively on the topic of celluloid. It had been featured insignificantly in a few minor categories on early advertising and toys, but overall the subject had been largely ignored.

Shortly thereafter, during the course of my studies, I was required to write a thesis on a subject of which I had little prior knowledge. Being well aware that pyroxylin plastic was a subject still widely unexplored by both the collector and scholar, I set to work gathering resources, only to find that very little information regarding celluloid and its inventor, John Wesley Hyatt, Jr., was readily available.

The quest for knowledge led me to contact Andra Behrendt, an Illinois collector of decorative celluloid boxes and albums. Andra's boundless enthusiasm for the subject and generosity in sharing her many resources were remarkable; she responded to my request for information by sending me a portion of her extensive collection and also providing me with several technical documents (in the form of related articles and book references) that I needed in order to get started on my research project. Furthermore, Andra put me in contact with Keith Lauer, historical archivist at the National Plastics Center and Museum in Leominster, Masschusetts.

A visit to Massachusetts in the summer of 1993 brought me to the National Plastics Center and Museum where Keith Lauer and I finally met face to face. His extensive knowledge regarding the matter of early plastics was indeed impressive, as was his personal collection of celluloid objects. I had never seen so many toys and novelties, utilitarian items, decorative goods, and advertising items assembled together in one place. They say "a first impression is a lasting one," and I must emphasize, it's true! I am still amazed at the extraordinary collection Mr. Lauer has accumulated throughout the years. In addition, the resource materials he has gathered while archivist of the N.P.C.M. provide numerous possibilities for a student of plastics history.

By the summer of 1995, I had finally gathered enough information to fulfill the I.S.A.C. thesis requirement. The story, "John Wesley Hyatt and the Invention of Celluloid," was published nationally in the June 19th edition of *AntiqueWeek*, a trade paper distributed by Mayhill Publications of Knightstown, Indiana. With this project behind me, it became obvious that Mr. Lauer and I should join forces to write an extensive work on the history and applications of the first commercially successful semi-synthetic thermoplastic – celluloid.

Perhaps the reason for celluloid's great success as a material had to do with the conservative approach with which the Hyatts marketed their product; carefully adapting and establishing celluloid as an alternative material for traditional substances before moving on to new applications. This is clearly evident with its establishment as a replacement for Vulcanite in denture plates, celluloid's primary use for the first five years. By 1875, when celluloid was introduced as an alternative for expensive luxury materials in fashion accessories, the impact of mass production was felt in both industry and consumerism.

Among the most significant changes were those felt in industries where traditional skills were replaced by the mass production of molded plastic articles. Craftsmen, who had been trained as horn and shell smiths soon found themselves in competition with machinery that mass produced items in minutes, when previously it had taken hours of skillful handiwork.

The social impact of celluloid's introduction as an imitation for expensive luxury materials was equally significant; it bridged the gap between the wealthy and the working classes. For the first time in history, all people could indulge in owning elegant looking jewelry and accessories, even if they couldn't afford the genuine article.

Celluloid was by far one of the most significant inventions of the nineteenth century. It gave birth to the modern plastics industry of the twentieth century, which today is continuing to advance our standard of living the world over; and just as celluloid found a multitude of uses from the late 1800s through the 1920s, modern plastics are finding useful applications in art, industry, consumerism, science, and medicine.

Early plastics are a wonderful and vast subject, a matter that deserves the respect and attention of serious antiques dealers and collectors. It is hoped that this book will further the appreciation for the material that had over 25,000 different applications ranging from the most personal of accessories – dentures – to the most influential social medium of the twentieth century – cinema film.

"The story of plastics does not end. To it there is no conclusion."

Reginald L. Wakeman, 1947

Acknowledgments

American Plastics History Assoc.
206 N. Mill Street
Chestertown, MD 21620

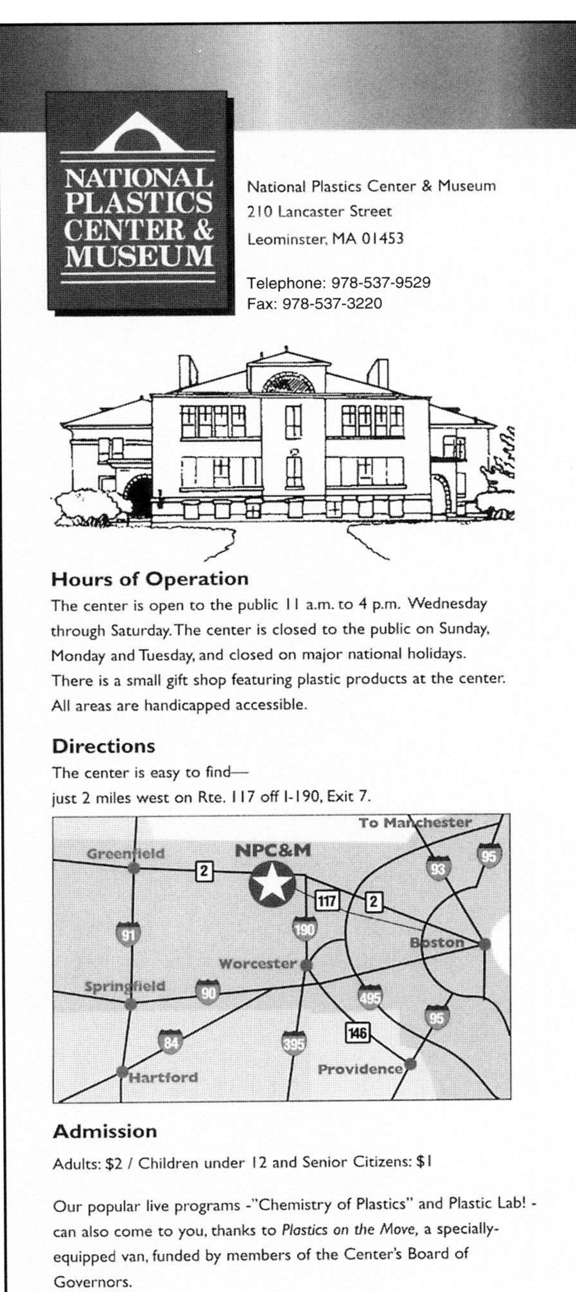

Supplemental resources and materials regarding the research for this project were graciously provided through many individuals and organizations. We would like to acknowledge the contributions of the following:

Isao Iwai

Bert Cohen

Joan Van Fleet

Koichi Sekiguchi

The Hagley Library

The Kramme Sisters

Dr. Melvin Wolk

Kay Beaulieu

Andra Behrendt

The Robinson Family

Jared Truscott

Lucille Mauro

Elizabeth Barclay

The Pelletier Family

John and Gail Dunn

MaryLou Holt

Reese Howe

John W. Hyatt, III

Helen D. Golubic

Cindy Orris

Terry Leffler

Dotty Maust

Rev. Charles Kelly

Diane Saylor

Christie Romero,
Jewelry Historian

William Winburn,
Dental Historian

Ellen T. Schroy

Harry L. Rinker Sr.

Harry L. Rinker, Jr.

Ben Z. Swanson, Jr., D.D.S

M. Phil – Director,
National Museum of
Dentistry, Baltimore

Keith Lauer – Archivist,
National Plastics Center
and Museum

Allegheny Antiques Gallery,
Windbur, PA

Karen's Memory Lane
Antiques, Jennerstown, PA

Somerset Antiques Gallery,
Somerset, PA

Diane and Ernie Hollsopple,
Auctioneers, Hollsopple, PA

Merle Mishler, Auctioneer,
Davidsville, PA

History of Celluloid

John Wesley Hyatt and the Invention of Celluloid

John Wesley Hyatt, Jr. was born in Starkey, Yates County, New York, on Nov. 28, 1837, the son of John W. Hyatt, Sr. and Anne Gleason Hyatt. (John Sr. had been named after the famous Methodist Evangelist John Wesley and was ardently religious.) The Hyatts had a family of seven children; three girls and four boys, of which John Jr. was the next to youngest.

In the village of Starkey the Hyatts owned and operated the town's blacksmith shop. As a child, John Jr. helped with the family business and at an early age became fascinated with machinery and its operation. In school he was especially bright, excelling in mathematics.

When John was 15 years old, his parents sent him to Eddystown Seminary where they hoped he would prepare for a life in the ministry. John, however, had other ideas and a year later, dropped out of seminary and headed west toward the bustling city of Chicago where his older brother Isaiah had settled.

John W. Hyatt – inventor of Celluloid, father of the modern plastics industry

By 1854 at the age of 17, John was in Illinois working as a printer's apprentice. He stayed there for several years, often finding work with the help of his older brother Isaiah, who was an editor living in nearby Rockford. While in Illinois, Hyatt met and married a young Chicago woman named Julia D. Philleo.

On Feb.19, 1861, J.W. Hyatt was issued a patent for his first invention, a kitchen knife sharpener. On June 17, 1862, the ambitious 24-year-old received his second patent, #35,652 Improvement In Knife Or Scissor Sharpener, based on the invention he had patented the year before.

Shortly thereafter, Hyatt and his wife returned to the Albany, New York, area where he found work as a journeyman printer. It was sometime in 1863 that John saw a newspaper advertisement that caught his attention and sparked his creative interest. Phelan and Collander, the nation's largest billiard supply company, was offering the handsome reward of $10,000 to the first person who could create a suitable ivory substitute for use in billiard balls.[1-3]

Fueled by the promised reward money, Hyatt accepted the challenge. Working in the print shop by day and experimenting nights and weekends, he diligently sought to develop an ivory substitute and become the winner of the cash reward. In September of 1865, Hyatt made application for a patented process of manufacturing billiard balls using a combination of shellac and ivory/bone dust, layered over a core of wound fiber. When the patent was granted on October 10, 1865 (#50,359), he took action to protect his interest; within a few months he and his trusted friend Peter Kinnear formed the Hyatt Billiard Ball Company.[4] Together they developed machinery and manufacturing techniques for the production of wound fiber core and shellac composition billiard balls. The year was 1866.[4]

A short time after this development, personal tragedy struck the Hyatt household; Julia, John's 26-year-old wife, contracted pneumonia and died on October 9, 1867, leaving behind her grieving 29-year-old husband.

Undaunted by his loss, Hyatt continued to experiment in hopes of improving on his invention. Since his billiard balls lacked the characteristics and density of true ivory, he continued to experiment with familiar materials such as sawdust, paper flock, gum shellac, and varnish. Over the course of time, he successfully developed a composition material that was patented on April 14, 1868 (Pat. #76,765), Improvement In Compositions For Billiard Balls and Other Articles.

Hyatt also developed a pressed wood composition that had potential as a molding material. With the help of his older brother Isaiah, he formed a small family business which would profit from the substance. In 1868, along with younger brother Charles, the Hyatt Mfg. Co. was established at 29 Quackenbush St. in Albany for the production of pressed composition dominoes and checkers.[5-7]

Meanwhile John continued his job as a printer, while spending as much time as possible in his search to invent artificial ivory. As with many wonderful inventions, it was an accidental discovery that lead to his eventual success.

While working in the print shop one morning, Hyatt reached for the collodion bottle, only to find that the solution had tipped over and spilled.[8] Expecting to clean up a sticky mess, what he discovered instead was a dried piece of solid collodion about the size and thickness of his thumbnail. John observed that the density of the material resembled that of the ivory he had so earnestly been trying to duplicate. Realizing the significance in his findings, he exclaimed "Eureka!" at his discovery. It was the breakthrough Hyatt needed and from that day forward, he turned his full attention toward experimenting with solid and liquid collodion.

Hyatt set to work developing a billiard ball that consisted of a solid center made from paper flock and shellac, coated with a thick layer of collodion mixed with bone and ivory dust. Although there were obvious drawbacks with the new ball, Hyatt patented his process (U.S. Pat. # 88,634) and began production in a small factory he called the Albany Billiard Ball Co.[9-11]

Around this time, problems associated with the new billiard balls began to surface. Hyatt had received a letter from a billiard saloon proprietor in Colorado who shared his concerns: It seems that more than once a lighted cigar had come in contact with the balls, causing a serious fire. He also mentioned that occasionally the violent contact of the balls resulted in a loud BANG!, like that of a percussion guncap. The saloon operator stated that he did not care so much about it, but that instantly every man in the room pulled a gun.

By 1868 the enterprise, located at Grand and Plain Streets, was in full operation. Peter Kinnear, Hyatt's associate from the Hyatt Billiard Ball Co., was put in charge of the factory operations so that he could devote himself to improving upon his invention.

Over time Hyatt developed a method of casting a celluloid composition material into a mold; he also developed machinery to turn the balls on, making them a perfect sphere. Hyatt's Improved Pool Balls were packaged in wooden boxes that featured a trademark illustrated on the lid.

In his quest to find solutions to the problems associated with the use of cellulose nitrate, Hyatt continued to work diligently, patenting three different improvements on solid collodion between April and May of 1869. During this time he consulted with his older brother Isaiah, convincing him to leave Chicago and return to Albany in order to assist with the experimentation.

Several challenges lay ahead for John and Isaiah; they needed to find a solvent that would make solid collodion pliable, and they also needed to develop methods for making the resulting compound moldable. Isaiah had heard of others who had experimented with camphor, the white crystalline resin derived from the camphora evergreen tree, and he suggested that John give it a try.[12-15]

Hyatt combined collodion and camphor under normal conditions, then applied heat to the compound. What resulted was immediate success in making the mass soft enough to mold or cast. Hyatt had finally ascertained the methods that would result in the world's first commercially successful semi-synthetic thermoplastic.

The Hyatt brothers immediately registered their discovery with the United States Patent Office and on June 15, 1869, received a joint patent for the fundamental invention of pyroxylin plastic. It was titled "Improved Method Of Making Solid Collodion" U.S.P. #91,341.

Printers frequently used a bottled liquid product to protect their hands while working. Commercially the solution was available as "New Skin," a liquid court plaster, but technically it was collodion, a mixture of cellulose nitrate and ethyl alcohol. When brushed on the hands, liquid collodion dried into an elastic, waterproof film which created an invisible coating. It worked like a second skin that protected the hands of printers from ink and paper cuts.

This photograph was taken around the turn of the century at the Albany Billiard Ball Company at Grand and Plain St. in the city's south end. The manufacture of Hyatt's Improved Ball began at the factory around 1875 and later in March of 1877, the company became an official licensee of the Celluloid Mfg. Company of Newark.

Isaiah proceeded to take samples of the solid collodion material to the American Hard Rubber Co. in hopes of interesting them in the new substance. They responded by sending their employee, Professor Charles A. Seeley to the Hyatts' workshop in Albany.[16]

When Professor Seeley arrived in Albany, the Hyatt brothers conducted their process of manufacturing a solid piece of pyroxylin plastic by mixing pulp collodion with camphor and applying heat and pressure. Seeley, a trained chemist, was impressed with the invention, but not the method of manufacture. The inflammability of cellulose nitrate posed a serious hazard to the Hyatt brothers.

Professor Seeley kindly advised them that "if accidentally or otherwise they were to apply a little too high a temperature, the quantity with which they were dealing would inevitably destroy them, along with the building and adjacent property."[17]

Seeley then suggested to the Hyatts that their material had potential as a replacement for hardened rubber in the manufacture of dental plate blanks. Since solid collodion was clear in its original form, various fillers and pigments could be added to imitate the natural color of the gums. Taking Seeley's advice, the Hyatt brothers set to work developing a market for their moldable pyroxylin plastic. Fortunately, the timing was just right for the introduction of this new material, which they decided to call Celluloid.

For years hardened rubber had been used successfully as a denture blank material; however, when the Goodyear Dental Vulcanite Co. purchased the patent rights, they began to impose expensive fees upon the substance.[18] In addition, the rising cost of rubber, due to the popularity of the bicycle craze and the demand for this commodity for tires, made Vulcanite an ever increasing expense for dentists who owned large practices. Thus the stage was set for the introduction of Celluloid dentures.

1869 was a busy year for the Hyatt brothers. Charles was overseeing production of game pieces at the Embossing Co.; Isaiah left Illinois and returned to Albany in order to help with the newly patented plastic material and 31-year-old John, widowed two years earlier, remarried on July 21st to Anna E. Taft. All the while, John W. and Isaiah S. Hyatt continued to work on perfecting the recipe for their new semi-synthetic thermoplastic and on July 12, 1870 – U.S. Pat. #105,338 "Improvement In Treating And Molding Pyroxylin," was issued to the brothers. The three claims of this patent were: 1. The grinding of pyroxylin (nitrocellulose) into a pulp. 2. The use of finely ground camphor added to the pulp and then heated to activate the solvent action. 3. The use of pressure during the heating and cooling process.

It was Isaiah Hyatt who named the new invention "Celluloid." Two different explanations of the naming exist:

National Plastics Center and Museum

This German-made machine was imported into the United States during the 1920s. It was designed for molding celluloid denture plate blanks.

National Plastics Center and Museum

Celluloid Hyatt Pocket Billiard Balls with original box manufactured at the Albany Billiard Ball Co., Albany, New York. $300.00+.

one is that the word is a contraction for "colloid of cellulose." Another states that it is a contraction of the word "cellulose" and the Greek word "oid" which means "like."

In 1870 the Hyatt brothers established the Albany Dental Plate Co. at 151 Eagle St., for the manufacture of Celluloid denture blanks.[19] To add credibility the new material, Samuel S. White, the well-respected publisher of "Dental Cosmos" and president of the S.S. White Dental Co. in Philadelphia, endorsed the product and became its sole distributor. Flasks and heating machines were invented and through trial and error, pyroxylin plastic became a successful alternative for hard rubber and gutta percha in denture base production.[20]

Ben Swanson – Trade cards; W. Winburn – Denture

A completed celluloid upper plate with porcelain teeth. Both trade cards offered patrons the opportunity to purchase celluloid dentures.

> Several pages of testimonials are found in an 1878 Celluloid Mfg. Co. Instruction Manual for dentists. The following are excerpts from the booklet:
>
> *"I have used celluloid as a base for artificial teeth for several years with great satisfaction. It is durable, and does not warp or change its form, provided the conditions are strictly complied with. My patients are delighted with it." — I.J.Wetherbee, DDS, Boston, MA, Mar. 23, 1878*
>
> *"Celluloid is an excellent base for artificial teeth and has given excellent satisfaction to 200 of my patients who are wearing it. I use it for artificial palates and noses, and for the latter it is very much better than rubber." — A.S.Dudley, MD, Salem, MA., Mar. 20, 1878*
>
> *"I think celluloid the best base for artificial teeth I ever worked, and I have used everything. I can make a set of teeth in the shortest time of anything I ever worked, and in half the time I can with rubber. It is the strongest plate also." — J.I. Fosdick, LaPorte, IN., Feb. 12, 1878*
>
> *"Do you feel satisfied with celluloid?, I seem to hear you ask. I answer that I would not give $5.00 for a rubber license. I would not have rubber in my own mouth on account of the heated feeling. I have broken two rubber plates in the time I have worn one of celluloid. It is healthful, cleanly, strong, unchangeable and beautiful". — B.B. Chandler, Boston, MA, Feb. 11, 1878*
>
> *"I esteem celluloid of such inestimable value to the profession, that I should regard it as criminal not to give my unqualified testimony in its favor, which, after using it for more than three years, it affords me pleasure to do. After overcoming a few difficulties at first, I like it better every plate I make, and consider it superior to every other plastic material for dental plates." — D.Burrill, Freeport, IL, Feb. 8, 1878*
>
> *"Three years since I took celluloid in hand, I have used it ever since in rather a large practice. I have no trouble in working it – less in fact than in using rubber. I would not return to the use of rubber if I could get license free, and get the rubber thrown in. Having been 40 years in a large practice, I know what I am talking about." — D.D. Dickinson, MD, Boston, MA, Feb. 4, 1878*

Courtesy Ben Z. Swanson, Jr., DDS; M.Phil, Director Museum of Dentistry, Baltimore

Advertising Celluloid as a use for denture material to the public took place through the medium of trade cards. Although rare, on occasion a card can be found that mentions the use of this material. Harvard Dental Parlor of Boston and Queen City Dentist of Cincinnati were two such patrons of celluloid as an alternative material for dentures, the cost ranging $5.00 – $10.00.

The Pyroxylin Plastics Industry in America

By late 1872, Isaiah successfully convinced several wealthy New York capitalists, Joseph Larocque, Tracey Edson, and Marshall Lefferts, to back the new plastic material. Lefferts, the primary financial investor[21], was especially attracted to the possibilities of celluloid, as it had unlimited potential as a molding material.

In the winter of 1872 – 1873, the Hyatts moved to Newark, New Jersey, and established the Celluloid Manufacturing Company in a five-story brick building on Mechanic St. Employing 150 workers, they commenced the production of raw celluloid stock in block, sheet, and rod form. In 1873, Celluloid became a registered trade name with the U.S. Patent Office; exclusive rights for its use were granted to the Hyatts' and the Celluloid Manufacturing Company.

Two years later in 1875, a devastating fire caused Hyatt to relocate his plastics works to the outskirts of Newark. The Celluloid Mfg. Company set up shop in an old cradle factory and the production of celluloid resumed. The owners also began construction of a large complex of brick buildings in the vicinity of Broad and Ferry streets, adjacent to the old cradle factory. This site later became the heart of Newark's industrial district.

Throughout the 1870s, an array of utilitarian and ornamental applications for celluloid unfolded as the Hyatt Brothers improved on production methods and machinery for their wonderful pyroxylin plastic. One of celluloid's greatest assets was its ability to successfully imitate expensive luxury materials. Since it was clear in its original state, various dyes and fillers could be added during the production process, making celluloid a remarkable imitation of expensive ivory, tortoise shell, coral, jet, and amber.

In the year 1878, Isaiah traveled to Paris where he started the French Celluloid Company. When he returned to America in the early 1880s, the brothers turned their attention to developing a more efficient method of purifying the water used in the production of celluloid.[22] Together they established the Hyatt Pure Water Company in 1881, patenting their unique filtering process in 1884. Sadly, it was shortly after this that the collective genius of the Hyatt brothers abruptly ended. Isaiah died in March of 1885, leaving John to continue the work alone.

The success of celluloid as a quality imitation material spawned tremendous growth within the infant plastics industry. In spite of its dangerously flammable nature, by the mid 1880s several companies were in business producing pyroxylin thermoplastics, identical in composition to celluloid, but marketed under their own registered trade names. For more information on the history of the plastics industry see the section titled The Big Four and Ill-fated Fifth on page 15.

Patent battles ensued between Hyatt and those who imitated his inventions. Companies which started with inexperienced help frequently manufactured inferior products or due to the ignorance of the dangerous materials used in manufacture, burned to the ground. Even the Celluloid Manufacturing Company experienced several devastating fires, but they always recovered and went on to become the most important manufacturer of plastics in history.

Between 1872 and 1880, 16 different companies were licensed by the Celluloid Manufacturing Company for the production and distribution of various finished goods and novelties made from the new manmade plastic. The following is a list of those companies, their finished celluloid product, and the date they were licensed.

Oct.	01, 1872	Samuel S. White – Celluloid Dental Plate Blanks
Feb.	12, 1873	Celluloid Harness and Trimming Co. – Martingale Rings
Jan.	26, 1874	Edward C. Penfield – Truss Pads
Nov.	20, 1874	Meriden Cutlery Co. – Knife Handles
Nov.	21, 1874	Isaiah Hyatt and The Celluloid Brush Co. – Dresserware
Sept.	01, 1875	Emery Wheel Co. – Emery Wheels
Sept.	18, 1875	Spencer Optical Mfg. Co. – Eyeglass Frames
Dec.	22, 1875	Celluloid Novelty Co. – Collars and Fancy Goods
Mar.	01, 1877	Albany Billiard Ball Co. – Hyatt Improved Ball
Mar.	09, 1878	Celluloid Waterproof Cuff and Collar Co.
Oct.	23, 1878	Celluloid Hat and Trimming Co.
Oct.	31, 1878	Celluloid Fancy Goods Co. – Finished Novelties
Nov.	30, 1878	Celluloid Shoe Protector Co.
Dec.	12, 1878	Celluloid Piano Key Co. – Piano Keys
Apr.	01, 1879	Celluloid Veneer Co. – Sheet Veneer
Mar.	01, 1880	Celluloid Surgical Instrument Co. – Handles

Several other companies were also licensed to produce and distribute finished articles with plastic supplied by the Newark-based manufacturing company. Although dates are not available, the list includes:

The Celluloid Show Case Co. – Veneers
J.B.Oelkers – Fancy Goods
Denison Brothers Organ Stop Co. – Organ Pulls and Knobs
The Celluloid Letter Co. – Die Cut Letters and Numbers
The Celluloid Stereotype Co.
The Celluloid Corset and Clasp Co. – Waterproof Boning and Clasps
The Celluloid Varnish Co.

Executives and employees of the Celluloid Manufacturing Company of Newark, New Jersey, during the early 1870s.

This illustration shows the Celluloid Manufacturing Company's facility in Newark.

Andra Behrendt/NPCM

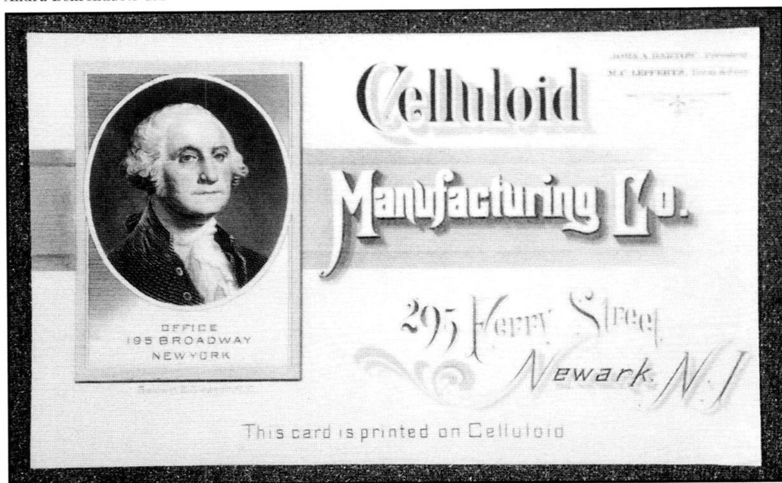

This Celluloid Manufacturing Company business card, produced by Baldwin and Gleason, on imitation ivory grained celluloid sheet, bears the name of Marshall Lefferts, primary financial investor for the Celluloid Manufacturing Company of Newark, New Jersey.

Photograph Courtesy of John W. Hyatt, III.

The gold Perkin Medal was awarded to John Wesley Hyatt at the age of 77 by the Society of Chemical Industry, May, 1914.

John W. Hyatt continued his efforts to improve the methods of manufacturing celluloid and went on to develop a number of other significant inventions relating to its production. In addition to the water purification process, introduced in 1881, he also devised a type of roller bearing to reduce friction on machinery and moving parts. As a result, he founded the Hyatt Roller Bearing Company of Harrison, New Jersey, which later became a division of General Motors. By the turn of the twentieth century, Hyatt was further engaged in the development of several new machines and methods to advance industry.

In 1914, the Society of Chemical Industry recognized the 77-year-old inventor by awarding him the solid gold Perkin Medal for his outstanding contributions to the field of industry and applied chemistry. This was indeed an honor, as in reality John W. Hyatt was actually a self-taught inventor rather than a scientist with a learned understanding of chemical theory.

Other Hyatt inventions included a machine for turning billiard balls in 1870; a machine for making slate blackboards in 1875; a substance using bone and silica, called Bonislate, which was used in billiard balls and knife handles, in 1878; a method for solidifying hardwoods for use in bowling balls, golf heads, and mallets, in 1878; a sewing machine capable of sewing 50 rows of stitches simultaneously (used for machine belting and to manufacture mattresses) in 1900; a machine for cold rolling and straightening steel shafting in 1901 and in 1989 – 1901, a sugar cane mill designed to extract juice more efficiently than those presently used.

On May 10, 1920, John W. Hyatt died of heart failure at his home in Short Hills, NJ. He was 82 years old and left behind two sons, Ralph and Charles, and his wife of 50 years, Anna Taft Hyatt. Overall, Hyatt received 238 patents issued in his name, with 77 of those directly relating to the manufacture of celluloid.

In 1973 the Billiard Congress of America recognized Hyatt for his outstanding contribution to the sport by inducting him into their Hall of Fame. In 1992, with the opening of the National Plastics Center and Museum, Hyatt was inducted into its Plastics Pioneers Hall of Fame. In 1995 the John Wesley Hyatt Society was established for the purpose of raising annual financial support for N.P.C.M.

The Big Four and Ill-fated Fifth

Celluloid, Arlington, Viscoloid, Fiberloid, and American Zylonite

Development of the Pyroxylin Plastic Industry in the U.S.

Any account of the development of the cellulose nitrate industry in this country must include references to the early work done in England and how it relates to our American effort. A quote from *Landmarks of the Plastics Industry* states:

"The history of the plastic industry, like that of many others, consists mainly of long periods of gradual progress, relieved every now and then by a sudden leap forward."

As we've explored the development of the early pyroxylin plastics industry, this truth has become more obvious. One man's efforts were built upon by the next and after many years of trial and error a successful new material – celluloid – was born.

It is sometimes difficult to note the year a new material was discovered, developed, or invented. Would the date be that of first experiment, formal announcement, commercial production, or introduction into the market economy?

John Eklund, curator of the Department of the History of Science, National Museum of American History, Smithsonian Institution has noted:

"These dates are somewhat arbitrary since few inventions really occur in a single year. At the least there is a development phase when some form of the polymer product exists but the processes are not yet fully worked out; the formulation is usually not the same as when the product is being made in market quantities." ...and so it is with celluloid. Therefore, the authors have chosen to date the material by the time of first production and general availability.

Cellulose Nitrate and Parkesine

Experimentation in the field of nitrocellulose had been conducted by Schonbein, Pelouse, and other Europeans interested in chemistry and invention during the early 1800s. Most of these pioneers directed their efforts toward the use of nitrocellulose as an explosive, or as collodion for use in photography. However during the early 1860s in Birmingham, England, there lived a metallurgist turned inventor whose name was Alexander Parkes.

Parkes managed to use cellulose nitrate along with various oils and solvents as a moldable plastic substance. He called his invention Parkesine and proceeded to fashion a variety of small novelty items from the material. In 1862 a variety of Parkesine novelties, combs, buttons, boxes, and other products, were displayed at the International Exhibition in London and also at the Paris Universal Exhibition. Parkes was awarded an honorary medal for excellence of product and the *Birmingham Daily Mail* hailed Parkesine as "A Wonderful Substance." In 1865 Alexander Parkes was granted a patent for his semi-synthetic plastic material.

Parkes believed that he could produce his plastic substance quickly and at a very low price. Between the years 1864 and 1866 he formed the Parkesine Company Ltd. and proceeded to manufacture his plastic material at the factory of George Spill, a waterproof cloth manufacturer, in Hackney Wick, London. Spill's brother Daniel became an associate of Parkes, learning the art of making pyroxylin compounds and eventually becoming managing director of the firm.[23]

Unfortunately, in an attempt to exploit Parkesine, production methods at the factory did not include the purest form of raw materials; unrefined cellulose fiber and reclaimed solvents were used in order to manufacture the product as inexpensively and quickly as possible. The result was an uncured finished product that was a commercial failure.[24] Articles made of this cheaply produced Parkesine warped, discolored, and broke easily and by 1868, the Parkesine Company Ltd. was out of business.

Celluloid

Near the time of the Parkesine failure, John Wesley Hyatt, an Albany, New York printer and inventor, accepted the challenge of the nation's largest billiards supplier, Phelan and Collander, to invent a suitable material for replacing ivory in the manufacture of billiard balls; the company offered the impressive prize of $10,000 for the accomplishment. History does not record that Hyatt ever received any money from Phelan and Collander; however he did invent a method of producing billiard balls and in so doing, introduced a material that had been continuously manufactured for the past 130 years.

The material, named Celluloid by John and his older brother Isaiah Smith Hyatt, was the first commercially successful semi-synthetic pyroxylin thermoplastic. In 1870, the Hyatt brothers, at the suggestion of Charles A. Seeley, formed the Albany Dental Plate Company for the purpose of making and marketing celluloid denture blanks.

For detailed information concerning the applications of celluloid, see the section titled John Wesley Hyatt and the Invention of Celluloid on page 8.

The Celluloid Manufacturing Company, 1872 – 1890

Meanwhile, Isaiah Hyatt convinced several wealthy investors to back the new plastic material, and in the winter of 1872–1873, they moved to Newark, NJ where the Celluloid Manufacturing Company was established on Mechanic Street. During this time, the Hyatts were also issued a patent for the first injection molding machine for plastics. In 1873 the word Celluloid was registered as the pyroxylin plastic's official trade name.[25]

The Celluloid Manufacturing Company produced and supplied cellulose nitrate plastic stock to a number of establishments that were licensed to use the Celluloid trade name as a prefix to their particular product or finished article. The gradual granting of these licenses served to test the acceptability of celluloid for a variety of products and also to spur the creation of new uses, with little or no risk to the Celluloid Mfg. Co. Of the many licensees, several prospered while others failed, but nevertheless, celluloid became established as a reputable product. For a complete list of licensees and their specialties, see page 12.

Competition in Pyroxylin Plastics

The gradual successes of the Celluloid firm did not go unnoticed. By the 1880s, the infant plastics industry had begun to expand, and serious competitors were beginning to enter the picture. However, before we set the stage for the development of American pyroxylin plastics, let's first return to England and take an objective look at the events surrounding the failure of Parkesine.

Xylonite and Ivoride

After the closing of the Parkesine Works, Daniel Spill, the former associate of Alexander Parkes, made his reentry into the field of plastics. In 1869 around the same time Hyatt was applying for patents related to his pyroxylin plastic, Spill reformulated the Parkesine recipe using a purer form of raw materials. He named the resulting pyroxylin plastic substance Xylonite and registered his enterprise (situated on the premises of the former Parkesine Works and his brother's waterproofing business) as the Xylonite Company. However his product fared no better than Parkesine, perhaps because of skeptical consumers, and by 1874 the company collapsed.

Undaunted by this failure, Spill moved to a new site in Homerton and established the Daniel Spill Co. for the manufacture of Xylonite and Ivoride, an imitation ivory version of Xylonite.

In 1876 Spill made an agreement with L.P. Merriam, who built a small factory next door to the Xylonite Company, with the intention of manufacturing finished articles of pyroxylin plastic. By 1879 Spill and Merriam had merged their two businesses to become the British Xylonite Company, Ltd. Business was slow for the first several years, but in 1885 British Xylonite joined forces with Lewis L. Hyatt (no relation to the American inventor of celluloid), who had been marketing waterproof linen collars and cuffs in France. From that time forward, business for British Xylonite improved; however a devastating fire caused the production of pyroxylin plastic to be resumed in Suffolk in 1887.

However, the story of Xylonite does not end there because a complicated patent situation regarding Daniel Spill and John Hyatt during the early 1870s had a direct impact on the American pyroxylin plastics industry.

Spill vs. Hyatt

In the year 1875, Daniel Spill filed suit against the Celluloid Manufacturing Company for alleged patent infringement by Hyatt. The case, which accused Hyatt of purloining the use of camphor as a plasticizer, came before the Honorable Judge C.J. Blatchford in the U.S. Circuit Court for the Southern District of New York. After five harrowing years of litigation, in 1880 Judge Blatchford reached a decision in favor of Daniel Spill. This victory opened a door of opportunity for Spill to profit, and he sold his Xylonite patents to Leroy L. Brown of Massachusetts, owner of the Graylock Paper Mills.

Under license of Spill and British Xylonite, Leroy L. Brown formed the American Zylonite Company in Adams, Massachusetts, in 1881.[26] Two years later in 1883, the first American Zylonite products were commercially introduced including combs, brushes, waterproof linens, and small novelties.[27]

Celluloid Absorbs Zylonite

In 1884 however, a turn of events led Judge Blatchford to reverse his previous court decision; it seemed that Daniel Spill had imitated Alexander Parkes' invention of Parkesine concerning the use of camphor as a plasticizer in the manufacture of pyroxylin plastic – the very thing that Spill was accusing Hyatt of doing.[28] With the decision reversed in favor of Hyatt, Spill was legally defeated. He left America, returning to England where he died of diabetes a few year later in 1887.

On Jan. 1,1891, the Celluloid Manufacturing Company changed its name to the Celluloid Company when it absorbed several of the small licensed firms in Newark, as well as the financially struggling American Zylonite Co. of Adams, Massachusetts.

Celanese Corporation

The Celluloid Company continued to manufacture pyroxylin plastics from their Newark-based factories throughout the first two decades of the twentieth century. It was acquired in the late 1920s by the Celanese Corporation.

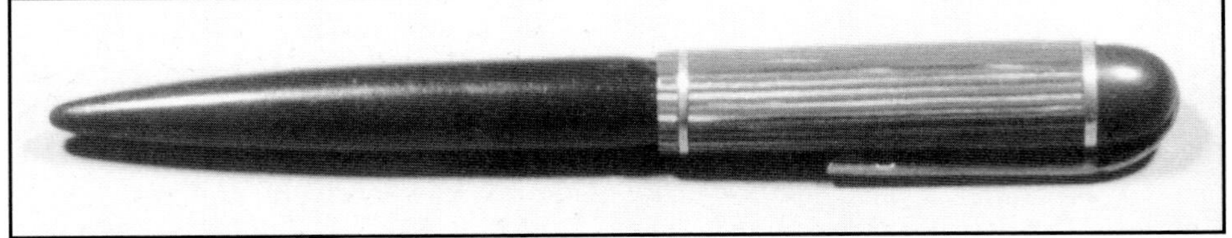

This Eversharp Skyliner fountain pen was designed by Henry Dreyfuss of Celanese Corporation. It was a best seller for the firm throughout the 1940s. Produced in a variety of colors and metal combinations and made of two-tone striped and solid celluloid, it is believed to be the last Eversharp pen manufactured from domestic pyroxylin plastic.

The Celanese Corporation of America was formed in 1918 by two Swiss brothers, Henri and Cecile Dreyfuss, who had been working for the British government during WWI manufacturing cellulose acetate dope to coat the wings of airplanes. After Hyatt's death in 1920, Celanese gained controlling stock in the Celluloid Corporation, finally acquiring it completely in 1927. The Celluloid Division of Celanese was active in the manufacture of vanity and dresser set articles throughout the latter half of the 1920s and into the 1930s, giving the tradename Arch Amerith to the line of pyroxylin plastic articles.

The merger of Celluloid Corporation and Celanese was completed in 1941 and the new title Plastics Division, Celanese Corp. of America was adopted in 1947. After having made celluloid in the Newark plant for over 77 years, the Celanese Corporation ceased production of pyroxylin plastic in 1949 and in 1950 they dropped the celluloid tradename.

Arlington Company, 1895 – 1915

The string of events leading to DuPont's entry into plastics begins with the introduction of the Merchant's Manufacturing Company and a pyroxylin plastic material they called Pasbosene. The company was founded by a group of Newark businessmen in 1881, who sought to break into the infant plastics industry. They had little knowledge of how to make cellulose nitrate however, and their product was commercially unsuccessful.

In 1883 the Merchant's Manufacturing Company merged with the Joseph R. France Co. of Plainfield, New Jersey, and reorganized under the name Cellonite Company. France had been nitrating cellulose since 1878, and although he had little knowledge of the manufacture of plastics, he did know how to make nitrocellulose. In 1886, with an experienced chemist on board, the Cellonite Company relocated to a small factory in Arlington, New Jersey, and proceeded to manufacture a better quality of pyroxylin plastic, which they called Cellonite.

In 1887, the Cellonite facility was destroyed by a devastating explosion and fire, a serious hazard associated with the manufacture of highly flammable cellulose nitrate plastics. The following year however, a new plant was built and the company reorganized for the production of pyroxylin plastic renamed Pyralin. The name of their firm was the Arlington Manufacturing Company.

Business was slow and competition from the Celluloid Company stiff, but an odd twist of events in 1891 served to establish the Arlington company as Celluloid's main competitor. After the Celluloid Company ruthlessly put American Zylonite out of business, the Arlington Manufacturing Company hired a large number of displaced Zylonite employees. Many of these workers had a great deal of experience in the pyroxylin plastics industry that had once flourished in the Adams plant, and as a result the new workers and supervisors were a great asset to the Arlington Manufacturing Company.

In 1893 a separate company was formed for the manufacture of Pyralin collars and cuffs and a factory built adjacent to the plastics plant. As the reputation of Pyralin grew, production increased and in 1895 the two compa-

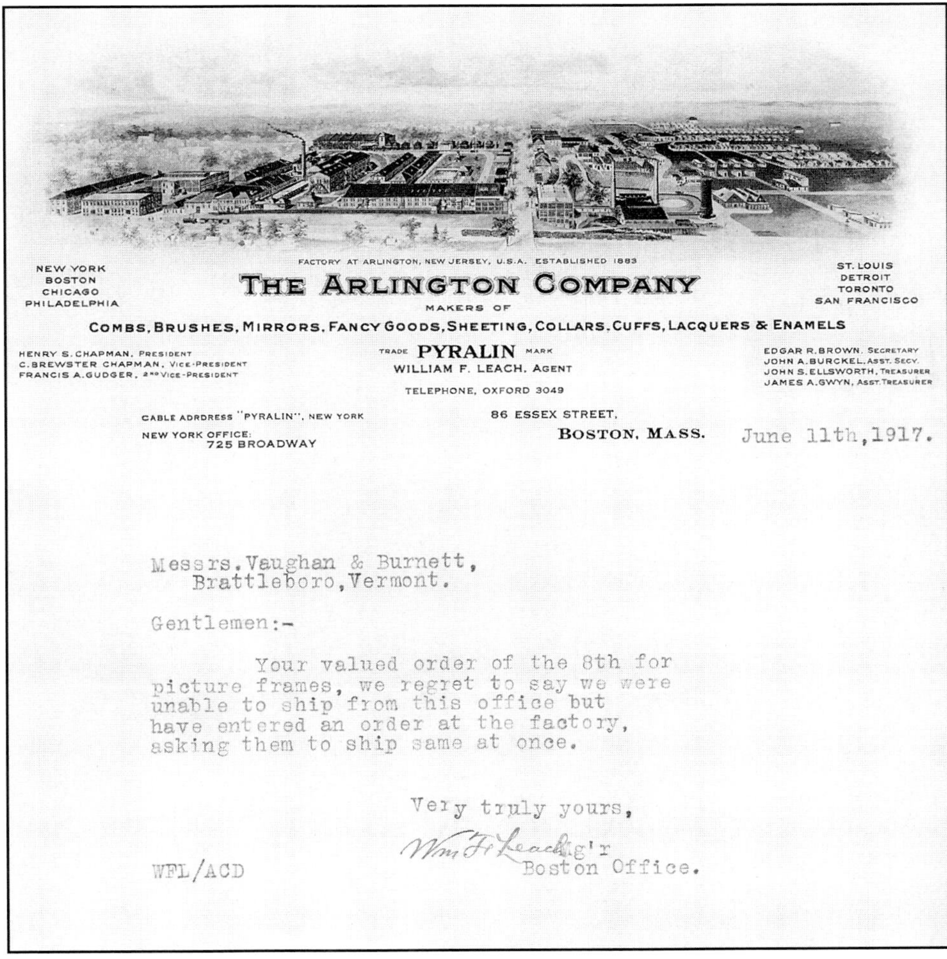
FACTORY AT ARLINGTON, NEW JERSEY, U.S.A. ESTABLISHED 1883

NEW YORK
BOSTON
CHICAGO
PHILADELPHIA

THE ARLINGTON COMPANY

ST. LOUIS
DETROIT
TORONTO
SAN FRANCISCO

MAKERS OF

COMBS, BRUSHES, MIRRORS, FANCY GOODS, SHEETING, COLLARS, CUFFS, LACQUERS & ENAMELS

HENRY S. CHAPMAN, PRESIDENT
C. BREWSTER CHAPMAN, VICE-PRESIDENT
FRANCIS A. GUDGER, 2ND VICE-PRESIDENT

TRADE PYRALIN MARK
WILLIAM F. LEACH, AGENT
TELEPHONE, OXFORD 3049

EDGAR R. BROWN, SECRETARY
JOHN A. BURCKEL, ASST. SECY.
JOHN S. ELLSWORTH, TREASURER
JAMES A. GWYN, ASST. TREASURER

CABLE ADRDRESS "PYRALIN", NEW YORK
NEW YORK OFFICE:
725 BROADWAY

86 ESSEX STREET,
BOSTON, MASS.

June 11th, 1917.

Messrs. Vaughan & Burnett,
Brattleboro, Vermont.

Gentlemen:-

Your valued order of the 8th for picture frames, we regret to say we were unable to ship from this office but have entered an order at the factory, asking them to ship same at once.

Very truly yours,
Wm F. Leach
Mg'r
Boston Office.

WFL/ACD

Merchant's Manufacturing Company and Pasbosene 1881 – 1883;
Cellonite Company 1883 – 1887; Arlington Manufacturing Company 1888 – 1895;
Arlington Company 1895 – 1915; E.I. DuPont de Nemoures 1915 – 1917

nies merged to become the Arlington Company. By the turn of the twentieth century, Pyralin had become established as celluloid's chief rival.

One of the important factors in the success of the Arlington Company was its highly competitive approach to marketing. In the early 1900s they established sales offices in Toronto, New York, Cleveland, Chicago, Boston, St. Louis, Detroit, Philadelphia, and San Francisco.[28]

In 1913 Arlington constructed a branch facility in Poughkeepsie, New York, to produce Pyralin combs, collars, cuffs, and toys. In that same year they also formed the Florida Essential Oils Company with the intent to raise camphor trees on 12,000 acres of land near Waller, Florida.[29]

DuPont

By 1915, the Arlington company was the largest manufacturer of pyroxylin plastic in the United States, producing nearly 40% of the total American output (Celluloid produced 25%; Fiberloid 25%; and Viscoloid 10%). In December of 1915, E.I. DuPont de Nemoures and Co. purchased the Arlington Company for the cash price of $6,700,000. At the same time, DuPont also bought the Norwich Paper Company of Connecticut; as tissue paper was the form of cellulose used in the making of Pyralin.[30]

In June of 1916, over one million pounds of cellulose nitrate burned in an inferno of flames that reached one hundred feet into the air above the Arlington plant in New Jersey. The following year DuPont dissolved the Arlington facility and production of Pyralin was transferred to other DuPont departments.

In the 1920s, DuPont also purchased the Della Celluloid Company of Italy from its owner Dr. Silvio Mazzuchelli. However, political situations in 1936 concerning Benito Mussilini, who took a dim view of foreigners controlling companies in Italy, caused DuPont to resell the company to its original owner.

Viscoloid Company, 1901 – 1977

The story of the Viscoloid Company of Leominster, Massachusetts is an important one and of particular interest to collectors, especially those who specifically collect such items as fancy celluloid hair ornaments or blow-molded dolls and toys.

Viscoloid is somewhat unique in its beginnings since all of its founders had been involved, in one way or another, with the natural plastic material, horn. During the early 1880s four businessmen, Alexander Paton, Bernard W. Doyle, Ludwig Stross and Paul Rie became familiar with one another through various connections in the horn industry. Stross and Rie were partners in the Albert Ochse Company of Paris, the largest dealer of horn in the world.

Bernard Doyle, a Leominster native, had traveled extensively throughout South America, Mexico, and Europe with Albert Ochse in the quest to buy quality horn. When supplies in America began to dwindle, Ochse and Doyle joined forces and founded the Horn Supply Company with the intent of processing cattle horn for the manufacture of natural plastic articles. Alexander Paton had organized the Paton Manufacturing Company in Leominster in 1879 to produce horn combs, buttons, and jewelry.

This quartet of businessmen formed the Sterling Comb Company for the manufacture of hair ornaments, dressing combs, and novelties. As the demand for hair ornaments grew, especially the high back Spanish style, a second business, the Harvard Novelty Company, was formed to help meet production needs.

While traveling in Europe during the late 1890s, Bernard Doyle became familiar with pyroxylin plastics. Upon returning to America in 1898, Doyle began a series of experiments with cellulose nitrate plastic and came to the conclusion that it had tremendous advantages over horn as a molding material.

With the continued growth and prosperity of the Paton Manufacturing Company, the Sterling Comb Company, and the Harvard Novelty Company, the owners decided to merge the three firms

This turn-of-the-century photograph shows a drilling crew as they worked on the Viscoloid well in Leominster, Massachusetts. The job was completed prior to the manufacture of pyroxylin plastic at a cost of $600. When finished, an unlimited supply of 60-gallons of pure water per minute was available through a 4" pipe. A storage tank with a capacity of 20,000 gallons was also installed when the well was drilled.

to form a single business with the intent of manufacturing pyroxylin plastic articles. In 1901 the four men met at the Delaware Club, directly across the street from the E.I. DuPont headquarters in Delaware, and organized the Viscoloid Company.

The process of making pyroxylin plastic involved the use of cellulose, which was treated with nitric and sulfuric acids and alcohol. The result was cellulose nitrate, which then had to be washed with pure water – water that was free of iron, sulfur, and any organic particles or substances. To obtain the large amounts of quality water needed, the founders of Viscoloid hired a drilling rig and crew to dig a 200 ft. deep well prior to the date of first production in December of 1901.

At the time Viscoloid began production, the type of cellulose used in the manufacturing process came in the form of double bleached cotton yarn. This yarn was subjected to heat in a hot air chamber where it was thoroughly dried, then run through a cutter that chopped it into tiny pieces. The cut-up cellulose fiber was then placed in large jars and soaked in a nitric and sulfuric acid solution. After a chemical change had taken place and the cellulose was fully nitrated, the jars were emptied and the cellulose nitrate put into large 1,200 gallon tanks of water where it was washed repeatedly, up to 15 times. Once the acid residue had been thoroughly cleaned from the nitrated cellulose, the material was cut up a second time, put into vats, and mixed with camphor, then treated with alcohol to make a pyroxylin compound. After thorough mixing, the material was then ready to be dyed and processed into sheets and blocks.

In 1902, just one year after the Viscoloid Company produced their first sheet of pyroxylin plastic, another Leominster industry was born, the Handifold Toilet Paper Company; their first sheet of tissue paper measured 64 inches wide and 60 feet long. J.G. Jarvis, superintendent of Viscoloid, was quoted in the newspaper as saying, "This class of paper can be used as a basis for manufacturing the Viscoloid, instead of cotton yarn which is now being used, if it could be gotten just as cheaply."[31] The Handifold management replied to Jarvis's comment by stating they were indeed prepared to make tissue paper for the manufacture of cellulose nitrate by Viscoloid Company.

Viscoloid quickly became established as a major company in the manufacture of pyroxylin plastic stock and finished articles. The numerous comb shops in Leominster began to mold

Handifold Tissue advertisement

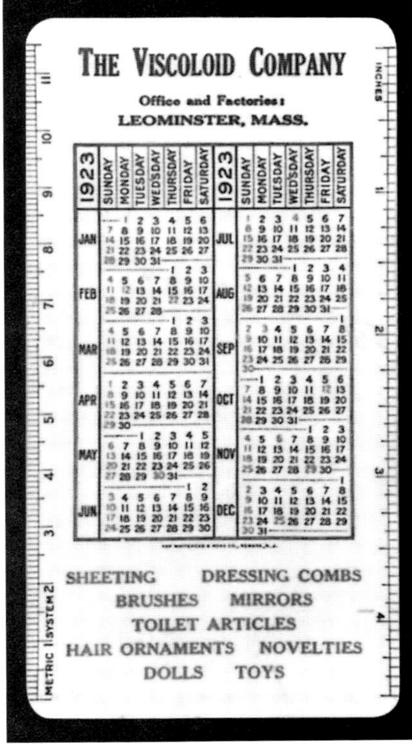

1923 Viscoloid pocket calendar printed on pyroxylin sheet

Viscoloid plant

In 1925, DuPont purchased the Viscoloid Co. of Leominster, Massachusetts, changing the name to DuPont Viscoloid Co., Inc. In that same year the DuPont Poughkeepsie plant was closed and its Pyralin product line of collars, cuffs, and toiletware was transferred to the DuPont Viscoloid facility in Leominster. The following year DuPont purchased the Pacific Novelty Company as well. This photo shows the top portion of the Dupont Viscoloid Company letterhead.

Viscoloid in place of horn for the production of dressing combs and hair ornaments. By 1910 however, changing fashion caused a serious decline in the use and sale of fancy imitation tortoise shell hair ornaments. As a result, the company was forced to recognize the need for other product lines and began the manufacture of toilet articles and dresserware.

It wasn't until after 1914 that the Viscoloid Company began to market toys made of pyroxylin plastic. Prior to this time, most of the toys in America were manufactured in Germany and imported into the United States. However, when World War I broke out, trade with the Germans abruptly ceased.

At that time Viscoloid seized the opportunity to enter the toymaking business. They hired German-born artist Paul H. Kramme as a designer in 1914 and quickly became the most prolific of pyroxylin plastic toy manufacturers in America. By the 1920s Viscoloid's toymaking department alone employed 350 workers.

The toys made by Viscoloid were usually manufactured by the blow molding process – a technique in which two thin sheets of Viscoloid were placed in a mold and steam was blown between them, softening the material and forcing it to take the form of the mold.

Viscoloid made nearly every variety of domestic and wild animal in this fashion, as well as a great many floating birds and fish toys. Their other products include holiday novelties, rattles, and figural character toys. The marketing of these Viscoloid products was done by the Pacific Novelty Company of New York City. The firm had been organized in 1891 by Joseph Gutman and eventually became the largest distributor of Viscoloid hair ornaments and novelties in America.

In 1928 and 1929 DuPont called some of their finest pyroxylin plastic toiletware Lucite, branding each individual piece with the new tradename. It should be clearly understood that this particular material was cellulose nitrate plastic – the same material as Pyralin – and not the acrylic plastic DuPont introduced in 1936. The acrylic material now known as Lucite was first called "Pontalite" when it was introduced in 1936. In 1934 the Viscoloid Corporation discontinued the manufacture of pyroxylin plastics; however they continued to market articles made from the existing stock throughout the 1930s. DuPont Viscoloid continued to operate in the plastics industry until November of 1977.

Collector Caution

A special note of interest concerning the introduction of cellulose acetate toys: At some point in the late 1920s, the Viscoloid Company sold their toy molds to Irwin Cohn of Leominster. Cohn continued the Viscoloid line of toys but in the 1930s began to use nonflammable cellulose acetate (CA) plastic sheets rather than cellulose nitrate. Irwin toys made from CA plastic in Viscoloid molds can sometimes be identified by the whiteness or brightness of the molded material. The Irwin trademark, a circle with a banner through the center, was also added to a number of the Viscoloid molds.

Fiberloid Company, 1894 – 1938

The early beginnings of the Fiberloid Company can be directly traced to the formation of the Lithoid Manufacturing Company; however it is necessary to first mention an earlier organization, the Lignoid Fancy Article Manufacturing Company. Lignoid was formed in Newark, New Jersey, in 1878, and two years later the company moved to Newburyport, Massachusetts.

It is currently not known what happened with the Lignoid Fancy Article Mfg. Company as it seems to fade away in historical records. However, there is a possibility, but no documented proof, that the Lignoid firm was reorganized to form the Solid Fiber Company.[32]

The Solid Fiber Company of Newburyport, operated by Edward F. Coffin, was an established producer of cellulose nitrate sheet stock. In 1884, Silas Kenyon, George Tapley and J. D. Parsons of the United Manufacturing Co. of Springfield, Massachusetts, a paper collar and cuff enterprise, merged their business with the Solid Fiber Company of Newburyport for the manufacture of waterproof cuffs and collars. In January of 1888 Silas Kenyon, George Tapley, J. D. Parsons of Springfield, and Julius Levine, a financial backer from New York, assumed control of the Solid Fiber Company and reorganized the firm as the Lithoid Corporation.

The new enterprise carried on operations for several years producing their brand of pyroxylin plastic – Lithoid – for the manufacture of waterproof collars and cuffs, as well as sheet stock for piano keys. Then in the early 1890s, the company went out of business; however the machinery and factory facilities were left intact. Shortly thereafter, the businessmen previously involved in the manufacture of Lithoid decided once again to engage in a pyroxylin plastic venture. In 1894 they formed the Fiberloid Company of Maine and proceeded to manufacture a nitrocellulose plastic material they called Fiberloid. Operations were successfully carried out in the Newburyport facility until after the turn of the twentieth century.

In 1904 the Fiberloid manufacturing plant was completely destroyed by a raging fire. The following year a new factory complex was built on a 16-acre tract of land along the Chicopee River in the Indian Orchard section of Springfield. In 1911 the name of the company was changed to the Fiberloid Company of Massachusetts.

By 1914, Fiberloid had doubled its plant capacity and was said to have been responsible for one-quarter of the total cellulose nitrate production in the United States, a production output equal with that of the Celluloid Company. In 1916 the name was changed to Fiberloid Corporation.

Throughout the 1920s, Fiberloid Corporation's reputation as a manufacturer of quality pyroxylin plastics continued to grow and production increased. The line of goods marketed including toiletware, cutlery handles, automobile curtains, toothbrushes, bathroom accessories, fountain pens, golf club faces, advertising novelties, jewelry, imitation leather, and cuffs and collars. By 1930 the Indian Orchard facility consisted of 40 buildings, all protected against fire by their own fire department, with three inexhaustible water supplies. A cafeteria and emergency hospital were also located on the grounds.

In 1933 the Monsanto Chemical Company of St. Louis purchased 14% interest in the company and five years later completely absorbed the company; in 1938 Fiberloid became the Plastic Division of Monsanto.

The Ill Fated Fifth
American Zylonite, 1881 – 1890

In early 1881 the American Zylonite Company was formed by Leroy L. Brown of Adams, Massachusetts, who had purchased patents from British Xylonite with the intent of manufacturing pyroxylin plastic under license of Englishman Daniel Spill, the developer of Xylonite.[33] Edward Worden in his volume *Nitrocellulose Industry* notes that the American name was pronounced "zy´-low-nite," the "zy" as in enzyme, while the English name was pronounced "zil´-o-nite," the "il" as in Spill.

Brown was the owner of Graylock Paper Mills in Cummington and had a ready source for the cellulose fiber used in the making of cellulose nitrate. For two years following the organization of the firm, Brown and his employees worked tirelessly building a complex to manufacture raw pyroxylin plastic and finished articles from the material he called Zylonite.

In the summer of 1883 a variety of American Zylonite goods were finally placed on the market. The product line included combs, brushes, collars, cuffs, toys, handles, shoe horns, curtain rings, surgical instruments, chess pieces, doorknobs, manicure implements, piano keys, and much more. These finished goods were all products of the Zylonite Brush and Comb Co.; the Zylonite Collar and Cuff Co.; the Zylonite Novelty Company; and United Zylonite Co.

The Zylonite facility was considered one of the largest pyroxylin plastic facilities in the world. Taking into consideration that 126 employees worked in the packaging department alone making cases and boxes for Zylonite products, it must have indeed been an awesome enterprise.

The growth of the Zylonite Company was due to many factors, but one of the most important attributes to Zylonite's success was the contributions of George M. Mowbray, the companies' technical manager and chemist. Mowbray came to North Adams to furnish the explosives used in the construction of the Hoosic Tunnel that moved the railroad from the east to the gateway of the west. His expertise in the manufacture of nitroglycerin and anything related to nitration was what landed him a position as chief chemist with Zylonite. There were also a number of other important men in the history of

This circa 1895 photograph shows a group of workers standing in front of a trolley car that ran between the towns of North Adams, Zylonite, Renfrew, and Adams.

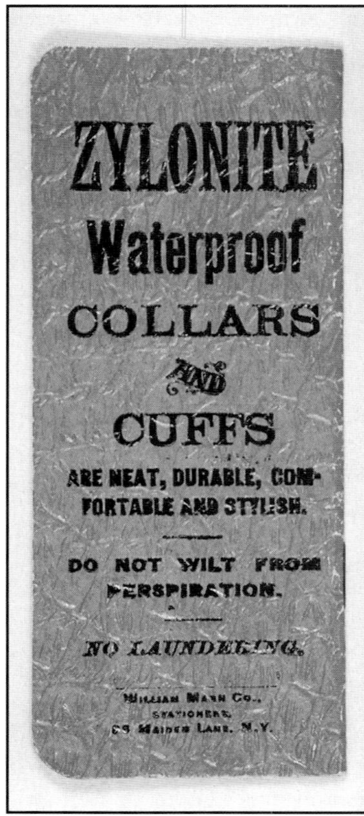

American Zylonite pocket notebook advertising waterproof collars and cuffs. The names Hanover and London clearly associate the product with their English roots, the Xylonite Company. American Zylonite operated under license of the British firm from 1881 – 1890. Cuff and collar production began in 1884.

This beautifully molded toiletware is seen throughout the Celluloid Company catalogs dating from 1892 through 1889. However, upon close examination the name Zylonite can be seen imprinted on the metal part of the nail file.

American Zylonite including J.G. Jarvis, who had started his career in plastics with John W. Hyatt and J.B. Edson, who also left the Celluloid Company to work in the Adams firm.

The area surrounding the Zylonite factories was eventually developed for the employees and their families, expanding to include a school, church, post office, rail station, and fire department; the village itself was called Zylonite.

In the mid 1880s, American Zylonite began to experience financial difficulties due to an unfortunate series of events. Patent litigation over the court battle between Englishman Daniel Spill of Xylonite vs. John W. Hyatt of Celluloid caused the North Adams firm to lose over one million dollars.[34]

By the end of 1890, American Zylonite was in such serious financial difficulty that the Celluloid Company of Newark, New Jersey, bought the facility for $950,000. Abruptly on January 1, 1891, the factory was unexpectedly closed leaving more than 525 workers unemployed overnight.

To make matters worse, the Celluloid Company moved in and completely cleaned the place out, destroying much of the old machinery, while salvaging the best for their plant in Newark. Devastated workers were forced to uproot their families and seek employment elsewhere.[35] The local paper referred to the Celluloid Co. as "the soulless Newark concern."

The zylonite "stock in work," which would have included a wide variety of finished articles, was also packed up and taken to Newark where it was incorporated into the current stock of the Celluloid Company.

Endnotes

1. According to the book *Albany, Capital City on the Hudson*, 12,000 elephants were slaughtered annually for the intent of making ivory pool balls from their tusks. Ivory was indeed an expensive commodity, for not only was it becoming scarce, it was reported that for every two elephants killed, one man lost his life.

2. During the early 1860s, English billiards master Michael Phelan wrote in his book *Game of Billiards*, "if any inventive genius could discover a substitute for ivory, he would make a handsome fortune for himself."

3. It was the American Billiards Industry that added incentive to the search for an ivory substitute by offering the impressive prize of $10,000. Unfortunately, there is no documented evidence to support that Hyatt ever received the promised reward money for his invention of celluloid.

4. Est.1866 – The Hyatt Billiard Ball Co. by Hyatt and Kinnear; renamed the Albany Billiard Ball Company and re-established in a small factory at Grand and Plain Streets in Albany's south end in 1868. It remained at that location until after WWI when the factory was moved to 408 Delaware Ave.

5. On June 15, 1869, Hyatt was granted yet another patent for one of his inventions; Improvement In The Manufacture of Dominos, Pat. # 91,235.

6. The Hyatt Mfg. Co. grew at a steady pace and as checker production increased, the enterprise split into two divisions: the Hyatt Mfg. Co., which relocated to a factory on Beaver St. in Albany, where John (still employed as a printer) acted as superintendent overseeing the production of base materials for the game pieces; and the Embossing Co., which was located at 4 and 6 Pruyn St. with 28-year-old brother Charles acting as president.

7. By 1871 the Embossing Co. was firmly established as a reputable manufacturer of boxed dominoes and checkers. As the company expanded its line of merchandise to include educational toys and games, they outgrew the original locations and moved to 23 Church and 58 Liberty St. in Albany. By 1884 the Embossing Company of Albany became one of the nation's most successful game producing business. The Embossing Company was bought out by Halsam in 1957.

8. Collodion was a liquid pyroxylin solution – cellulose nitrate, ether, and ethyl alcohol – which was discovered by Boston chemist Waldo Maynard in 1847. It was used extensively in early photography and also by the medical profession as a type of invisible bandage.

9. In addition to the fact that the balls were extremely flammable, other problems were also associated with the use of collodion coating: a thin paper-like "artificial skin" formed on the balls as the liquid collodion evaporated, and dirt quickly adhered to the surface of the balls when they were used.

10. Hyatt's invention quickly became the most successful alternative to ivory in billiard ball manufacture in spite of the early problems associated with them. The introduction of Hyatt's Improved Billiard Ball (a cast Celluloid composition) in 1875 put an end to the shortage of expensive ivory balls.

11. The social significance of Hyatt's invention is worthy of mention; it bridged the gap between the wealthy elite who played the sport of billiards in their upper class parlors and private clubs, making the game accessible to the middle and working classes as they patronized saloons and pool halls that offered the game as a novel recreation.

12. Englishman Alexander Parkes invented and patented Parkesine in 1861. It was a moldable pyroxylin plastic that employed the use of various oils and solvents, including camphor.

13. Parkesine was first introduced to the public at the London International Exhibit of 1862 where it was awarded a bronze medal for Excellence of Product.

14. Parkesine could be made transparent or opaque and was used as an imitation ivory material. It was flexible and waterproof, a suitable replacement for expensive coral, tortoise, and ivory in hair combs, buttons, jewelry, medallions, and a host of other utilitarian and ornamental applications.

15. In an attempt to supply consumers with an economical replacement for traditional materials, Parkes sought to reduce the cost of Parkesine by using the cheapest raw materials he could find, lowering the cost from $16.00 per pound to 12¢ per pound by the mid 1860s. Unfortunately, this was Parkes' downfall; the result was an inferior plastic material that was doomed to fail, and by 1869, production of Parkesine halted.

16. Seeley had firsthand experience with collodion; during the Civil War he worked for the U.S. government making the solution for medical use. In addition, Seeley had even been issued a patent for its improvement in 1868. (US Pat.#79,261 – Improvement In Solidified Collodion).

17. Source: Society of Chemical Industry, Perkin Medal Acceptance Speech, J.W. Hyatt, May 1914.

18. In those days much controversy surrounded the use of hardened rubber in dentistry, thanks to the work of the Goodyear Dental Vulcanite Company. Rubber and gutta percha had been used quite successfully for denture base materials since the early 1850s; however in 1864 Dr. John A. Cummings was issued a patent for the complete process of making rubber dentures. He sold his patent to the G.D.V. Co., which in turn required that all dentists using Vulcanite in the manufacture of dentures be licensed by the company, paying a yearly fee amounting to anywhere between $25.00 and $100.00. In addition, a second fee was required for each denture that was formed, the amount determined by the number of teeth set into each plate. Nevertheless, about 5,000 dentists purchased licenses from GDVC, as they were skilled in working with rubber prior to Dr. Cummings' patent. Some however, reverted to using gold as a denture base material while still others sought out new substances to replace Vulcanite.

19. It was from 1870 through 1873 that denture plate production was the primary use for Hyatt's pyroxylin plastic material. Later when the Celluloid Mfg. Co. of Newark, NJ was established, SS White became the first official licensee of the firm. However, during the first several years of production, there were serious problems associated with the use of celluloid. Unfortunately, dental plates made from the material often discolored, frequently warped and lost teeth, absorbed odors, and tasted offensive when hot food or liquid came into contact with them. This was in part due to a lack of experience by dentists who molded the Celluloid blanks into a fitted denture, and partly due to the fact that celluloid was in its early stages of development. Over time however, the material was perfected and by the late 1870s, dentists had become skilled in producing quality celluloid dentures at a fraction of the cost of alternative materials such as gold and hardened rubber.

20. Marshall Lefferts of NYC was not only the chief financial backer of the Celluloid Mfg. Company, he was also actively involved in the business. He filled the offices of both secretary/treasurer and president and was also instrumental in developing several methods for manufacturing celluloid articles. Working closely with Hyatt, Lefferts applied himself to the field of pyroxylin plastic, eventually receiving 10 patents regarding the production of Celluloid finished goods.

21. At the time, water was held in large tanks to which various coagulants were added and agitated. The water had to stand for up to 24 hours as the impurities settled to the bottom before it could be used. The Hyatts conceived the idea of adding coagulants to water, then filtering out the impurities as the water made its way to the factory through various supply pipes. The patented their unique filtering process in 1884.

22. Daniel Spill, born in 1832, was the son of a Unitarian minister and the brother of George Spill who had a waterproofing business. The traditional method of treating cloth with rubber had been employed by the Spills; however, during the mid 1860s, when Parkesine was introduced as the new wonder material, the Spills had an interest in it as a waterproofing agent. Daniel convinced Parkes to join forces, but instead of developing a product for the waterproofing business, Spill became the managing director of the Parkesine Co.

23. It should be understood that the formula for Parkes' earliest plastic products was considerably different from that manufactured at the Parkesine Works in Hackney Wick, London. Because the earliest articles of Parkesine were made with purified ingredients, the quality was much better. Parkes' attempt to produce the substance at a fraction of the cost is what doomed his product to failure.

24. The word celluloid was a contraction for cellulose and colloid, or as others state, cellulose and oid – a Greek word meaning "like."

25. The history of American Zylonite begins on page 21.

26. It was also in 1883 that the Celluloid Company forced Crolithion Collar and Cuff Company of Maine, a small waterproof linen manufacturer, out of business following patent litigation.

27. Camphor was an essential ingredient used in making celluloid and most of it came from the forests of Formosa. The Japanese realized the importance of this export substance and by 1899 had secured an imperial monopoly on their camphor. The price was drastically raised, which prompted many attempts to secure alternative supplies. The Celluloid Company purchased thousands of acres in Florida to plant camphor trees. However the thrip, an insect which loved to feast on camphor tree leaves, infested the plantation and doomed the attempt at producing American camphor.

28. Arlington Company had an office in Canada, of which John Chantler of Toronto was the head. In 1916, Chantler convinced DuPont to purchase the Toronto collar and cuff manufacturing company of A.B. Mitchell. After the acquisition, the organization was called the Arlington Co. of Canada.

29. About 5,000 acres of trees were planted in an effort to offset the Japanese monopoly in the camphor trade. The camphor trees began to flourish until they were attacked by leaf-eating insects called thrips. The pests doomed the efforts of Arlington to supply their own camphor and in 1921 the plantation was abandoned.

30. At an earlier date the Arlington Co. had obtained an interest in the White Springs Paper Co. of Nutley, New Jersey.

31. Jarvis had worked with John Hyatt in the manufacture of celluloid, and by the time he came to work for Viscoloid, he had 30 years experience in the pyroxylin plastics industry.

32. There is currently no evidence to cite which proves that the Lignoid Co. became the Solid Fiber Co. Robert Friedel in his book *Pioneer Plastic*, speaks of the Lignoid Fancy Article Mfg. and their move to Newburyport and further stated that the same became known as the Fiberloid Company.

33. Earlier Daniel Spill had brought a suit against John W. Hyatt for patent infringement concerning the formulation of his pyroxylin plastic – the case was finally decided by Judge Blatchford in favor of Spill in 1880. This decision gave Spill the opportunity to sell his patents to L.L. Brown for the formulation of American Zylonite. Later, in 1884, Blatchford reversed his decision; this reversal was the chief cause of Zylonite's eventual failure. Adding to the situation was the bankruptcy of the New York bank that held Zylonite's assets.

34. In 1884 when Judge Blatchford reversed his earlier decision concerning the Spill vs Hyatt case, the company suffered financially – eventually losing over one million dollars in patent litigation. Coupled with a New York bank failure, the American Zylonite Company was doomed.

35. At the time that American Zylonite Co. was closed, the Arlington Company was experiencing manufacturing difficulties. The company hired a good many experienced supervisors and workers for employment in their New Jersey facility.

Celluloid in Fashion

Introduction

Perhaps celluloid's greatest asset in the 1870s and 1880s was that of an imitation material. Since it was clear in its original form, various additives and dyes could be added in order to produce an array of colors. It is well known that celluloid's initial purpose was as a substitute for elephant ivory; however, other expensive and scarce luxury materials were also duplicated and these were used to create a wonderful assortment of fashion accessories.

Celluloid first found a niche in fashion when the waterproof collar was introduced as an alternative to linen. Celluloid's special qualities, including ease of cleaning and lasting durability, made it a popular replacement for the textile goods that required repeated laundering, starching, and pressing.

During the early 1880s the makers of Celluloid found another application for their waterproofing material. Up until this time, corsets had been lined with whale bone stays which became brittle or steel ones that rusted and stained the fabric. The only way to prevent these problems was to remove the stays before laundering. By coating the metal parts of corsets with celluloid, they were rendered rust resistant and the life of these vital undergarments was extended.

The advertising for both waterproof collars and corsets can still be found in the form of trade cards. These bits of ephemera from days gone by give today's celluloid collectors a glimpse into the time when whimsical, charming, and sometime offensive images were used to tout the great virtues of the product they advertised.

Possibly the most popular area of celluloid collecting is that of fashion accessories. Since celluloid was made in imitation of luxury materials like ivory, amber, tortoise shell and coral, it gave all classes of people the opportunity to enjoy lovely, expensive-looking fashion accessories. Celluloid bridged the gap between the wealthy and working classes in late nineteenth and early twentieth century America.

Later, during the 1920s, technological advances brought about a pleasing pallette of colored and pearlescent effects to celluloid fashion accessories. These were used as a laminate over imitation ivory and amber, as well as offering a variety of non-traditional colors.

Celluloid production was discontinued in the United States during the late 1940s; however the Japanese continued to import many types of novelty items into this country throughout the 1950s.

Cuffs and Collars

Development

When they were first developed in the early 1800s, detachable linen cuffs and collars seemed a great help in the tiresome chore of hand scrubbing dirty laundry. Not only did they reduce the time spent washing, starching, and ironing, but they actually prolonged the life of a shirt. Eventually however, scrubbing soiled collars and grimy cuffs became a dreaded task. For those who could not afford the luxury of a laundry service, there was no alternative to the bothersome chore.

By the mid 1800s it was evident that an alternative for wearing traditional starched linen was needed. Bachelors who were not adept at washing and starching their own soiled linens, traveling salesmen, evangelists, and waiters were among those most likely to use cuffs and collars made of disposable or waterproof materials.

Out of this need grew the disposable cuff and collar industry, first introduced in 1859 when W. Lockwood patented his invention of a disposable, embossed linen paper collar for ladies. The idea was further developed by J. Barton, and in 1866 he introduced the men's reversible/ disposable linen look paper collar.

Although the paper industry produced only a small fraction of the cuffs and collars worn by American men, it remained an important part of the market since it provided consumers with a wearable alternative to linen at a fair price. Paper collars were relatively inexpensive, costing only a few cents, compared to a 25¢ textile collar; however, over time it became evident that they were not exactly an economical replacement. They readily absorbed moisture and dirt, losing their crisp white appearance. Although the collar was designed to be reversible, the number of times it could actually be worn was limited. As a result, paper became a convenient alternative to textile goods but was never really established as a permanent replacement for wearing fine linen.

As early as 1854, attempts were being made to develop a waterproofing substance to coat collars and cuffs. The efforts made by W. Hunt and G. Ray using lacquer and varnish were admirable, but unsuccessful in producing a comfortable imitation linen item. It wasn't until the mid 1870s, when sheet celluloid was introduced into the industry, that a successful waterproofing material was found.

Introduction of the Celluloid Waterproof Collar

Hyatt developed a method of laminating linen or paper between two ultra thin sheets of transparent celluloid. Then he built machinery to cut, heat, and bend the material into collars and cuffs. On December 22, 1875, the Celluloid Novelty Company was licensed for the manufacture of a wide variety of

The following excerpt is taken from a Celluloid Mfg. Co. booklet.

"Celluloid collars, cuffs and shirt bosoms constitute the largest line of goods manufactured by the Novelty Company. They have made their way, against strong opposition, the world over. The especial qualities which commend them are their exact resemblance to linen, their flexibility, their comfort to the wearer and the ease with which they can be cleansed and renovated for immediate use. They are thoroughly waterproof, elastic and durable in wonderful degree. Their foundation is fine linen, coated with a smooth and glossy surface of the purest white Celluloid, yet they are free from the exaggerated brilliance of finish which made the enameled paper collars of former days so objectionable to persons of fastidious taste. These goods are especially suited for warm climates or summer heats, and by their use the discomforts and untidiness of wilted and soiled linen may be easily avoided."

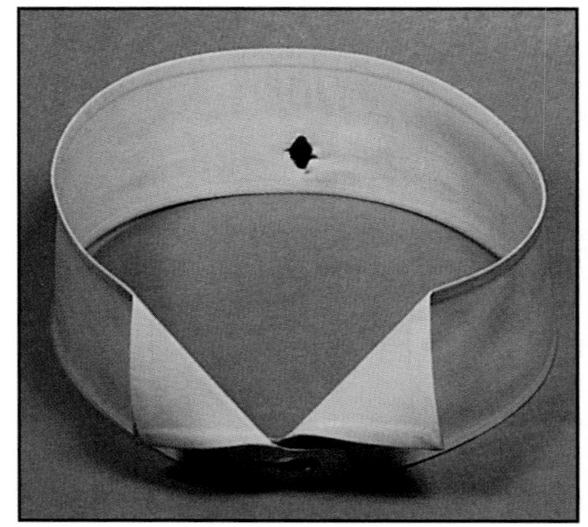

Celluloid waterproof collar.

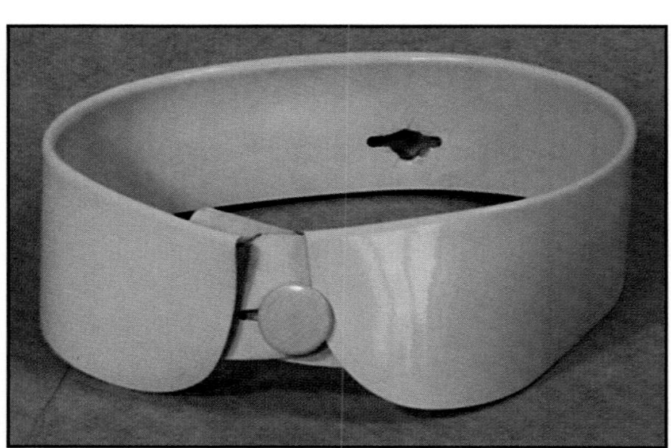

The collar featured here has a high polish finish. $15.00 each.

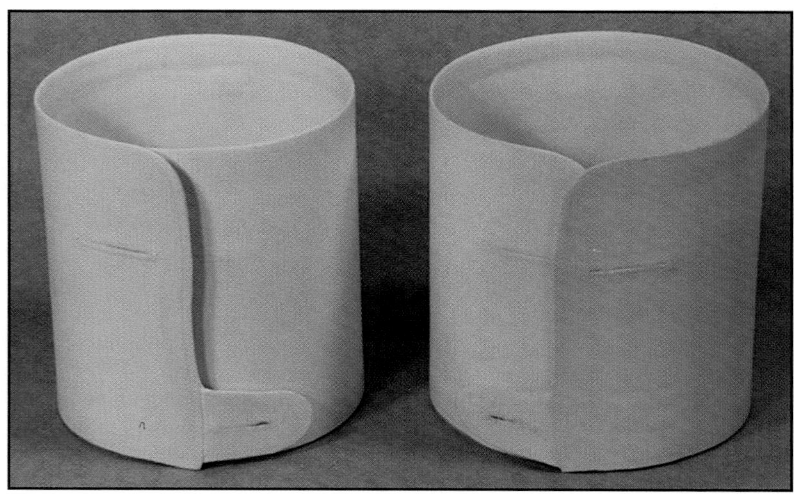

These cuffs are fashioned with an imitation linen finish. $15.00 each.

plastic goods; among the list of products offered were celluloid cuffs, collars, and shirt bosoms. The shirt bosom was a faux shirt front which could be strapped on over the shoulders then worn with a vest.

The popularity and demand for waterproof linens became so great that a separate business was established solely for their production. On March 9, 1878, the Celluloid Waterproof Cuff and Collar Co. was licensed to manufacture a variety of imitation linen goods including several styles of collar, cuffs, and full-length shirt bosoms. These items were printed with the official trade mark, an intertwined C, N, Co.

A variety of textures and finishes was produced for the manufacture of celluloid waterproof cuffs and collars including a silk pattern, an imitation linen finish, a mat finish, a plain smooth surface, and a high polish glossy finish.

While Celluloid Co. cuffs and collars are scarce, they are not impossible to find. Prices range from a few dollars each to $15.00, depending on condition and style.

Although they were a great success, waterproof celluloid collars and cuffs did meet with some resistance. Proper "upperclass" gentlemen preferred to wear traditional linen; the waterproof variety was scorned among the wealthy and actually denounced by such men's publications as the *Haberdasher*.

There were also other drawbacks associated with celluloid. Cracking and splitting along the folds and button holes of the firm plastic linens was a common nuisance, as was the annoying rattle of cuff buttons and studs in the button holes.

In order to stop the noise, Hyatt set the button holes on one end of the cuff at a greater distance apart than the opposing openings. When the ends of the cuff were overlapped, the buttonholes did not line up equally. As a result when the cuff button was inserted, the shank met with a certain amount of lateral tension that put an end to the irritating sound.

Another complaint against the celluloid collar had to do with its perspiration proof qualities, which ironically seemed to be the product's greatest virtue. Waterproof collars did not wick away moisture like linen did but rather repelled it. As a result on hot days they were quite uncomfortable to wear. Nevertheless, because they always retained their shape, a large percentage of the labor force chose celluloid over textile.

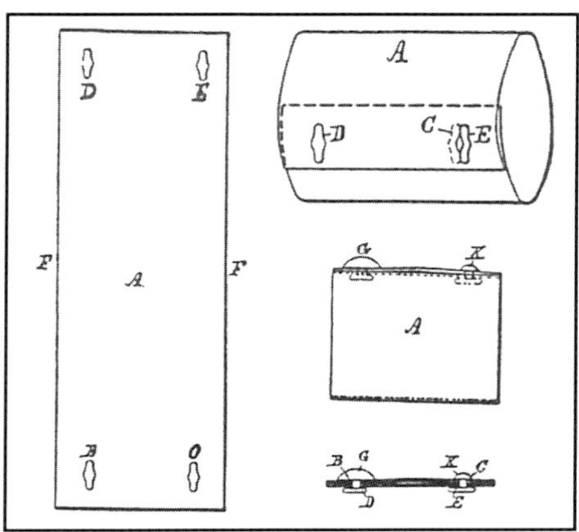

The Hyatt Non-Rattling Celluloid Cuff.

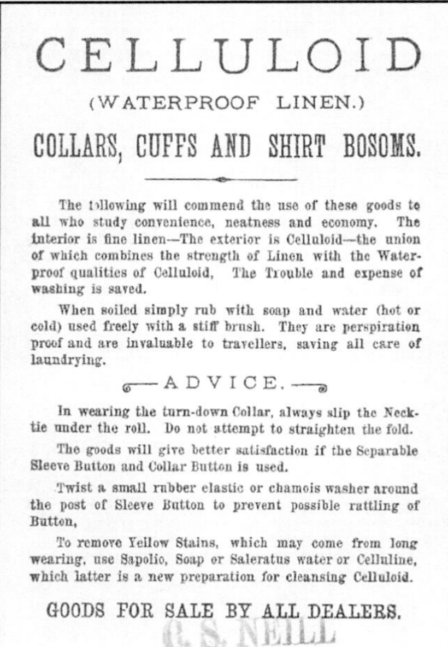

CELLULOID

(WATERPROOF LINEN.)

COLLARS, CUFFS AND SHIRT BOSOMS.

The following will commend the use of these goods to all who study convenience, neatness and economy. The interior is fine linen—The exterior is Celluloid—the union of which combines the strength of Linen with the Waterproof qualities of Celluloid, The Trouble and expense of washing is saved.

When soiled simply rub with soap and water (hot or cold) used freely with a stiff brush. They are perspiration proof and are invaluable to travellers, saving all care of laundrying.

—ADVICE.—

In wearing the turn-down Collar, always slip the Necktie under the roll. Do not attempt to straighten the fold.

The goods will give better satisfaction if the Separable Sleeve Button and Collar Button is used.

Twist a small rubber elastic or chamois washer around the post of Sleeve Button to prevent possible rattling of Button,

To remove Yellow Stains, which may come from long wearing, use Sapolio, Soap or Saleratus water or Celluline, which latter is a new preparation for cleansing Celluloid.

GOODS FOR SALE BY ALL DEALERS.

C. S. NEILL

The advice on this trade card instructs wearers to twist a small rubber elastic or chamois washer around the post of the sleeve button to prevent rattling.

Advertising

Advertising for celluloid linen goods included trade cards and advertisements in magazines and newspapers. A wide variety of novel themes and images was used to promote the special qualities of the product and reveal to us today how the manufacturers of waterproof linen sought to appeal to the general population.

Perhaps the most outrageous of advertising techniques used by the manufacturers of Celluloid Collars and Cuffs was the claim of special medicinal benefits for the wearer of waterproof linen goods. One such trade card exists in the Nation Archives in Washington, D.C. It shows a large, die cut fish bowl with bizarre claims on the reverse which state "when worn about the neck and pulse of the wrists, healing effects are imparted to throat ailments and lung complaints."

It is evident that the advertisers sought to exploit the use of their product by extolling the benefits of camphor as an essential ingredient in the manufacture of celluloid goods. Camphor was widely used in medicine at the time, and perhaps they sincerely believed their collars did indeed have curative powers. Nevertheless, it is a claim that had no basis in fact and such advertising practices were eventually regulated when the Pure Food and Drug Act of 1906 outlawed such ridiculous methods.

Eventually waterproof cuffs and collars were used throughout the civilized world. Abroad, the material from which they were manufactured became known as "American linen."

The Celluloid Co. priced their waterproof linens at approximately the same cost as high grade textile goods. However, the sensibility and economy of wearing celluloid cuffs and collars outweighed the fact that the cost was comparative, especially when the wearer was engaged in an activity that demanded extra durability. A cel-

CELLULOID

(Contagion Proof)

COLLARS, CUFFS, AND BOSOMS.

A Most Important Discovery!

Although CELLULOID COLLARS have been before the public for the past three years, and their especial qualities as to durability, economy, and general excellence have been thoroughly tested and indorsed by the million, it is only recently that it has been discovered that they serve an important use in warding off contagious diseases, and effectually curing all throat complaints and eruptions of the skin.

This is not surprising to the inventor, nor ought it to be to the wearer, when it is known that *camphor* (one of the best remedial agents known) enters largely into the composition of Celluloid. Testimonials are being continually offered from parties who have given the collars a steady trial, and who have heretofore suffered from the many throat and lung diseases extant, that their use has effected a permanent cure of these deadly ills, and that they now would not *dare* wear any other than the Celluloid Collar. Astounding as this may seem, it is a fact which can be abundantly verified. The manufacturers, therefore, feel it to be their simple duty to recommend their use, and would ask the public to inquire of the Gents' Furnishing Stores for the Celluloid Collars and Cuffs, and give them a fair trial. Should the reader be unable to find these goods at the regular stores, the undersigned (N. Y. agents) will, upon receipt of price, forward samples by mail to any address, as follows:

CELLULOID COLLARS.

	Size.	Price.
Novelty (stand up)	13½ to 17½	25 cts.
" "	18 to 20	35 "
Ajax (turn down)	13½ to 17½	40 "
" "	18 to 20	50 "
Opera (stand up)	14 to 17½	25 "
Army and Navy (stand up)	14 to 17½	25 "
" "	18 to 18½	35 "
Victor (corners turned down)	14 to 17½	25 "
Ladies' (stand up)	12 to 15	25 "

CUFFS.

	Size.	Price.
Champion (ends cut)	8 to 11 in., per pair,	50 cts.
Peerless (square)	8½ to 11 " "	50 "

BOSOMS.

Ventilated .... 75 cts.

Liberal discount to the trade.

SILLCOCKS & COOLEY, 4 Maiden Lane, N. Y. City.

This advertisement found in the June 4, 1881, issue of *Harper's Weekly* expresses the same sentiment found on the trade card currently in the Warsaw Collection, National Archives.

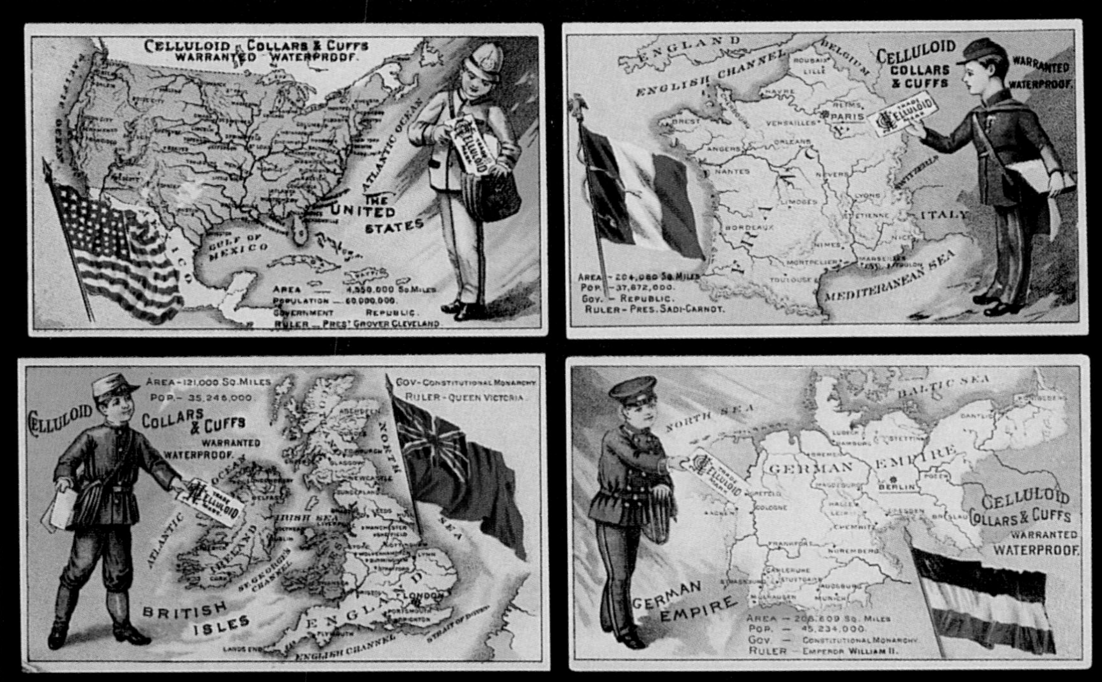

This series of trade cards dates between 1885 – 1889, (as indicated by the acting president of the United States, Grover Cleveland). Each card features a particular country and national flag, important statistical information, and an appropriately dressed mail carrier delivering the message of waterproof linens. Each card measures 2¾" x 4", and they range in price from $10.00 – $18.00 each.

Some trade cards extolled the unique waterproof virtues of Celluloid Collars and Cuffs with whimsical images of frogs, elves, and ducks playing in water. These 2" x 4" trade cards are printed on thick paper cards with the advertising pitch on reverse. $8.00 – $12.00 each.

Other images in advertising promoted the durability and sensibility of wearing long-lasting waterproof linens. The concept of children playing with cuffs and collars in water sent the subtle message that practically nothing could destroy the crisp white appearance of celluloid waterproof linens. Japanese illustrations can be found in advertising after 1885, a trend that was popularized with the success of Gilbert and Sullivan's opera, The Mikado. These trade cards are 3⅛" x 4" and printed on thick paper cards with the advertising pitch on reverse. $12.00 – $18.00 each.

In 1883, Palmer Cox introduced The Brownies whose likenesses became popular in advertising by 1890. This trade card features three of Cox's characters in fashionable attire, each wearing a collar appropriate for his style of dress. $25.00+.

From left to right: Undaunted by the elements, this fashionably dressed fisherman enjoys sporting success, thanks to the use of celluloid shirt bosoms – which enable him to continue his sporting activity in style and comfort. $12.00 – $15.00; images of handsome bachelors dressed in trendy clothing hinted of fashion correctness, self assurance, and sex appeal. This example sends a clear message that nothing can harm this smug chap's advances, as long as he is wearing celluloid waterproof linens. The matching suit, complete with a fashionable Prince of Wales pea jacket, was popularized beginning in the early 1870s. $12.00 – $15.00.

luloid item lasted for years, it never lost its color or shape, it never frayed or became worn around the edges, and it never needed laundering. Compared to the cost of disposable paper items and genuine linen goods, celluloid cuffs, collars, and shirt bosoms were a real bargain.

Laundering Problems and Solutions

During the late 1880s the Celluloid Co. devised an advertising campaign focusing primarily at the high cost of laundering linen. They promoted celluloid waterproof items as a superior product over traditional textiles by emphasizing their unique qualities. Celluloid collars, cuffs, and shirt bosoms never needed to be laundered, starched, or ironed; sweat and grime were easily wiped away with soap and water after wearing; and they always retained their crisp white appearance regardless of how often they were worn.

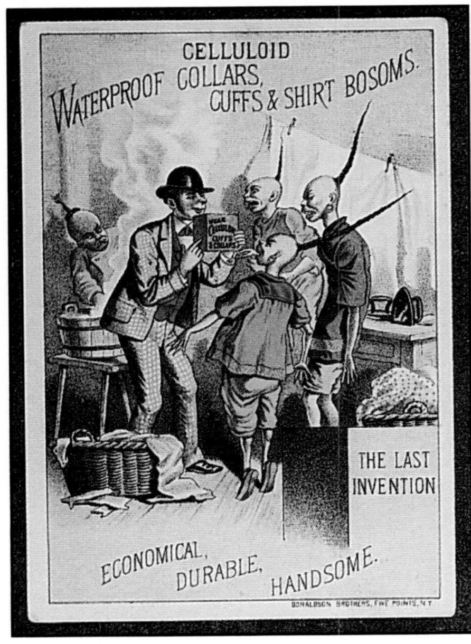

An exaggerated response of horror by Chinese laundry men as they are faced with a box of celluloid cuffs and collars by a grinning American man. $25.00+.

Two trade cards expressing anti-Chinese sentiment through the depiction of gleeful American — "Melican" — men flaunting their celluloid collars and cuffs to unemployed Oriental laundrymen. While the emphasis may seem prejudice to us today, this form of advertising was merely a tactic bent on arousing the patriotic loyalty of second generation Anglo American consumers. $25.00+. each.

Using the Chinese Immigration Exclusion Act of 1882 as a means to exploit their product, the Celluloid Co. attacked the Chinese laundry business fervently. This folding trade card, known as a metamorphosis card because it changes the image, shows a Chinese laundry man demanding payment from a customer. The customer however, rises victoriously with collar in hand, fully attired in a suit with crisp white shirt bosom and cuffs. $30.00+.

In 1881 a Harper's Weekly advertisement claimed that by wearing celluloid cuffs and collars, consumers would be healed of contagious diseases, ailments of the throat, and skin rashes. Of course there was no "proof" that celluloid held such curative powers, but because of the camphor content, the makers obviously felt that such claims were legitimate.

Three pages from the Celluloid Co. catalogs dated 1895, 1897, and 1899 show the variety of styles and designs available. Theoretically, a gentleman could own a single shirt, yet make a variety of fashion statements by switching detachable cuffs and collars. The Ajax and Sterling brands were for formal occasions; note the wide opening for an ascot tie on the Ajax.

THE CELLULOID COMPANY. 65

Waterproof Cuffs, Collars and Bosoms.

STERLING

The success of the Waterproof Collars and Cuffs originally put upon the marked by this Company over twenty years ago has caused several imitations to spring up, and we desire to call attention to the several trade-marks adopted by us to distinguish our goods, and to point out that every piece manufactured by us has its distinctive trade mark printed upon it.

HYDE PARK.

"INTERLINED." TRADE CELLULOID MARK.

These goods are so well known that it is unnecessary to dwell upon their merits. While more expensive than the "solid" goods they are well worth the difference in price; being a *linen collar or cuff* covered on both sides with a thin sheet of "Celluloid," rendering them perfectly waterproof. They are the *standard* waterproof goods and are not made by any other manufacturer, and purchasers desiring these goods should accept only those having the above trade mark stamped upon them.

"WORLD'S FAIR." TRADE MARK. WORLD'S FAIR.

This is a line of "solid" waterproof collars and cuffs made from a single thickness of "Celluloid," with the buttonholes *reinforced*. They are handsome and durable, and next to the interlined goods above described the best goods in the market. These goods bear the above trade mark.

"VICTOR." VICTOR TRADE-MARK Waterproof.

A line recently put upon the market to meet the demand for *cheap* waterproof goods. They are made from a single thickness of "Celluloid" of same quality as the "World's Fair," but somewhat lighter in weight. These goods bear the trade mark as above shown.

AJAX

No goods genuine unless stamped with one of the above Trade Marks, and the words, "THE CELLULOID CO."

EUREKA.

In addition to the above the following Trade Marks are owned by this Company: "Zylonite," "Solid Fibre," "Lithoid," "Triton," "Empire," "Eclipse."

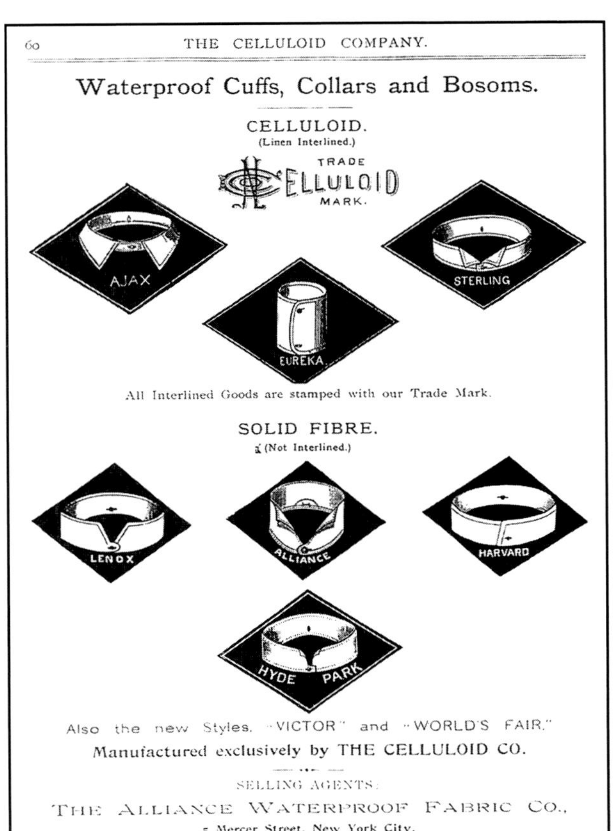
60 THE CELLULOID COMPANY.

Waterproof Cuffs, Collars and Bosoms.

CELLULOID.
(Linen Interlined.)
TRADE CELLULOID MARK.

AJAX
STERLING
EUREKA

All Interlined Goods are stamped with our Trade Mark.

SOLID FIBRE.
(Not Interlined.)

LENOX
ALLIANCE
HARVARD
HYDE PARK

Also the new Styles, "VICTOR" and "WORLD'S FAIR."
Manufactured exclusively by THE CELLULOID CO.

SELLING AGENTS:
THE ALLIANCE WATERPROOF FABRIC CO.,
5 Mercer Street, New York City.

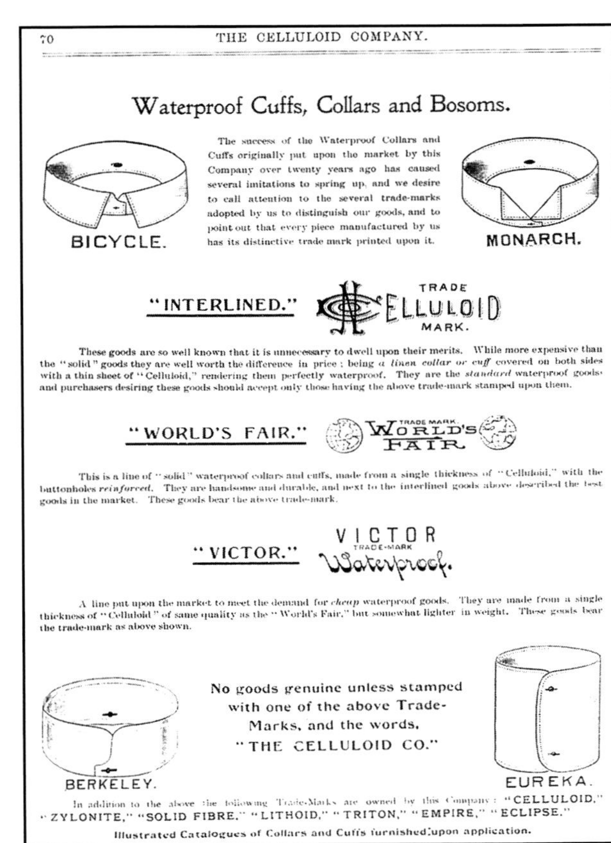
70 THE CELLULOID COMPANY.

Waterproof Cuffs, Collars and Bosoms.

BICYCLE.

The success of the Waterproof Collars and Cuffs originally put upon the market by this Company over twenty years ago has caused several imitations to spring up, and we desire to call attention to the several trade-marks adopted by us to distinguish our goods, and to point out that every piece manufactured by us has its distinctive trade mark printed upon it.

MONARCH.

"INTERLINED." TRADE CELLULOID MARK.

These goods are so well known that it is unnecessary to dwell upon their merits. While more expensive than the "solid" goods they are well worth the difference in price; being *a linen collar or cuff* covered on both sides with a thin sheet of "Celluloid," rendering them perfectly waterproof. They are the *standard* waterproof goods and purchasers desiring these goods should accept only those having the above trade-mark stamped upon them.

"WORLD'S FAIR." TRADE MARK. WORLD'S FAIR.

This is a line of "solid" waterproof collars and cuffs, made from a single thickness of "Celluloid," with the buttonholes *reinforced*. They are handsome and durable, and next to the interlined goods above described the best goods in the market. These goods bear the above trade-mark.

"VICTOR." VICTOR TRADE-MARK Waterproof.

A line put upon the market to meet the demand for *cheap* waterproof goods. They are made from a single thickness of "Celluloid" of same quality as the "World's Fair," but somewhat lighter in weight. These goods bear the trade-mark as above shown.

BERKELEY.

No goods genuine unless stamped with one of the above Trade-Marks, and the words, "THE CELLULOID CO."

EUREKA.

In addition to the above the following Trade-Marks are owned by this Company: "CELLULOID," "ZYLONITE," "SOLID FIBRE," "LITHOID," "TRITON," "EMPIRE," "ECLIPSE."

Illustrated Catalogues of Collars and Cuffs furnished upon application.

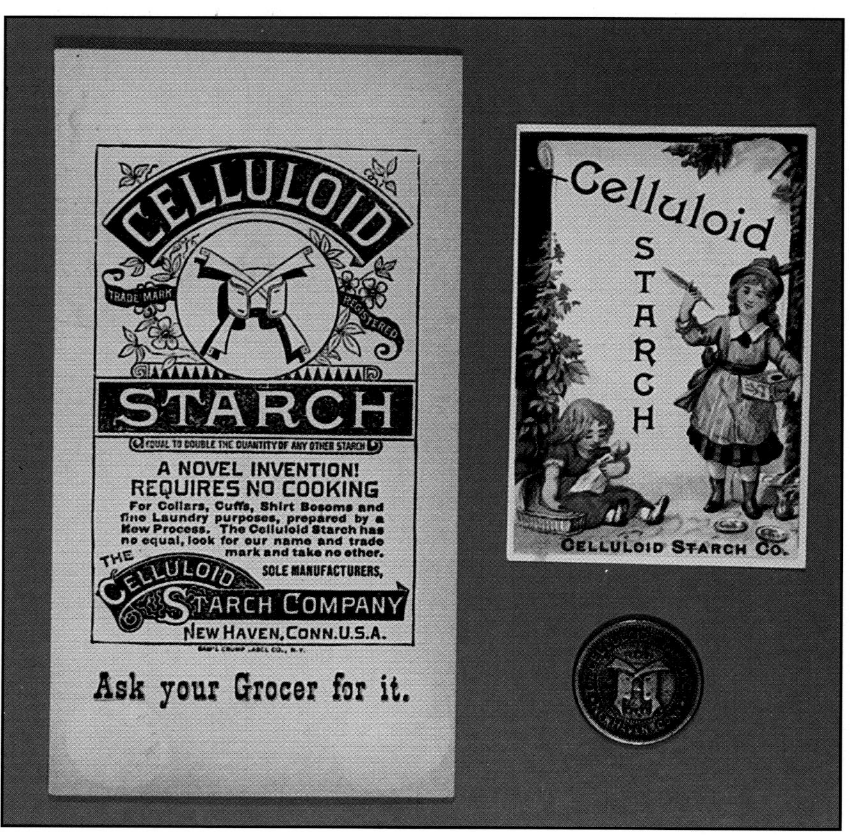

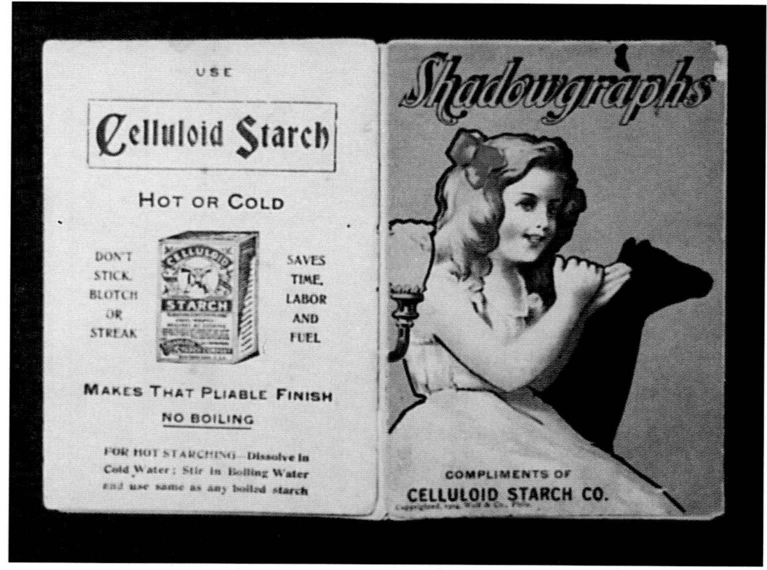

The unopened box of laundry starch is the only non-plastic product known to bear the registered Celluloid tradename. No price available on boxed starch or token. Trade cards $12.00 – $15.00.

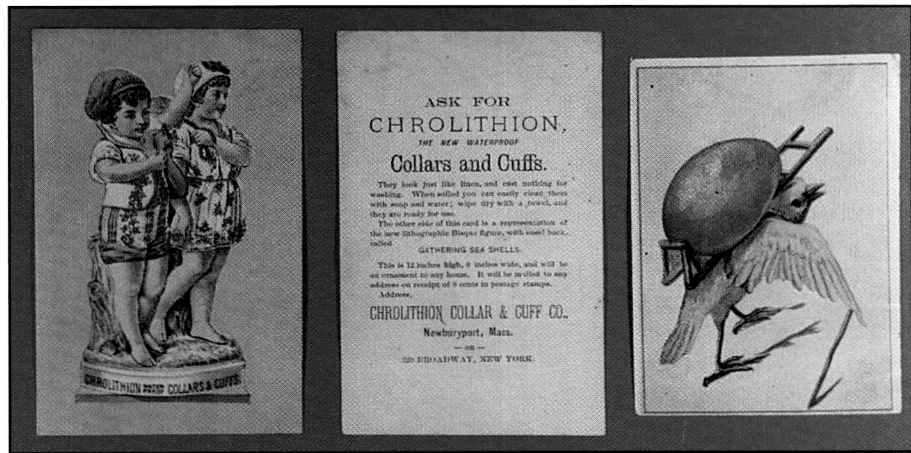

Chrolithion trade cards with reverse advertising pitch. $8.00 – $15.00 each.

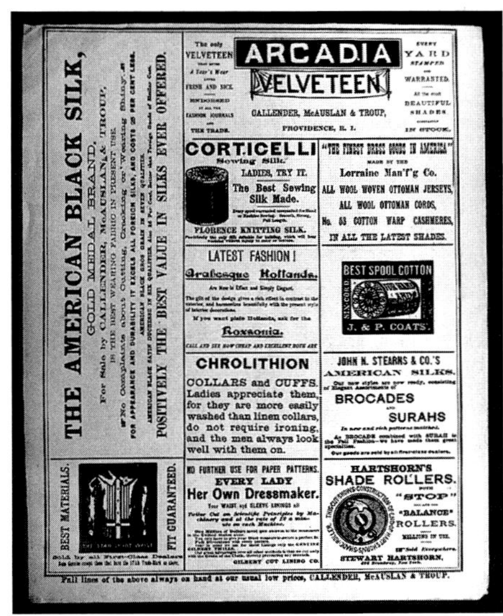

This Chrolithion collars advertisement, located in the lower center, is found on the back page of some sheet music.

Competition Within the Industry

Once celluloid became established as a successful waterproofing material for detachable cuffs and collars, others sought to capitalize on the invention. By the early 1880s several other firms began manufacturing waterproof linens as well. Unfortunately, a confused patent situation prevented Hyatt from exercising much control over the growing industry, resulting in stiff competition.

Chrolithion

The Chrolithion Waterproof Collar and Cuff Company was established by James Libby in Newburyport, Massachusetts, sometime during the early 1880s. Enough advertising remains today to substantiate a viable market for Chrolithion products. However, in 1883 Libby was challenged by Hyatt in court and found guilty of patent infringement and the Chrolithion Waterproof Collar and Cuff Co. was dissolved.

American Zylonite Collars and Cuffs

The Zylonite Collar and Cuff Company of Adams, Massachusetts, was established in 1884 by Leroy L. Brown using pyroxylin plastic manufactured at the American Zylonite works under a license issued by English inventor Daniel Spill.

Two English titles of Zylonite waterproof linens, the Hanover collar, and the London cuff, are clearly associated with the fact that Zylonite was manufactured under license of Englishman Daniel Spill, creator of British Xylonite.

In 1885, German immigrant and American Zylonite employee Emil Kipper of Adams, Massachusetts, was issued Pat. #322,729 for an improvement to waterproof Zylonite Collars or Cuffs. The following excerpt is from section 15 of that patent: "*to strengthen the edges and the button holes of such articles and also the article itself; and to that end, secured along the edge or around the button hole a piece of membranous substance – such for instance as gut skin, bladder, eel skin, various kinds of fish skin, the intestines of the ox, known as gold beater's skin, and like substances – the membranous substance being preferably contained between sheets or pieces of the Zylonite.*"

Unfortunately, very few Zylonite items remain today because the cuff and collar company was in business for such a short period of time, 1884 through 1889. Therefore, it is not known if Kipper's unusual technique was successfully applied to strengthen the weaknesses in Zylonite's waterproof linens. It is however, an amusing bit of historical insight into materials and their uses during the late nineteenth century.

Arlington Collars and Cuffs

The Arlington Cuff and Collar Co. was incorporated in 1886, just one year after the establishment of its parent company, Arlington Manufacturing in northern New Jersey. The production of waterproof Cellonite and Pyralin cuffs and collars became so successful that Arlington brand became Celluloid's chief rival in the trade.

The production of Arlington Waterproof Cuffs and Collars was not limited to the manufacture of pure white imitation linen, as seen in the example shown in the trade card on page 38 (left and center). Items made of Pyralin or Cellonite could also be produced with a colorful variety of designs and patterns. This manufacturing technique was devised by Joseph R. France and is described in his patents #249,142, dated Sept. 8, 1887, and #392,794, dated Nov. 13, 1888.

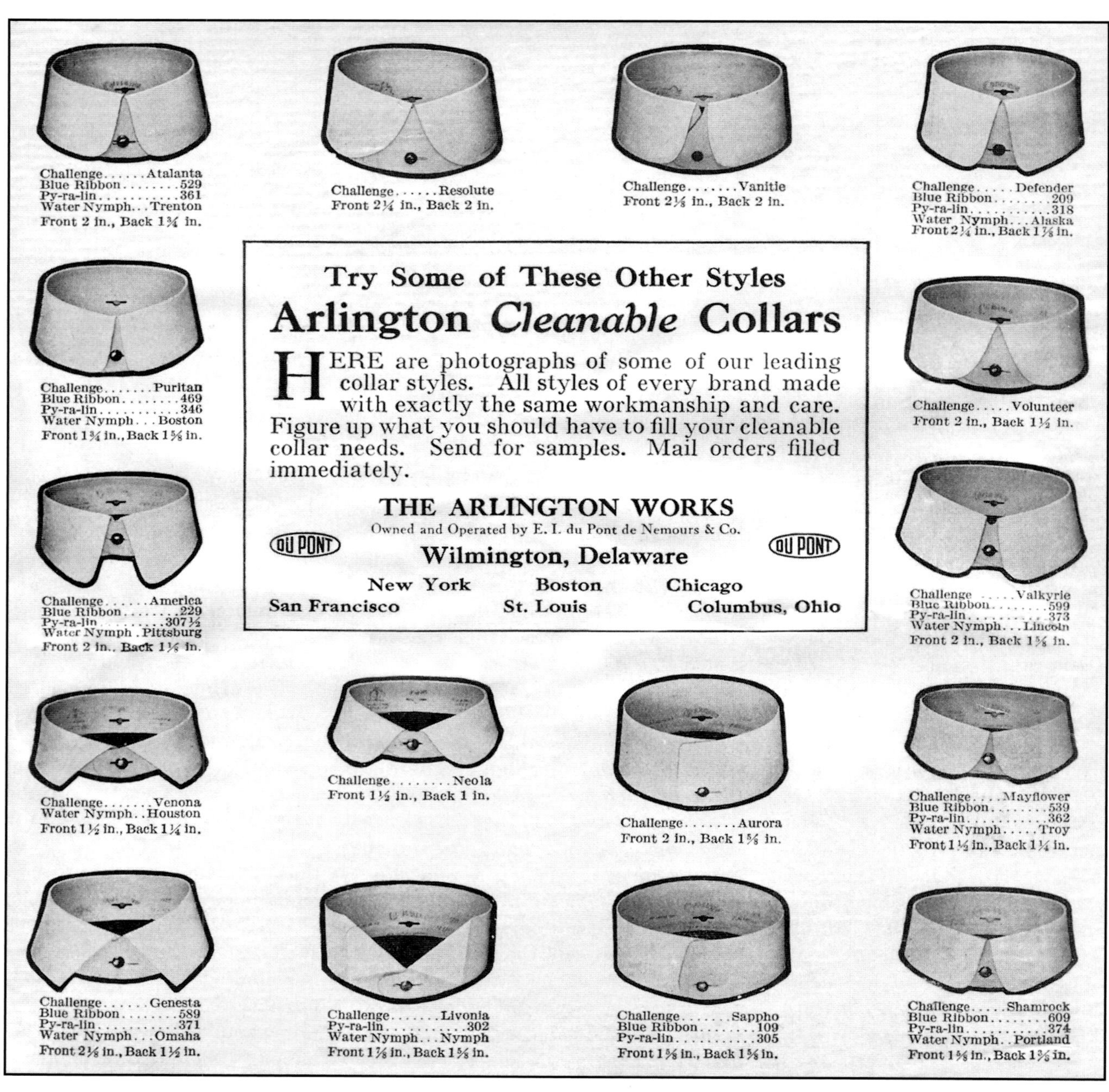

Arlington Cleanable Collars advertisement chart. The DuPont oval trademark on the chart indicates that these collars date after 1915, the year DuPont bought the Arlington works.

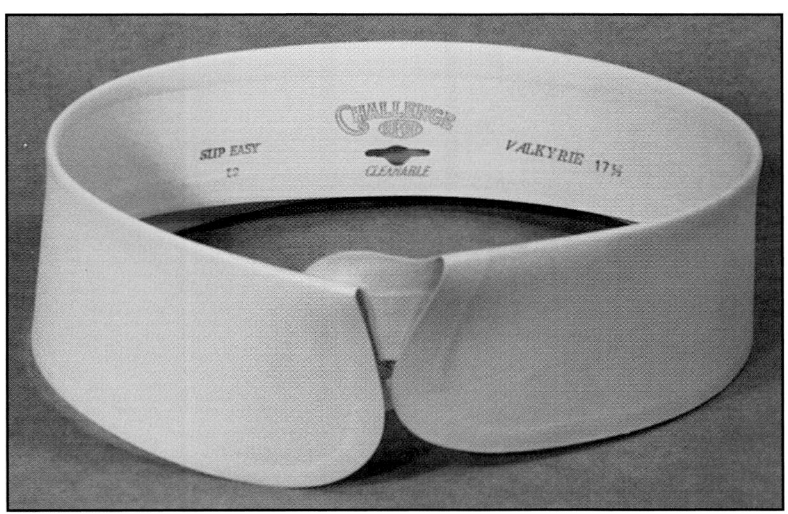

The Challenge Valkyrie shows little evidence of wear as the writing is still clearly visible, excellent condition. $12.00+. Note the DuPont oval trademark just above the button hole on the inside back of this collar. It is also shown on the previous page, fourth column, third down.

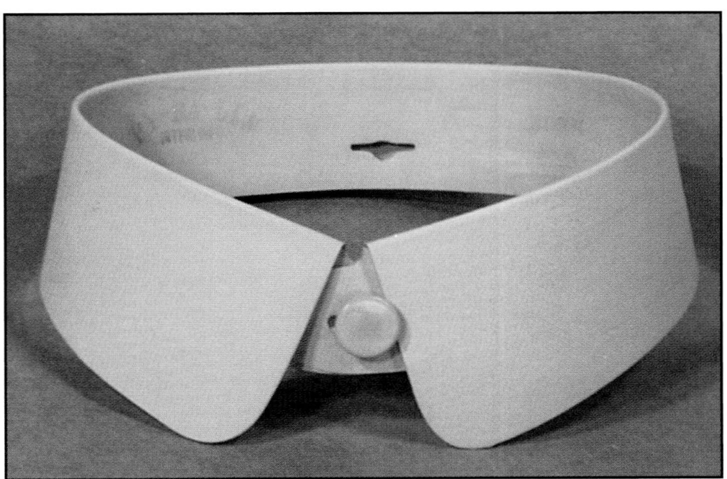

The Pyralin Collar was titled Challenge America and marked 307, Py-ra-lin Interlined on the inside back left. $12.00+. It is also shown on the previous page, first column, third down.

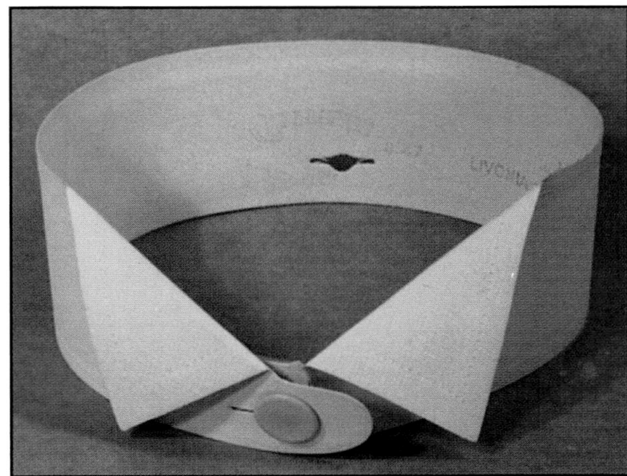

The Arlington Collar was titled Challenge Livonia. $12.00+. Formal turned-down wing tip collars were introduced in the early 1890s and remained popular for decades. It is also shown on the previous page, second column, bottom.

Front of Arlington Waterproof Cuffs and Collars trade card illustrates a variety of designs and patterns made.

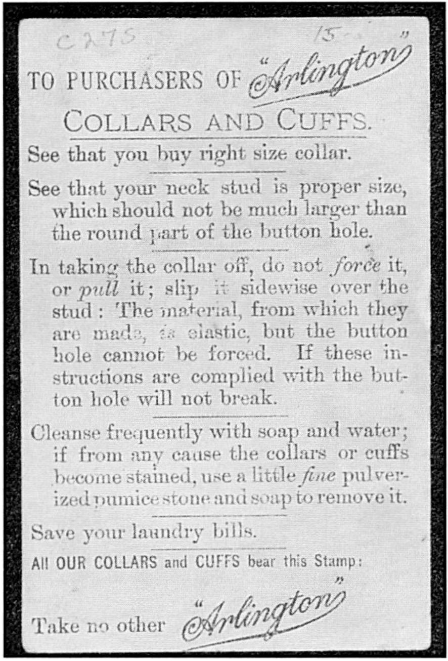
TO PURCHASERS OF "Arlington"

COLLARS AND CUFFS.

See that you buy right size collar.

See that your neck stud is proper size, which should not be much larger than the round part of the button hole.

In taking the collar off, do not *force* it, or *pull* it; slip it sidewise over the stud: The material, from which they are made, is elastic, but the button hole cannot be forced. If these instructions are complied with the button hole will not break.

Cleanse frequently with soap and water; if from any cause the collars or cuffs become stained, use a little *fine* pulverized pumice stone and soap to remove it.

Save your laundry bills.

All OUR COLLARS and CUFFS bear this Stamp:

Take no other "Arlington"

Advertising text on reverse side of the Arlington Waterproof Cuffs and Collars trade card.

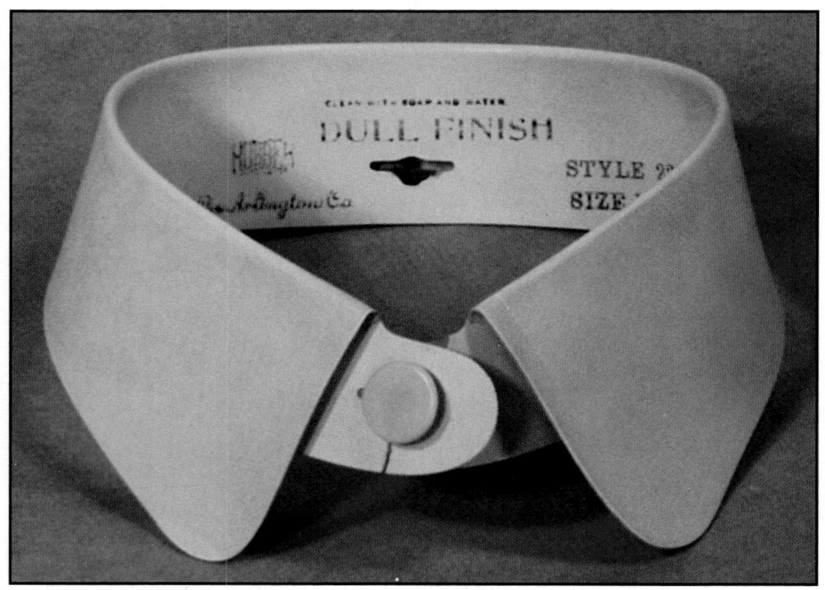

The Arlington Company dull finish waterproof collar shown here reminds wearers that it may be cleaned with soap and water. Also note the cracked and split buttonhole, a problem associated with the less than flexible openings. Regarding condition, $3.00.

Relating to the production of collars, cuffs, and shirt fronts from Cellonite or other Pyroxylin Compounds, the following excerpt is taken from Joseph R. France's second patent and refers to the fabrication of decorated material:

"Such articles being imprinted with any desired pattern, such as wide or narrow stripes, rings, polka dots or any fanciful pattern – in imitation, both as to design and color, of the linen or percale shirts, collars and cuffs now extensively worn."

The Lithoid Mfg./Solid Fiber/ Fiberloid Company

The Lithoid Mfg. Company was established in Jan. 1888 when the United Manufacturing Co. of Springfield, Massachusetts, leader in the paper collar industry, joined forces with the Solid Fiber Co. of Newburyport, Massachusetts. The Lithoid Co. operated for two years producing waterproof cuffs and collars using the registered trade names Solid Fiber and Lithoid. After their short production period, the company sold out to Hyatt, relinquishing cuff and collar production to the Celluloid Co. of Newark.

Shortly thereafter, the original founders of the defunct Lithoid Mfg. Co. ventured once again into the pyroxylin plastics industry. They reorganized under the name the Fiberloid Co. and began production of plastic in a two-story brick building in Newburyport. By 1904 the company had successfully grown out of their factory and found it necessary to relocate. A large modern plastics plant was built on a 16-acre tract of land in Indian Orchard, Massachusettes. Fiberloid continued to expand and became an established producer of waterproof cuffs and collars within the industry. Their products were trade marked with the brand names Litholin and Champion.

This circa 1911 advertisement for Fiberloid products was taken from *Munsey's Magazine*. It touts the virtues of waterproofed Litholin Collars and Cuffs.

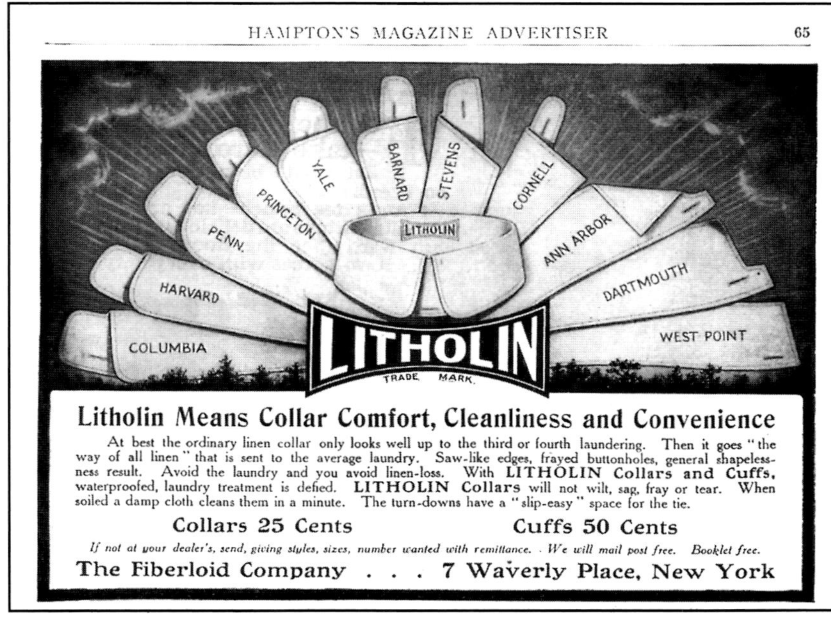

This circa 1910 advertisement for Fiberloid products was taken from *Hampton Magazine*. It shows a variety of scholarly sounding designs.

The cuffs and collar shown here were manufactured by the Fiberloid company, which marked their products with the trade names Champion Waterproof and Litholin. $15.00 per cuff pair or collar.

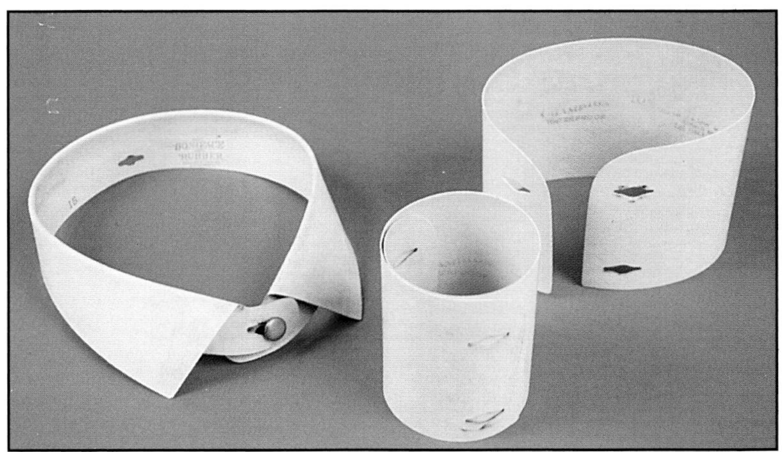

C.E. Buckley

By the turn of the twentieth century, competition within the American waterproof cuff and collar industry was growing. In 1901 the Viscoloid Co. of Leominster, Massachusetts, was founded by Bernard W. Doyle to manufacture pyroxylin plastic called Viscoloid. Eventually Viscoloid Co. also began to manufacture waterproof cuffs and collars. Later a former Viscoloid employee, Cornelius E. Buckley, went into production of the items for himself. His waterproof cuffs and collars were branded with the trademark "C.E.Buckley – Leominster – Massachusetts."

In regard to the establishment, the following story was related by James Buckley, a current resident of Leominster and the son of C.E. Buckley: Many years ago while on a hunting trip in Alaska, James was traveling through a small town when his eye caught a glimpse of what appeared to be a set of cuffs and collars in an antique shop window display. Curiosity drew him into the establishment where he inquired about the items. He was told by the proprietor that they had been discovered in an abandoned miner's shack, way up in the mountains. When Buckley asked to

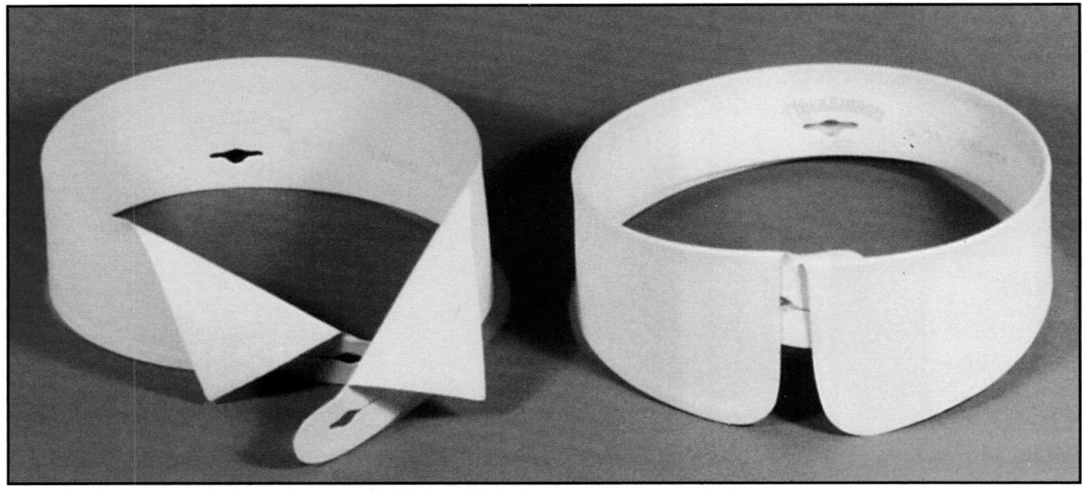

Two different styles of collar manufactured by C.E. Buckley in Leominster. An elongated slit adjacent to the button hole would have reduced the chances of cracks and splits caused by forcing a stud through the tiny opening. Unused condition, $12.00+ each.

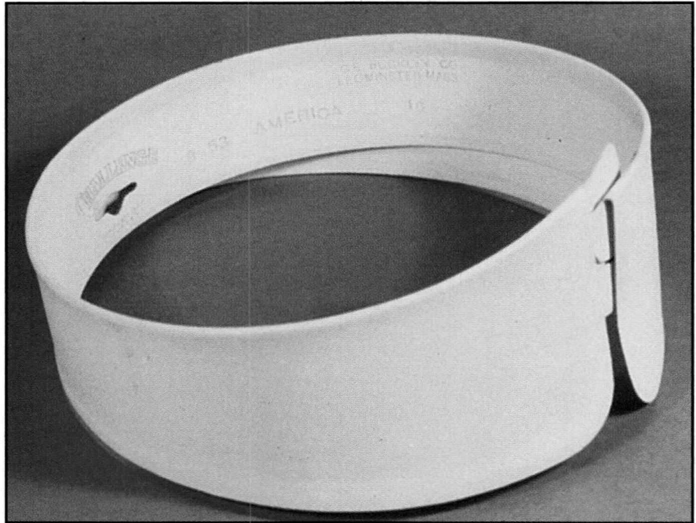

The Challenge-America collar shown here is similar to the DuPont/Arlington brand, however it is marked with the name C.E. Buckley, Leominster, Massachusetts.

This box contains a selection of C.E. Buckley waterproof collars in a variety of sizes and styles.

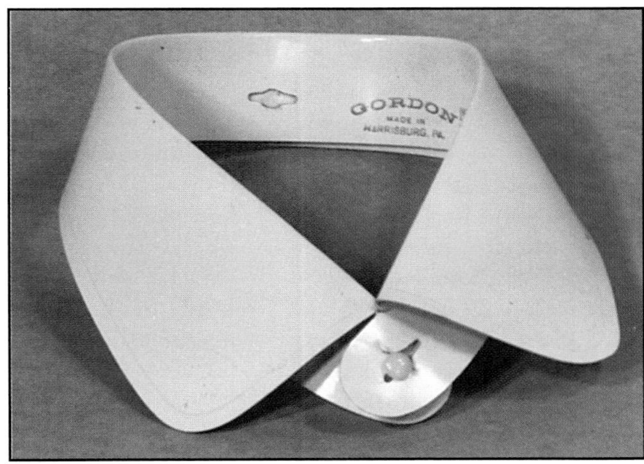

This waterproof collar is clearly marked Gordon, Made in Harrisburg, Pa., and titled "Lehigh" (the name of a nearby university). It is a folded example with embossed imitation stitching along the edge. $12.00.

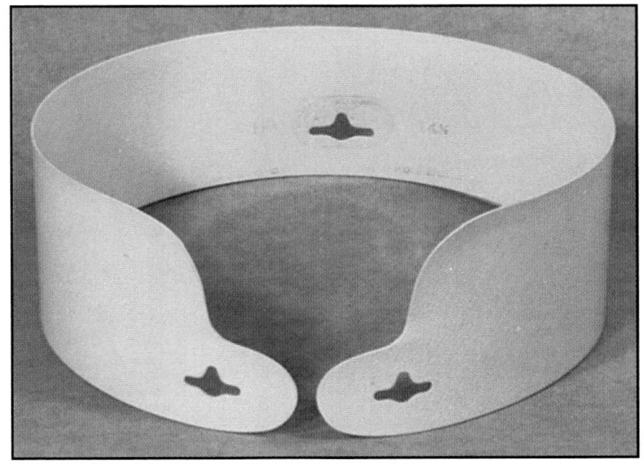

This collar is cut from a single flat sheet of glossy celluloid and has faux stitching embossed into the edge. Trademark on the inside shows a light blue spool of thread with the words "Willimantic, Collar Thread City" surrounding the back button hole. It is called the Era, size 14. $10.00.

see the items, he observed that they were indeed cuffs and a collar of the waterproof variety, and furthermore were branded with the C.E. Buckley trade mark. They had been manufactured by his father's own firm thousands of miles away in Leominster, Massachusetts – the very town he was from. Coincidence or fate? James purchased the set, returning them to their place of origin.

Unknown Manufacturers

Little is known of the Empire, Munson, or SLA Rated Cuff and Collar companies of Albany, New York. The 1905 Thomas Register lists them as a producer of waterproof linens. A 1906 Celluloid Company catalog claimed rights to the Empire trademark, as well as two other unknown trademarks, the Triton and Eclipse brands, so it is a possibility that they were absorbed by Celluloid just as Solid Fiber and Zylonite were.

Summary

Records show that an incredible 20,000 tons of pyroxylin plastic were manufactured annually for the production of waterproof cuffs and collars. Remarkably, this figure represents nearly half of all the plastic manufactured annually by the turn of the century. In addition, by the year 1900, the U.S. Patent office had issued over 50 different patents relating to the invention or improvements of waterproof cuffs and collars. Of these, John Wesley Hyatt was awarded 11 patents.

The entire detachable cuff and collar industry flourished throughout the first two decades of the twentieth century. It wasn't until the Great Depression of the 1930s that shirt styles were forced to change and the once thriving industry ceased.

Waterproof Corsets

Introduction

Corsets were considered a necessary part of female attire throughout the 1800s. In both city and country, women and girls – sometimes as young as 8 years old – squeezed their bodies into the steel framed undergarments in order to have an alluring and stylish figure.

Since it required another person to lace a corset, the process of getting dressed was long and uncomfortable. As a result, ladies began to wear the rigid undergarments day and night. The popular belief that one's figure would lose its shape if unbound also helped to perpetuate the practice. Ladies slept in their corsets, bathed in their corsets, and probably made love in their corsets more often than not!

Because steel stays had a tendency to rust and stain the fabric of the corset, they had to be removed before laundering, then sewn back into place every time. Eventually corset makers covered the steel stays with kid or other material – however within a relatively short period of time these absorbed the odor of perspiration and became quite offensive.

Alternative materials were sought and the use of horn and whale bone became successful substitutes because they were strong and flexible. (Whale bone was a plentiful by-product of the whale oil industry and was economical as well as readily available.) While these materials were water and perspiration proof, there was a drawback – over time the substances became brittle and frequently splintered or snapped.

Lily Langtry, famed English stage star, 1880–1900, was admired for her beauty and talent. She was so conscious of maintaining her curvaceous figure she popularized the practice of bathing in a corset.

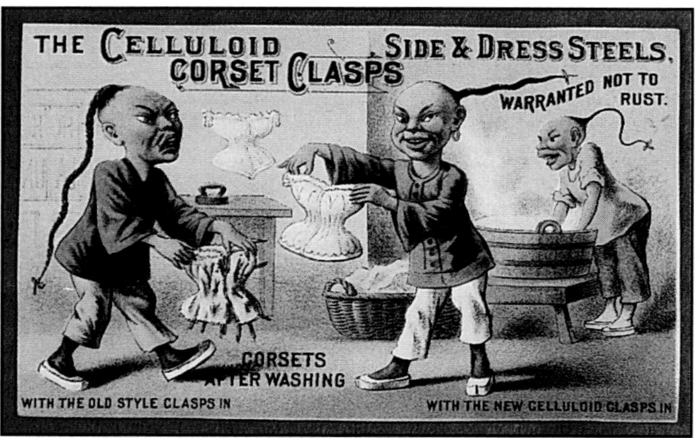

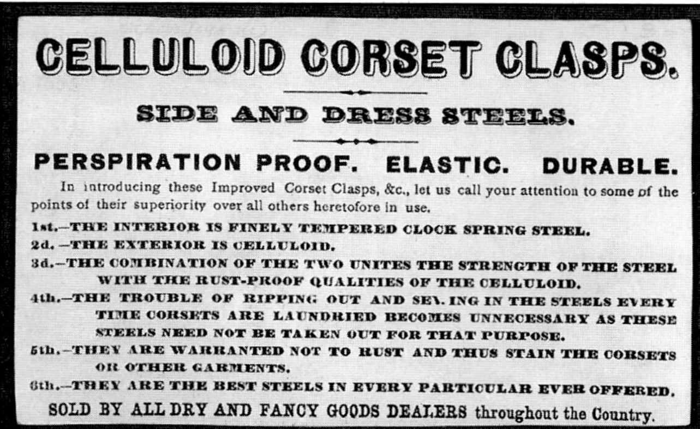

CELLULOID CORSET CLASPS.

SIDE AND DRESS STEELS.

PERSPIRATION PROOF. ELASTIC. DURABLE.

In introducing these Improved Corset Clasps, &c., let us call your attention to some of the points of their superiority over all others heretofore in use.

1st.–THE INTERIOR IS FINELY TEMPERED CLOCK SPRING STEEL.
2d. –THE EXTERIOR IS CELLULOID.
3d.–THE COMBINATION OF THE TWO UNITES THE STRENGTH OF THE STEEL WITH THE RUST-PROOF QUALITIES OF THE CELLULOID.
4th.–THE TROUBLE OF RIPPING OUT AND SEWING IN THE STEELS EVERY TIME CORSETS ARE LAUNDRIED BECOMES UNNECESSARY AS THESE STEELS NEED NOT BE TAKEN OUT FOR THAT PURPOSE.
5th.–THEY ARE WARRANTED NOT TO RUST AND THUS STAIN THE CORSETS OR OTHER GARMENTS.
6th.–THEY ARE THE BEST STEELS IN EVERY PARTICULAR EVER OFFERED.

SOLD BY ALL DRY AND FANCY GOODS DEALERS throughout the Country.

Chinese trade card, front and back. This early 1880s trade card illustrates the superiority of corsets boned with celluloid over those with steel stays. The Oriental laundryman was a common theme of advertisers during this time as so many Chinese had immigrated into the United States. $20.00 – $30.00.

What was needed was a durable, waterproof alternative to bone, horn, and steel. In 1880, Marshall Lefferts of the Celluloid Manufacturing Company made patent application for celluloid corset and dress stays. The initial patent, #238,927, was issued on March 15, 1881, and made claims that celluloid was a far superior product, over all other materials, for corset stays; its greatest virtue was that the stays did not need to be removed before laundering and the appearance and form of the article would not be damaged by immersion in water.

The Truth About Health and Corsets

It was well known by the late 1800s that corsets disfigured the bone structure of women who continually wore them. The normal shape of ribs and pelvis were so distorted that women often were unable to give birth and died during childbearing. The organs were squeezed tight and forced up into the misshapen rib cage causing lack of appetite and shallow breathing. Fainting was a common occurrence.

Many doctors disapproved of corsets and strongly advised their female patients against wearing them because of the unhealthy effects on the body. Nevertheless, vanity prevailed and the tightly cinched hourglass figure remained as popular as ever. With the advent of Charles Dana Gibson's ideal beauty – the Gibson Girl – the style became more alluring than ever and the practice of tightly binding one's waist continued.

In 1880 the Warner Brother's Company began to manufacture corsets with Coraline stays. Coraline was a brand of pyroxylin plastic that had been used for the manufacture of imitation coral jewelry for a short time – but now the manufactures found a far more profitable use. By boning corsets with plastic Coraline stays, they were rendered waterproof as well as more flexible – and therefore much more comfortable to wear. One can't help but feel the idea was copied from the Celluloid Corset and Clasp Co., but because the word "Celluloid" was never mentioned, Warner's managed to market and sell a great many waterproof Coraline corsets.

Today, Warner's is still in the business of manufacturing undergarments for ladies, however Coraline corsets are a thing of the past. Even though they were manufactured well into the 1920s, an example is yet to be found.

CELLULOID CORSET CLASPS.

SIDE AND DRESS STEELS.

PERSPIRATION PROOF. ELASTIC. DURABLE.

In introducing these Improved Corset Clasps, &c., let us call your attention to some of the points of the superiority over all others heretofore in use.

1st.—THE INTERIOR IS FINELY TEMPERED CLOCK SPRING STEEL.

2d.—THE EXTERIOR IS CELLULOID.

3d.—THE COMBINATION OF THE TWO UNITES THE STRENGTH OF THE STEEL WITH THE RUST-PROOF QUALITIES OF THE CELLULOID.

4th.—THE TROUBLE OF RIPPING OUT AND SEWING IN THE STEELS EVERY TIME CORSETS ARE LAUNDRIED BECOMES UNNECESSARY AS THESE STEELS NEED NOT BE TAKEN OUT FOR THAT PURPOSE.

5th.—THEY ARE WARRANTED NOT TO RUST AND THUS STAIN THE CORSETS OR OTHER GARMENTS.

6th.—THEY ARE THE BEST STEELS IN EVERY PARTICULAR EVER OFFERED.

SOLD BY ALL DRY AND FANCY GOODS DEALERS throughout the country.

Frog Ladies trade card front, and back. The trade card for the Celluloid Corset and Corset Clasp Co. features the ever popular image of frogs. What it lacks in artistic pizazz, it makes up for in the wonderfully bizarre and comical message (remember this was a day when outrageous and false advertising was rampant): The theme involves a conversation among bathing females – verifying that the corsets were waterproof; it features a hidden male admirer behind the reeds – confirming that the figure of wearers was alluring; the admiration of the swimmer's companion, "What a pretty form, Maud, what has happened?" shows that even women will notice the change in one's physical appearance; and furthermore the lady frog who is unable to swim (probably because of some female health complaint) joins in and claims they cure malaria, a dreaded disease spread by mosquitoes which would normally have been swarming in a swamp. Rare trade card, $45.00+.

Dr. Warner's Coraline Corset trading cards. By advertising their product as "Dr. Warner's Coraline Corset," Warner Brothers led the consumer to believe their brand of corset was more healthful for the wearer. After all, if a doctor endorsed the product, then it must not be bad for the user.

Early twentieth century advertisements showing naked children playing with water and corsets; from the advertising section of *Munsey's Magazine*, 1903.

A twentieth century advertisement from *Munsey's Magazine*, 1903, shows a child paddling through water while floating on a Warner's rust-proof corset. This brand was boned with pyroxylin plastic stays called Coraline.

Blissful Dreams trade card. Since ladies wore their corsets almost all of the time, sleeping was especially uncomfortable. This trade card appealed to the comfort factor of resting in a flexible Warner Brothers Coraline Corset. Both trade cards $8.00 – $10.00.

306 **SEARS, ROEBUCK & CO., (Incorporated), Cheapest Supply House on Earth, Chicago.**

Unfinished Skirt Patterns.

These Skirt Patterns are put up in pieces just the right amount to make a skirt. They are sold at very close prices, and are listed by us for the benefit of those who have the time or inclination to do the work at home.

No. 23621 This is an All Wool Skirt Pattern, of ample material to make a skirt of any size wanted. Comes in red and black, blue and black, or gray and black, with narrow and wide stripes. We can furnish it in plain brown if desired. Comes full 40 inches wide. It is made of very choice quality of material, and after the skirt is made up at home, it would equal anything that you could secure at a retail store at from $1.50 to $2.00.

Our special price, per pattern.....................69c

No. 23622 This is an All Wool, Strictly Non-Shrinkable Skirt Pattern. It is very closely woven, and is a quality that is very durable and warm. Comes in red and black, blue and black, or grey and black, with narrow and wide stripes.

Our special price, per pattern.....................78c

No. 23623 This is an extra quality, very fine All Wool Skirt Pattern, and we can furnish it in a variety of combinations, such as blue and black, red and black, or black and white, with narrow and wide stripes; or, if so desired, we can furnish it in large checks. This skirt after made up would equal anything your local dealer would ask $2.00 for.

Our special price.....................95c

No. 23624 We offer a very excellent quality of Mixed Flannel Skirting, with neat woven border of same goods in stripes. This when made up makes an exceedingly warm and durable skirt. The goods are all closely woven stuff, and we consider the pattern one of the choicest bargains we offer.

Our special price, per pattern.....................90c

CORSET DEPARTMENT.

A Corset Weighs about 15 Ounces.

Our efforts to make the corset department one of the foremost departments of our vast establishment have not been in vain. We now sell several thousands of corsets weekly. Taking care to sell nothing but good corsets that we can guarantee, no matter how low the price, and at all times selling corsets at prices way down, has built up our business in this line.

We directly control the manufacture of a great many of the corsets we sell, and are in a position to see that the material is good, the fit perfect and the corset durable.

If you want to buy one Corset as cheap as your local dealer buys one or more dozens, send your order to Sears, Roebuck & Co.

Please order corsets by **waist measure only.** Corsets are numbered by actual waist measure. If measure is taken outside of dress, deduct two inches for dress, and this will give you the correct size to order. **Do not order by bust measure.**

Dr. Warner's Four-in-Hand Corsets

No. 23631 Boned with Coraline. High Hip for ladies with large hips whose corsets break down at the sides. Just the corset for such people. It is worth four times the price to any one so troubled. It is easy fitting and adds grace to the figure. Comes in drab only. Sizes 18 to 30. Per pair......75c

Warner's 333 Corset.

No. 23632 Boned with Coraline. Extra long waist, medium form. A very popular corset, made of heavy jean with three boned strips of fine sateen. Beautifully shaped and a very comfortable, easy fitting corset. Colors drab or black. Sizes 18 to 30.

Price.................75c

Dr. Warner's Health Corset.

Boned with Coraline.

No. 23633 Made in Two Lengths, medium and long waist; adapted to ladies deficient in bust fullness, and those desiring bust support. For both slim and stout figures. The special features of this corset are the Coraline busts, which are light and flexible, and give to any lady an elegant figure, and assure a well fitting dress. This corset, with constant improvements, has been before the public for seventeen years, and has been worn by over six millions of ladies, a success never attained by any other corset. Colors: white, drab or black. Sizes 18 to 30. Price.................$1.00

No. 23634 Extra Long Waist 6 Hook Corset made of the best quality satin handsomely embroidered, a corset that will give satisfaction and one of the best corsets that we handle; drab or black.

Price, per pair........ 90c

BALL'S STYLE B.

No. 23635 The Most Comfortable Corset Ever Made. They need no "breaking in," has a coiled wire elastic section which yields to every movement of the wearer. Ball's corsets are boned with Kabo, made of fine quality jean; white and drab only. Sizes 18 to 30.

Price.........75c

Extra sizes 31 to 36. Price..$1.00

KABO STYLE 110.

No. 23636 A Corset of Perfect Form that will not stretch, break, roll up or pucker; extra long waist; made in white, French drab and black sateen. Sizes 18 to 30. Price.........75c

Extra sizes 31 to 36.

Price...............$1.00

NOTE—If you require a corset larger than size 30, order from those we quote in extra sizes. Ordinary corsets are made in sizes 18 to 30 only.

Kabo Style 110

Dr. Warners' Coraline Corsets.

No. 23637 Made in Medium Length Waists. Adapted to ladies of average figure. This corset has been before the public for fifteen years, has the largest sale and gives the best value and best service of any dollar corset ever manufactured. Made in two thicknesses of fine corset jean, heavily boned with coraline in a manner that prevents the corset from losing its shape, and makes it absolutely unbreakable. The hip is extra stayed with clock spring side steels. Colors; drab or black. Each $0.75

Extra large sizes, 32 to 36, 25 cents extra.

Dr. Warners' Abdominal Corset.

No. 23638 Boned with Coraline. Adapted to ladies with either full or slender figure desiring a corset long below the waist, to give abdominal support. Made with extension steels, side lacings and elastic gores on each side. Colors, drab or black. Sizes 18 to 30.

Price...............$1.25

Extra large sizes, 31 to 36 inches. Each.......$1.50

Special Sewing Machine Catalogue Free.

Nursing Corset.

No. 23639. Nursing Corset. The most sensible, convenient and comfortable nursing corset made, well stayed on the sides, but very pliable over the sensitive parts of the body; the opening permits the use of nipple without the least inconvenience; made of fine jean. Colors, white or drab; size, 18 to 30. Price....85c

No. 23641 Ladies' Perfection Waist; made of fine sateen; soft puffed busts; clasp front. Colors white, black or drab. Sizes 18 to 30.

Price.........................90c

ALWAYS GIVE WAIST MEASURE WHEN ...ORDERING... CORSETS.

No. 23642 Young Ladies' Corsets, suitable for girls 13 to 17 years of age; made of good jean; nicely corded, with shoulder straps. Colors white or drab; sizes 18 to 26 waist measure. This corset in appearance and durability is equal to goods that retailers sell at a very much higher figure. Each........40c

No. 23644 Warner Corsets, No. 65. Boned with rust proof, made of fine corset jean striped with sateen. The bust is flexible, but sufficiently rigid to give form to the figure. Silk embroidered white, drab or black.

Price.........................75c

No. 23646 Best Quality Jeans Corset, striped with sateen, bone bust, two side steels, 6-hook clasp, embroidered at top and bottom; in shape, appearance and durability equal to any $1.00 corset; unquestionably the best corset ever produced for the money we ask. Colors; white, drab or black.....................50c

No. 23648 Exposition, perfectly shaped and a fine fitting Corset, equal to any retailed at 80c; made of heavy jean, striped with sateen, wide zone, double bust, two side steels. Colors: white, drab, cream or gold.................40c

TENNIS AND CROQUET SETS AT POPULAR LOW PRICES IN SPORTING GOODS DEPARTMENT. REFER TO INDEX.

Sears Roebuck and Co. catalog page. This catalog page taken from the 1897 Consumer Guide shows a variety of styles and sizes of Dr. Warner's Coraline Corsets. The average cost was 75¢ while the most expensive example sold for $1.50.

Jewelry

The earliest forms of jewelry and accessory products were manufactured at the Celluloid Novelty Company, of Market Street in Newark. Licensed on December 22, 1875 by the Celluloid Mfg. Company, this establishment was the first to produce personal adornments from pyroxylin plastic. A circa 1887 Celluloid Company brochure, held at the National Archives in Washington, D.C., lists an extensive array of fancy articles including armlets, breast pins, bracelets, crosses, charms, watch chains, earrings, jewelry, necklaces, pendants, shawl pins, sleeve buttons, shirt studs, scarf pins, and rings.

The earliest jewelry reflected traditional Victorian era design. Realistic animal images, often carved from true ivory or genuine onyx, were reproduced in imitation celluloid. Mourning brooches, previously fashioned from jet or vulcanite, were sometimes molded in black celluloid. Bracelets, necklaces, pins, and ornamental hair combs were produced in imitation amber, coral, ivory, and tortoise shell and were frequently embellished with traditional decorative methods like inlaid metal or paste jewels.

The cameo has been a favorite jewelry form since the middle of the Victorian period. Traditionally carved from a variety of materials including shell, lava, coral, jet, and ivory, the profile of a beautiful woman is the most common interpretation found today.

Very little of the earliest celluloid jewelry is available for today's collector. When it is found, positive identification is nearly impossible because no trademarks are evident. Old company catalogs provide some clues to date and manufacture of certain jewelry forms, however they are rare and difficult to access for information. The best way, therefore, to date old celluloid jewelry is to study Victorian and Edwardian era materials and design, keeping in mind the progress of celluloid development.

Remember that the earliest vintage jewelry reflects the excellent imitative qualities of celluloid as a substitute for expensive luxury materials. This was a day when the working and middle classes enjoyed owning expensive looking items, even if they weren't the real thing.

A circa 1887 Celluloid Company brochure, held at the National Archives in Washington, D.C., boasts:

"These goods are in close imitation of coral, ivory, malachite, tortoise shell, amber, turquoise, lapis lazuli, agate and cornelian, with combinations in colors to which there is no limit. The beauty of these products is not surpassed by the originals of which they are counterfeits. Even to the eye of the expert they appear as remarkably perfect specimens of the natural substances they supplant. Their superiority over the genuine articles they represent is marked in many respects, but especially in their moderate cost. A few dollars invested in Celluloid bijouterie equals, in effect, hundreds expended in the purchase of genuine products of nature, and the closest scrutiny can scarcely detect a difference."

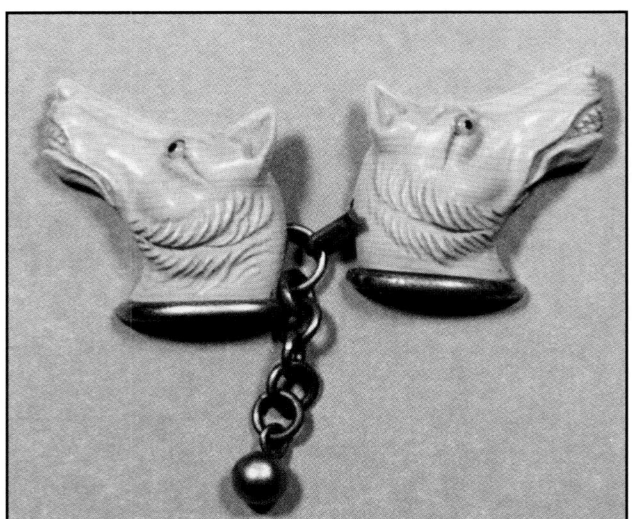

Celluloid cape or fur clasp. Circa 1885. Similar form found in the Celluloid Novelty Company catalog. Each molded ivory grained wolf head is 1" across and 1⅝" wide and features inset glass eyes and hand carved detailing. Metal closure and trimming are brad fastened to the celluloid, most likely attached while the piece was still pliable. This is also a fabulous example of the striation technique used to imitate the natural grain lines of elephant ivory. A rare and unusually early item, $175.00+.

National Archives, Washington, DC

THE CELLULOID COMPANY. 57

SLEEVE BUTTONS.

ONE DOZEN PAIRS IN A BOX.

Prices per Gross Pairs.

No. 1. 8 25 — No. 2. — No 2. 9 50 — No. 4. 12 00 — No. 6. 9 50 — No. 7. 8 25

No. 8. 9 50 — No. 9. 16 50 — No. 10. 12 00 — No. 11. 12 00 — No. 12. 12 00

No. 13.—Assorted Patterns. 14 25

No. 14. 15 00 — No. 15. 12 00 — No. 16. 9 00 — No. 17. 21 00 — No. 18. 12 00 — No. 19. 13 50

No. 20. 12 00 — No. 21. 12 00 — No. 22. 12 00 — No. 22. 12 00 — No. 24. 15 00

MADE IN ALL COLORS.

Cuff button page. This page from an early Celluloid Company catalog shows the type of realistic / grotesque images popular in jewelry motifs during the late Victorian period. Note the imitation onyx in the top row and the intricate detailing of realistic animal images; a special point of interest is the miniature glass eyes that were unique to the Celluloid Co. Such finely crafted items are difficult to find today, therefore collectors who do own such examples consider themselves fortunate. Starting at $45.00+ pr., anything less is a real bargain; Be prepared to spend upward to $80.00 pr. for examples w/glass eyes.

Neoclassical profiles were made popular by Roman cameo carvers who produced jewelry for the tourist trade. This rectangular brooch measures 2" x 1" and is fashioned from ivory grained celluloid attached to an imitation amber base. $55.00+.

Dotty Maust

1" x 1" faux shell cameo of a pretty woman with flowers in her hair. The slightly turned-up nose is associated with carved cameos of later vintage. No setting, $30.00.

These circa 1890 beads reflect a style reminiscent of the lavaliere that was so popular around the turn of the century. The necklace is 19" long and fashioned from a variety of shaped imitation coral beads with brass filigree embellishments. The small beads are linked together by chain, as are the large round and oblong beads, which are strung on a long wire. $150.00 – $200.00.

Christie Romero

These hinged bracelets in plain cream colored celluloid are inlaid with ornate metal decorations that imitate the piqué posé technique used to embellish tortoise shell and true ivory during the late nineteenth century. $125.00 each.

Perhaps the earliest of organizational pins, this circa 1887, 1" x 1" WCTU bow pin belonged to J.P. Robinson's great-grandmother, Sarah Augusta Farrington. The Women's Christian Temperance Union was founded in 1874 to educate boys and girls against consuming alcoholic beverages. $65.00+.

Gail and John Dunn

This finely detailed piece is molded in imitation ivory and applied to faux shell, which is attached to a filigree Art Nouveau style pendant trimmed with intricate tiny gold tone beads. Imitation ivory beads of varied sizes are strung to make a lovely 20" long necklace. $110.00.

2¾" long black bar pin, with a center oval cameo of a pretty woman, manufactured from "Persian Ivory;" probably intended to imitate the mourning jewelry that was fashioned from jet during the late Victorian period. $85.00 with original card.

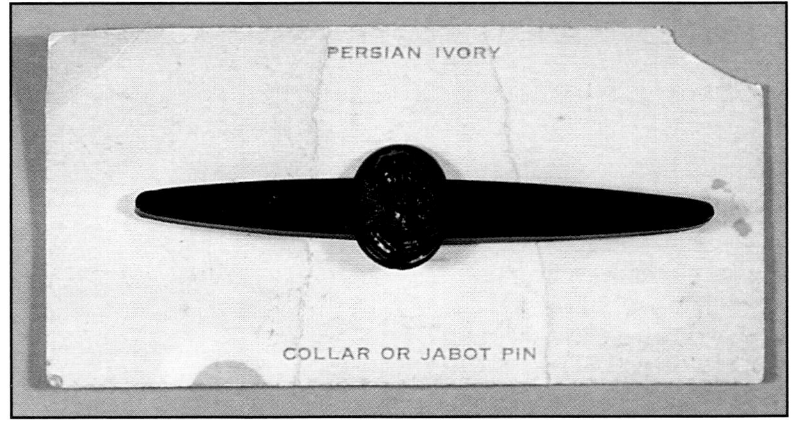

Three black celluloid cameos of varying sizes – all feature the profile of a beautiful woman. The smallest cameo in the center is set in an ornate metal frame. $25.00 – $45.00 each.

In 1889 an important technique for laminating paper with clear sheet celluloid was developed. This method created opportunity for photographers and advertisers, who seized the chance to introduce the public to a new form of personal adornment.

Another important development about this time was the introduction of celluloid photographic film by George Eastman. His transparent Kodak film and portable cameras brought about a new era in photography, making the hobby of picture taking accessible and affordable to the general population. By the end of the 1890s, small celluloid coated photographs were being used for personalized jewelry forms. Brooches and pins, like the ones shown here, were available from several firms for the reasonable price of about $9.00 per one dozen pins.

Most of the celluloid jewelry available to today's collector was manufactured during the first three decades of the twentieth century. In the early years, manufacturers embellished faux tortoise, amber, and ivory with applied molded decorations or painted motifs. Keep in mind that the decorations were subtle and meant only to enhance the beauty of the celluloid itself.

In 1915 the laminating of two contrasting colors of celluloid became widely used. The technique, though widely applied to the manufacture of dresserware, can also be found in some jewelry forms.

Helen Golubic

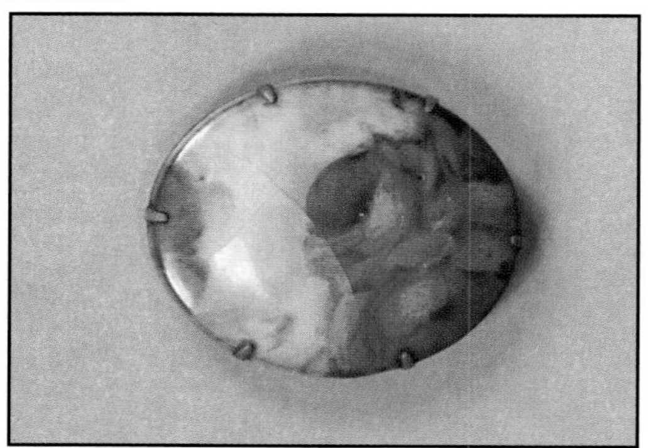

The oval brooch pictured here measures 1¾" x 2⅛" and is fashioned from laminated printed floral paper in shades of yellow, red, and green. Note the tiny stress cracks that have appeared in the surface of the celluloid sheet, which has been applied over a slightly dome-shaped metal disc, then attached to a flat metal back with prongs, C-clasp. $35.00 – $45.00.

Helen Golubic

Left, 2¼" photo brooch of a beautiful girl; twisted metal trim. $65.00+; right, double photo pin of husband and wife; metal with blue enamel decorations. $45.00+.

The novelty of having one's image reproduced on a brooch or pin became the rage and before long, advertisements for inexpensive pinback buttons and stick pins began to appear in magazines and newspapers. While this type of celluloid jewelry is indeed a novelty, it lacks appeal to many collectors because the image shown has very little personal meaning.

Novelty photo jewelry was used to commemorate historical events, celebrate birthdays, anniversaries, and promote politics and fraternal organizations. These examples feature the various forms available around the turn of the century. $15.00 – $20.00.

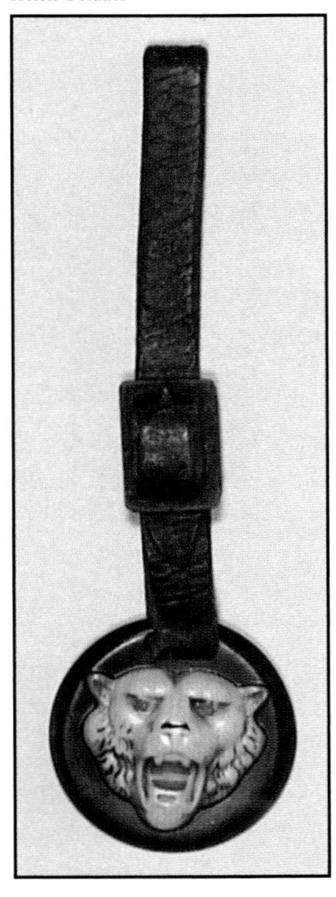

Circa 1915 celluloid watch fob, 5" long w/strap; 1¼" imitation tortoise shell disk w/grained imitation ivory lion's head, painted features. $45.00 – $50.00.

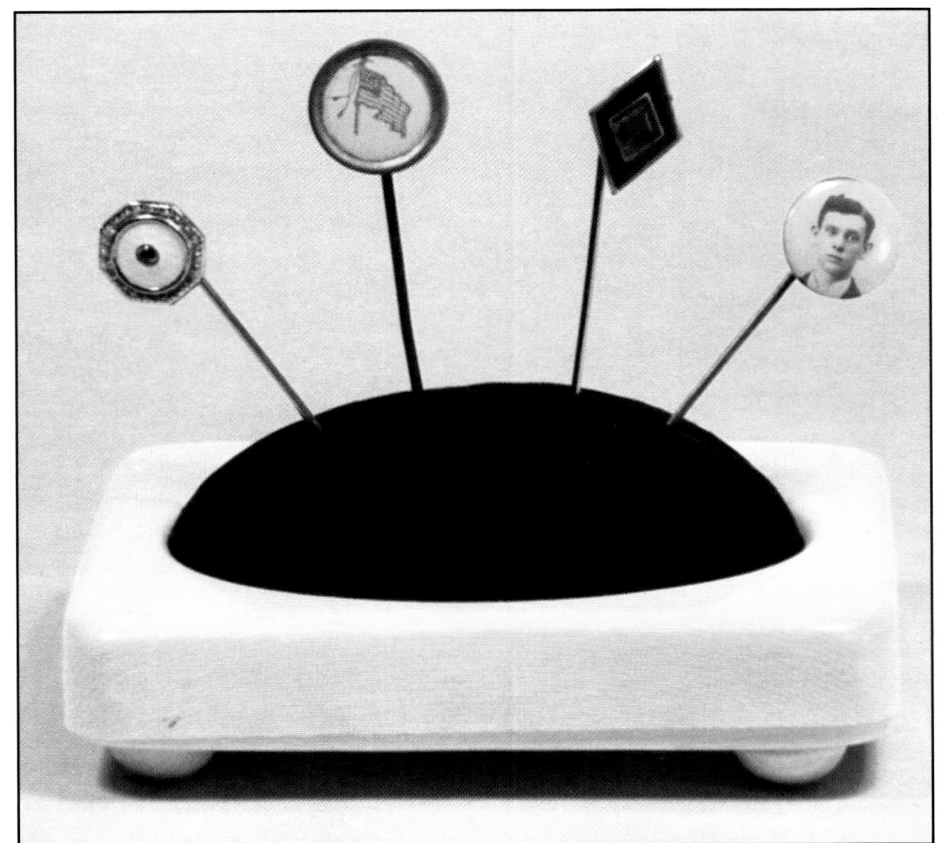

This collection of stick pins features an array of decorative techniques using sheet celluloid; faux ivory grained sheet w/rhinestone $25.00; patriotic flag motif is celluloid coated printed paper, $25.00; diamond-shaped pin with black sheet celluloid and faux gem, $20.00; photo pin, $15.00. Pincushion is black velveteen mounted in an oval celluloid frame. $25.00 – $30.00.

Helen Golubic

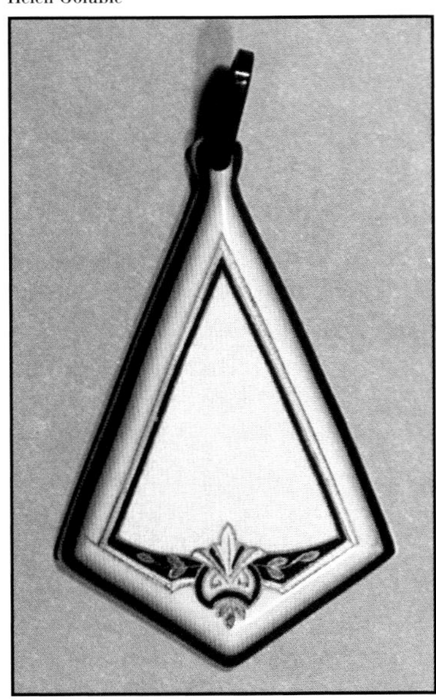

Circa 1920s, 3¼" kite-shaped pendant, laminated layered black and ivory grained celluloid features a striking Art Nouveau/Art Deco design. Hand painted black and gold decorations. $85.00 – $120.00.

Helen Golubic

The unusual 3¼" dia. bracelet shown is fashioned from round, oval, and elongated links in varied sizes. The largest links are laminated amber on top of cream celluloid. $35.00 – $45.00.

Cuff links with lever closures. Round, imitation amber sheet over alternating white celluloid and ornate metal circles, $15.00 – $25.00; collar button covered in imitation tortoise shell celluloid, pointed gold plated lever finding, $3.00 – $5.00; octagonal silver tone framework with imitation ivory sheet celluloid and center rhinestone, lever closure, $20.00 – $25.00.

These delicate bar pins, circa 1920, feature dainty applied floral decorations. 3" long ivory grained rectangular pin w/painted pink and green rose motif, C-clasp closure, $20.00. 2¾" uncommon amber bar pin w/circular center, embellished with tiny blue celluloid flowers and green paint, $35.00 – $40.00. 2¾" oblong ivory grained bar pin w/applied center coral celluloid rose and painted leaves, $25.00.

The Roaring Twenties

It wasn't until the years that followed WWI, that bold colors and glittery decorative treatments began to replace the simple beauty of materials found in nature. The war had brought about many changes in society, which in turn had a great impact on the ladies of America; with their men away at battle, American women suddenly found themselves liberated from the antiquated restrictions of fashion and society. They entered the work force in non-traditional roles, donating their steel corset stays toward the building of a battle ship and cutting their long, flowing hair into stylish short bobs. As the war ended, the Roaring Twenties dawned, and along with it, women's right to vote. It was the advent of the Progressive Era, a bright new beginning that was boldly expressed in the decorated celluloid jewelry that is so readily available to today's collector.

Perhaps the most beloved symbol of the Roaring Twenties is the flapper, whose rebellious fashion sense drew the attention of young and old alike. Her flamboyant image, seen portrayed on page 53 on two celluloid pieces, remind us of an exciting yet turbulent time; a time when the Prohibition Act restricted the opportunities for society, in general, to whoop it up.

In 1925, Howard Cartier opened King Tut's Tomb, revealing to the world a vast treasure trove of Egyptian antiquities. The discovery inspired a trend in jewelry design that included such motifs as hieroglyphics, scarab beetles, pharaoh and sphinx images, as well as an array of other related embellishments.

Egyptian Revival jewelry and accessories began to make their appearance in the late 1920s and early 1930s and the period has remained a popular theme of collectors throughout the decades. Several of the pieces shown here display the fascination with King Tut by the prominent use of a pharaoh's head, an especially desired image.

For those who enjoyed the bright, bold fashion colors of the Roaring twenties but wanted to remain respectable, the rhinestone studded bangle was just the thing. Manufactured in a wide range of translucent and opaque colors, bangles in a variety of widths were decorated with contrasting stones.

Ann Frick

The owner of this flexible 1920s snake bracelet purchased it years ago when she first admired it in the window of Glosser Brothers' Department Store in Johnstown, Pennsylvania. She found it fascinating, primarily because at that time only "vamps" wore such outrageous jewelry; as a result her bracelet was never worn, for she was a respectable girl. Serpent fashioned from embossed ivory colored celluloid with green and red dyed surface, further decorated with rhinestones. $125.00 – $150.00.

The unusual bright red 2" x 1¾" two-piece container could have been used as a compact for face powder – or even rouge, which was not only used to redden the lips and cheeks, but also to "rouge the knees" of gals unashamed at showing a bit of leg, a daring and mischievous display of feminine naughtiness. The ivory grained, dome top brooch is of the same dimensions as the compact and also has the identical flapper image stenciled in red, yellow, and blue, although it is difficult to perceive colors on the red example. $85.00 – $120.00 per item.

Helen Golubic

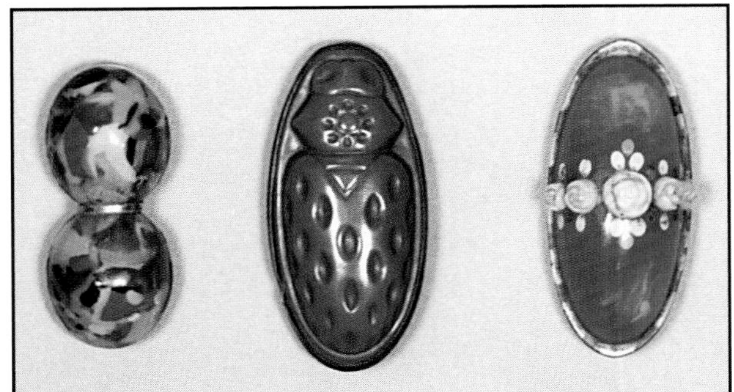

Unusual oval dome top pins, manufactured from two separate pieces of celluloid that have been cemented together, of similar construction as the larger flapper example. This technique, usually found on buttons, makes an attractive pin. What is special about these three are their colors. Marbleized translucent red, opaque green, and "end of day," (made from scraps) are not often seen in jewelry. The green beetle brooch is quite possibly an Egyptian Revival piece manufactured during the very end of the decade, after the opening of King Tut's Tomb. 1¾" x¾" end of day, double dome pin with silver center band, flat ivory back, one-piece finding w/U-shaped latch. $25.00. 1⅝" green embossed beetle brooch with metal bezel and back, modern safety clasp. $45.00 – $55.00. 2" x⅝" marbleized red dome pin with center band of graduated ivory roses, applied painted pink, blue, and green dots, back is flat with 2 pc. C-clasp finding. $35.00.

This glitzy two-piece buckle is molded in translucent amber celluloid, then studded with blue rhinestones; it features the fabulous design of two birds coming together in the center. $55.00 – $75.00.

Helen Golubic

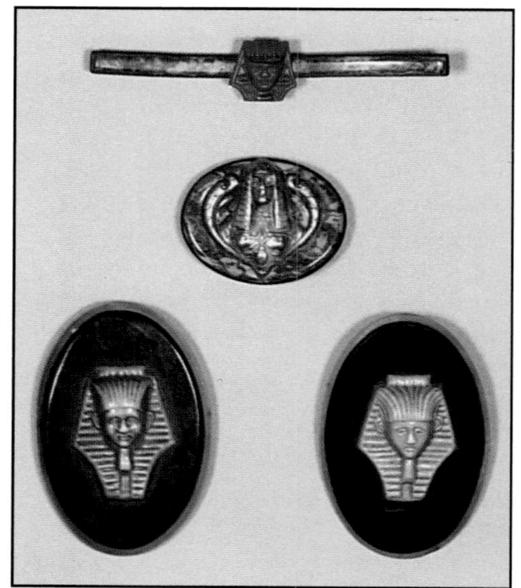

3" long bar pin with red pharaoh head in center; pin is two-tone celluloid laminate of black with a swirled green, yellow, red, and blue surface, C-clasp finding, $50.00 – $65.00. 1" x 1⅛" oval two-tone celluloid disc in black with variegated swirl surface, metal embossed image of Egyptian woman is washed with green paint to give it a look of patina, C-clasp finding, $55.00. 2 – 2" x 1" oval black and gray laminated base w/attached pharaoh image, the darker example is fashioned into a belt buckle while the lighter one has a pin back. Both $55.00 – $65.00 each

A variety of bangles. $25.00 – $40.00 for a single row of stones. $55.00 – $60.00 for a double row of stones. $85.00 – $125.00 for multiple rows of stones or those that exhibit special designs.

Helen Golubic

3¼" x 1" one-piece molded buckle, black celluloid w/detailed Egyptian temple scene incised into surface, applied red, green, and yellow painted details. $75.00.

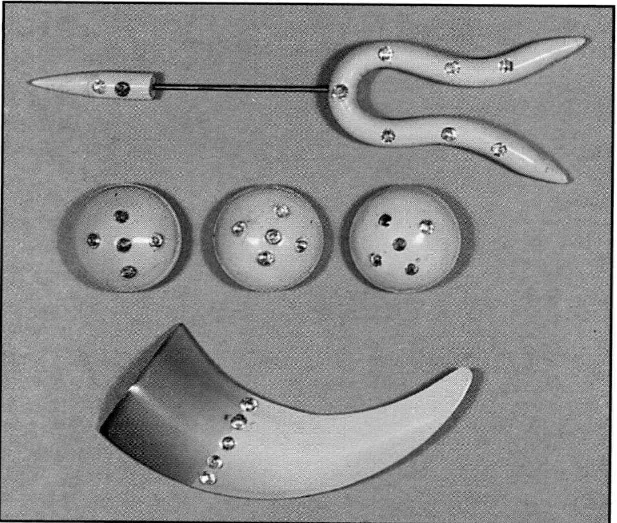

This collection of rhinestone studded cream colored celluloid jewelry could be considered subtle yet fashionable. 4¼" U-shaped hat or coat pin, $35.00; ¾" diameter buttons w/rhinestones – set $15.00; 3" tusk-shaped two-tone brooch with division line set in rhinestones, $22.00.

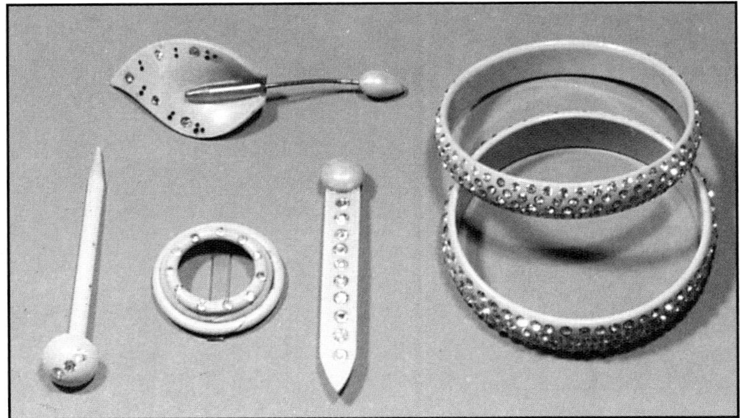

3" calla lily coat or hat pin w/amber center and black dots, set w/rhinestone trim, $25.00 – $30.00; 3" long hat ornament, circular top has 3 set rhinestones, $12.00 – $15.00; 1" dia. scarf ring, three graduated circles set w/rhinestones, $12.00 – $15.00; 3" ivory grained pin w/circular top and rhinestone studded elongated narrow point, $18.00 – $22.00; 9⁄16" wide bangle w/4 rows small rhinestones and 9⁄16" wide cream bangle w/4 rows of medium sized rhinestones, both $65.00+.

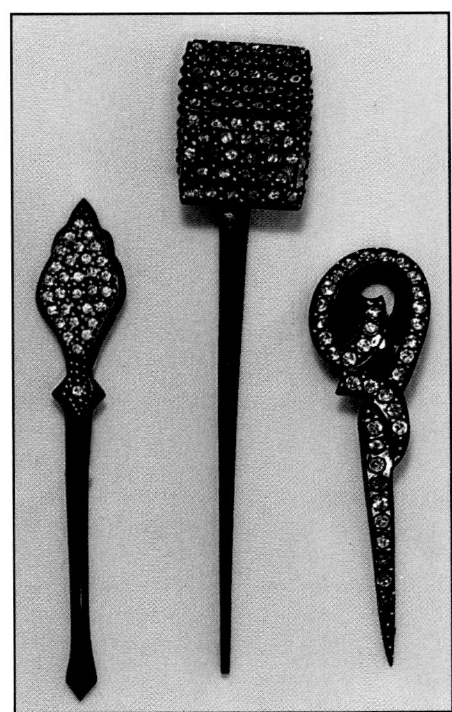

Two elongated Art Modern lapel pins, 4¼" and 3", flank a 6" hair ornament. All pieces feature a striking rhinestone and white dots motif. $45.00 – $55.00 each.

Helen Golubic

Three circa 1930s whimsical flower/leaf items. The 5" elongated leaf is a flattering hat or coat ornament; the flowing center stem exhibits two tiny thread holes, on either end, for sewing the accessory to a garment, or attaching it to a hat. $35.00. The whimsical leaf and flower brooches are fashioned from thick black celluloid and set with rhinestones. Incised lines are further enhanced by the application of white paint. $35.00 – $45.00.

C. Orris

Circa 1930 collection of Art Modern and Art Deco style black celluloid pins with studded rhinestones and painted decorations; a favorite among plastic jewelry collectors. Prices generally range from $35.00 – $55.00 each.

Assortment of rhinestone decorated accessories in contrasting black and cream celluloid. 3⅛" x 2¼" oval-shaped barrette, laminated black over cream celluloid, carved to reveal alternating colors, exhibits carved filigree and rhinestones, an example of tremendous craftsmanship. Marked Made In Germany, $65.00. 3" x 1" two-piece laminated black and cream buckle with flower motif, white and red rhinestones, $45.00; 3" flowing V-shaped pin w/white painted decorations, 8 rhinestones, C-clasp, $30.00; 3" long cream and black scarf ring with pointed black tips set w/rhinestones, $20.00; 1¾" black and cream oval buckle w/rhinestones, $12.00; 3" tusk-shaped pin, painted black and cream, set with dividing rhinestones, $22.00 – $25.00.

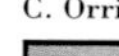

C. Orris

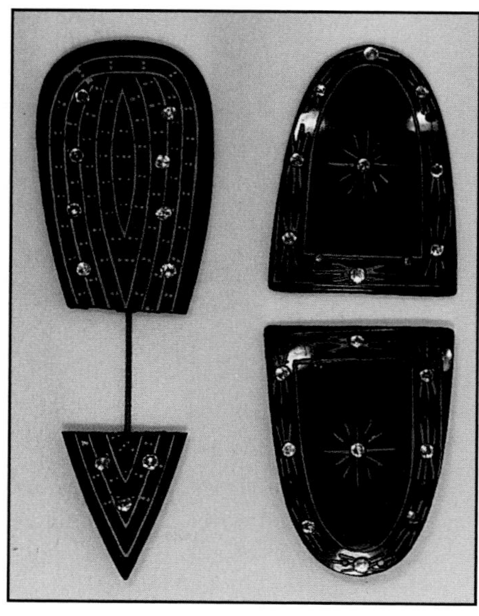

Two large black accessories with scored lines and rhinestones; both coat pin and buckle are 4¼" long. $30.00 – $40.00.

Christie Romero

Circa 1925 black celluloid pendant and earrings set w/striking Deco style feather motif in rhinestones with red, blue, and topaz enamel paint. $125.00 set.

Helen Golubic

Shoe buckles and clips could easily be attached to a simple pair of flats or pumps and were an ingenious way to dress up a simple pair of shoes. These examples, circa 1930s, feature stunning decorations; contrasting topaz colored rhinestones on black, and a glittery decorative laminate – which was developed in the mid 1920s by the Celluloid Company and called Goldalure. $25.00 – $30.00.

Introduction of Pearlescence

In 1924, William Lindsey, chemist at the Celluloid Company, discovered that by applying warm mercury to the surface of celluloid, a chemical reaction was created that resulted in a beautiful pearlescent effect.

Prior to this, jewelry manufacturers had used the age-old pearlizing method of coating celluloid with multiple layers of a pyroxylin solution containing ground fish scales and/or mica. It was a process that required several days of preparation, as up to 27 layers of the fish scale solution had to be applied in order to obtain the desired effect.

Lindsey called his new synthetic finish "H-Scale," a term he derived from the chemical symbol for mercury "Hg" and "scale" in reference to the use of ground fish scale in creating pearlescent effects.

By the end of the 1920s, colorful pearlescent laminated celluloid was introduced commercially and quickly became all the rage. Jewelry designers enhanced imitation ivory, amber, tortoise shell, and jet with the shimmering finish in an array of pastel tones accented with bold colors.

Buttons and buckles were an affordable way to accessorize a plain dress. Buttons were manufactured in mass quantities from a variety of methods including solid molded celluloid; decorated sheet celluloid wrapped over metal framework; two-piece, hollow dome top buttons; and molded or two-piece figurals.

Buckles were the quickest way to add a bit of glitz to a plain outfit. There are two basic styles represented here, two-piece buckles that are joined at the center by a clasp, which also have slots on either edge for connecting to a belt; and one-piece buckles that usually feature a divided open center. There are however, exceptions to the rule like the two buckles featured in the collection of Egyptian Revival accessories.

Buttons and buckles can be found exhibiting a great variety of colorful decorating techniques. Because they are relatively small objects, they are easy to store and display. In addition they are plentiful and still quite affordable; therefore a collection of such celluloid accessories can be assembled for a relatively affordable price.

The separable cuff buttons shown on page 60 were invented in 1914 and became so popular after WWI that sales surpassed 4 million pairs a year by 1920.

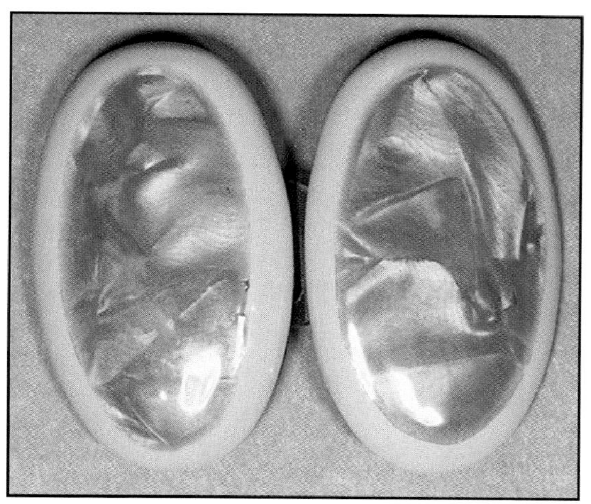

Double 2" x 1" oval buckle, each piece molded from thick ivory grained celluloid w/laminated pearlescent surface. Translucent amber celluloid hook and clasp applied to back. $30.00.

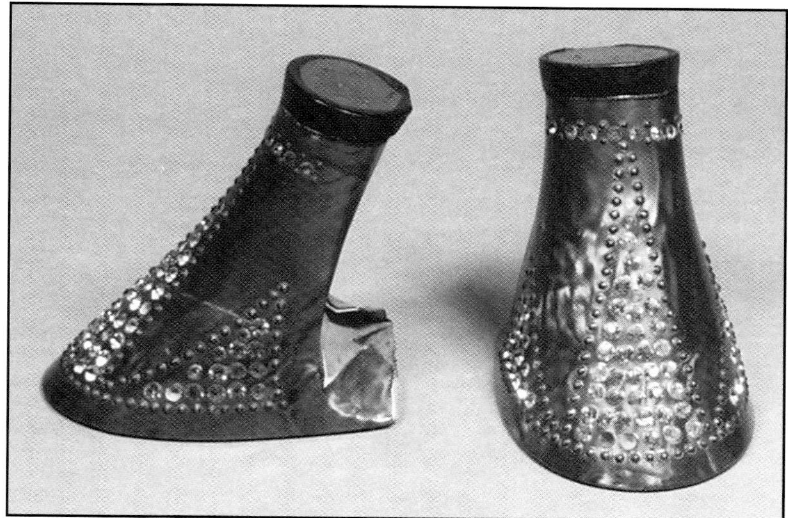

These shoe heels are fashioned from a wood base that has been covered with gray pearlescent sheet celluloid and studded with rhinestones. Although some of the stones have since fallen out, the heels are still worthy of mention. Fashionable accessories like shoes, purses, and hat ornaments completed a lady's stylish outfit and further enhanced the appearance of her jewelry.

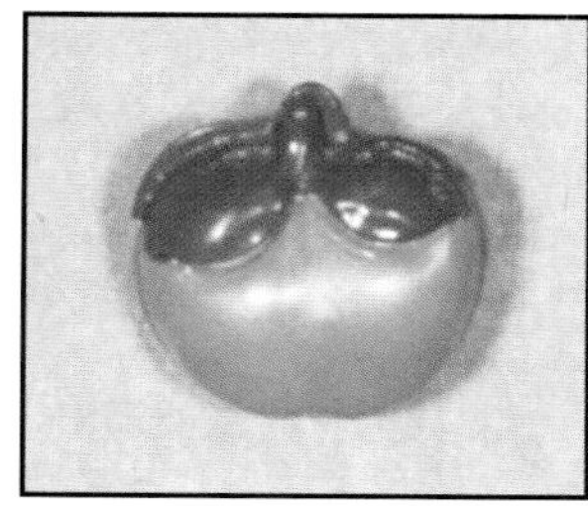

This whimsical apple figural is hollow and made from two pieces of sheet celluloid; pearlescent surface is further decorated with green paint, translucent celluloid shank on reverse. Set $6.00.

This wonderful assortment of buttons includes those manufactured from an array of pearlescent celluloid. Small examples can be had for as little as 25 cents each while larger buttons with pearlescent effects in patterns, swirls, polka dots, or special designs can run upward of $4.00 each.

This striking 3" Art Deco turban or hat ornament reminds one of the feathers that flappers often wore in their bandeaux. The amber pearlescent finish is further enhanced with painted chevron designs in green, orange and black. Tiny thread holes are at the top and bottom for sewing to an article of clothing. $45.00.

These dome top pearlescent buttons are fashioned from decorated sheet celluloid, which is shaped then housed in a metal shank framework. Small, 50¢ – $1.00 each; medium, $1.00 – $2.00 each; large, $2.00 – $4.00, depending on design.

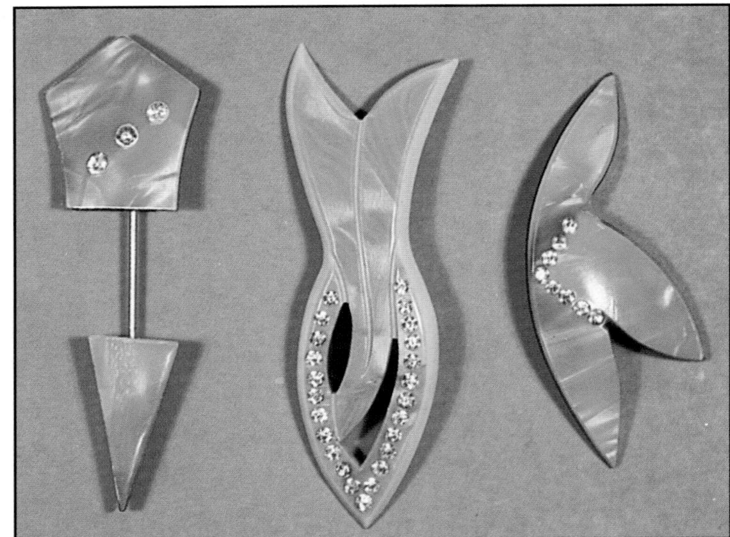

Collection of cream pearlescent accessories studded with rhinestones; 2¾" two-piece stick pin hat ornament; 2¾" fish-shaped lapel pin w/open cut work and rhinestone trim; 2⅛" three point crescent pin. $20.00 – $25.00.

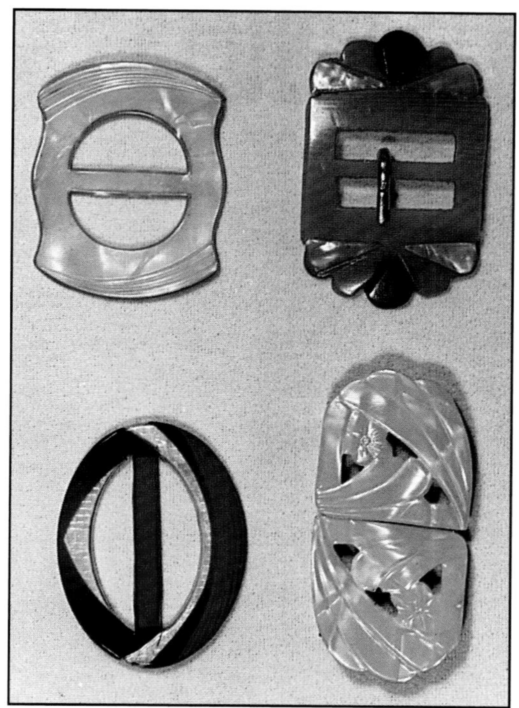

The two buckles on the left are fashioned from colored and pearlescent sheet celluloid applied over a thin metal frame. The lower right buckle is a solid two-piece, pearlescent finish example with molded floral motif. Upper right buckle is cut from a thick dark amber celluloid sheet and is finished with pearlescence and black trim; a metal belt hole fastener is joined to the center divider. Buckles are shown smaller than actual size. \$8.00 – \$12.00 each.

These brooches display a shift in decorative motifs from the dramatic contrast of Art Deco/ Modern designs and colors to the elegant whimsey associated with the latter part of the 1930s. Note the romantic silhouettes portrayed in the top two brooches. \$30.00 – \$45.00 each. 1¾" x 1⁄12" rectangular brooch in cream pearlescence w/applied painted silhouette in black. 2" x 1" oval brooch in amber pearlescence with black swan silhouette and gold painted trim. 2" x 1" oval brooch, cream pearlescence w/house scene, all surface painted except the clouds. 1⅞" x 1" purple pearlescence with a row of purple rhinestones and hand painted swan motif.

Art Deco and Art Modern designs are a favorite among jewelry collectors. This 3" long half circle hat ornament exhibits all the qualities that make a piece highly desirable: two-tone amber celluloid base w/laminated red and cream pearlescent finish, rhinestone trimming, and screw bottom teardrop of white pearlescence. \$45.00. 2" x 1" dia. mottled green celluloid dome top buckle, fashioned from two half circles applied to a metal base and joined in the center by a metal clip; pointed trim and center line studded with rhinestones. \$45.00.

Four pairs of separable cuff buttons on original card, circa 1922. The Jem Snap Link was similar in design to the Kum-a-Part buttons. Original card w/buttons in octagonal, square, or round shapes, and a variety of colored celluloid: purple, green, black, and brown. $30.00 per pair on card.

Two pairs of separable cuff buttons on the original card. Kum-a-Part was the registered trade name of Baer and Wilde Co. (later to become SWANK) of Attleboro, Massachusetts. The wonderful shapes and colors used in these examples are reflective of the modern colors and styles associated with the mid 1920s. $40.00 – $50.00 on original card.

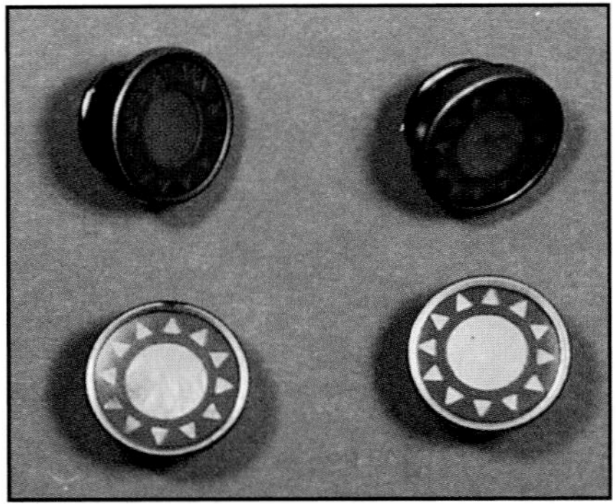

This pair of separable cuff buttons feature mother-of-pearl centers that are covered with a layer of perforated brown celluloid in a sun ray pattern, then further covered with clear sheet celluloid. Marked "Baer and Wilde" these separable buttons were manufactured in Attleboro, Mass., around 1918. $20.00+.

The story has been told that the inmates at a particular prison spent time fashioning rings out of old pyroxylin plastic toothbrush handles. While there is a possibility that such rings could have been made (since celluloid is a thermoplastic and easily manipulated when the right amount of heat and pressure is applied), it is obvious that fancy rings of this caliber could not have been produced from recycled toothbrushes. Various molding machinery and volatile chemical preparations were necessary when fabricating such intricate items. In addition, precise combinations of laminated and pearlescence effects could not have been successfully manipulated without a certain expertise regarding the applications of celluloid.

Helen Golubic

Collection of rings manufactured from a variety of techniques including laminated celluloid in ivory graining, layered with solid colors and pearlescent; celluloid covered photos; imbedded initial in clear celluloid. Photo rings, $45.00; multicolored laminated and pearlescent rings, $65.00 – $85.00; initial rings under clear celluloid, $55.00.

Novelty Jewelry

Beginning in the 1930s, whimsical novelty designs began to appear on inexpensive pins and brooches. While some featured silhouette decorations, others were fashioned to represent inanimate objects and still others were made in the image of animals, insects, birds, and people. Today, collectors of celluloid jewelry desire figural pins with amusing decorative treatments.

It was around the early 1930s that inexpensive Japanese jewelry in imitation coral and cream celluloid began to appear in a wide array of forms; bangle bracelets, brooches, rings, pins, earrings, barrettes, pendants, dress clips, and buckles. Trade with the Japanese ceased throughout the years of WWII, but with the Occupation of Japan between 1945 – 1952, a great deal of celluloid was imported into the United States.

After WWII ended, the Japanese relied upon their celluloid industry to help rebuild the economy. During the 1945 – 1952 occupation, thousands of inexpensive novelty pins and rings were produced and exported into the United States. The molded floral brooches on page 65 are similar to the style, which is frequently embellished with hand painted detailing. Often Japanese celluloid has a thick, shiny appearance.

Collector Caution: Lea Stein Jewelry
During the 1950s, Lea Stein, a French jewelry designer, produced a wide variety of novelty brooches and pins from cellulose acetate). Most Stein pins feature ultramodern designs in wonderful colors, contrasted with ivory grained cellulose acetate. Known forms include large, hollow blow-molded two-tone turtles, stylized foxes, modern automobiles, Indian profiles, various stylized and modern female profiles, bell hops and sailors with dangling arms, and multi-colored laminated hearts. Although they look like celluloid, they are not and buyers should beware. See explanation of cellulose acetate on page 66.

Helen Golubic

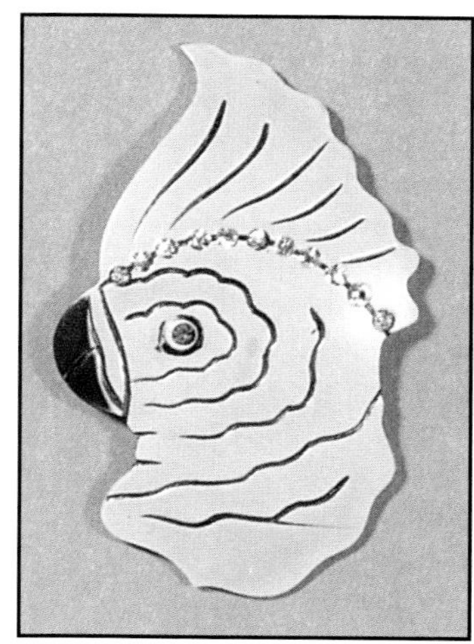

2¾" pink cockatiel with incised feather markings painted with black enamel, crest is ornamented w/rhinestones and eye is a celluloid bezel set green rhinestone. A highly collectible form associated with the Art Deco movement $55.00.

Helen Golubic

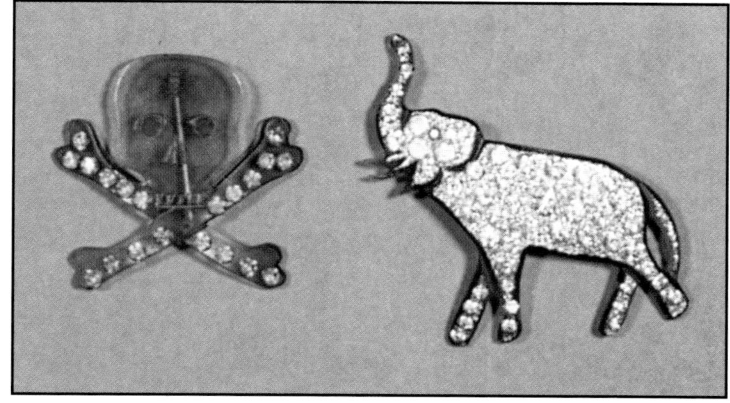

Circa 1930s novelty pins fashioned from pale amber celluloid; the 2¼" elephant is coated with a glittery surface and pavé set with rhinestones, the raised trunk is a traditional symbol of good luck. $35.00 – $40.00. The skull and crossbones pin is set with amber and red rhinestones, and the teeth and nose are incised. An unusual motif that is desired by collectors. $45.00 – $55.00.

Helen Golubic

This wonderful red embossed fireman's hat is fashioned from two pieces of unusual red celluloid and is 2⅜" long x 2" wide. The words "Put Out My Fire" add to its appeal. $45.00+.

Important Celluloid Developments Relating to Jewelry

1874 Patent issued for imitation coral
1874 Celluloid Mfg. Co. chemists develop imitation tortoise shell, amber, and jet.
1882 Inlay of color pigments in celluloid developed for jewelry
1883 Development of imitation ivory graining
1884 Patent issued for pearlescent effect on celluloid by using ground mica in pyroxylin base.
1888 Process of print transfer on celluloid patented
1889 Development of laminating printed paper with celluloid sheet. Development of embossing techniques perfected
1891 Artificial horn perfected
1893 Imitation onyx perfected
1898 Imitation marble perfected
1899 Imitation mosaic, cloisonné and champlevé enameling
1902 Patent for setting rhinestones in celluloid issued
1914 Laminating two thick colors of celluloid developed
1924 Synthetic pearlescence, H-Scale, developed
1925 Commercial introduction of colored pearlessence
1927 Non-flammable, cellulose acetate plastic developed

Helen Golubic

2¼" tall, die cut girl figural with embossed detailing on dress and painted green trim. Manufactured from very thin, red sheet celluloid (an uncommon color). Pins fashioned from it are of particular interest to collectors. $30.00+.

The neoclassical profile of a woman on this brooch is very similar to the example of earlier vintage shown in the beginning of this section. However, the quality of this 2" x 2" oval cameo with open lace edging is sorely lacking in comparison to the earlier piece. Embossed from thin sheet celluloid, discoloration in the form of yellow streaking can be observed throughout the lace edging. Tiny brown spots, which indicate contaminants in the batch of celluloid when manufactured, are evident around the offset profile. In addition, the finished quality of this piece is poor – note the unclean edges around the filigree border. $15.00.

1¾" tall football player, kicking position, football at end of stickpin is ¾". Two-piece, die cut figural from thick cream celluloid sheet with hand painted detailing. $40.00 – $50.00. 2" tall novelty pin of girl on skis, die cut from thick cream colored celluloid sheet with wonderfully painted detailing. $40.00 – $55.00.

These pendants are both die cut from sheet celluloid; the dancers measure 1⅜" x 2" and the ivory grained silhouette of a lady in a frilly dress is 1¹⁄₁₆" x 2". Both pendants are suspended from black satin ribbon and both range in price between $25.00 – $35.00.

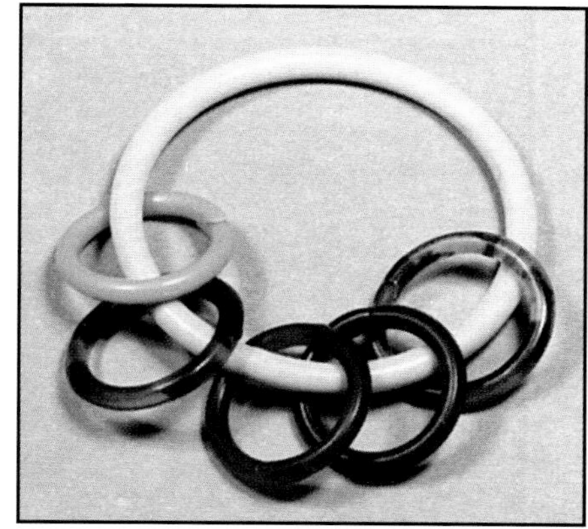

This cream colored celluloid ring is a salesman's sample of multi-colored round links. Green, tortoise, blue, and black. Circa 1930.

The oval link chain is a fine example of the type of work that was done at home by employees of the Viscoloid Company in Leominster, Mass. The chain consists of two types of links; plain solid ovals and split ovals. These links were hand joined by women who took the materials home and assembled them in their spare time. Payment was determined by the length of finished chain.

Helen Golubic

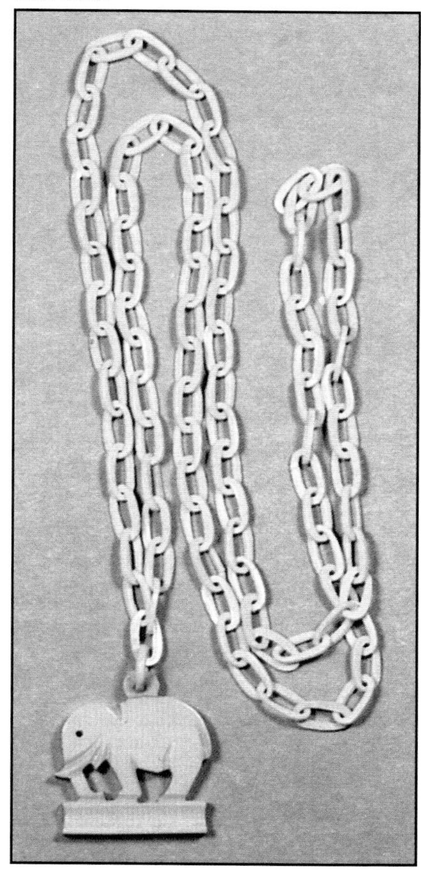

1/8" thick imitation ivory grained pendant, 1¼" wide x 1⅛" tall, in the form of an African elephant w/hand carved detailing so realistic it could fool the naked eye. Pendant is suspended from a 16" long, oval link ivory grained chain. Complete, $65.00+.

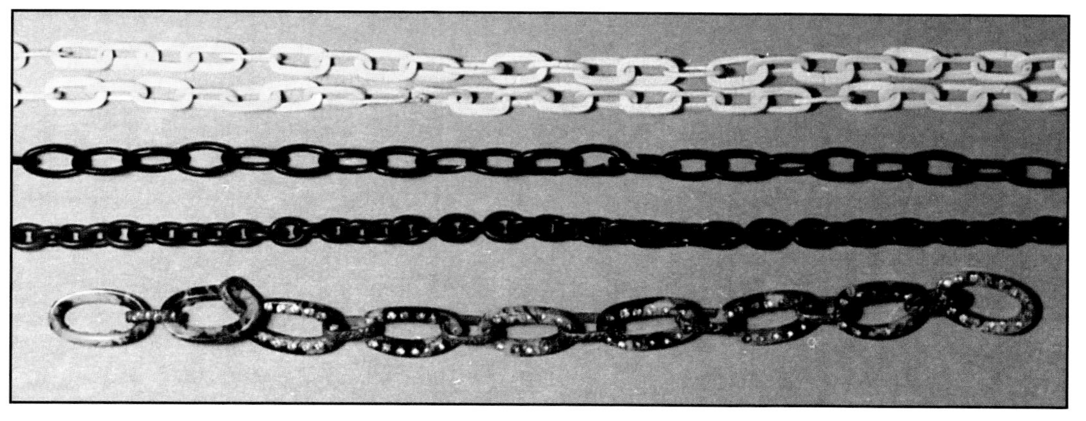

Four different types of chain manufactured in celluloid. The smallest section is a variegated brown and yellow celluloid that has been studded with rhinestones.

Marked Japanese 1¾" floral pendant, $20.00; rose earrings w/gold tone findings, $12.00 – $15.00; ¾" and ½" wide bangle bracelets, $25.00 – $35.00; 2-pc. 3¼" imitation coral rose buckle w/jeweled trim, $30.00.

This molded Japanese brooch shows a female profile, framed by a hand painted floral border, a decorative technique used after WWII. The thick, shiny celluloid coupled with garish colored accents is a far cry from the intricately molded detailing of the earlier cameos featured in this section. $20.00.

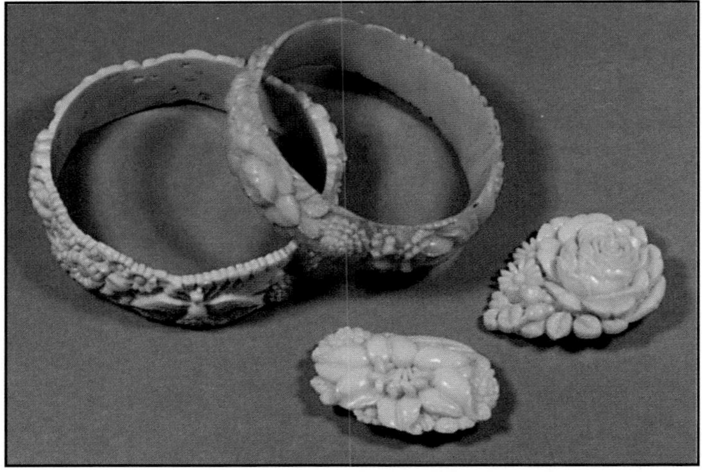

⅞" wide floral bangle and 1" wide floral bangle in cream celluloid, $25.00 – $35.00 each; lily dress clip and 2" wide pointed rose dress clip, both $15.00 – $20.00.

Helen Golubic

These two bow pins were tied into shape while the celluloid rods from which they were fashioned were still pliable. 1¾" x 2" opaque green double bow w/dangling heart charms, $25.00. 1¾" x 1" translucent mottled brown and amber with center knot set with rhinestones. $18.00 – $20.00.

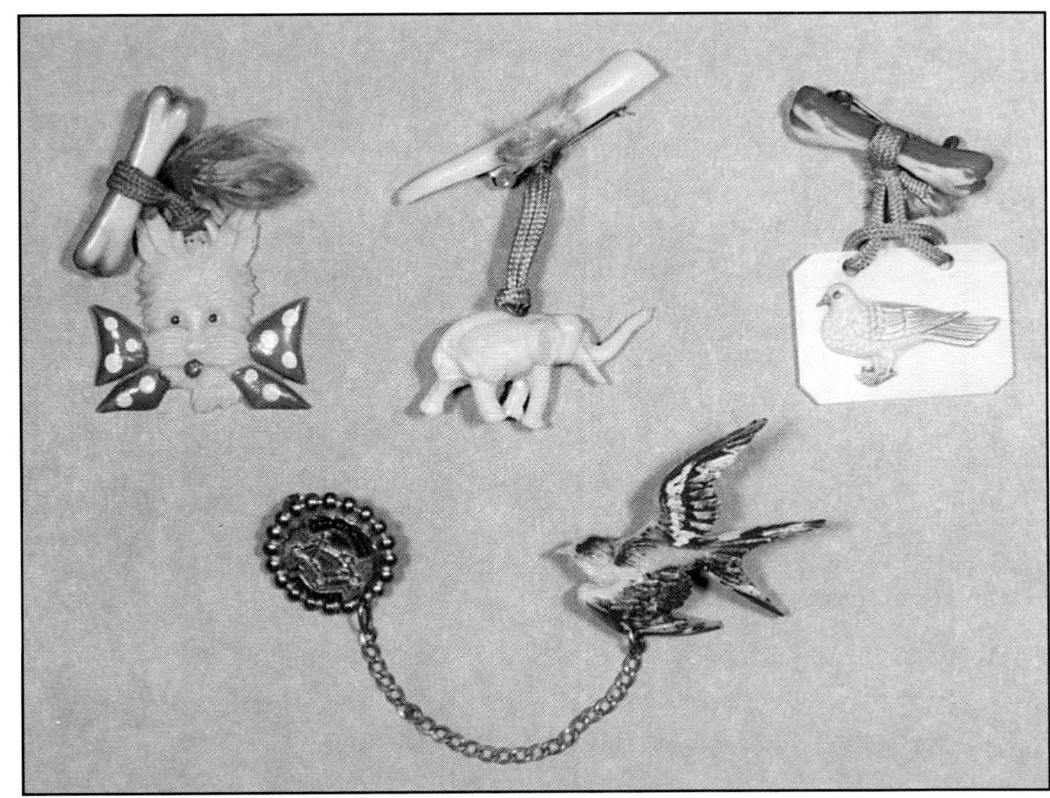

Cute pins with dangling charms were inexpensive children's novelties during the late 1940s and 1950s. The Scottie dog has been a favorite collectible since the 1930s. (Scottie dog motifs were inspired by President F.D. Roosevelt's Scottish terrier Falla.) This later example wears a large blue polka dot bow and is suspended from a 2" bone, $12.00. 1¾" rectangular charm w/molded dove w/hand painted highlights in pink and blue, suspended from a bone pin, $6.00 – $8.00; 2" tusk w/dangling elephant charm, $6.00 – $8.00; molded 1¾" bluebird pin with hand painted highlights, marked on the pin back Made in Occupied Japan, linked by a gold tone chain to a souvenir pin from Fort McHenry in Baltimore, Md. $18.00.

Collector Caution: Lea Stein

Recently it has come to the authors' attention that French designer Lea Stein worked with cellulose acetate and not cellulose nitrate as many had believed. The imitation of celluloid in her jewelry items is remarkable and can fool the eye. Buyers should be aware they are not collecting celluloid when they purchase jewelry designed by Lea Stein. See page 66 for an explanation of cellulose acetate.

Baskets and flowers are collecting categories that have gained much attention in recent years. The examples shown here have nicely molded details and applied paint. The findings are marked JAPAN. Note the painted detailing. 2¼" wide pink basket with flowers in pink, yellow, and green, $45.00. 2¼" rectangular Oriental style filigree brooch w/center floral design and painted highlights, $30.00. 1" wide miniature purple basket w/cream colored posies and green leaves, $30.00. 1⅞" floral pin with pearlized pastel paint, $25.00.

This whimsical Lea Stein dog pin in navy blue and grained ivory is one of the less common pins available. Note the metal pin back on this brooch is marked Lea Stein, Paris, and sunk into the cellulose acetate. Reproduction Lea Stein jewelry has recently surfaced; however on the new items, the pin back is glued to the cellulose acetate instead of set into it.

Cellulose Acetate Plastic

During the 1930s, nonflammable cellulose acetate – CA – thermoplastic was introduced as a substitute for the highly inflammable celluloid (cellulose nitrate) that reigned supreme for over 60 years as a beautiful moldable material for imitating luxury substances.

It is difficult to distinguish the difference between these two plastic materials by sight because many of the celluloid jewelry forms popular during the late 1920s and early 1930s began to surface in acetate as well. Some ways to distinguish the materials apart is color – CA was frequently manufactured in brighter colors, like orange red, bright pink, blue, and yellow – and its bright white color is a sharp contrast to the mellow cream color of pyroxylin plastic.

The density of acetate plastic differs only slightly from that of pyroxylin, but it usually appears that acetate is thicker than celluloid.

A hot water test will sometimes reveal the true identity of plastic materials, but exercise caution – the surface of acetate plastics can turn cloudy when exposed to very hot water. Exposing a small portion of the plastic to hot tap water will release identifying odors – celluloid generally smells of camphor while acetate has a sharp acrid odor. Be aware however that camphor substitutes were used from time to time, so just because an item doesn't smell of camphor does not mean it is not pyroxylin plastic.

Hair Ornaments

Beginning in the mid 1700s, ornamental hair combs became popular as a lady's fashion accessory. They were carved from a variety of substances including wood, bone, mother-of-pearl and ivory, as well as two natural plastic materials, horn and tortoise shell.

Leominster, Massachusetts, was the center of natural plastics comb manufacture in America throughout the eighteenth and nineteenth century. Skilled craftsmen produced both dressing and ornamental hair combs from cattle horn and tortoise shell. The process was painstakingly long, as these materials needed to be harvested and cleaned, then processed for use before they could be manipulated into shape.

Although horn was a plentiful by-product of the meat and leather industries, it was sometimes difficult to work with because it frayed and splintered easily. First it had to be cleaned and softened in boiling water or oil, then split and flattened in a press before it was ready to be crafted into a comb blank. Horn came in a variety of shades ranging from white and golden, to orange and deep brown. It could be clarified (made translucent) and dyed to imitate choice shell.

Tortoise was somewhat easier to work with because it did not fray and broken pieces could be fused together by heat and pressure. Both the back and underside of the shell was used to manufacture haircombs; the back produced a deep mottled brown-orange product, and the underside yielded a luxurious golden blond or amber shell. However, the marine species from which it came, the Hawksbill turtle, began to dwindle in number after decades of continual harvest. The threat of extinction was ever present, and with it came the need for a new material.

By the mid 1870s, comb manufacturers began to recognize the potential of semi-synthetic pyroxylin plastic as a material for hair ornaments. Celluloid was soon found to be superior to natural horn and tortoise shell for the ease with which it could be manipulated and because it could be dyed in imitation of the finest luxury materials.

With celluloid, the laborious preparation of natural plastics was abolished, and what had once taken days to manufacture could now be produced in a matter of hours. One factory alone could turn out up to 200 fancy plastic combs within a 24-hour period, and there was no shortage of material.

Heated comb cutting machines were used to soften horn and tortoise shell into hair combs. A charcoal fire was kept in a chamber at the base of this particular machine, in order that the cutting plate maintained a temperature consistent with keeping the natural plastic materials pliable for cutting.

When comb makers began to use semi-synthetic celluloid as a substitute for horn and tortoise shell, changes needed to be made. Because celluloid is made from cellulose nitrate and is highly inflammable, the threat of fire was ever present. Many factories had suffered devastating blazes, so in order to prevent a disaster from happening, if the tools they were using generated any heat, machine operators were required to work under a mist, or steady stream of water.

Nation Plastics Center and Museum Exhibit

Charcoal heated comb cutting machine was invented by Deacon Ward M. Cotton.

Celluloid comb production flourished in the numerous shops of Leominster which was known worldwide as "The Comb City." This early twentieth Century photograph shows the Standard Comb Company and presumably, their employees. Note the patriotic bunting draped along the building. Perhaps this was an employee celebration, as those shown are certainly not dressed for labor.

By 1906, the Leominster City Directory lists the following comb manufacturers:

- Blodgett and Co.
- Columbia Comb Co.
- Damon Co.
- Earl and Co.
- WD Combs
- Goodale Comb Co.
- Howe Comb Co.
- Kingman and Co.
- FB, Leominster Comb Co.
- Newton and Merriman
- Paton Mfg. Co.
- Pickering Metcalf Co.
- Sterling Comb Co.

In the comb manufacturing town of Oyonnax, France, three major companies were established to exclusively produce celluloid hair ornaments:

- La Societe Industrielle de Celluloid
- L'Oyonnaxienne
- L'Oyonnithe

Elsewhere, several other firms also produced ornamental combs:

- The G. Petitcollin and Co. of Etain, France
- Rheinische Gummi und Celluloid Fabrik
- Neckarau-Mannheim of Mannheim, Germany
- Aberdeen Co., Scotland

Method of Manufacturing Celluloid Combs

The production of celluloid combs began with the delivery of cured plastic slabs from a supplier to the comb factory. These measured 1.30 meters by .60 meters (approximately 50" x 19½") and ranged in thickness and color. Upon its arrival, the celluloid passed through several different processes before the final product was ready for market.

Detailing – The slabs of celluloid were cut into smaller sections possessing the external contour of a comb. Cutting methods included the use of a saw or a press which cut the comb blank by means of a lever-operated punching blade.

Tapering – This consisted of thinning out the comb blank in the area of the teeth. The process was done by means of a toothed cutter rotating at a high speed.

Cutting out – The comb blank was secured by a clamp and the teeth cut out, either by hand or mechanically with a small circular saw.

Dressing or trimming – The teeth of the comb, which were cut straight across the bottom from the circular saw, were now rounded and tapered by hand. The trimming was done with a triangular file and a widening tool.

Engraving – The corners and edges of the comb back were finished and smoothed using a mill revolving at a high speed. The craftsman ornamented the comb at this time if a border or design was necessary.

Pouncing – This operation consisted of rounding and smoothing the rough edges which were left by the dressing and engraving tools. The comb was immersed in pulverized pumice mud or ash, then pressed against a cloth polishing disc which revolved up to 900 times per minute, until all surfaces were smooth.

Curving – It was during this step that ornamental hair combs acquired their shape. The comb was softened by steam heat or immersion in hot water, and then placed upon a curved wood or metal mold where it was held in place until it cooled. This was usually done by skilled women who realized the value of a well-shaped ornament.

Varnishing – This process involved quickly dipping the comb into and removing it from an acetic acid solution which gave it an overall shiny brightness. The comb was then air dried on wicker framework.

Polishing – This was performed using a revolving disc fashioned from chamois or linen and a paste buffing compound made from ash, grease, and tripoli, a fine limestone powder.

Ornamentation – This final process, also called mounting, involved the decorating of hair combs by the application of metal ornamentations, paste jewels and paint.

The Late Victorian Era

Throughout their production, hair ornaments have been designed to compliment the popular hairstyles and fashion trends of the day. During the 1860s and 1870s in both England and America, women wore very dark clothing.[37-38] As a result, the deep mellow tones of tortoise shell were highly favored for hair combs.

The earliest of celluloid back combs were produced in imitations of luxurious looking tortoise shell. Manufacturers created an array of beautiful duplications in mottled and blond shades. The combinations of colors ranged from variegated browns, golden amber, and rich orange tones. So remarkable was the imitation of that found in nature, it was nearly impossible to distinguish from the real thing.

The first celluloid combs had dimensions that were nearly as tall as they were wide. The shape was slightly curved with a row of uniform multiple teeth. Ornamentation included molded designs, carving, engraving, prong set artificial gemstones, and inlaid or brad-fastened metal work.

These combs are becoming increasingly difficult to find with teeth and ornamentation undamaged. Years of use, exposure to hair dressings, and the natural breakdown of celluloid all contribute to the shortage of fine quality, late Victorian era hair ornaments.

As the nineteenth century was coming to a close, exciting changes were taking place. In America, the nation had recovered from the Civil War and industry was booming; it was a time of peace and prosperity. Entertainment and recreation were on the rise, with new and exciting opportunities available to both men and women. Perhaps the most influential force behind the changing fashion trends were the opera and theater.

In England, Victoria's son Edward and his lovely Danish wife Alexandra had been attending social functions and entertaining at Marlborough House since his widowed mother had dropped

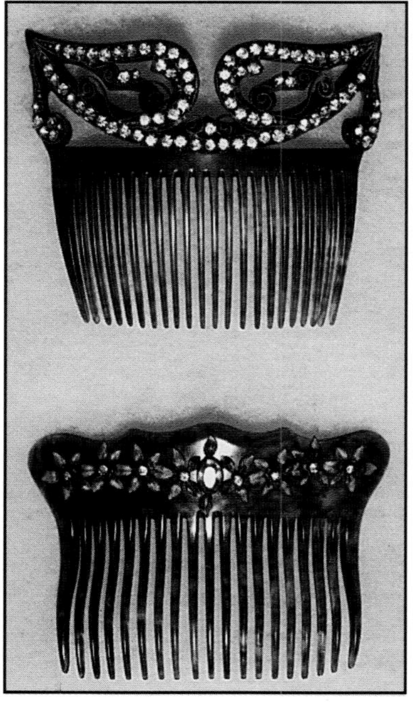

3" x 4¼" imitation tortoise backcomb, metal framework with prong-set rhinestones, intricate curlicues, 22 curved teeth. $95.00+. 3" x 4¼" imitation tortoise backcomb with beveled scallop edge, metal flowers with prong-set rhinestones/faceted pink oval imitation gemstone in center, 19 curved teeth. $95.00+.

Helen Golubic

4" x 5¼" imitation tortoise backcomb with tinted metal work showing leaves, flowers, and scarab beetles; prong-set rhinestone trim along top edge. Decorative motif probably influenced by the Egyptian Revival of the late nineteenth century. $100.00 – $125.00. Not all early combs were decorated in such a fashion; these examples are the exception. Most combs were manufactured with molded decorations that were sometimes further enhanced with hand carving.

4" x 3¼" embossed side comb for wear with the Gibson Girl hairstyle, sturdy and thick graduated prongs helped to keep hair firmly in place. Art Nouveau molding, very dark imitation tortoise shell. $25.00 – $35.00.

3" x 3" imitation tortoise backcomb w/molded Art Nouveau naturalistic design of swags and leaves on a stippled background, 18 slightly curved teeth. $40.00 – $50.00.

6" x 3¾" imitation tortoise backcomb with lace and plume motif. Slight curve to comb and teeth. $35.00 – $40.00.

4" x 3¼" embossed imitation tortoise back comb with naturalistic cattail design. $25.00 – $35.00.

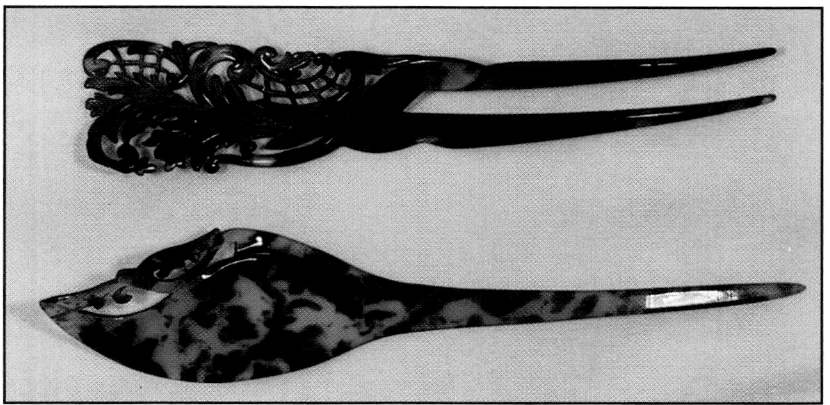

These elegant looking ornaments were worn on the side whenever the hair was piled high upon the head. Most often found are those of the two-prong variety, but single pick ornaments are also available; they were used to pierce the fashionable top knots and chignons of the late nineteenth century. 6" single prong hairpin in fine imitation tortoise shell for wear in elegant upswept coiffures. $18.00+. 6" double prong hair ornament with carved out lattice work and leaf spray design. $25.00+.

out of such activities. Their influence was felt throughout English society and by the 1880s, Edward and Alexandra were regarded as the accepted social leaders, although Queen Victoria was still on the throne.

Conventional styles began to shift from somber dark colors to lighter, brighter hues. Illustrator Charles Dana Gibson's beauty ideal – the Gibson Girl – became popular throughout America. In England, Princess Alexandra's influence was felt; she wore pastel gowns, light colored jewelry, and her hair was fashioned in an upswept style.

It wasn't long before hair ornamentation expanded to include the backcomb, single- or double-prong ornamental pin, and sidecomb. The prongs on these ornaments are quite different from their earlier Victorian counterparts, which could number up to 22 separate teeth. Instead, the amount of prongs was reduced to anywhere from 3 to 8; they were also much sturdier, being longer and wider in order to anchor the upswept Gibson Girl hairstyles.

Several factors come into play concerning the introduction of light colored clothing and accessories during the last few years of the Gay 90s and into the twentieth century. In addition to the fact that a new century had dawned, so had electric lighting which illuminated the lives of mankind in more ways than one. Before long, dark overbearing colors were exchanged in favor of lighter, more feminine looking garments. Accessories of plain imitation tortoise were also on the decline as women preferred lighter, brighter adornments to compliment their new look.

According to an Arlington Company report, by 1911 the hair fashion of wearing imitation tortoise shell ornaments changed and women no longer wore combs as profusely. The sale of tortoise pyralin sheet declined dramatically. This is evident as the majority of collectible hair combs readily available today were produced after the turn of the century, during the teens and through the twenties. Imitation ivory, pale mottled and blond imitation tortoise, and amber tones were molded into a fabulous array of ornaments, many bearing a variety of decorative treatments.

During the late teens and into the early 1920s period, plain old-fashioned imitation amber, ivory, and tortoise shell were abandoned in favor of combs decorated with vibrant colored rhinestones. Bold contemporary shades like red, topaz, blue, and green were introduced to pale imitation tortoise shell or amber. Some celluloid combs were further enhanced with painted detailing. The effect ranged from delightfully whimsical to elegantly sophisticated.

Dotty Maust

Two turn-of-the-century single prong ornaments, both fashioned from plain cream colored pyroxylin plastic. The filigree pick is 7" tall with a twisted prong and the plain twisted pick is 7" tall. \$22.00 – \$26.00 each.

Edwardian era backcomb, 5⅝" tall, imitation grained ivory, five curved prongs topped with a regal looking filigree crest; seven points are crowned with ¼" diameter solid cream colored spheres. Purchased in England, circa 1900. \$85.00+.

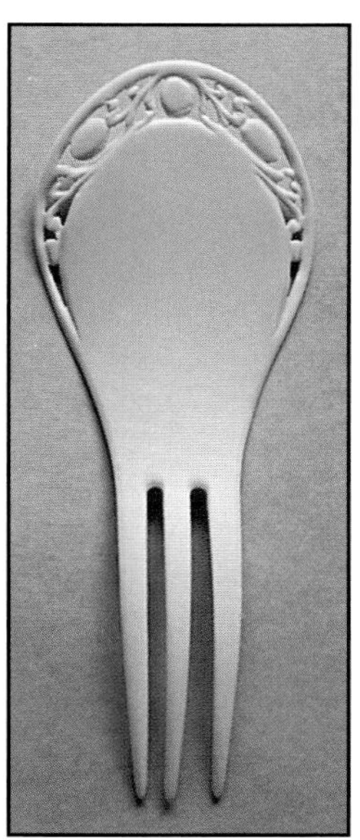

A simple yet elegant chignon comb, 5" x 3", in cream colored celluloid. $25.00 – $30.00. Note the long, slightly curved prongs.

5" x 4" cream backcomb w/intertwined flowers and vines forming a heart motif. Such filigree was popular after the turn of the century throughout the years of WWI. $40.00 – $50.00.

John and Gail Dunn

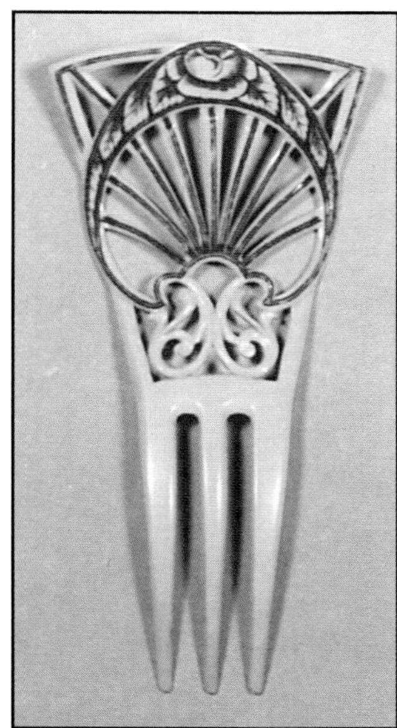

6" tall ivory chignon comb, three prongs, w/etched rose motif. The style displayed on this ornament is associated with the Art Deco movement, so there is a real possibility that this comb dates into the mid 1920s. $50.00– $65.00.

Common hairpins for keeping the hair style secure: Grip-Tuth triple prong hairpins in "Pin-Tainer" dispenser box; loose U-shaped dark brown hairpins; Wellmade wavy hairpins of 1930s vintage. These were the type of hairpin that was meant to be invisible while holding the hair in place. Boxed Grip-Tuth pins, $25.00 – $30.00; loose hairpins, $50¢ each; Wellmade Hairpins on original card, $6.00 – $8.00.

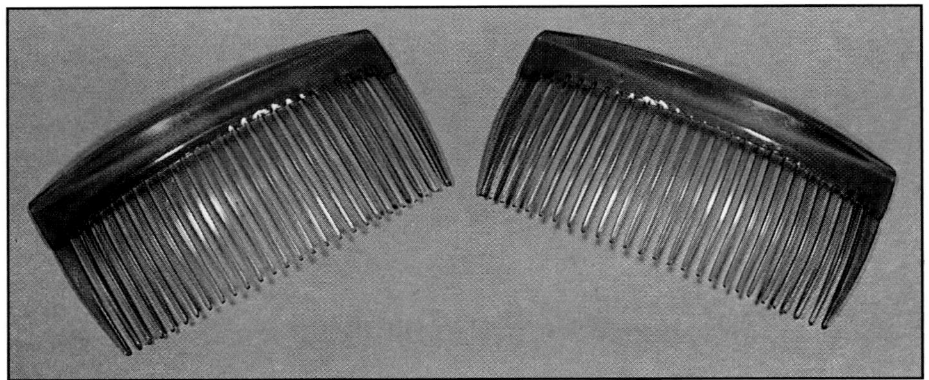

This simple pair of amber colored sidecombs would have been suitable for day-time wear. Plain and functional, they would have complimented the lovely decorative two-prong pin nicely. $12.00 per pair.

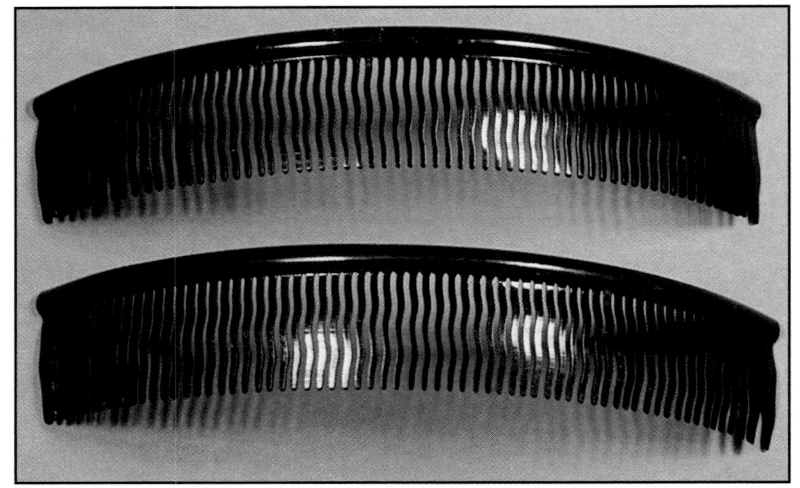

These purely functional 5¾" long x 1¼" wide, curved sidecombs were designed to fit snugly against the head as an aid in holding twisted coils of hair in place. The reverse of each comb is marked with a warning to users that they were highly inflammable. $2.00 each.

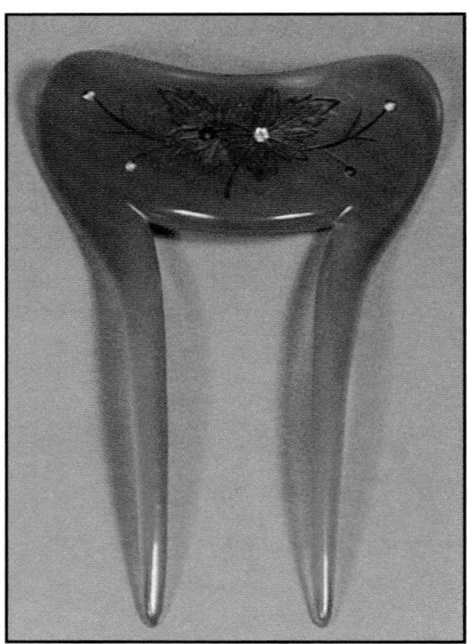

This thick, amber colored hairpin measures 4¼" tall and features an engraved leaf design set with five tiny rhinestones. The ornament is subtle enough to have been worn during the day. $50.00.

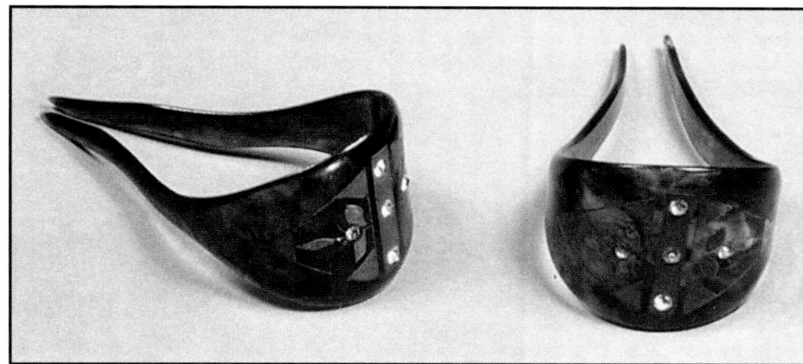

These circa 1920 ornamental, wide curve pins measure 3" long and 1¼" at the widest part. They are fashioned from imitation tortoise celluloid and painted with golden geometric shapes enhanced with rhinestones. $35.00 per pair.

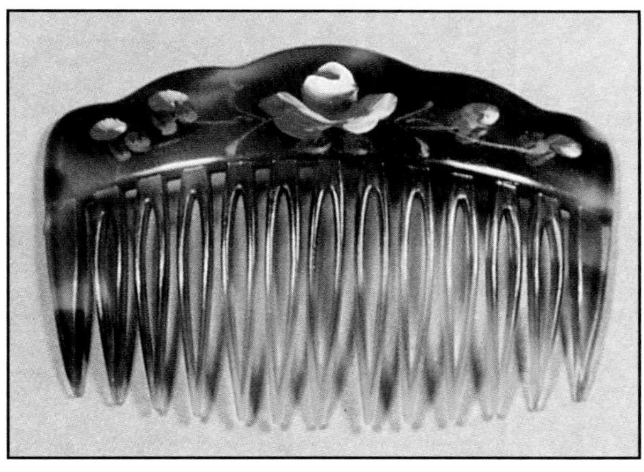

This 3" long x 2" wide imitation tortoise shell side-comb is decorated with a pretty hand painted floral motif. It is marked "Modele Deposse France" on the reverse. $12.00 – $18.00.

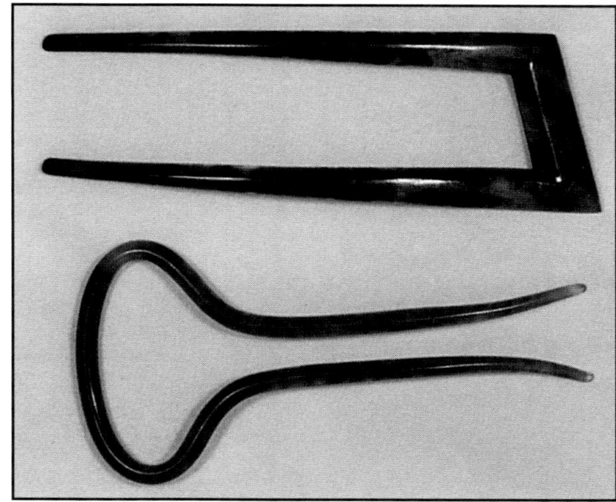

It was a common thing during the first decade of the new century for ladies of high social standing to enhance their natural hair with "switches" that could be purchased. These functional 5" long, shaped fastening pins were a necessity when it came to anchoring braids or switches securely onto the head. $4.00 – $6.00.

The translucent amber color seen in these hair ornaments is a beautiful representation of the golden gem for which it is named. However, what collectors may not realize is that the underside of tortoise yielded a beautiful mellow amber colored natural plastic; it was called blond tortoise and was used in comb production also. 5" long ornamental pins fashioned from ¼" wide amber celluloid. Hand applied floral motif. $20.00 – $28.00 per pair.

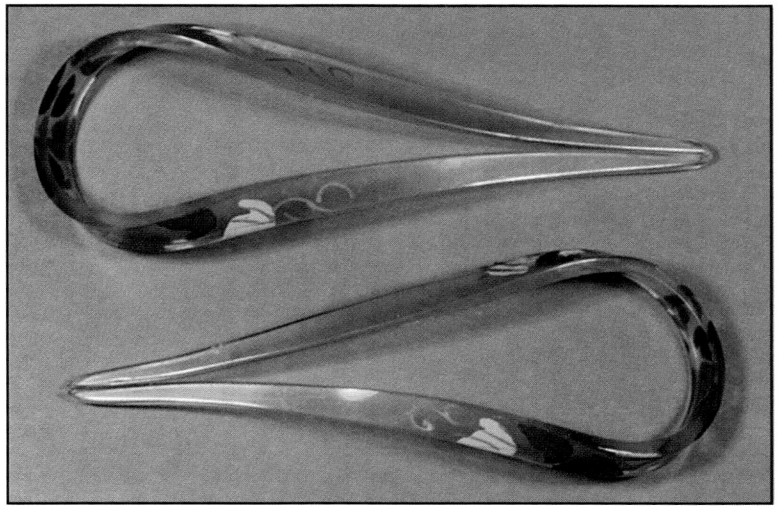

Consolidated Safety Pin Co. advertisement, 1900.

L. Shaw advertisement, 1900.

L. Shaw advertisement from *Munsey's Magazine*, 1902.

MUNSEY'S MAGAZINE ADVERTISING SECTION.

HUMAN HAIR GOODS

Retailed by Mail at Wholesale Prices.

FIRST QUALITY SWITCHES.

1¾ oz., 18 in.	$1.00
2 oz., 22 in.	1.50
1¼ oz., 22 in.	2.00
2½ oz., 24 in.	2.50
3 oz., 26 in.	4.00

Gray, Blonde and peculiar shades 25 to 100 per cent. extra.

All Switches made from **finest French Cut Human Hair, Natural Color** and **Guaranteed Not to Fade.** All short stem. Send sample of hair and size wanted. We will match perfectly in color and send to you Prepaid on **Approval by mail or express.** If entirely satisfactory remit the cost, otherwise the goods to be returned to us. We are **Importers and Leaders in Hair Goods** and carry only the **Finest and Latest Styles. Comparison** with others will prove that our goods are **superior** and **cost less.** Goods positively as represented. We find **"Honesty the best Policy."** For **Reliability** we refer you to **Dun** and **Bradstreet's.**

The latest **Transformation Pompadour** which can be used as a covering for gray hair, or take the place of the old fashioned wig. Made of natural curly hair. Price, $8.00 and up, according to shade.

The latest **Stemless Switch** made on a ring foundation, which does away with the top and stems. Naturally wavy, 22 in. long, $5.00; others from $8.00 to $15.00.

Illustrated Journal with instructions pertaining to latest styles in Hair-dressing, sent on receipt of 10c. postage.

Switches made of your own Combings, $1.00.

Made of natural wavy hair. Each . . . . . $3.00 others up to $10.00

PARISIAN HAIR CO., 5th Floor, 62 State St., Chicago.

Circa 1907 L. Shaw advertisement shows the variety of human hair goods that could be purchased in order to enhance the current style. Long fastening pins were needed to anchor the switches, small pins were necessary to secure the natural hair around the false hair, and ornamental pins and combs were used to complete the overall look. Note the beautiful variety of styles and ornamentation shown in the circa 1900–1902 advertisements. In recent years, the hairpin has become an invisible styling aid, but around the turn of the century not only was it used to hold the coiffure in place, it could also be decorated and used as an ornament for evening wear.

A patent for mounting stones directly into warm celluloid was issued in November of 1902 to Martin H. Brown of Meriden, Connecticut (US Pat. #714,447). Prior to this, stone decorations were cemented into place or prong set in metal framework, then riveted onto the celluloid item. Brown's method of setting decorative stones in celluloid was simple and effective:

1. A recess was formed in the plastic for each stone, the recess being slightly smaller than the stone to be mounted.
2. The article to be decorated was softened by heating and the stones embedded in the warm, pliable celluloid.
3. As the object cooled, the plastic contracted around the stones and held them tightly in place.

This method was also used for embedding metal decorations in celluloid.

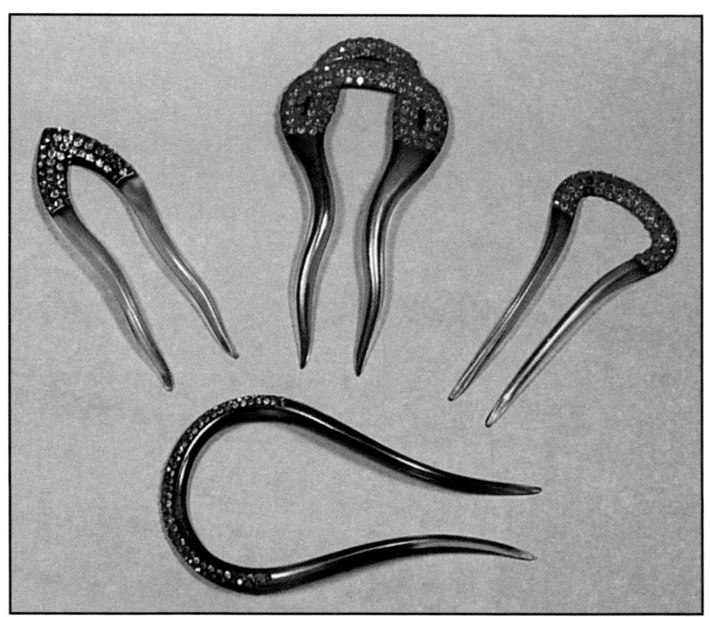

The four amber hairpins seen here each display a different ornamental shape, but similar decorative treatment. They would have been worn during evening events as ornaments so glitzy would never have been acceptable for the day. They added a splash of color to the upswept hairstyle as they sparkled and glinted in the glow of electric lights. $12.00 – $18.00 each.

Care should be taken to closely examine hair ornaments decorated in this fashion, as missing or damaged rhinestones reduce the value of an item. Liquids should never be used on combs set with rhinestones; it can run behind the glass, tarnish the foil backing, and dull the brilliance of the stone. Note the slight tint of color behind these examples, which no longer sparkle. When purchased in the spring of 1993, this ornamental back comb had a very small, 2 cm. crack in the center of the celluloid. It was obvious the item was in the early stages of deterioration, so as an experiment, it was washed thoroughly in soap and water, then put away. Within a relatively short period of time, six months, it became obvious that the foil finish and coloring behind the stones had been damaged beyond repair. In addition, the tiny crack grew into a large split with a number of tiny fine lines shooting out from the center. Within a year the formation of crystals had developed. Today the piece is quickly crumbling away as the disease is spreading throughout the pyroxylin plastic.

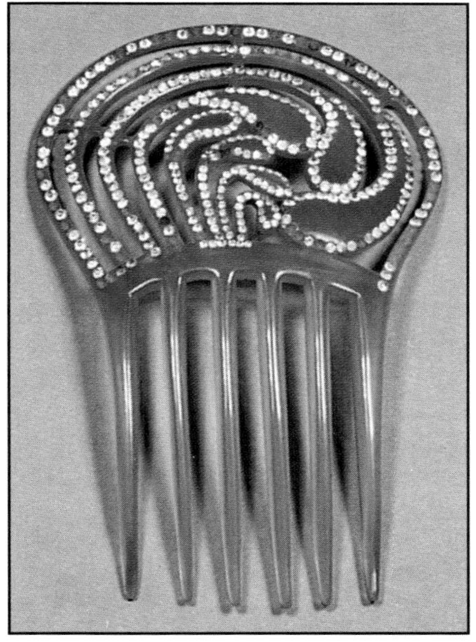

Missing rhinestones and traces of foil remain on this pale amber backcomb and are obvious upon first glance. However, when a comb is embellished with colored paints and matching rhinestones, damaged areas are less noticeable. Therefore, examine decorated combs closely before purchasing. If desired, missing stones can be replaced with a pyroxylin based adhesive.

This collection of decorated ornaments exhibits the range of decorative treatments popular after WWI. 4" amber pin, curve painted bright blue and set w/matching rhinestones, $18.00 – $25.00; 4" mottled imitation tortoise sidecomb w/set stones and white painted dots, $15.00 – $25.00; 4" pale amber and laminated black celluloid chignon comb w/green stones and white dots motif, $18.00 – $25.00; 5" deep amber three-prong chignon comb w/filigree center, studded w/red stones, $18.00 – $25.00.

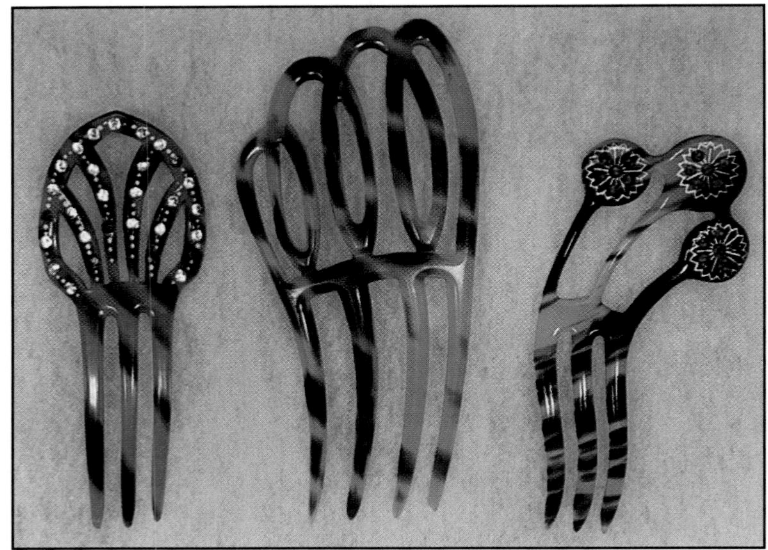

These whimsical combs display slender, flowing lines in imitation tortoise shell; two have been accented with white paint and rhinestones. 4¾" chignon backcomb w/Art Deco motif, embellished with white dots and rhinestones, $35.00 – $45.00; 5" four-prong, flowing elliptical looped pattern; back or side ornament, $20.00 – $30.00; 4¾" curved three-prong back or side ornament, whimsical floral motif studded with green rhinestones, $35.00.

The Beginning of the End

Following WW I, progressive political and social freedoms began to affect the nation's women. Eager for a liberating change in fashion as well, many modern women embraced the styles portrayed by those popular on the silver screen. It was in 1919 that the influence of one beautiful starlet, coupled with the action of the media, resulted in a fashion trend that swept the country with incredible consequences. The following excerpt is from the book *More Than Meets The Eye, The Foster Grant Story* by Glenn D. Kittler.

"Irene Castle had her hair bobbed. When this event occurred, it made headlines across the country and it became the kickoff for the Roaring Twenties. Some people thought it was charming. Some people thought it was daring. Some people thought it was shocking. To the people of Leominster, an industrial town in the heart of Massachusetts, it was downright catastrophic. The manufacture of combs and hair ornaments was the town's major industry and Leominster was already known as America's Comb Capital. Now Irene Castle decided to cut her hair and Leominster was thrown into turmoil. Everybody knew that the women of the country would quickly follow the example of this beautiful celebrity who, with her husband Vernon had become the leading exponent of ballroom dancing and the ultimate arbiter of how to dress while doing so. Overnight half the comb factories in Leominster shut down. Thousands of people were suddenly out of work.

There was one man in Leominster who refused to let his life be ruined by the whimsical decision of this elegant hoofer. He was Samuel Foster, Jr. He was thirty-eight years old at the time. He was married, he had a teenage son and every cent he owned was sunk into a new business he had recently started. He made combs and hair ornaments. As Leominster shook under the staggering blows struck by a delightful woman who was merely exercising her female prerogatives, Sam Foster calmly told his worried staff, "So all right. We'll make something else."

The Roaring Twenties

The advent of the Roaring Twenties brought about a drastic change in hair fashion and the ornaments with which to compliment the new styles. For women who followed the lead of Irene Castle, the use of hair combs became a thing of the past; however, there are always exceptions, and on special occasions some women were known to strap an ornamental comb to their short hair with ribbon or a bandeau.

For those who were not influenced by movie stars but preferred to keep their hair long, the French chignon was in vogue. Worn as a knot of hair at the nape of the neck, it was a hairstyle perfect for side and long-toothed back combs.

Striking Art Deco, Art Nouveau, and Modernistic designs began to appear, merging with advancing decorative techniques to create glitzy faddish accessories. Pale amber ornaments were embellished with brightly colored enamel paints or laminated with black celluloid, then set with contrasting glittery rhinestones. The effect could be stunning.

The mid 1920s brought the introduction of two striking decorative treatments; Goldaleur, a sparkly glitter suspended in clear pyroxylin plastic, and H-Scale, a shimmering synthetic pearlescent finish in an array of colors. Both methods were developed by researchers at the Celluloid Company.

These new techniques created many dramatic possibilities for decorating fancy hair accessories and jewelry. When used alone or in combination with solids and laminates, the effect was stunning. As seen at bottom right on page 79, the brilliant reflection of light on the tiny specks of glitter is splendid.

One of the most significant developments in the decorating of celluloid objects was the discovery of a synthetic pearlescence in 1924 by William Lindsey, a chemist with the Celluloid Co. Prior to his invention, the technique of making pearl finish on celluloid involved repeated applications of ground fish scale to an article's surface. When Lindsey discovered that the chemical reaction of mercury on celluloid resulted in a beautiful frosted effect, he patented the technique and named his formula H-Scale, (using the chemical symbol for mercury, Hg, and the former fish scale method). Upon the Celluloid Company's commercial introduction of H-scale in 1925, demand for accessories in combination of traditional colored celluloid and a contrasting layer of colored pearlescence came into favor. By the end of the decade popular shades included green, blue, aqua, lavender, pink, peach, and gray.

Because women have always loved to decorate their hair, thin side combs and small barrettes were introduced for those who chose to wear the stylish, short bob. An array of decorative techniques was used to embellish the tiny accessories including combinations of laminates, solids, pearlescence, rhinestones, and paint.

The latter years of the 1920s saw a brief revival of interest in large Spanish style back combs in imitation tortoise shell, amber, and translucent colors. Worn draped with a mantilla or fastened to the head with a band of ribbon, the comb had a striking effect whether the wearer had flowing long tresses or a fashionably short bob cut. Most of these large flamboyant combs were mass produced in Leominster for export to Mexico, Spain, and South America. Although American women did mimic the fad for a time, it was short lived and the Great Depression of the 1930s brought an end to the era of fancy celluloid hair combs. The bottom photograph on page 82 was taken on location in Spain during the 1924 filming of the movie "The Bandolaro." The combs were most likely produced in Leominster.

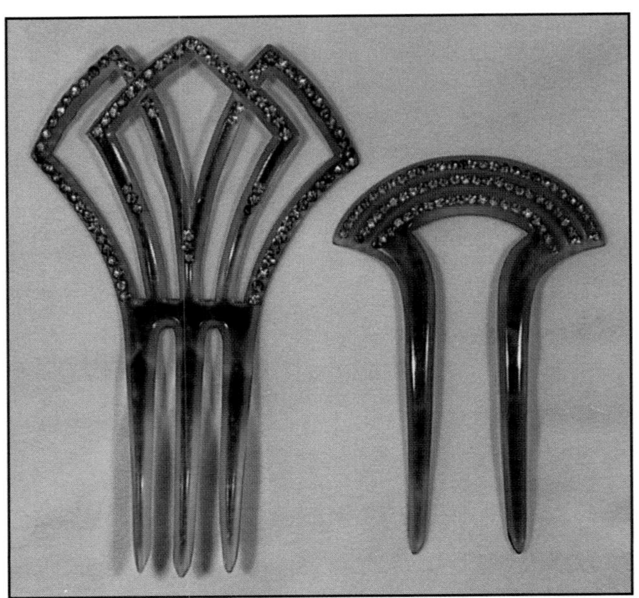

These striking Art Deco style hair ornaments are a fine example of the rhinestone studded decorations that became so popular during the Roaring Twenties. Small, $25.00; large, $35.00 – $45.00.

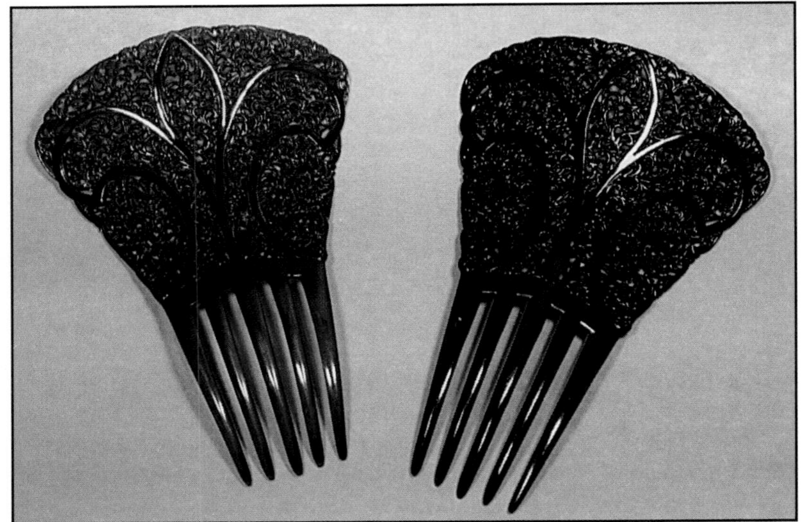

The zest for color during the 1920s led to the demise of solid color imitation ivory and tortoise hair accessories. Most hair ornaments had a variety of decorative treatments applied to the surface; however these 7" translucent green and black chignon combs with trefoil and lace motif are an exception. The decorations are molded directly into the back comb; the design is similar in style to the ivory heart and lace comb at the beginning of this chapter. $40.00 – $50.00 each.

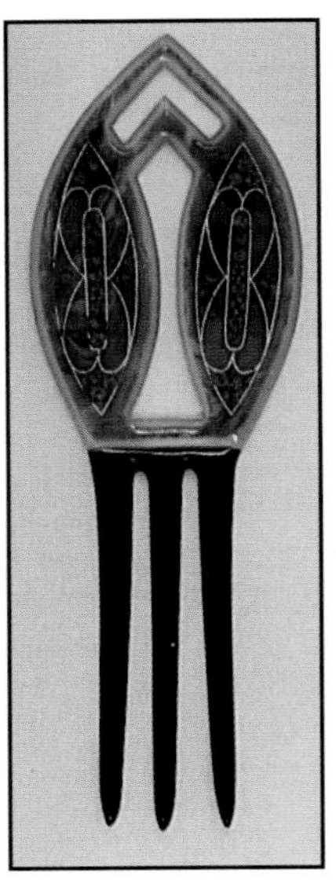

Contrast became the rage during the latter part of the 1920s and this delightful Art Deco chignon ornament is a wonderful example of the blending of materials and style. Opaque black prongs cemented to a pointed oval top in imitation tortoise further embellished w/incised lines painted white and red rhinestones. 5¼" tall, $55.00 – $65.00.

Helen Golubic

The three-prong black comb with a modernistic plume and the double-prong ornament with Art Deco style openwork are simple and elegant. Black was a popular color for jewelry and accessories, but most often it is found with some sort of decorative embellishment like tiny white lines, dots, or rhinestones. Both, $50.00.

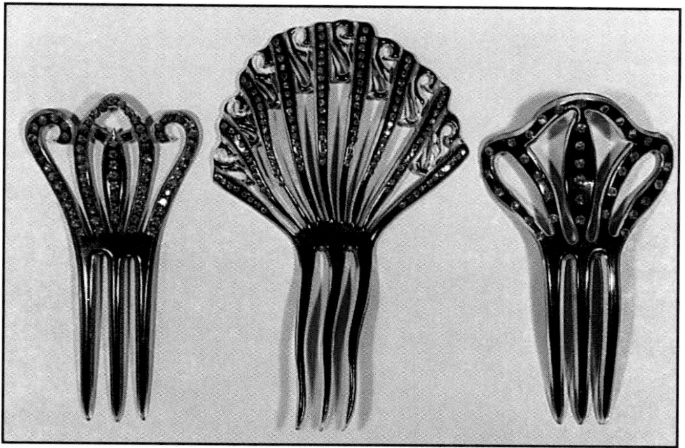

These fancy examples are done in pale translucent amber with black celluloid laminate; beveled carving along the edges reveals a two-tone effect. The treatment is topped off with blue rhinestones. Small, $55.00; large, $75.00.

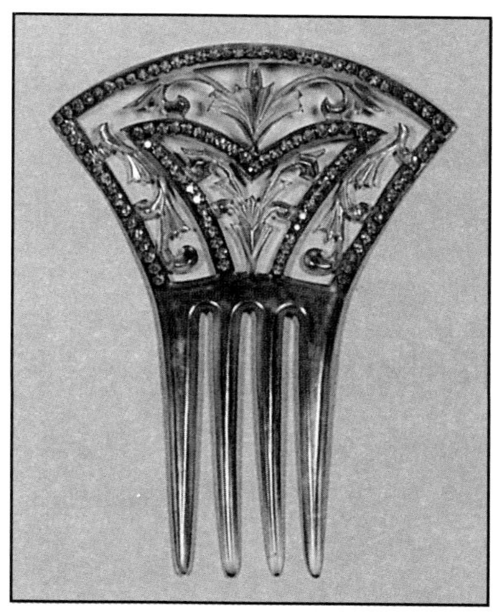

The same decorative technique is seen on this amber and tortoise laminated comb with pale blue rhinestones. The carved detailing on the openwork shows variations in dark and light tones where the tortoise laminate has been whittled away. Circa 1925 $55.00+.

Helen Golubic

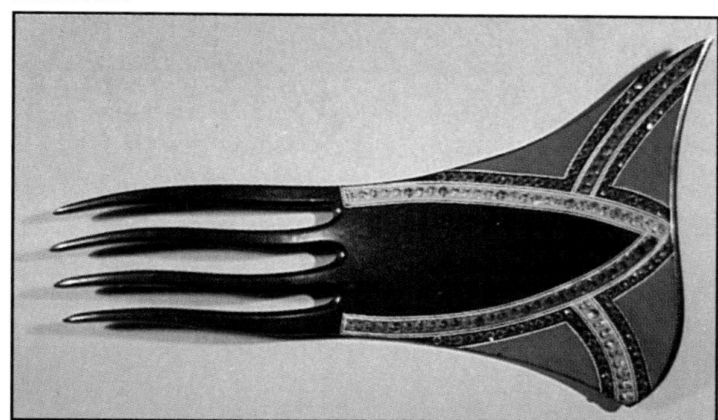

This absolutely fabulous example of Art Deco/Modernistic style is 6" long and 4¾" across. Underneath the deep tones of blue and red enamel paint is an ivory grained celluloid comb. Channel set division lines are painted in topaz, green, and blue, then set with matching rhinestones. $185.00 – $210.00.

Helen Golubic

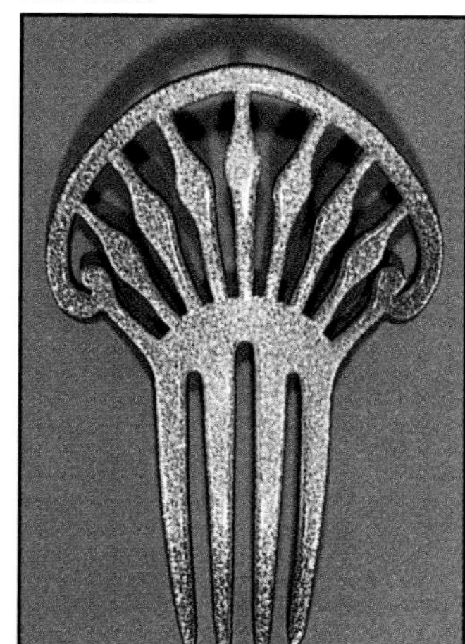

This dazzling backcomb is decorated with a glitter and pyroxylin laminate called Goldaleur. The decorative technique can also be found on other small accessories and some dresserware items. 4¾" tall, $95.00 – $120.00. These new techniques created many dramatic possibilities for decorating fancy hair accessories and jewelry. When used alone or in combination with solids and laminates, the effect was stunning. As seen here, the brilliant reflection of light on the tiny specks of glitter is splendid.

Helen Golubic

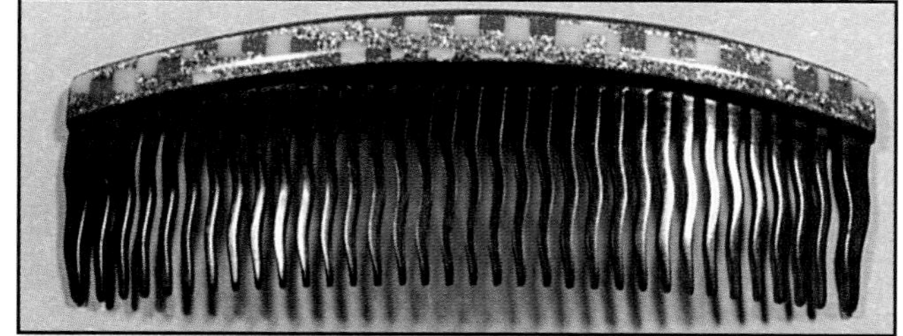

3¾"x1⅓"x4" curved, wavy tooth side comb. Decorative strip along top edge is a pattern of solid ivory w/glittery red and green checkerboard design. $35.00.

Tiny barrettes were the best way to decorate a stylish short haircut. These four ornaments are decorated with the glitter laminate technique developed by the Celluloid Co. during the mid 1920s. Note the application of rhinestones and the striped effect on the rectangular example. $8.00 – $12.00 each.

This collection of oval, translucent amber barrettes features a colorful variety of pearlescent finishes including gray, blue, red, and ivory. Each item is further decorated with contrasting rhinestones. $8.00 – $12.00 each.

While the style of this comb reminds one of the earliest form of celluloid backcombs, mainly because of the multiple row of small teeth, its pale amber color decorated with swirled synthetic gray pearlescence is an indication that the comb was made after 1925. 4" wide, $50.00 – $65.00.

Helen Golubic

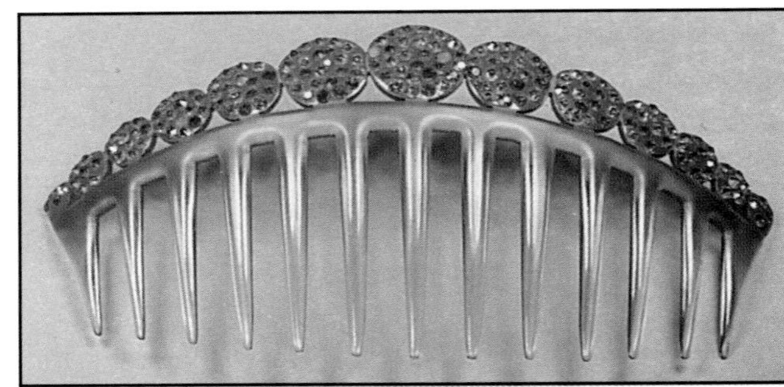

While this pale frosted amber comb with round green rhinestone studded circles looks as if it should be worn as a tiara, the curve of the teeth indicate it would have been worn in the back of the hairstyle. $65.00+.

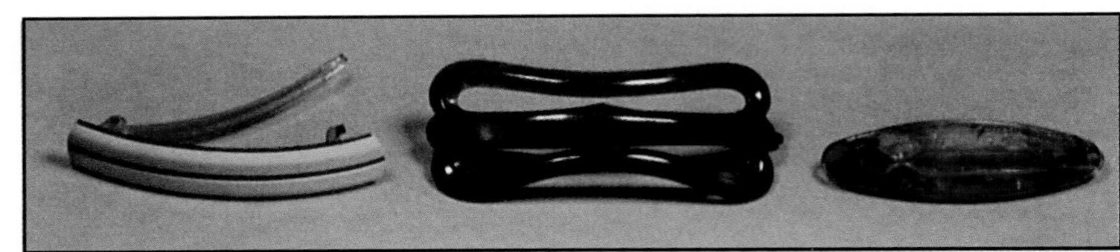

Three barrettes, circa 1925, feature an amber w/ivory laminate; imitation tortoise shell; and oval amber barrette. Such undecorated examples are relatively inexpensive and can usually be found for less than $1.00.

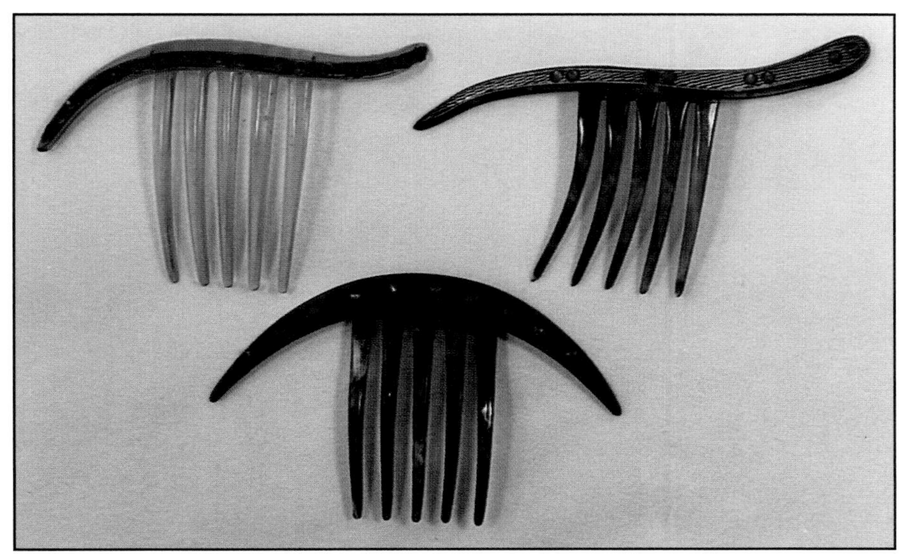

Three shaped side combs of amber and imitation tortoise, with pearlescence and rhinestone trimming. $20.00 – $30.00 each.

Helen Gobubic

This 6" decorated backcomb shows a flying bird set in flashy blue rhinestones against the delicate pale amber rays of frosted celluloid. $85.00+.

Helen Gobubic

Synthetic pearlescence was introduced after 1925 as a shimmering decorative treatment for accessories and dresserware. This striking backcomb is reminiscent of the fancy styles popular during the late Victorian period; however the stunning teal blue color is evidence that this example is a modern interpretation of an old form. The swirled pearlesent finish and matching stones are layered over a light shade of variegated green celluloid. $85.00 – $120.00.

Helen Gobubic

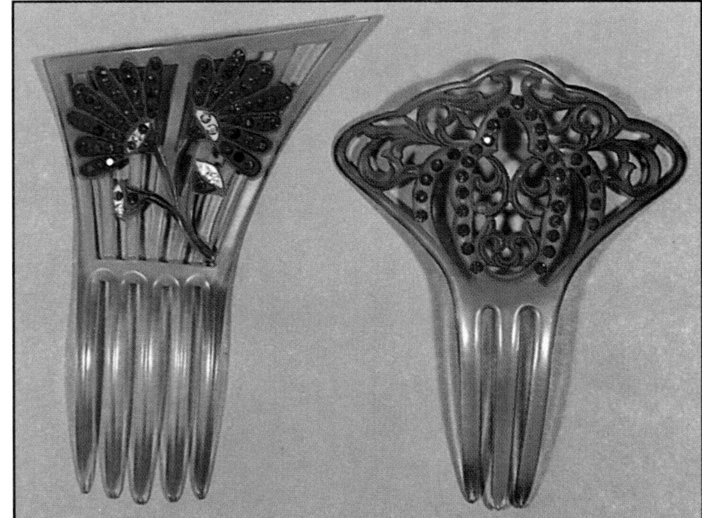

Two whimsical chignon combs in pale amber with contrasting rhinestones. The decorated areas on the combs have a frosted matte surface, while the prongs are smooth and shiny. $55.00 – $65.00 each.

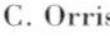

C. Orris

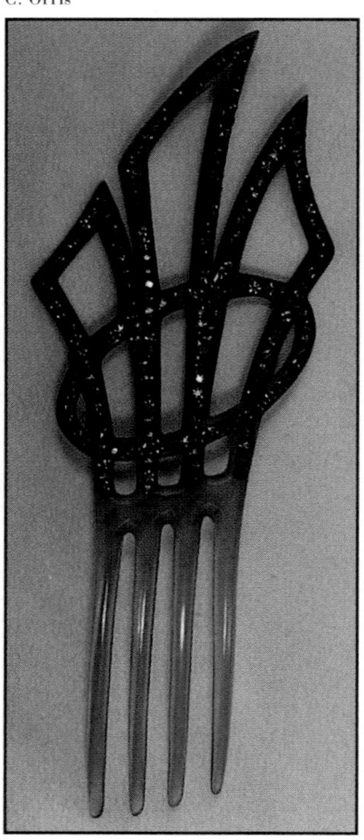

7¼" Art Moderne chignon comb in amber with blue enamel and turquoise channel set rhinestones, futuristic design with offset oval. $65.00 – $85.00.

C. Orris

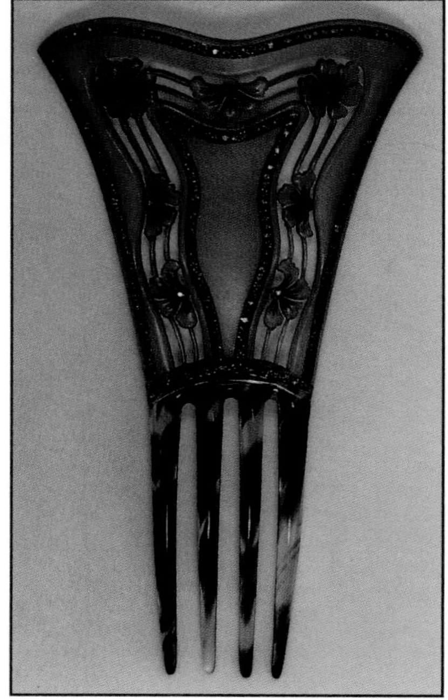

The gentle curve of the comb teeth ensured that the ornament would fit snugly against the head. Pale amber with floral motif and blue rhinestones. $65.00 – 85.00.

This photograph was taken on location in Spain during the 1924 filming of the movie "The Bandolaro." The combs were most likely produced in Leominster.

This photograph shows the difference in size between the traditional ornamental backcomb (left) and a Spanish style backcomb. Both varieties were manufactured in Leominster during the late 1800s and again in the mid 1920s when there was a revival of the style.

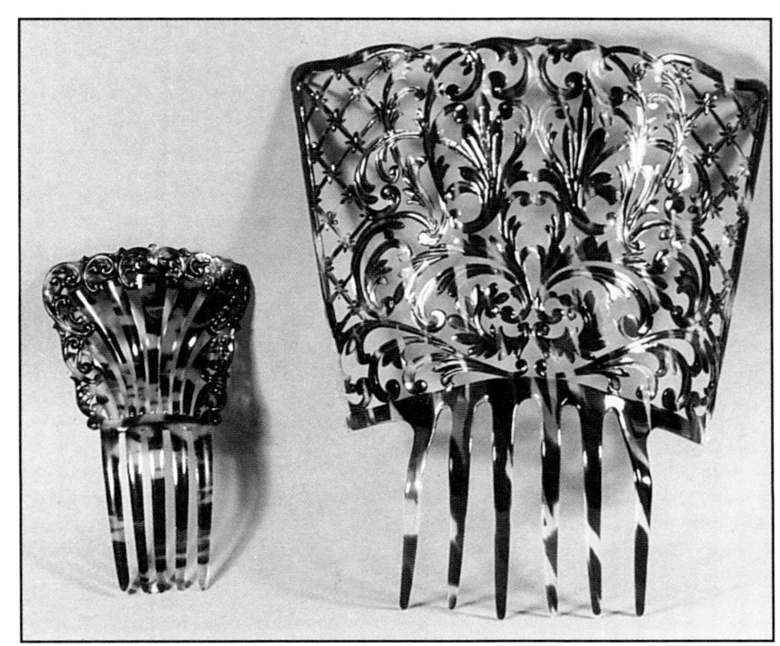

With short hair equally as popular as long hair, ornament manufacturers were soon creating colorful barrettes using the same decorating techniques found on large ornaments. The top row of larger barrettes includes two imitation tortoise examples with red and green rhinestones and metal clasps. The top center barrette is fashioned from pale amber and layered with black paint and dark blue rhinestones. The lower two barrettes are also made from amber with a painted surface studded with stone, however the clasp on the back is plastic. Small, $2.00 – $4.00; medium, $4.00 – $6.00; large, $8.00 – $10.00.

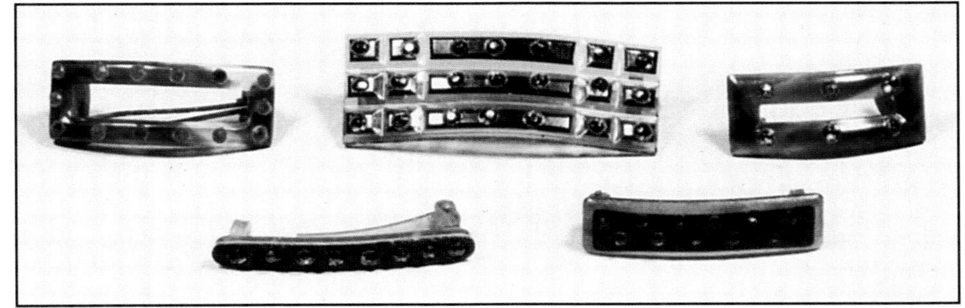

Linda Clawson

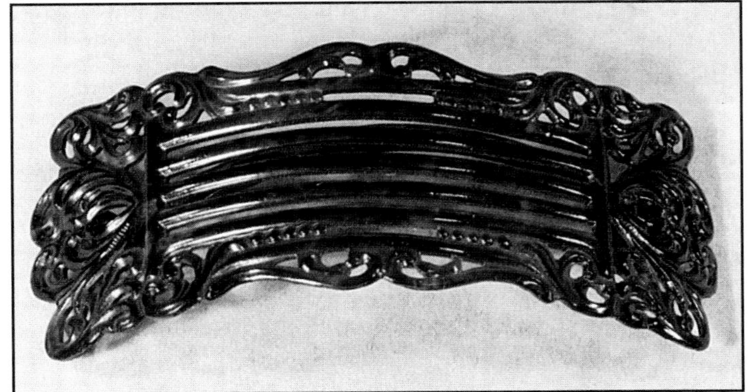

Imitation tortoise shell filigree barrette for wear in long hair. Shown actual size. $25.00.

Hatpins and Holders

By the 1880s celluloid had become a popular medium for ladies' long shanked hatpins and a great many of them have survived intact today. On October 23, 1878, the Celluloid Manufacturing Company licensed the Celluloid Hat and Trimming Company of Newark to produce millinery articles from plastic stock supplied by the parent company. Although no other information has survived concerning this enterprise, the mention of their name is found among the list of licensees in the Celluloid Company records at the National Archives in Washington, D.C. It leaves no doubt with a name like "Hat & Trimming Co." that their products must have been decorations for the fashionable bonnets that were worn throughout the late Victorian and Edwardian eras.

The first patent for sheet celluloid was awarded to Hyatt in 1878, the very year the Hat & Trimming Co. was licensed. While imitation tortoise shell and amber celluloid had been produced since 1875, ivory grained celluloid didn't make its appearance until 1883. It was also around this time that the first imitation pearlescence was developed using ground mica. Blow molding became popular around the turn of the century. (It wasn't until 1902 that a method of embedding rhinestones was developed; prior to this time rhinestones were prong set into decorative celluloid items.) Lastly in 1915 the fusing of two different colors was perfected.

Hatpin holders fashioned completely of celluloid are somewhat illusive. While many were made in vase styles to compliment dresser sets and had a dual purpose, the woven holder is a rare find. The Pickering Company of Leominster produced woven items of this nature after the turn of the twentieth century, although there is no way of identifying this hatpin holder as one of their items.

Support rods are fixed into a weighted base and thin strips of sheet celluloid are interwoven in the basket weave style. A wide sheet of celluloid lines the inside of the holder to reinforce the conical shape. The molded scalloped edge along the top is fitted with two sets of holes, the inner row for holding hatpins, and the outer row for fastening the supporting rods. These are secured in place with small celluloid beads which add a decorative touch.

The hatpins in the woven holder include a great variety of novel designs that can still be found today. Each example employees a different manufacturing technique; sheet celluloid was die cut or crimped into a variety of shapes, blow-molded celluloid was used to make hollow decorations, and thick pieces of celluloid were molded and used in combination with other materials.

Woven hat pin holder, 7" tall, \$125.00. 7" striped black and cream fused celluloid, shuttle shaped pin. \$65.00+. ¾" dia. solid celluloid ball, mottled red and cream. \$55.00+. 9" imitation tortoise shell, ribbed blow-molded to a point. \$35.00+. 8¾" imitation amber convex oval with fitted brass disc showing phoenix bird motif. \$105.00. 8" imitation tortoise shell, ribbed blow-molded tear drop. \$35.00+. 8" ivory grained pleated conical sheet topped with an ivory grained circular dome. \$45.00+. 8" Pearlescent ivory question mark, ground mica pearlescent finish. \$65.00+.

5" tall ivory grained holder, rectangular pyramid base. \$25.00 – \$35.00. 6" tall ivory grained oval cameo, w/applied trimming. \$155.00. 10" tall, cream colored solid celluloid egg w/rhinestones. \$55.00 – \$60.00. 8¼" tall, reverse painted black and gold teardrop. \$90.00 – \$95.00.

John and Gail Dunn

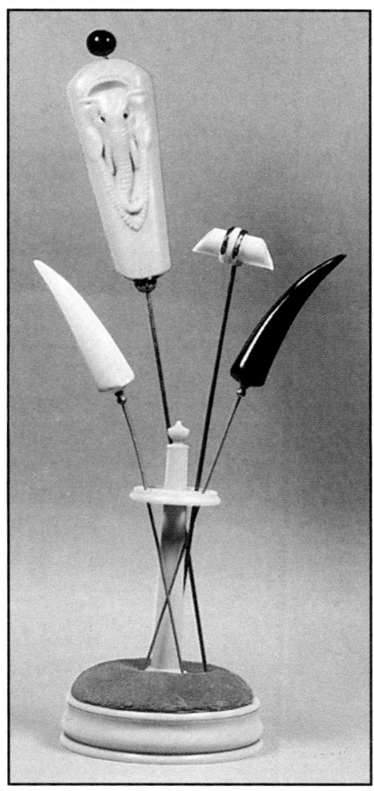

6" tall round ivory grained hatpin holder w/center spire and circular holder, cranberry velvet cushion. $150.00 – $175.00. 8¼" tall tusk-shaped hatpins, black or grained ivory. $25.00. 8" macaroni-shaped ornament w/black stripes. $50.00 – $55.00. 12" shank w/5" ornament, celluloid Asian elephant head, black glass eyes and bead on bottom and top. $200.00 – $235.00.

John and Gail Dunn

5" tall ivory grained tubular holder. $45.00 – $50.00. 7¼" hatpin w/pale green elongated heart ornament. $50.00 – $55.00. 6¼" hatpin w/dangling egg ornament in green pearlescence. $50.00 – $55.00. 7" hatpin w/ivory and green ornament, balls on spires. $65.00 – $75.00.

John and Gail Dunn

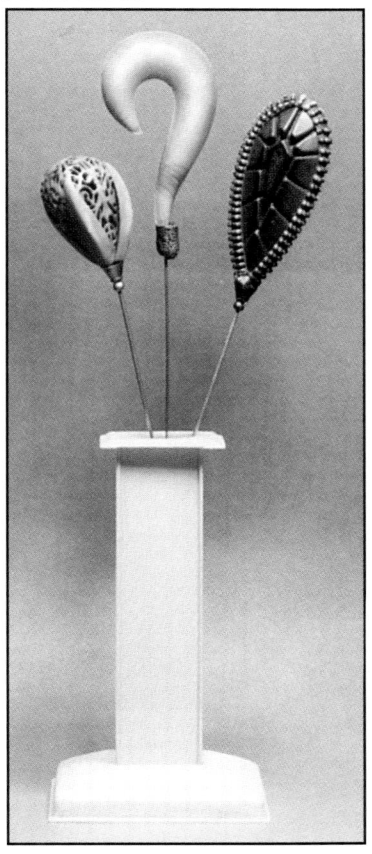

6" tall ivory grained square hatpin holder w/square pyramid base. $55.00 – $60.00. 7¾" tall hatpin w/black celluloid teardrop w/applied bronze paint, rubber ornamental trimming. 60.00 – $65.00. 8" tall hatpin w/ivory pearlescence celluloid question mark. $55.00 – $60.00. 7" ivory filigree egg w/4 celluloid petals, sienna enamel paint. $65.00 – $70.00.

Purses, Purse Frames, Compacts, and Accessories

Purses
The variety of celluloid purses, purse frames, and vanity bags seems endless. Because ladies vanity items are widely collected, the price of items in this category reflect the going prices collectors will pay. Many excellent reference books have been published on this subject.

The round solid celluloid purses (shown at bottom and on the next page) open up like a clam shell and are dated to 1925 because of pearlescent finish. The straps are leather, and all findings are celluloid.

John and Gail Dunn

4" x 4" basket weave purse w/link celluloid chain; mottled grain ivory and green. $350.00 – $375.00.

Helen Golubic

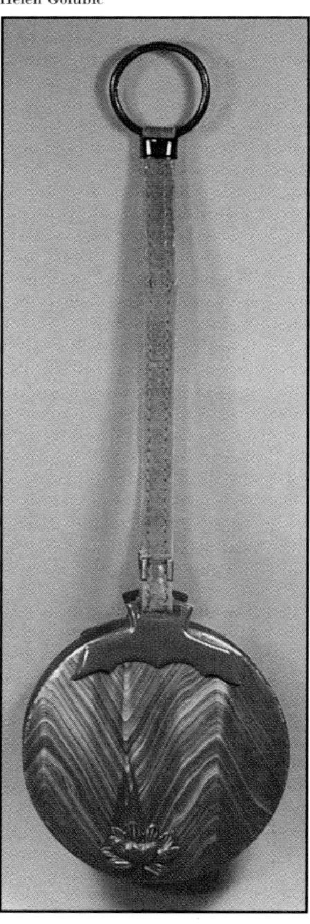

4" dia. purse, 5" leather strap; variegated pearlescent maroon surface w/maroon strap holder and applied maroon flower w/green and yellow paint. Clamshell type, mirror and blue satin lining inside. $150.00.

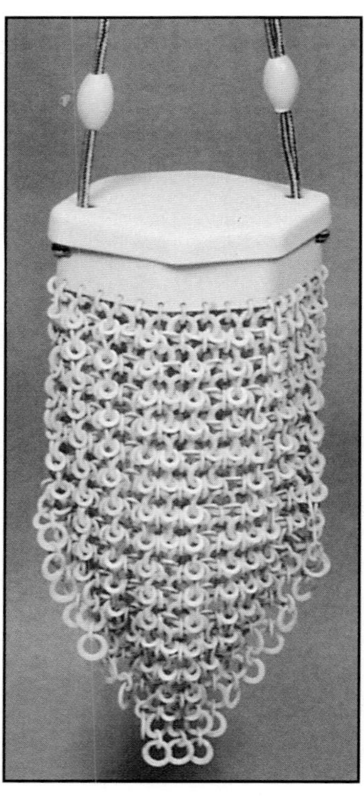

These purses are made from hundreds of tiny round links that have been put together. The solid celluloid frames are pierced to accommodate the links and a satin lining. 8" long circular mesh purses, ivory and mottled green w/applied flower decorations in red and blue. $200.00 – $225.00.

John and Gail Dunn

2" dia. octagonal purse in pearlescent gray w/attached perfume; powder and puff w/mirror $200.00 – $350.00.

Helen Golubic

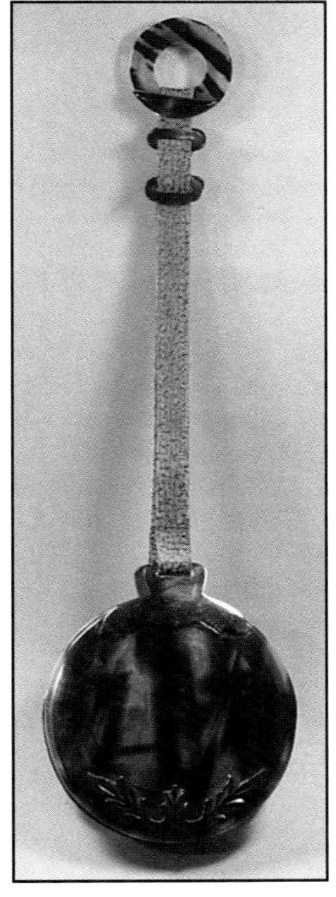

4" dia. round clamshell type purse; imitation tortoise shell with sides of imitation ivory; leather strap w/celluloid findings and finger ring; applied celluloid leaf decoration. $150.00.

John and Gail Dunn

5" celluloid diamond-shaped purse, oval cameo clasp, mottled variegated green, brown, and ivory. Inside is mirror, powder w/puff and chrome scent vial. $250.00 – $400.00.

2¼" dia. vanity powder box, floral motif in green, brown, pink, and blue; black edges. $250.00 – $475.00.

4" x 2" black vanity box w/rhinestone design, both sides open. Center divider in cream celluloid. $200.00 – $425.00.

3¼" dia. black vanity box w/red trim and rhinestone decoration; mirror and puff inside. $250.00 – $400.00.

3" dia. round vanity box; black and cream w/rhinestones; plunger clasp; inside powder, puff, and lipstick. $200.00 – $375.00.

3" dia. orange vanity box w/push knob, circular and floral rhinestone motif; inside mirror, powder and puff. $250.00 – $450.00.

Purse Frames

Ornamental celluloid purse frames with molded, engraved, or painted decorations are almost as valuable as the entire purse. Those which reflect special themes are more desirable than plain frames; unadorned celluloid frames in imitation ivory, tortoise shell, amber, and jet can sell for as little as $18 in some antique malls and shops. For the exceptional frames shown here, anything under $65.00 is a bargain.

The absolutely fabulous purses seen on page 90 are from the John and Gail Dunn collection and are believed to be French in origin. They are fashioned from various textiles with ornate celluloid frames. Because these are so rare, there is no price available, but if any collector of celluloid objects should come across such an example for under $500, it would be considered reasonable.

Dome top purse frame, ivory with painted orange flowers and green leaves. $150.00+.

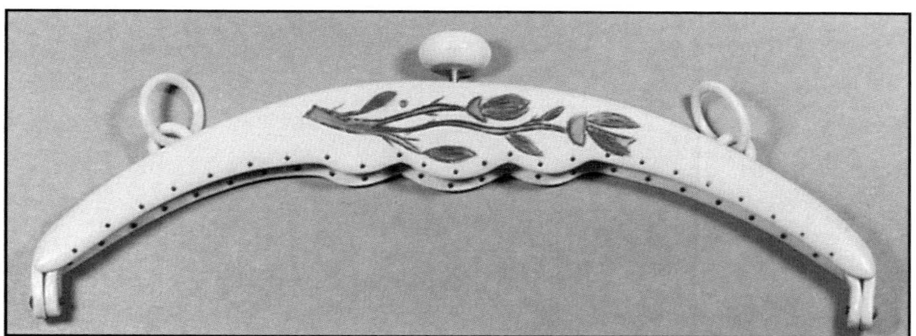

8" crescent-shaped purse frame w/push button and carved and painted fuchsia flowers. $75.00+.

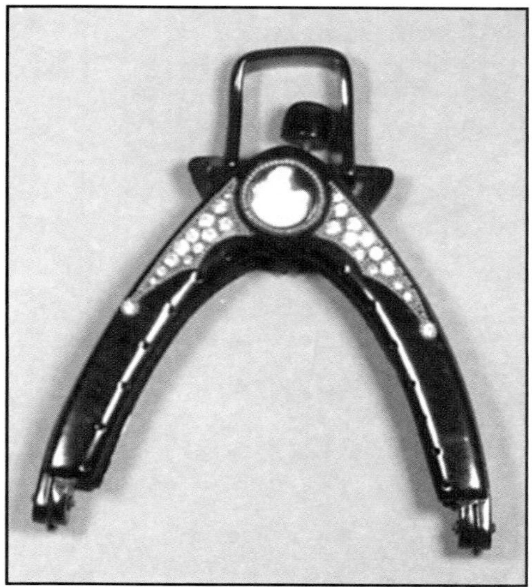

4" black pointed horseshoe-shaped frame w/rhinestones and Neptune motif. $100.00.

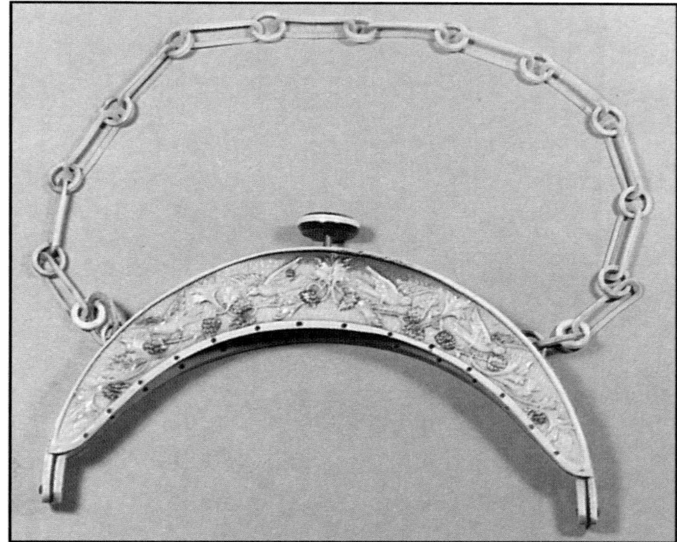

5" crescent-shaped purse frame w/blackberry and bird motif. Ivory w/painted decorations, push button clasp and link chain. $100.00+.

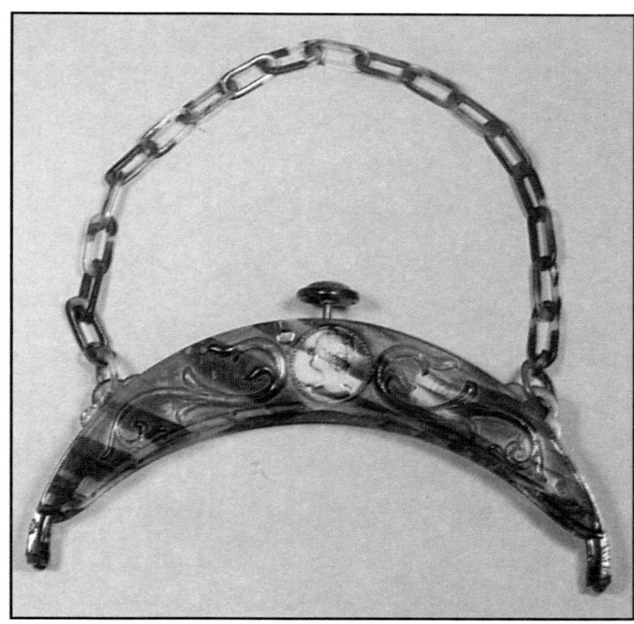

6" imitation tortoise shell crescent frame w/cameo center motif. Push button closure, linked chain. $110.00.

6¼" Egyptian motif purse frame; ivory w/applied orange and gold paint. $120.00.

Green velvet bag w/4" dia. red rose and leaf celluloid frame. #35 on inside of frame. Rare, no price available.

9" tall purse; ornate celluloid frame shows red haired child embracing a greyhound dog; rose motif on sides; mirror on bottom. Made in France. Rare, no price available.

3" female frame w/peach gauze skirts. Frame is woman with gown and feathers in head. Rare, no price available.

Compacts & Purse Accessories

Celluloid compacts have been used since the Roaring Twenties when gals began to rouge their cheeks and apply lipstick. The examples that are shown here were all made in the late 1920s. It is suggested that collectors who wish to focus on this particular category refer to Roselyn Gerson's books on the subject, printed by Collector Books.

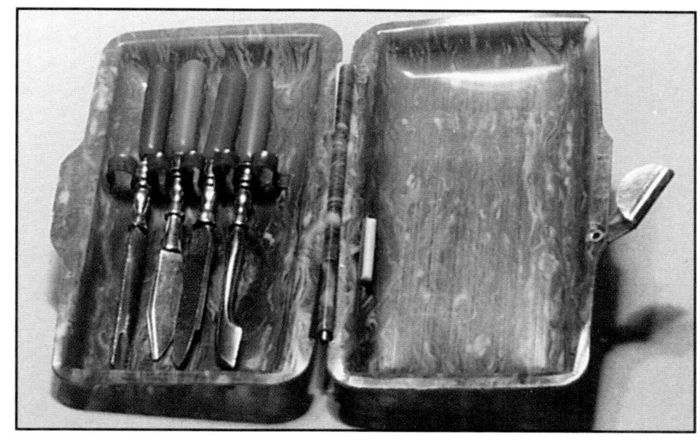

3¼" x 2" variegated green case w/miniature manicure set, 4 implements. $25.00 – $30.00.

Three compacts of unusual design, left to right: cream colored celluloid two-piece powder compact w/butterfly and flower decorations under translucent celluloid lid, $35.00; rectangular metal souvenir compact w/celluloid over printed paper, Magnolia Gardens, Charleston, S.C., $18.00; octagonal metal compact with pearlized celluloid lid insert painted with pink and green floral motif, $25.00.

Large round compact with cream pearlescent celluloid, monogrammed wtih the letter "M," and the smaller rectangular example with applied rhinestone decoration. Both circa 1930. $25.00 – $35.00 each.

Two French-made cigarette lighters with pearlized sheet celluloid covering, pale purple and pale blue-green. Rare and unusual. $45.00 each.

The small souvenir square and round compacts shown here are made from metal with a printed celluloid lid. Because so many of these novelty items were manufactured for the tourist trade, they are still plentiful and relatively inexpensive. Three round compacts w/Wash. D.C.; American Flag; Lovers; two square w/Statue of Liberty and Wisconsin Dells. $15.00 – $25.00 each.

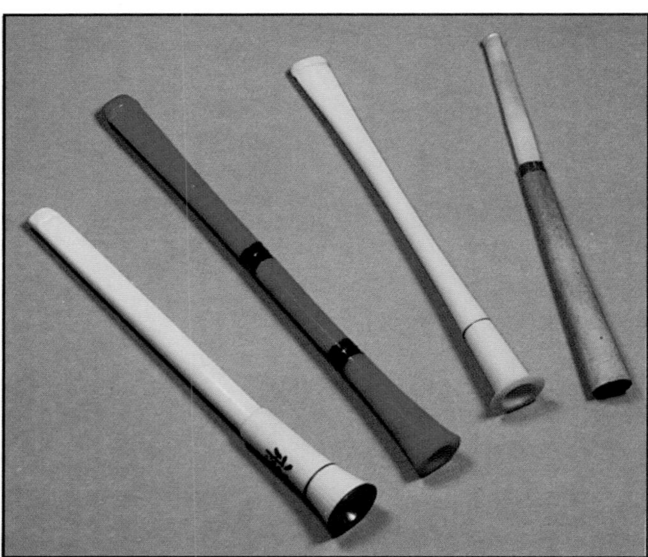

It seems ludicrous that any manufacturer of celluloid objects would have chosen to produce cigarette holders from cellulose nitrate plastic given its flammable nature, nevertheless here they are. The fact that we show four different examples leads one to believe that they were somewhat common. Cigarette holders, left to right: ivory grained w/Japanese motif; red w/black stripe; plain ivory grained and celluloid mouthpiece with cardboard holder. $38.00 – 45.00 each.

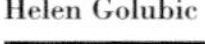
Helen Golubic

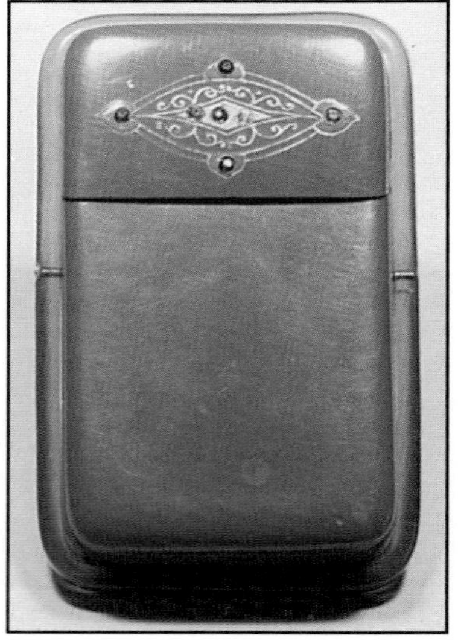

3¼" x 2" celluloid cigarette case; blue w/amber trim, green and white rhinestone motif. $35.00 – $45.00.

John and Gail Dunn

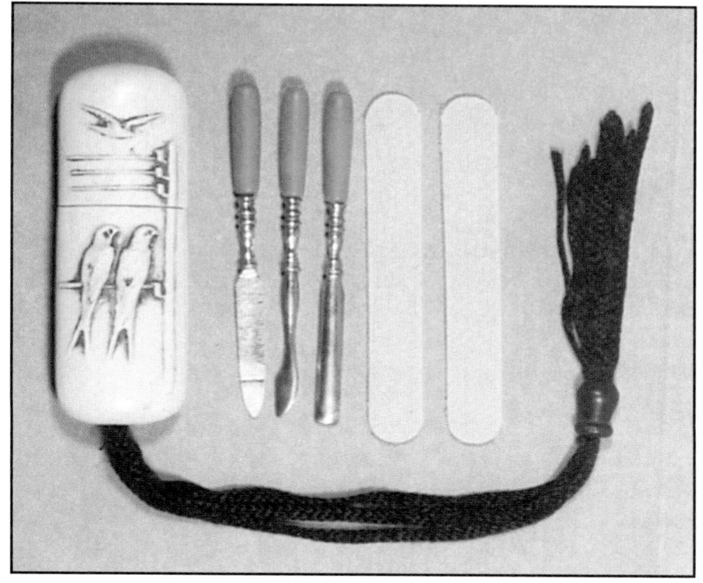

2¾" miniature manicure set; nicely detailed cream colored case with swallows on telephone line; coral handle implements and emery boards. $65.00.

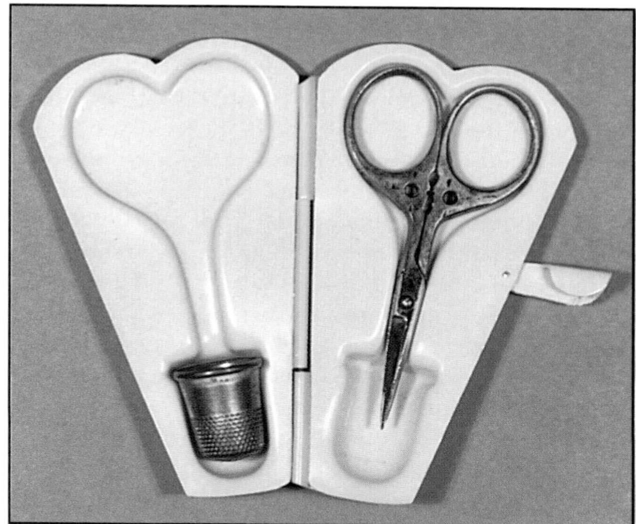

Cream colored folding holder of sturdy celluloid w/sterling and gold plated scissors and thimble, marked Germany. $75.00.

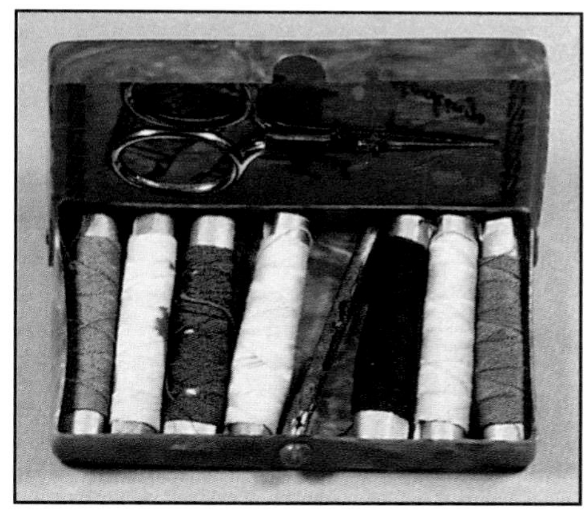

3¼" x 2" mottled blue sewing kit with needles, thread, and scissors, $22.00.

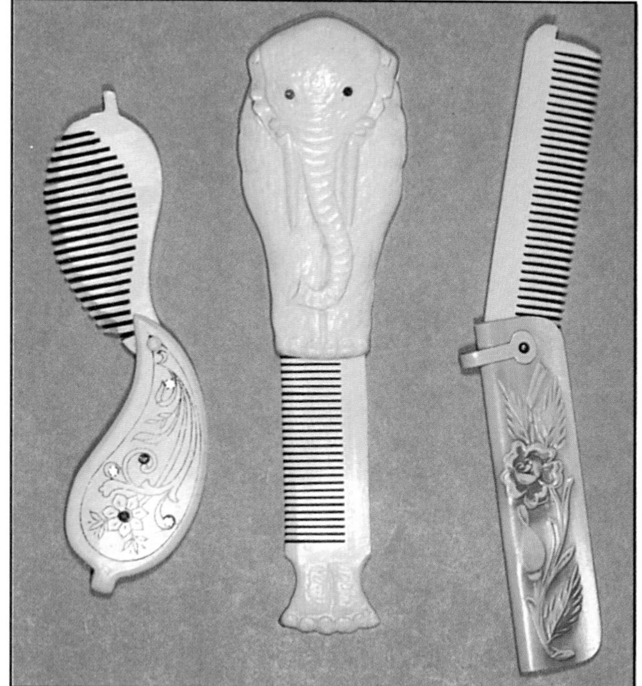

The three folding novelty combs shown here include a teardrop shape that measures 2¼" long, decorated with incised floral motif and rhinestones; elephant with green rhinestone eyes, feet pull out to reveal comb; rectangular comb with embossed floral design highlighted with gold tone paint. $18.00 – $25.00 each.

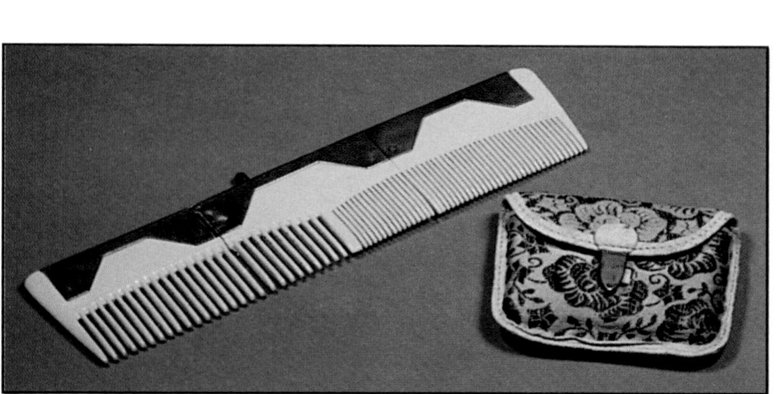

German-made folding comb, three parts with lock that slides into place securing sections, textile carrying case. $45.00.

Fans

Fans have been a popular ladies accessory item since the seventeenth century when Oriental merchants introduced them into trade with the West. While they were practical and essential for cooling and waving away insects during summertime and equally as useful in winter for fanning the flames of a fire, as fashion accessories they were used mainly by the wealthy upper class.

From the earliest of days, fans have been fashioned from every kind of substance known to man including wood, straw, bone, ivory, mother-of-pearl, fabric, paper, and natural plastics. Fan sticks were carved by hand until Alphonse Baude invented a machine to do the work in 1859, making fan production more efficient and less expensive.

During the 1860s, fans became popular fashion accessories as they were finally available to all classes of society. They were used at weddings and funerals, the opera, theater, and dances. In addition to complimenting the clothing and warding off hot flashes brought on by tightly laced corsets, fans were waved flirtatiously by available young women and often used to hide behind when undesirable suitors showed interest.

The development of sheet celluloid in 1878 and the availability of it to the accessory trade during the early 1880s brought even greater efficiency to the manufacture of fans. Rounded guard sticks were fashioned from rods of celluloid, while flat sticks were die cut and embossed from sturdy sheets. The earliest known dated celluloid fan is a souvenir of the 1,200th performance of Cecil B. Demille's play "Men & Women," Tuesday April, 12, 1892. The fan is a brisé style with alternating sticks of celluloid and cardboard; the celluloid is stamped with the names and signatures of actors in the show.

The earliest known patent for a fan utilizing celluloid was issued to Gabriel Kaiser on October 7, 1902, Pat. #710,465.

Decoration of a celluloid fan could include embossing and die cut designs, the addition of satin ribbon, tiny mirrors, paste jewels, feathers, decals, printed images, hand painting, finger loops, tassels, and chains. Many celluloid fans were also used as advertising media. Those which commemorate an historical event or feature colorful images of consumer products command a higher price than simply decorated generic fans.

Brisé (pronounced breez – a) is the type of fan made from flat overlapping sticks that are die cut from sturdy celluloid sheets. The sticks are held together by a rivet and sometimes a finger loop at the bottom of the fan. Satin ribbon or cord was woven or glued along the top of a fan to keep the sticks evenly separated. The thick end sticks of a fan are called guard sticks, and they are often embossed or decorated in some manner.

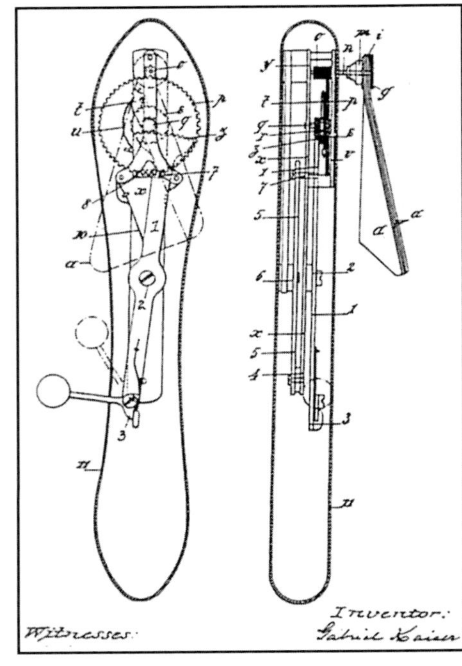

Fan patent #710,465, Oct. 7, 1902.

The three brisé fans shown on the next page are hand decorated with painted floral swags, a popular theme of the Edwardian era. Fans that have a chain attached to the finger loop are much harder to find and therefore more expensive.

7½" fan box, ivory grained celluloid with hinged lid. Box fits folded 7" fan without chain. Box only, $15.00.

10¾" open, 6¼" closed, brisé fan, cream color with decorative perforated celluloid sticks; hand painted apple blossom motif, 10" celluloid chain. $35.00 – $40.00.

10" open, 7" closed, brisé fan w/cream celluloid die cut sticks, hand painted w/violet swag motif, violets on guard, finger loop and pink ribbon, celluloid chain. $40.00 – $45.00.

Cockade fans are fashioned from two sticks with pleated linen or paper which opens to form a complete circle. This example dates from 1890 – 1900. 13" open, 9" closed, cockade pleated linen fan; cream colored celluloid sticks that are clasped together at the bottom. $50.00 – $65.00.

10" open, 6" closed, brisé fan with embossed and stamped gold neoclassical design; center medallion features a decal scene of two women which is enhanced with hand painting; celluloid finger loop and blue woven ribbon. $45.00 – $60.00.

Helen Golubic

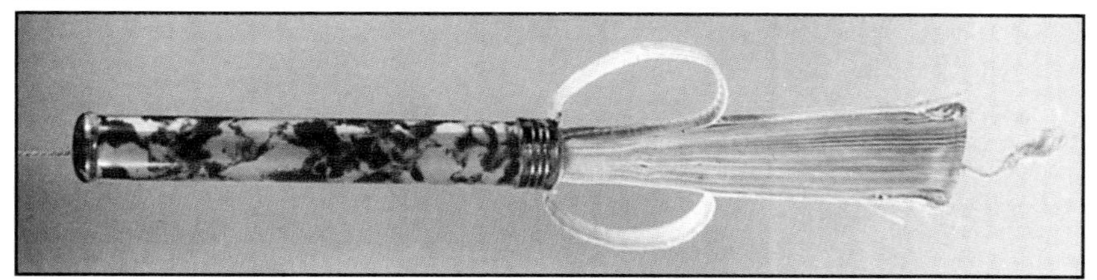

The imitation tortoise shell handle of this fan also serves as its case when a string is pulled and the pleated linen fan retracts. Originally this type of housing was used as an umbrella handle with a hidden fan inside. 5" imitation tortoise shell celluloid tube w/sliding 5" linen fan w/string pull. $30.00 – $40.00.

A fan that has no movable parts, like this circa 1920 example with a cream celluloid handle and loop topped with three black ostrich plumes, is called a "fixed" fan. It came into vogue just before WWI and enjoyed popularity throughout the Roaring 20s. 12" long, cream handle fan with black ostrich feathers. $20.00 – $30.00.

Large fans, such as the one shown, were used to compliment the exaggerated hourglass figure of the late Victorian era. In addition to being fashion accessories, fans were no doubt essential in keeping one as comfortable as possible while wearing a tightly laced corset. 23" open, 16" closed, 24 imitation tortoise shell sticks with graduated black ostrich feathers; horn loop with black grosgrain ribbon. Circa 1890. $65.00 – $85.00.

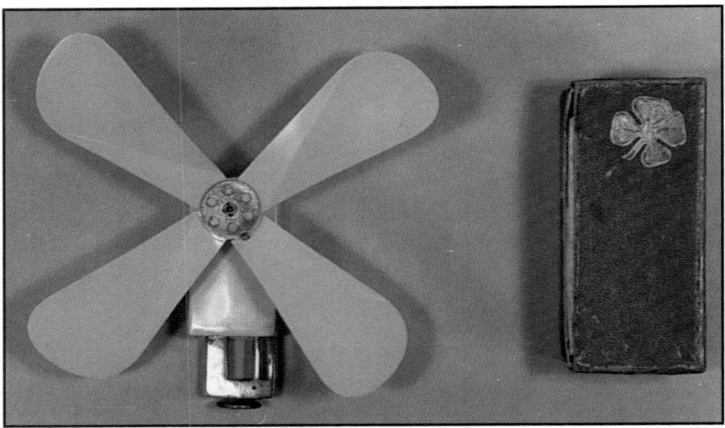

4¾", 4-blade, ivory colored folding mechanical fan, rectangular mechanism w/thumb plunger. "Depose/France" on metal part, original box w/4-leaf clover. $40.00 – $50.00.

4¾", 3-blade, variegated pearlescent brown fan, two finger plunging mechanism. Circa 1925. $35.00 – $45.00.

4⅜", 3-blade, ivory colored folding mechanical fan, round mechanism w/thumb plunger. "Carlo, Made in Germany" on metal parts. $35.00 – $45.00.

Optical

On September 18, 1875, the Spencer Optical Manufacturing Company of Mount Kisco, New York, was issued a license to use celluloid in the production of spectacle frames, lorgnettes, loupes, magnifiers, spectacle cases, holders, and wipers; frames were clearly the most important item on this list.

The pince-nez style was first introduced in the 1840s and remained the most popular type of eyeglasses worn by both men and women throughout the nineteenth century.

John Spencer issued a patent on October 14, 1879 for an improvement in the manufacture of celluloid rims and handles for the pince-nez style.

Until the introduction of celluloid, eyeglass rims had been manufactured of various materials including horn, tortoise shell, and hard rubber. An excerpt from a Celluloid Manufacturing Company brochure boasts of the benefits of using the new plastic.

> *Since 1876 Celluloid has been used by this Company for the rims of eye-glasses. It has been found to combine many advantages for this purpose. It is lighter than rubber, horn, shell or any other of the materials formerly employed. The rims are stronger and more durable than others. For beauty they surpass the ordinary tortoise shell, rubber and steel frames. They are not affected by atmospheric changes, and stand equally well in hot or cold climates. They do not corrode by moisture and are not tarnished by exposure to the fumes of acids. Consequently they may be constantly worn in many kinds of employment where frames or rims of other material soon become discolored and unsightly.*
>
> *Their durability and lightness are chief among these excellences. Although their first cost is a trifle above that of rims made from rubber, they are cheaper in the end, for they are almost indestructible. The number of eye-glasses yearly broken through carelessness in handling and from being permitted to drop upon floors is almost incredible. It is well nigh impossible to break a Celluloid rim unless by violence purposely applied and where economy is an object a rim of this material would be cheaper to the purchaser than any other commonly used, even if its cost were twice or thrice that at which it is offered.*
>
> *The factories of this company are at Mt. Kisco, N.Y., where nearly one half million eye-glasses and spectacles are annually made. At the Centennial Exhibition at the American Institute of 1879, and in numerous competitions throughout the country, the Spencer products have received high awards for superiority in all points of excellence. Their catalogue embraces glasses in every degree of quality, of great variety in styles and of extreme range in prices. They can fill every requirement in their department of an exceedingly useful art, and their manufacturers have won their way to nearly every corner of the globe.*

These trade cards, a most popular method of advertising, show Spencer Optical pince-nez eye glasses with celluloid rims. The trade cards, which range in price from $8.00 to $15.00, state that each pair was branded with the following information: S.O.M. Co. Pat. Mar. 13, 1877.

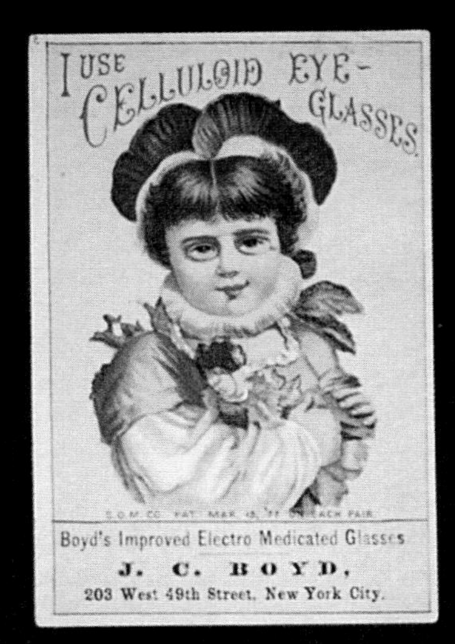

Pansy girl trade cards.

Ben Swanson

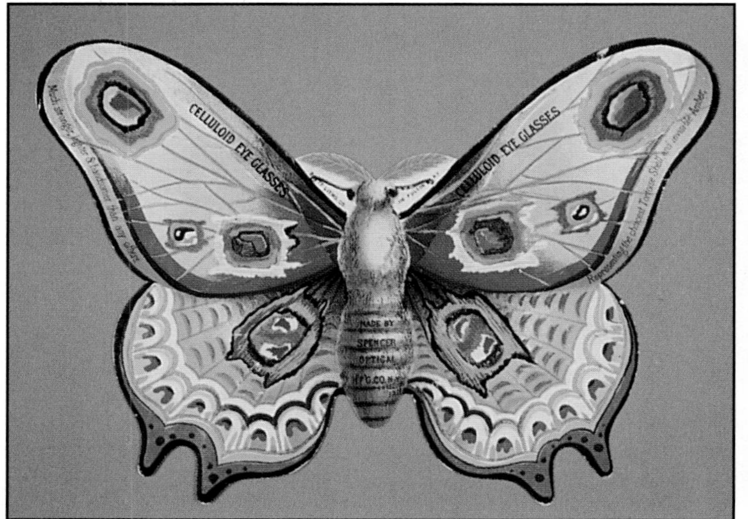

It wasn't until the 1880s that imitation mottled tortoise shell was introduced. This colorful 8¼" x 6" trade card boasts the great advantages of celluloid over shell, with a special emphasis on the dwindling tortoise population. $50.00.

The round imitation tortoise shell rims shown here were introduced into optical fashion around the turn of the century. The eyeglasses shown here sold for $5.00, as indicated by the original price sticker on the lenses.

By the 1920s, "Harold Lloyd" spectacles were considered the height of fashionable eye wear, as both men and women embraced the style. This respectable young lady looks rather studious in her round rimmed spectacles.

Harold Lloyd eyeglasses toy. After the turn of the twentieth century, celluloid became increasingly popular as a medium in fashionable eye wear. The style became all the rage when movie audiences around the country were entertained by Harold Lloyd, the famous silent movie comedian, who appeared in the round, black rim spectacles.

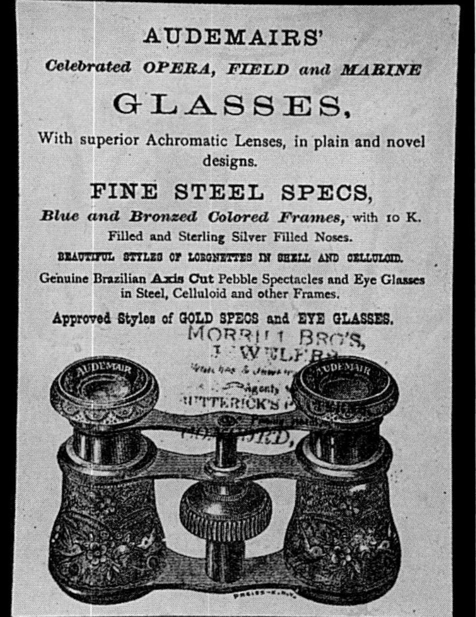

AUDEMAIRS'

Celebrated OPERA, FIELD and MARINE

GLASSES,

With superior Achromatic Lenses, in plain and novel designs.

FINE STEEL SPECS,

Blue and Bronzed Colored Frames, with 10 K. Filled and Sterling Silver Filled Noses.

BEAUTIFUL STYLES OF LORGNETTES IN SHELL AND CELLULOID.

Genuine Brazilian **Axis Cut** Pebble Spectacles and Eye Glasses in Steel, Celluloid and other Frames.

Approved Styles of GOLD SPECS and EYE GLASSES.

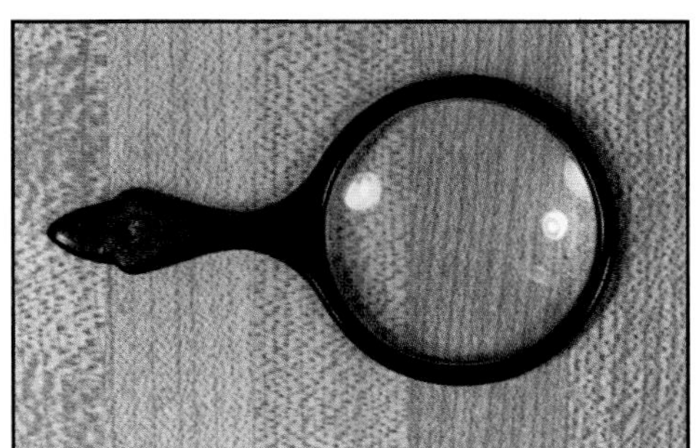

This trade card advertising a variety of Spencer products pictures a dog holding a single lens spectacle. The reverse lists a variety of goods including lorgnettes and eyeglasses in celluloid. $15.00 – $20.00.

The Texas Eye Shield, patented on Jan. 30, 1894, was a safety goggle rather than a corrective lens. Made from fine wire mesh and translucent celluloid they came in two styles, clear or green tint. Designed for protection from the elements while engaging in work or sporting activities, they were an inexpensive alternative to traditional leather and glass goggles.

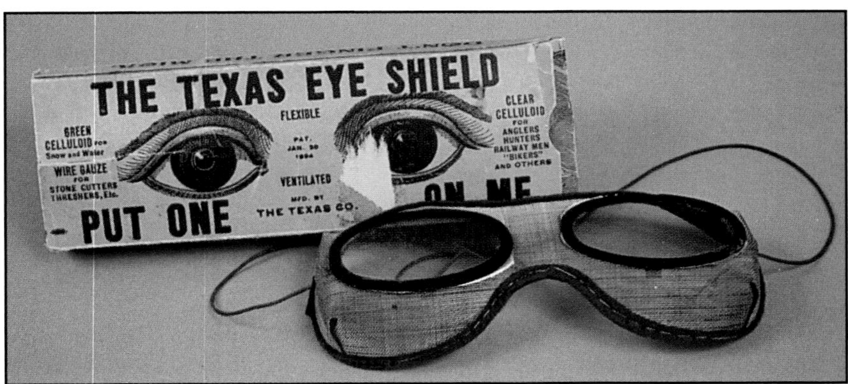

Chevalier Optician Opera Glasses, chrome, copper and celluloid, marked Paris, $85.00+.

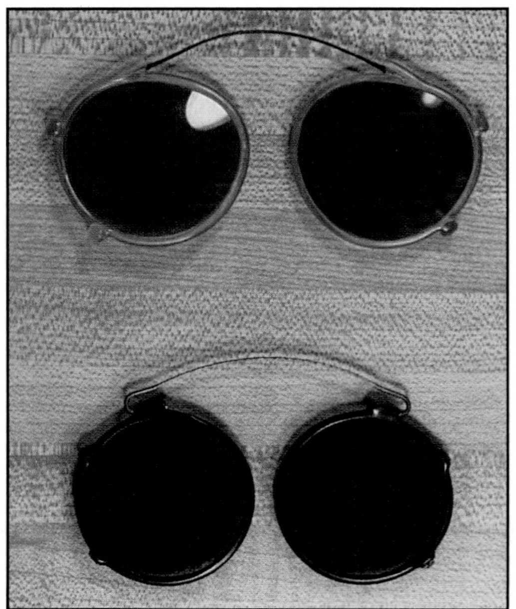

Attachable shades with frames of translucent amber, imitation tortoise shell, and jet black celluloid were designed to clamp onto the rims of eyeglasses. These lenses ranged in color from green to brown and were made of glass set in celluloid rims, which were held together by a piece of flexible steel. $5.00 – $8.00.

Endnotes

36. Throughout the mid 1800s, millions of Chinese immigrants came to the United States seeking gold or work on the railroad. Those unable to strike it rich or secure construction jobs soon realized the opportunity available to them. Desperate for work, they were willing to do whatever came their way, including service jobs. Before long, Chinese laundries began to spring up all over the country. At first the new businesses were welcomed, but as the economy weakened and laundry fees escalated, the sentiment began to change. In fact, so many Chinese were immigrating into the U.S. annually, by the early 1880s the government decided something had to be done to put a halt to the massive influx. The Chinese Immigration Exclusion Act was instituted in 1882 and again in 1884.

37. This was partly due to the passing of Queen Victoria's beloved husband Albert in 1861. Deeply grieved, Victoria went into mourning and society followed suit, joining her in somber attire.

38. In America, the Civil War was raging, tearing apart the nation. Black, the acceptable color of grief, and deep shades of brown and maroon, were the only proper colors to wear. Tortoise shell complimented the dark clothing that was fashionable during this period of time beautifully.

Vanity Items

Celluloid Grooming Implements

Personal grooming accessories and containers for cosmetics, perfumes, and ointments have been made since ancient times, however it wasn't until the late Victorian era that elaborate matching vanity sets for ladies' dressing tables became commonplace. These dresser sets were sometimes simple, consisting of a comb, brush and mirror, but they could also be very elaborate, including as many as twenty different components.

At first, the materials used to make vanity items were primarily glass and china, as well as finely crafted silver, ebony, ivory, bone, mother-of-pearl, and tortoise shell. But as the popularity of celluloid grew, so did its applications and by the mid 1870s, John and Isaiah Hyatt began to manufacture personal grooming implements using pyroxylin plastic.

By the early 1880s, the Celluloid Brush Company was in full operation producing an assortment of toiletry articles including tooth, clothing, hair and cosmetic brushes; mirrors and combs, soap and powder boxes, salve jars, and a limited assortment of small accessories, manicure implements, and button hooks.

An 1883 Celluloid Brush Company catalog features a limited selection of dressing items that were simple in design and color; pieces could be purchased individually in amber, shell (imitation tortoise), malachite, black, red, white, and blue.

The makers of celluloid struck gold with the introduction of pyroxylin plastic dresser sets and boudoir accessories. Celluloid was the perfect material for molding the wide array of articles in a fashionable vanity set; the shapes, styles, and colors were limited only by the imagination of the designers.

By 1889, the Celluloid Novelty Company had begun to manufacture ornately molded accessories for the Brush Company, adding to the list of available implements glove stretchers,

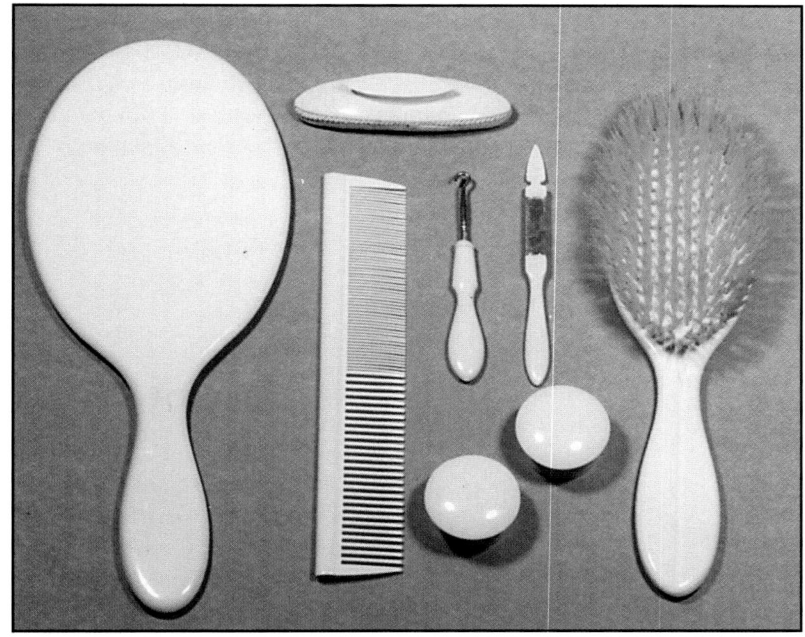

These "white" celluloid grooming implements were available beginning in the early 1880s from the Celluloid Brush Co. Store at 313 – 315 Broadway St., New York. This modest set includes a marked "Celluloid" 8" brush w/natural bristles; a marked "Celluloid" 10" beveled mirror; 7" comb; 3" nail polisher; 4" nail cleaner w/file; 3¾" glove button hook and two small powder/salve boxes. $65.00.

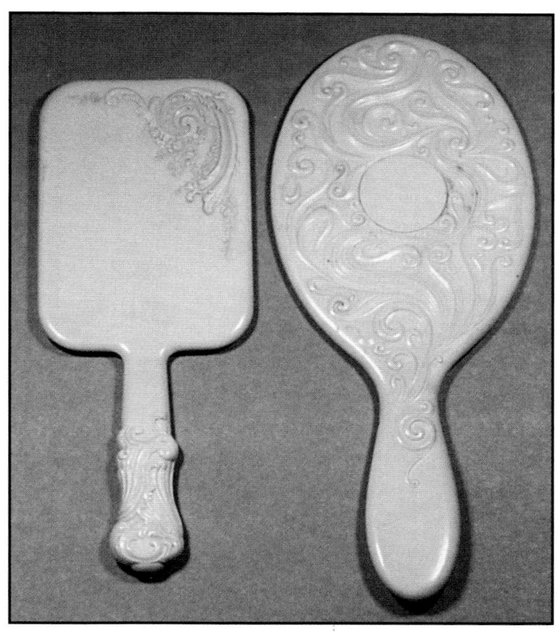

These two Celluloid Company mirrors exhibit the excellent molding properties of pyroxylin plastic. Both items are branded with the Celluloid trademark and date to the mid 1880s. $20.00 – $25.00 each.

powder shakers, small hinged boxes, shoe horns, and cosmetic brushes.

By 1892, the Celluloid Company had expanded their line of merchandise to include 38 different design styles and several elaborate matching vanity sets. As the catalog illustrations on pages 103 and 104 show, celluloid articles were so beautifully designed they rivaled valuable handcrafted ivory and silver. In this case, celluloid was not an inexpensive imitation material, but rather an extravagant alternative for the traditional substances used in fancy dressing articles.

The earliest of celluloid dresser items were most desired in imitation ivory with simulated graining. This was first accomplished by J. Edson in 1883 (USP# 283,225) when he devised a process of laminating thin, contrasting shades of opaque and translucent ivory colored sheet, together into solid blocks. When cut "across the grain," not only did this technique produce the desired striations, it was in fact a remarkable imitation of genuine elephant ivory.

The introduction of matched dresser sets in imitation grained ivory presented the manufacturer of pyroxylin plastic with a unique challenge; it became necessary to make the raw celluloid using a uniform mix of coloring, in order that all pieces in a set would match. Each day's production had to be exactly like that which had been manufactured before.

So successful was celluloid that others sought to capitalize on its potential. Rival companies were established in New Jersey and Massachusetts to produce pyroxylin plastic goods similar in composition to Hyatt's patented celluloid. Those that produced vanity items and dresserwares were: American Zylonite; Arlington Manufacturing (Pyralin); Arlington; Viscoloid Co.; and Fiberloid Company.

In 1878 John W. Hyatt was granted the first patent (#199,909) for the manufacture of dressing combs from celluloid. In it he states:

Celluloid has been found to possess many valuable properties which admirably adapt it to the construction of many devices, especially combs. Thus celluloid is easily molded or stamped when warm, and then, being cooled, retains the contour or shape it received when warm. It is not affected by cold, but retains its elasticity and flexibility at any climatic temperature. It is much stronger and less frangible than wood, hard rubber, or horn, lighter than metal and is not affected by oil or water and is moreover capable of assuming a very high polish, and of being colored in any manner desired, or made to represent ivory, tortoise shell or amber, and also malachite, lapis lazuli and various gems. The surface of the material is not harsh to the skin, while its flexibility and tenacity are such that a comb made of it can be bent into a circle without fracturing and then straightened into proper shape, the teeth of the comb being always perfectly flexible and elastic; nor would it be fractured by bending or by falling from a great height. Obviously none of the other materials above described would produce a comb possessing the many excellent qualities and inherent superiorities of a comb made of celluloid, which thus becomes a new and distinctive article of manufacture of great value.

These personal grooming implements in "white" are early examples of the finely detailed accessories advertised by the Celluloid Novelty Company in their 1892 Manicure Goods Catalog. It is believed that the original molds for this pattern were actually made by the American Zylonite Company and after Celluloid Co. acquired the firm, they continued marketing the pieces. The 3" x 1" nail polisher originally cost $2.50 per dozen; 1" dia. x 5⁄8" powder/salve box sold for $1.50 per dozen; 5" nail file was $2.50 per dozen; and the 3 5⁄8" cosmetic brush sold for $2.50 per dozen. The total combined cost of the four items shown was approximately 76¢. Today individual pieces with intricately molded patterns can exceed $10.00.

Christie Romero

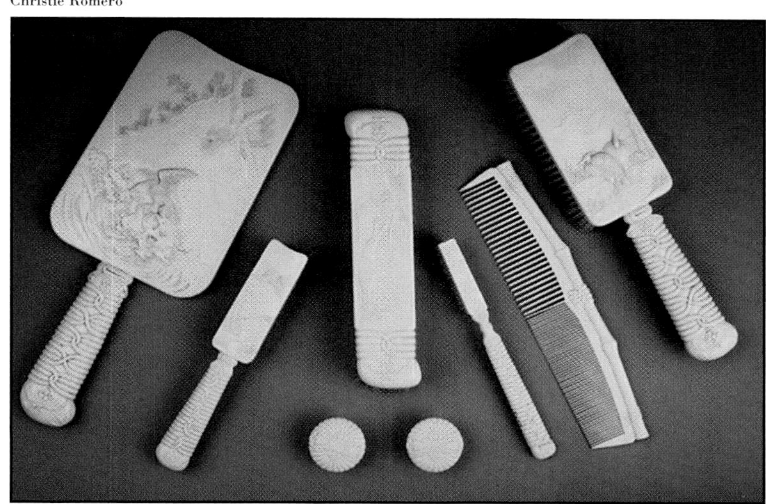

This beautiful light antique colored six-piece set was advertised in the 1892 Celluloid Company catalog. Two additional salve containers complete the set, which originally sold for $96.00, a costly sum prior to the turn of the century. Today its value is almost three times the original expense, as it is rare to find complete sets in such fine condition. As stated in J.W. Hyatt's 1878 patent, celluloid had indeed become a new and distinctive article of great value.

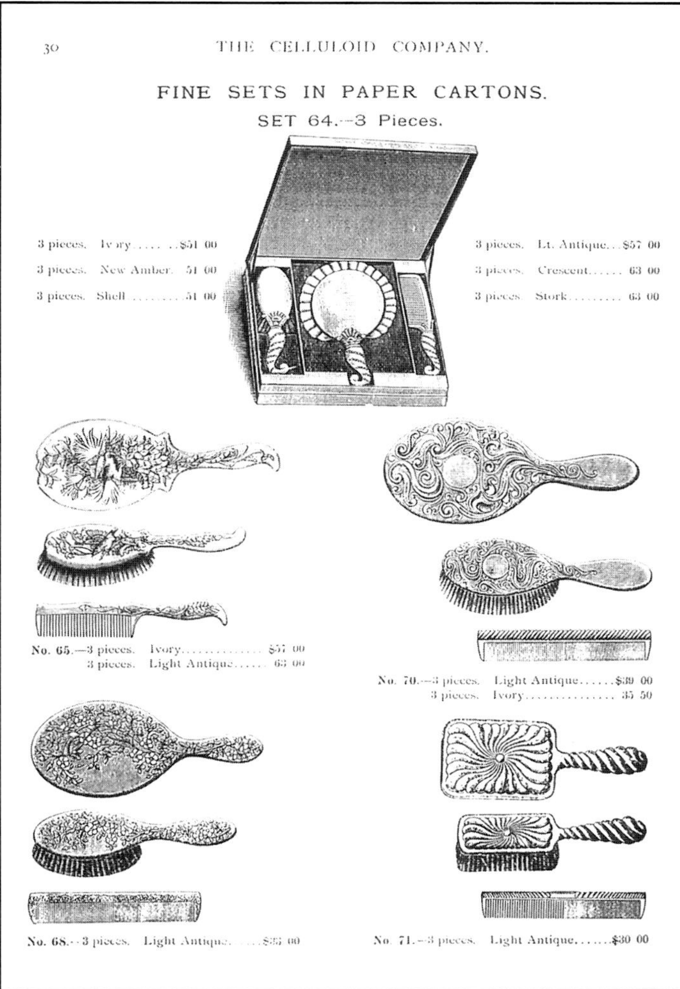

30 THE CELLULOID COMPANY.

FINE SETS IN PAPER CARTONS.

SET 64.—3 Pieces.

3 pieces. Ivory........$51 00
3 pieces. New Amber. 51 00
3 pieces. Shell..........51 00

3 pieces. Lt. Antique...$57 00
3 pieces. Crescent...... 63 00
3 pieces. Stork......... 63 00

No. 65.—3 pieces. Ivory.............. $57 00
3 pieces. Light Antique...... 63 00

No. 70.—3 pieces. Light Antique......$39 00
3 pieces. Ivory................ 35 50

No. 68.—3 pieces. Light Antique.......$55 00

No. 71.—3 pieces. Light Antique.......$30 00

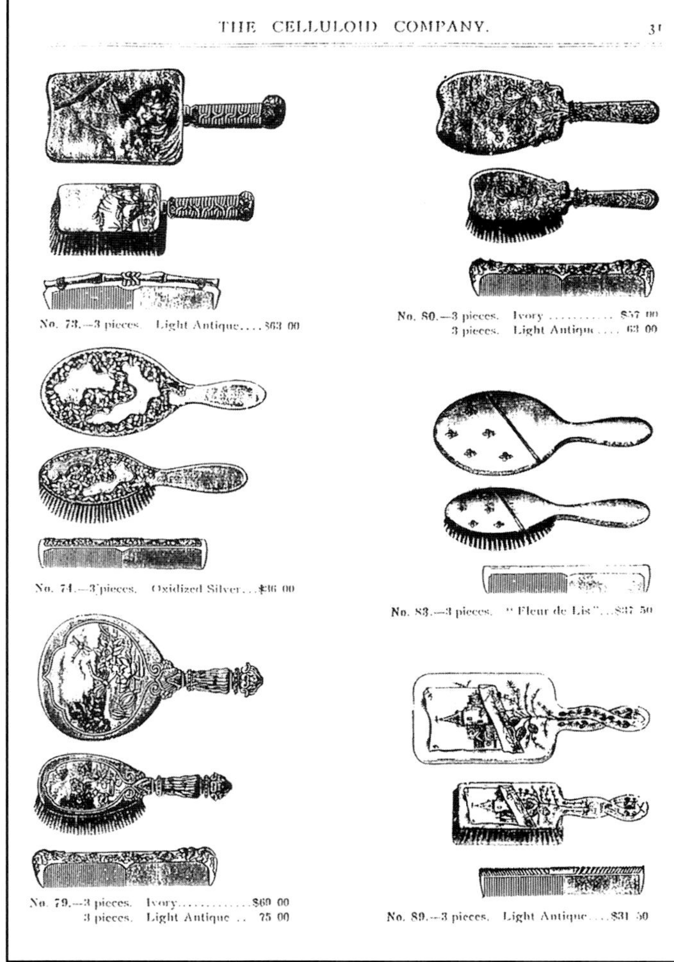

THE CELLULOID COMPANY. 31

No. 73.—3 pieces. Light Antique....$63 00

No. 80.—3 pieces. Ivory $57 00
3 pieces. Light Antique 63 00

No. 74.—3 pieces. Oxidized Silver...$36 00

No. 83.—3 pieces. "Fleur de Lis"...$37 50

No. 79.—3 pieces. Ivory.............$60 00
3 pieces. Light Antique .. 75 00

No. 89.—3 pieces. Light Antique....$31 50

Note the color selection of set #74 on page 31 in oxidized silver. Celluloid was not considered to be a cheap imitation of luxury materials, but rather a beautiful substance for making lovely, and expensive, accessories.

Vanity Items

Celluloid, Arlington, Zylonite, and Fiberloid all branded their dresser-ware products with appropriate trade names. Viscoloid is the only company known to have not registered their own brand name.

Dresser ware and personal vanity items made up a large portion of the finished goods produced by these companies. As a result vanity items are, without a doubt, the most available celluloid product for today's collector.

Trademarks can often be found branded on the finished articles and are clues to origin of manufacture and date of production. Trademarks were applied to finished articles by stamping with a hot die, which left an imprint that was filled in with black paint or paste. As with most antiques, those that bear a trademark are most desirable.

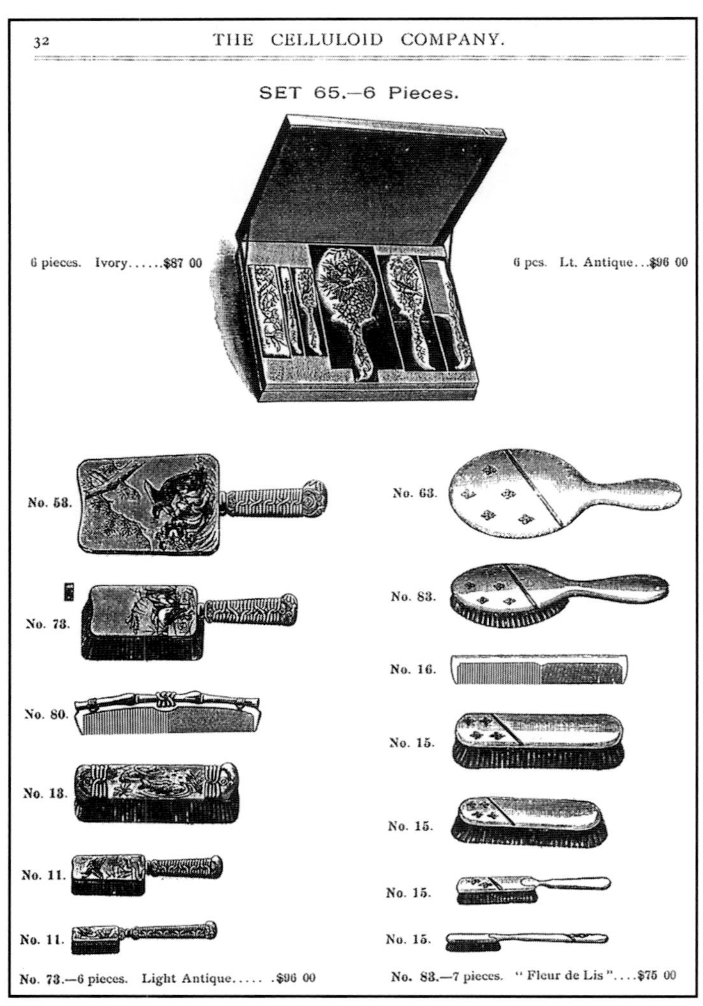

32 THE CELLULOID COMPANY.

SET 65.—6 Pieces.

6 pieces. Ivory......$87 00

6 pcs. Lt. Antique...$96 00

No. 58.

No. 63.

No. 73.

No. 83.

No. 16.

No. 80.

No. 15.

No. 18.

No. 15.

No. 11.

No. 15.

No. 11.

No. 15.

No. 73.—6 pieces. Light Antique..... .$96 00

No. 83.—7 pieces. "Fleur de Lis"....$75 00

A selection of 12 different three-piece matching vanity sets (with comb, brush, and mirror) were available at $30.00 to $69.00, while a boxed six-piece vanity set with naturalistic detailing could cost as high as $96.00.

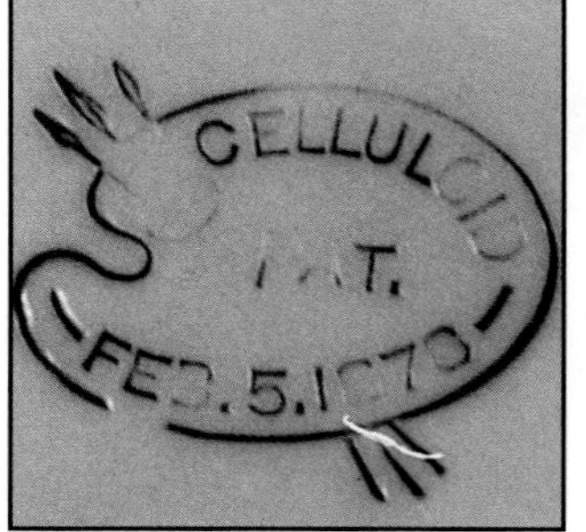

Tradenames or trademarks. Oftentimes the Zylonite tradename can be found imprinted in a location other than on the plastic itself, as is evident in the second photo above.

This toothbrush also bears the American Zylonite arrow trademark. Such marked items are difficult to come by since the company was in business for such a short period of time.

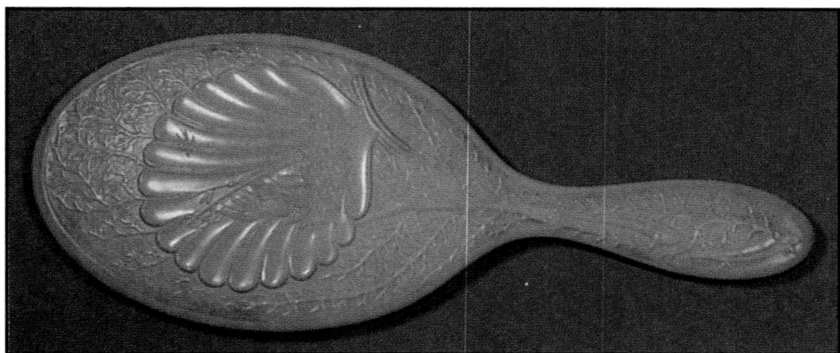

Not all American Zylonite items were simply designed. This beautifully ornate mirror has an all-over molded vine pattern and a shell center with the image of a sailboat, further evidence that Zylonite was a quality company.

Brush and mirror in cream colored Zylonite. NPA.

Arlington Co. called their brand of plastic Pyralin, a tradename derived from the word pyroxylin. The Pyralin mark can be found on a wide variety of vanity items and toilet articles because it was used by DuPont well into the 1930s.

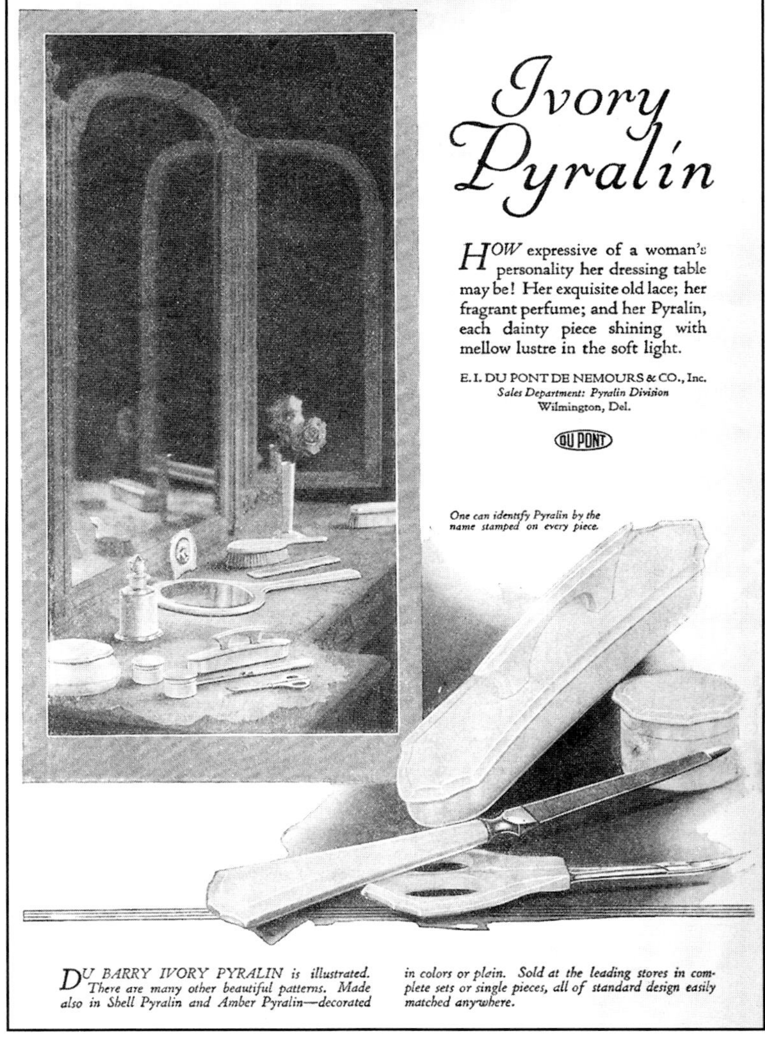

Circa 1925 Pyralin advertisement featuring the DuBarry line. Manufacturers of dresserware sought to introduce new designs annually and DuBarry was the Arlington Company's first and most popular.

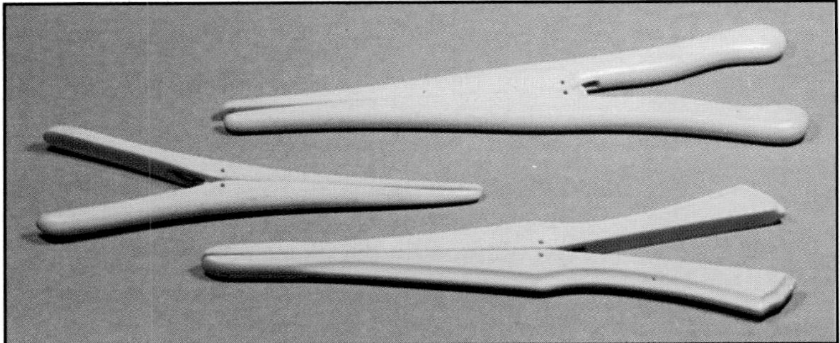

Although not evident in this photograph, the three glove stretchers shown here are branded with the Pyralin trademark. The various styles may reflect different years of production. $12.00 each.

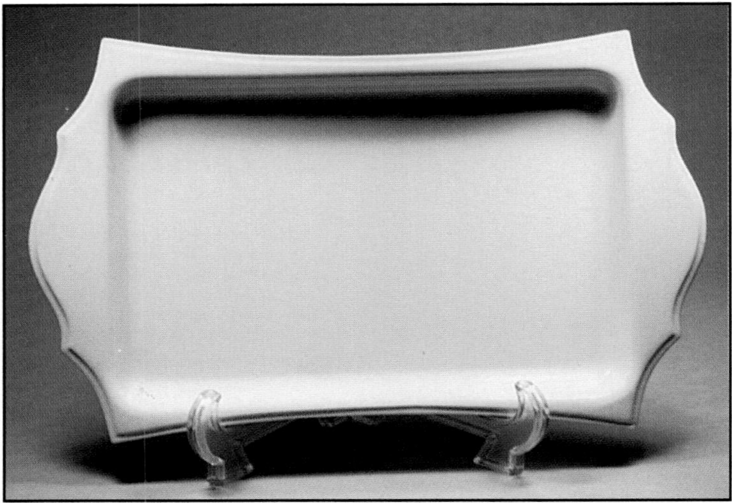

This wonderful dresser tray is branded with the Ivory Pyralin tradename. To find an example in such excellent condition is rare because often perfume and hair dressings stained the surface of the plastic. $25.00.

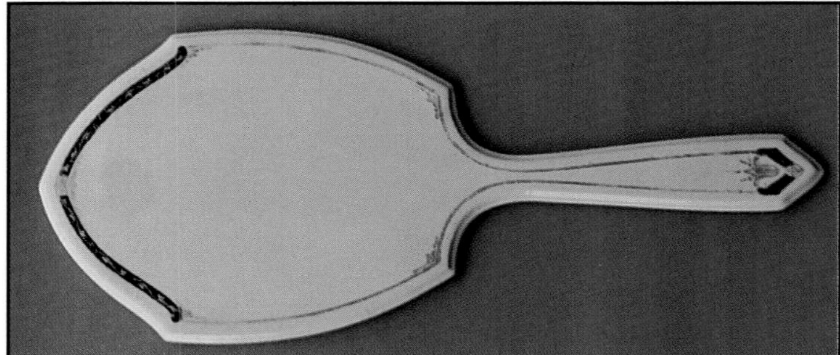

This lovely Fiberloid mirror is from the Cleopatra pattern in ivory. It is embellished with black and gold trim. Dating to 1925, the mirror came as a set in a gift pack that included a brush and comb. It could not be purchased separately.

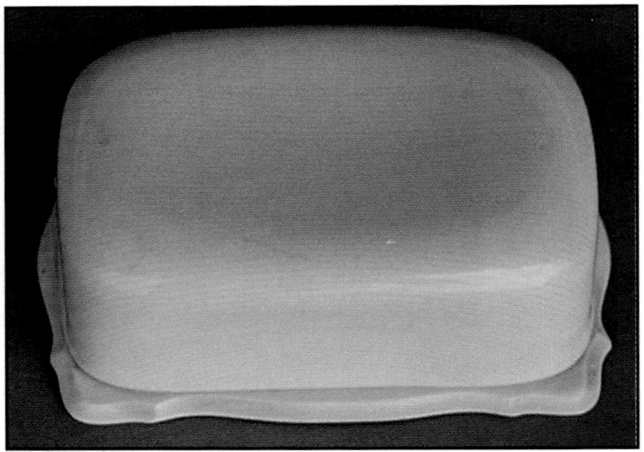

This soap box is branded Berkshire Ivory, Fiberloid's best line of pyroxylin plastic in imitation of elephant ivory.

Advertisement, Ivory Fiberloid.

Decorative Techniques

There were a number of decorative techniques employed in the making of vanity items. In addition to molding elaborate designs in relief, the second most popular method of decorating involved hand painting. A third technique involved engraving monograms into the surface of an item, then painting the initials with deep blue or black paint.

Generally a trademarked container is more collectible than one that is not branded. Other factors that affect cost include the addition of a powder puff and the condition of decorative embellishments.

Powder Boxes and Hair Receivers

Powder boxes and hair receivers were among the usual items on a lady's dressing table. The hair receiver, which has an open hole in the center of the fitted lid, was a necessary receptacle in the days when human hair was recycled into jewelry or sold for cash to wig makers. The usual method of saving one's "combings" involved removing the hair from brush or comb by neatly winding it around the index and middle finger, then slipping the twisted lock through the opening of the lid.

Three decorated powder boxes with hand painted floral and ribbon motifs. Blue forget-me-not floral decoration with trademark Arlington, $25.00. Pink and white flowers w/ribbon, unmarked; daisy motif in yellow and white, unmarked. $18.00 each.

2¾"h. x 2⅞" dia. powder jar w/lid; 3½" x 2" soap box. Ivory grained celluloid w/pink, white, and blue floral decorations. Set $25.00 – $30.00.

2" h. x 2" dia. powder jar w/lid and feather puff; 2½" x 3" soap box, ivory grained w/hand painted blue forget-me-not flowers. Trademarked easel w/Celluloid, Pat. Feb. 5, 1878. Set $45.00+.

The addition of a down puff, especially one of such fine quality, can escalate the price of a simple powder box by four times. This box and puff which includes a fancy celluloid and blue glass handle is valued at $65.00.

These fine examples of powder box and hair receiver are molded in imitation ivory grained celluloid and features 2" h. x 4" square shaped boxes and round fitted lids w/F monogram. Trademark French Ivory (possibly an import from the French Ivory Co. of Canada). $30.00 – $35.00 per pair.

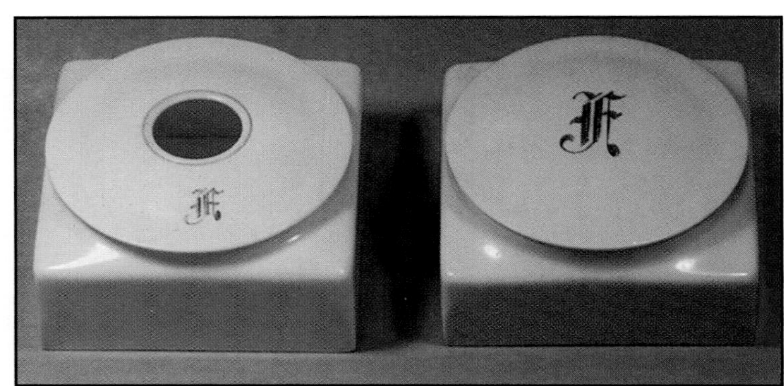

Pincushions with celluloid bases were often used on the vanity table to secure stick and hatpins. These three cushions represent the variety of styles available. Note the monogrammed "W" example. $12.00 – $15.00 each. Plain ivory grained vanity items with unusual shapes or odd embellishments are more difficult to find than those which are flat on the bottom.

2" h. x 4" dia. ivory grained powder box and hair receiver, tusk-shaped feet and pointed finial on lid, trademark Titterton, England. $35.00 – $40.00.

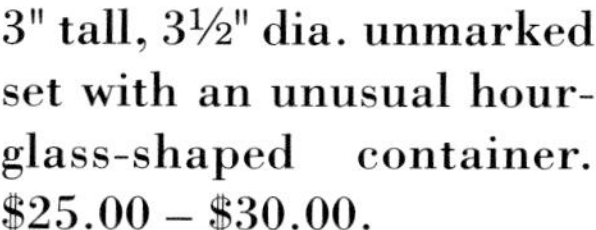

3" tall, $3\frac{1}{2}$" dia. unmarked set with an unusual hour-glass-shaped container. $25.00 – $30.00.

4" dia. ivory grained boxes w/$4\frac{3}{4}$" scalloped beveled lids, laminated with golden glitter over ivory grained celluloid. These were manufactured by the Celluloid Co. for a short time during the 1920s and were called Goldaleur or Silvaleur. Watch for glitter verdigris (green corrosion), which indicates a copper based material that may seep out of this type of decorative treatment. $30.00 – $40.00 per pair.

Pearlescence

By the late 1920s, pearlescent color was used in a variety of swirled and geometric patterns, as a laminate over translucent amber and solid colored celluloid. Imitation ivory and tortoise shell were no longer the most popular choices in dresserware.

Dorothy Maust

Five-piece amber and blue pearlescence, 5" x 9" scalloped rim dresser tray, 4" dia. Octagonal hair receiver w/hand painted rose motif., 7" button hook, 5" nail buffer, 5" scissors marked Germany. $25.00 – $30.00.

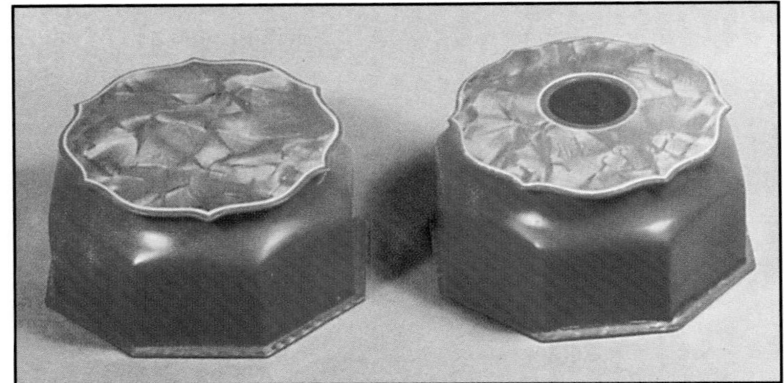

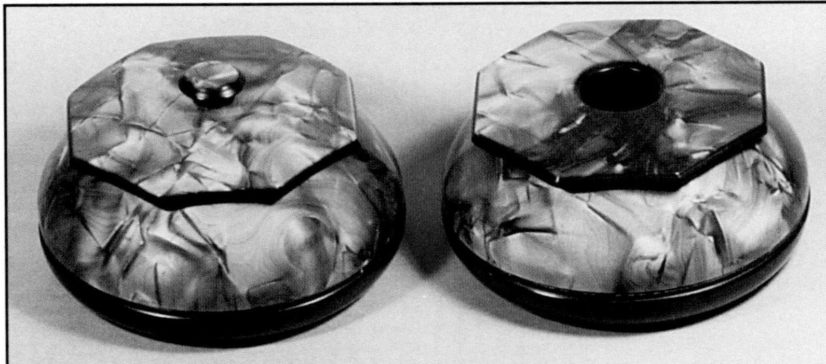

Brightly colored sets were first introduced in 1925 when artificial pearlescence was developed and color was all the rage. Note the octagonal shapes in these examples; bright orange octagonal base with contrasting pearlescent green lids/ octagonal set in gray and black pearlescence. $25.00 per set.

Unusual container shapes began to appear by the end of the 1920s, as shown in these peach pearlescent examples. The rectangular-shaped boxes are branded with the Fiberloid trademark while the pointed oval set is unmarked, yet attributed to Amerith as the Lotus pattern in peach pearl, circa 1929. $20.00 – $25.00 per set.

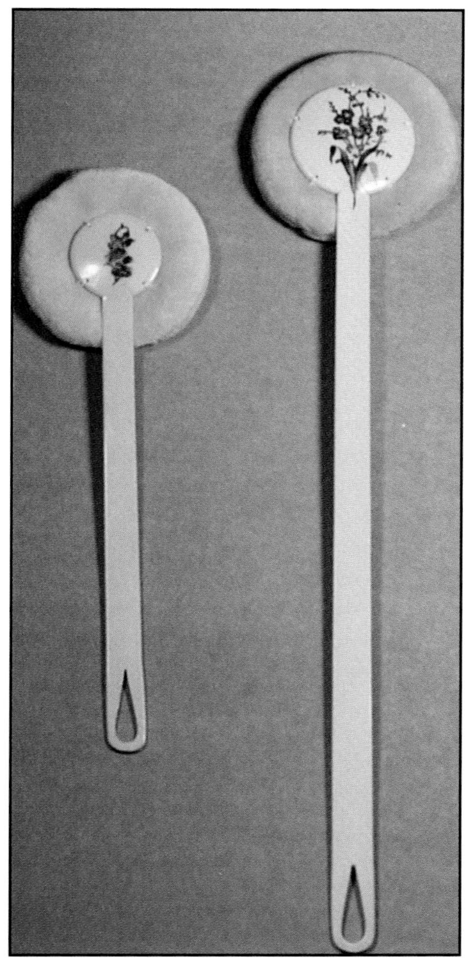

One way to apply powder to those hard-to-reach places was with a long handled puff. These 13" and 9" long powder puffs are fashioned from peach velour which is sewn onto a one-piece celluloid handle. Hand painted floral motifs. Small, Morning Glory; large, Forget-Me-Nots. $45.00 and $55.00.

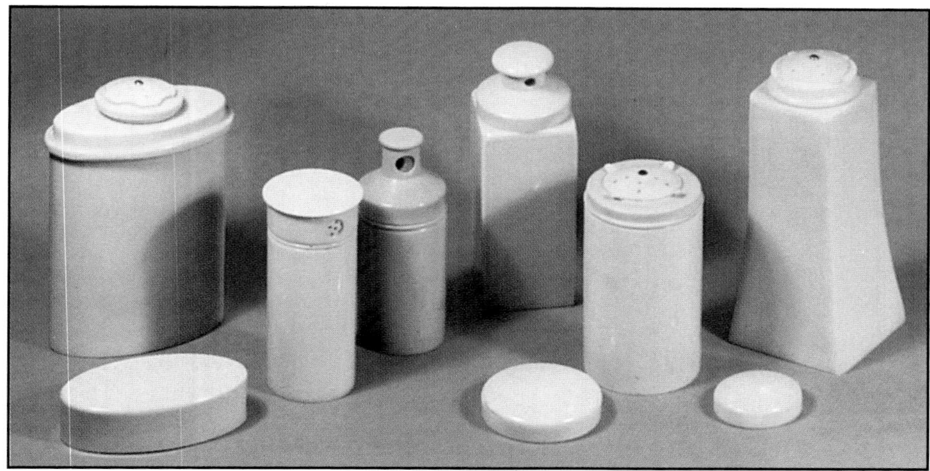

Examples of the wide variety of powder shakers that were manufactured in ivory grained celluloid. The earliest form, the largest plain round one (5th, right to left) was marketed as early as 1880 and remained a popular form through the 1920s. The two unusual forms on the extreme ends are the most valuable. Smaller containers range in price from $12.00 – $18.00 while the odd-shaped examples are in the $25.00+ range.

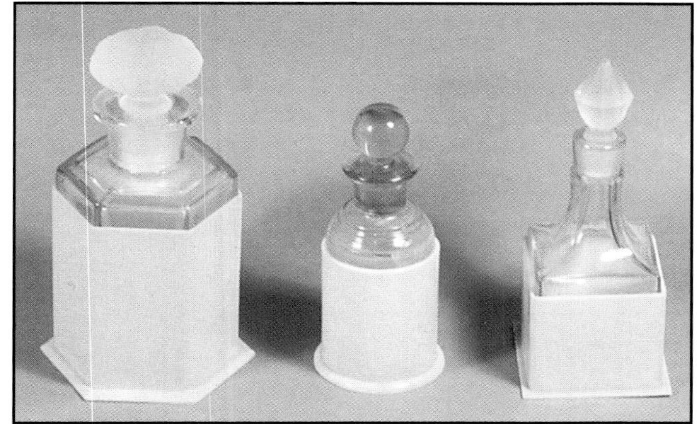

These wonderful holders were most popular after WWI, although they were manufactured much earlier. Note the example that is shown in the Ivory Fiberloid advertisement. $18.00 – $30.00.

These plain ivory grained dresser boxes are lined with velour and intended for storing gloves, hankies, jewelry, and hair accessories. They were manufactured through the 1920s but lost their appeal after the introduction of bold color during the middle of the decade. Small, $15.00 – $20.00; medium, $20.00 – $28.00; large, $25.00 – $35.00.

The addition of such novelty items as piano shaped jewel and trinket boxes added a touch of elegant whimsey to the dressing table. 3"h. x 5"w. piano jewelry box, imitation amber celluloid w/gold embossed trim and black/gold flowers, velvet lined. $35.00 – $50.00.

Novelty dresser boxes are difficult to find in good condition. All too often the repeated openings and closings of the lids have caused the celluloid to break. In excellent condition, this 5" tall ivory grained trinket box is made in the shape of a Victrola record player. Scalloped beveled edges, blue monogram, and sliding front door add to its appeal. A novel jewelry case for a lady's vanity. $55.00 – $65.00.

This unmarked rectangular box features a mottled opaque amber celluloid, decorated with painted engraving and amber rhinestones. This type of decorative treatment was often used in jewelry during the mid to late 1920s. $20.00 – $25.00

A 5" by 2" deep oval amber box w/decorated lid. The paper butterfly, grass, and milkweed silk are arranged in a pleasing fashion and held in place by a thick piece of clear celluloid. $25.00 – $35.00.

Vanity Trays

Many manufacturers of bureau sets offered trays made of celluloid for the orderly arrangement of various dresser items. However, often these solid celluloid trays are found with brown or yellow stains on the surface. This is the result of a chemical reaction due to contact with the alcohol in cologne, toilet water, or perfume. Unfortunately, these marks are permanent and cannot be removed by either washing with soap and water, or bleaching.

During the late 1920s, manufacturers of vanity sets conceived the idea of replacing the celluloid bottom with mirror or clear glass. This served a two-fold purpose: resistance to chemical damage and added attractiveness.

Today these trays can be found in a wide array of sizes and styles with a variety of decorative treatments sandwiched between layers of glass.

Small oval dresser tray, a milkweed silk and butterfly design sandwiched between two pieces of glass which are held in place by ivory celluloid framework. The handles are of translucent imitation amber. $18.00 – $25.00.

This novel dresser tray features the same decorative technique seen in the small examples. The tray bottom is made of white celluloid, upon which a print of a pretty girl and milkweed silk is applied, then covered with a glass insert. $35.00.

The two rectangular-shaped dresser trays shown here and the oval ones on top of the next page were made in the late 1920s when pearlescent color was fashionable. Each is decorated with engraved trim and features an oval-shaped center of lace under glass. $25.00 – $30.00 each.

The oval trays are made from translucent and opaque amber and include floral center Normandy lace doilies. $25.00 – $30.00 each.

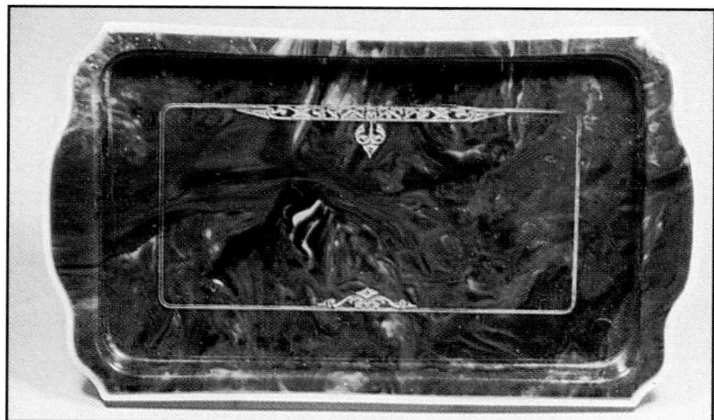

Imitation tortoise shell was popular during the late 1800s as a material for ornamental hair combs and eyeglass rims. It is the least common color for vanity items and dresserware. This rectangular tray in laminated ivory and imitation tortoise shell is further embellished with gold engraving in a pretty Art Nouveau design. $35.00.

At first glance, one might assume the toilet articles in this photograph are all part of a set, however just the opposite is true. It has taken years to assemble this small collection of imitation tortoise shell items. Upon close examination it is obvious that a variety of shell designs is evident. Left to right: trinket box, collar box, hairpin holder, hair receiver, toothbrush holder, soap box, nail buffer, shoe horn, folding comb, and razor case. Items range in price from $5.00 for the razor case to $20.00 for the unusually shaped hair receiver.

Dresser Sets

Complete dresser sets, especially early examples, are becoming increasingly difficult to find. Collectors should be aware that many sets were "married" over the years, therefore it is important to check individual articles for trademarks. Since several companies produced similar patterns, it is easy to mix and match pieces that compliment one another.

Remember that quality control ensured that the coloration of ivory graining was exact, so if the articles in a set are of different color variations, there is a very good possibility they did not start out together.

The DuBarry pattern in ivory Pyralin was first introduced in 1915 and throughout many years it remained Arlington's most popular line for dresser and vanity items. Although the name stayed the same, the decorative embellishments changed annually (much like a new model of a car). In the year 1928, Pyralin DuBarry was produced with a hand carved floral motif (shown on following page).

Arch Amerith was the tradename used by the Celluloid Corporation to describe their very best line of pyroxylin plastic toiletware. The trademark was first introduced in 1925 because the company trade name "Celluloid" had become generically used.

The most popular colors for Arch Amerith were pearl rose, pearl green, and pearl amber laminated over imitation ivory, black or translucent amber. Arch Amerith used an archway as their trademark.

This lovely circa 1910 ivory grained monogrammed set would have made a wonderful wedding gift. Each piece is engraved with a deep blue "G". The set also includes three graduated trays, salve and powder box, nail buffer, clock, frame, shoe horn, mirror, and clothing brush. Trademark Parisian Ivory, Loonen, France. $125.00.

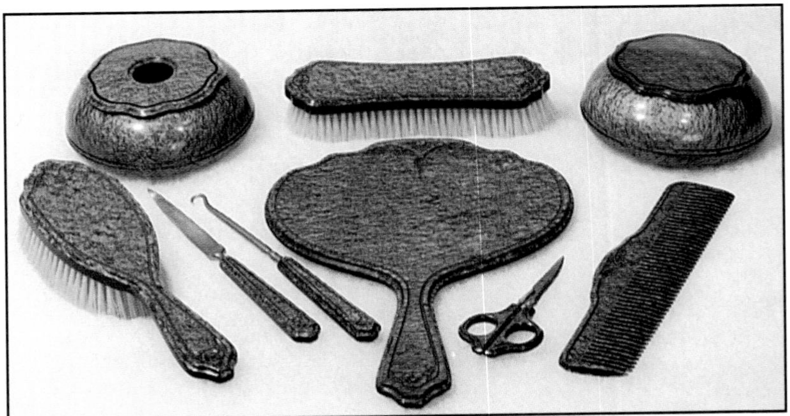

This set of Fiberloid dresserware in the Fairfax pattern dates to 1924. Many of the individual items have a small hand carved design, seen here in this detail photograph. Other items also featured in the company catalog include a matching dresser tray, jewel box, clock, frame, perfume, and pincushion.

NPCM

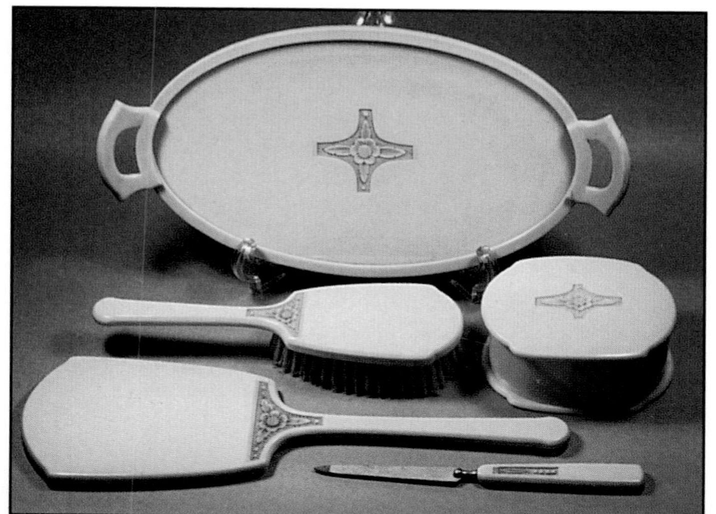

Originally this Du Barry set would have cost around $20.00; today it is valued at $75.00. The Pyralin is of the best quality and the tray and powder jar are lined with glass.

Arch Amerith trademark

This Arch Amerith dresser set, dated 1928, came complete in a satin-lined carrying case that was in deplorable condition, however, it did serve to protect the contents, keeping them pristine. The pattern name is Windsor, and the laminated color is described as "Pearl Amber." Originally this eight-piece set sold for $11.15. It was purchased for $45.00 several years ago.

NPCM

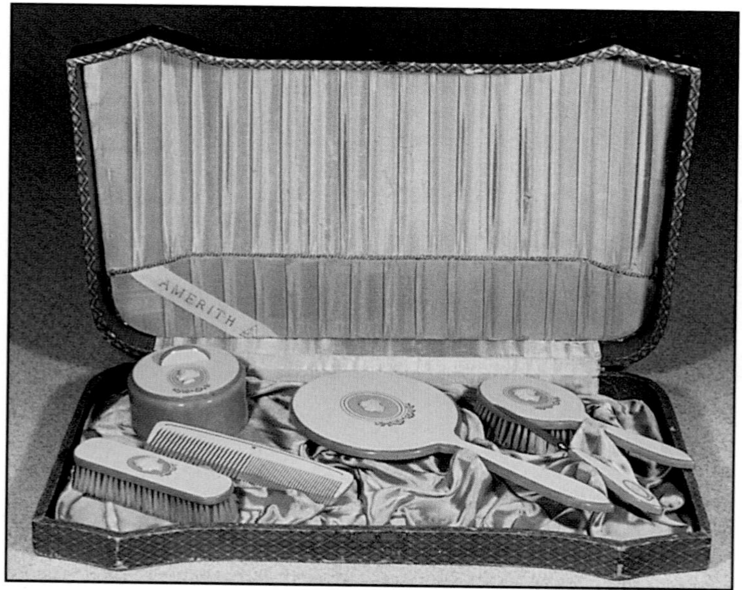

This boxed Arch Amerith dresser set is fashioned in the Melano pattern. Laminated translucent amber and ivory are further embellished with a pink celluloid oval and molded cameo profile. Circa 1930. The very best of the best! $175.00+.

NPCM

In July of 1928, DuPont introduced a new line of exceptional quality pyroxylin plastic that they named Lucite. In 1929, the company introduced 10 artistic designs, of which this four-piece set was one. Named Watteau after the famous French artist who painted the garden scene shown on the pieces, the set is complete with four pieces. It was molded by DuPont Viscoloid Corporation in Leominster. $125.00.

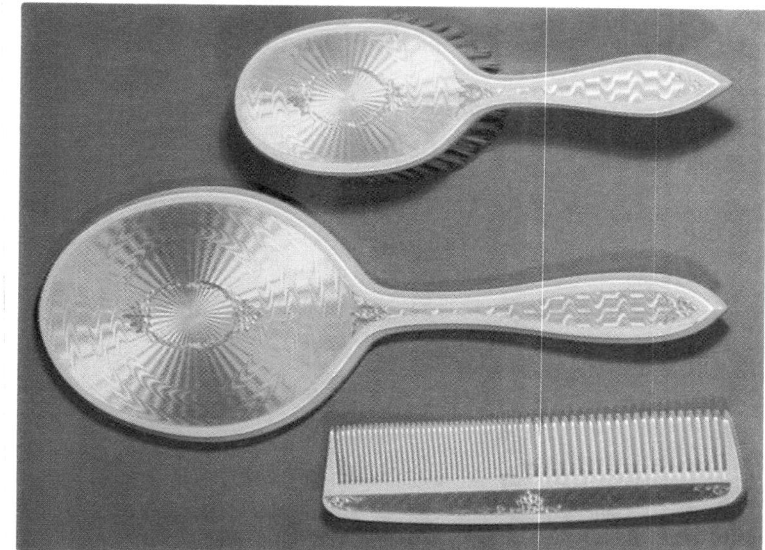

A stunning three-piece dresser set in golden yellow celluloid, fashioned to imitate the popular guilloche enameling done on mirror backs, compacts, and jewelry around the turn of the century. The set is currently housed at the National Plastics Center and Museum in Leominster. $75.00.

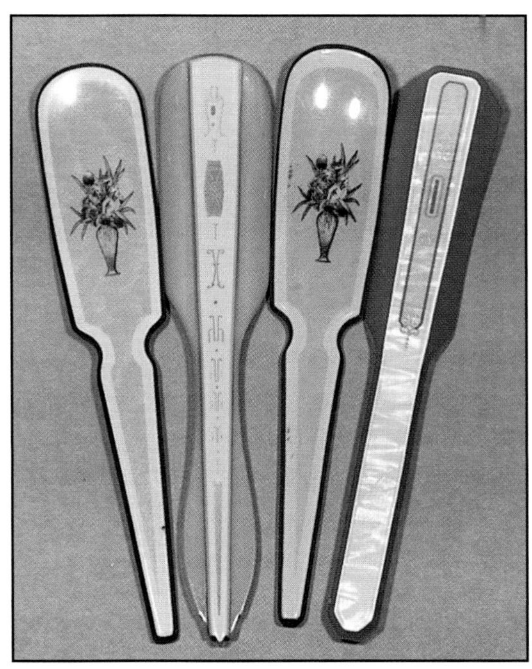

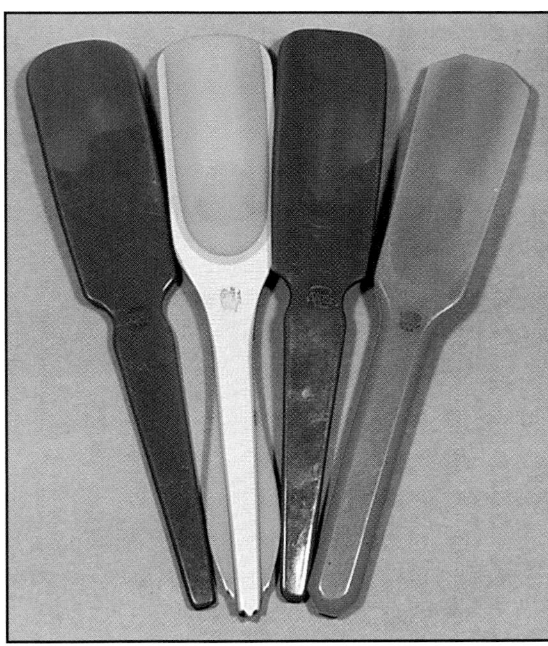

The four shoe horns illustrated here (fronts at top, backs below) were all manufactured around 1930 by the DuPont Viscoloid Corp. The pyroxylin plastic, called Lucite, was the very finest the company had to offer. The floral pattern is called Navarre, introduced in 1929, and the far right example in orange and pearlescent amber is the 1931 Adam pattern. Marked DuPont LUCITE USA. $12.00 each.

Circa 1930s, 11-piece amber and laminated green pearlescent dresser set includes a lace and glass bottom dresser tray, amber glass jar with matching lid, and a variety of manicure and toilet articles. Bright green became a popular color when artificial pearl effects were introduced during the latter part of the Roaring Twenties. $35.00 – $40.00. The majority of dresserware items manufactured during the 1930s were in laminated pearlescent colors.

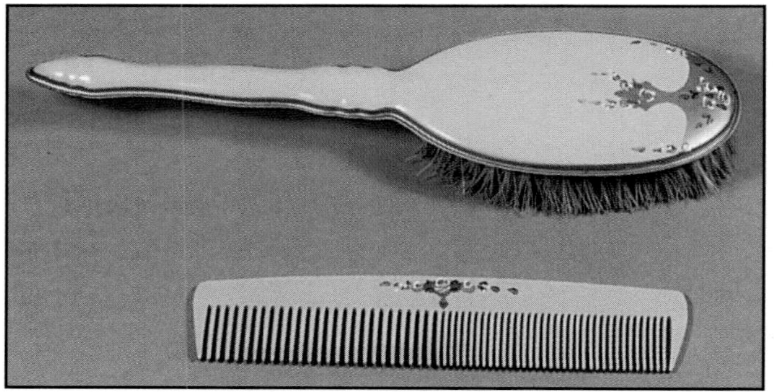

An early 1930s light pink brush and comb with gold hand painted trim embellished with roses. Around the early thirties, simple pastel colors began to appear, a pleasant change from the flamboyant pearl effects that had been so popular. Unmarked. $22.00 – $26.00 set.

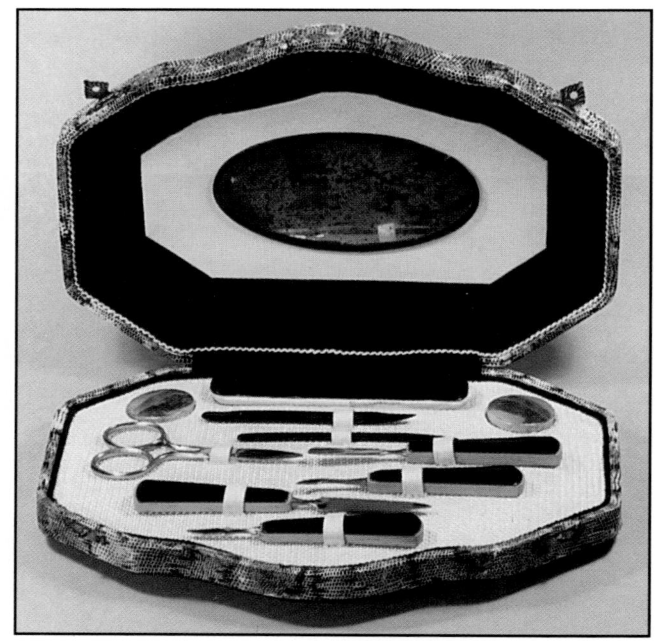

A circa 1930s manicure set in white birch wood, laminated with black celluloid. Unmarked, the set w/original box is valued at $18.00 – $20.00.

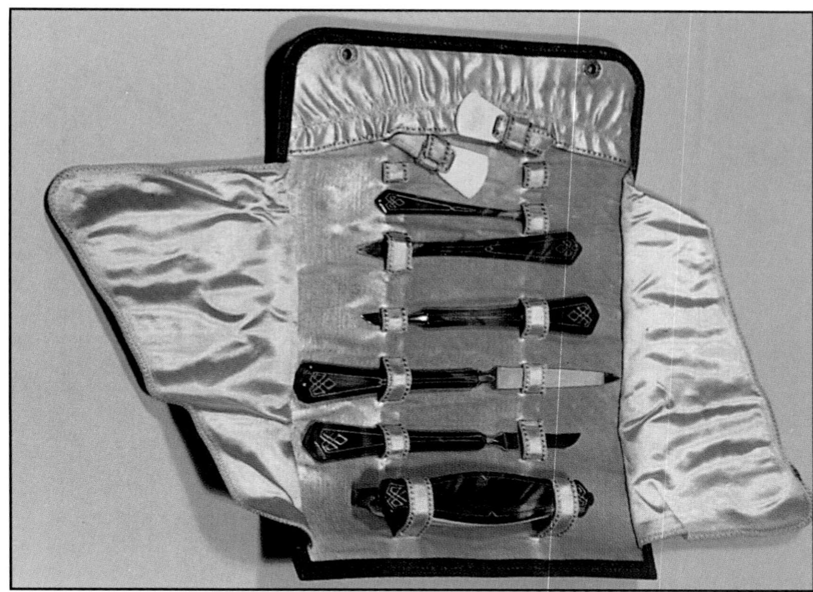

This pink satin-lined leather manicure roll features an array of imitation tortoise shell implements, engraved with gold designs. Imitation ivory pull tabs keep ribbon secure around tools. The scissors that belonged with this set had corroded around the metal and the celluloid had deteriorated and crumbled away. $28.00.

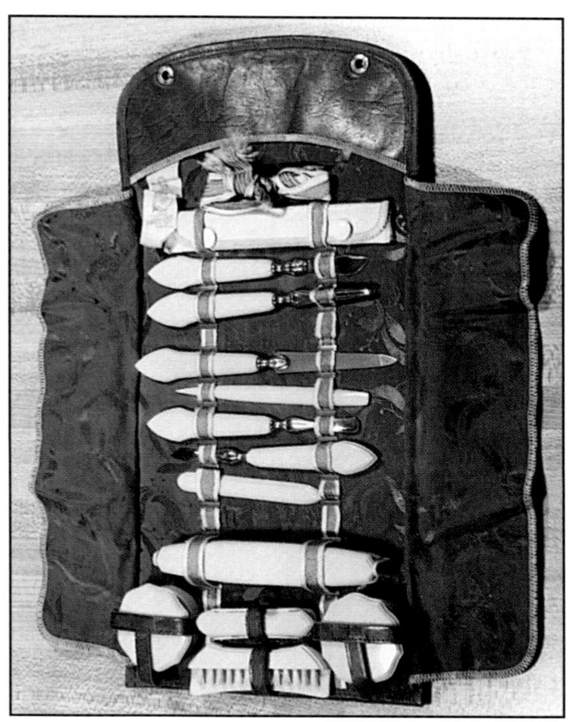

A green satin-lined leather roll is fitted with 13 manicure tools. Each item is branded with the French Ivory trade name. This set was most likely a product of Canada, where the French Ivory Co. was located. $40.00.

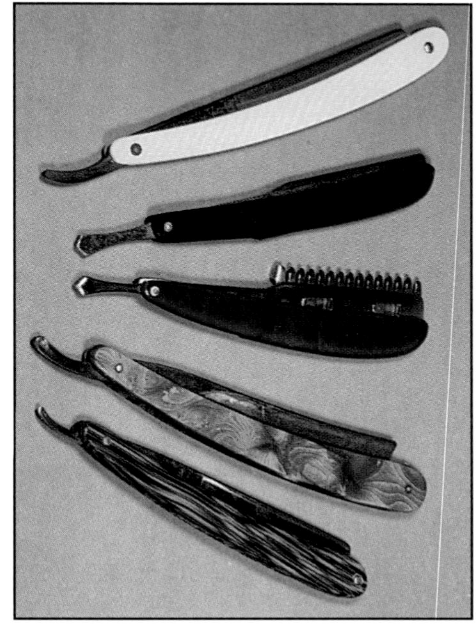

The variety of imitation materials executed in celluloid can be seen on these straight razor handles. They include ivory, jet, faux tortoise, pearlescent amber, and wood. $12.00 – $18.00 each.

Reese Howe. Photograph by Rebecca Barclay Pelletier

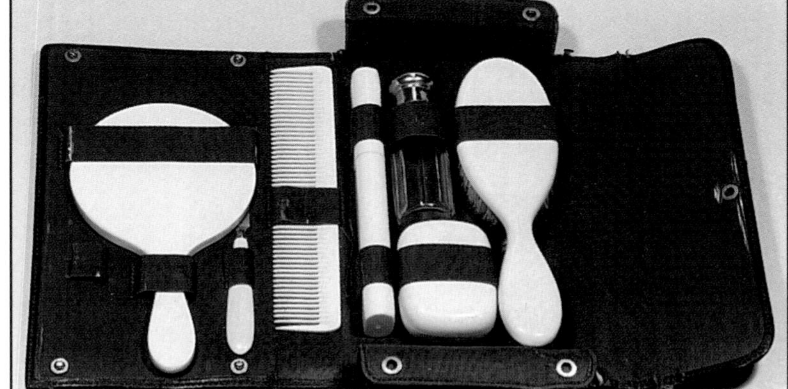

This unmarked ivory grained travel set features a mirror, brush, comb, toothbrush holder, soap box, manicure tool, and leaded glass bottle w/silver plated top. Blue satin lined leather case w/snaps. $55.00.

Exit 10 Antiques

This absolutely fabulous shaving mirror dates to the late 1890s and was manufactured in England. Made of imitation tortoise shell with a milk glass cup insert and adjustable mirror, it is a rarity and valued at $150.00+.

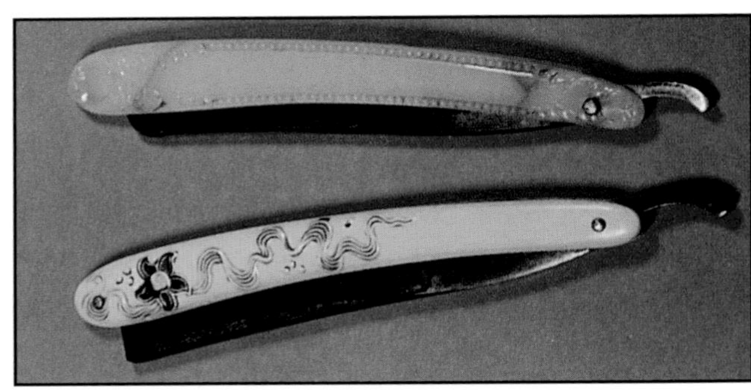

These two straight razors are but a sample of the molded designs used on the celluloid handles. Art Nouveau nudes, bamboo, flowers, and ears of corn are among the most commonly seen. $15.00 – $22.00 each.

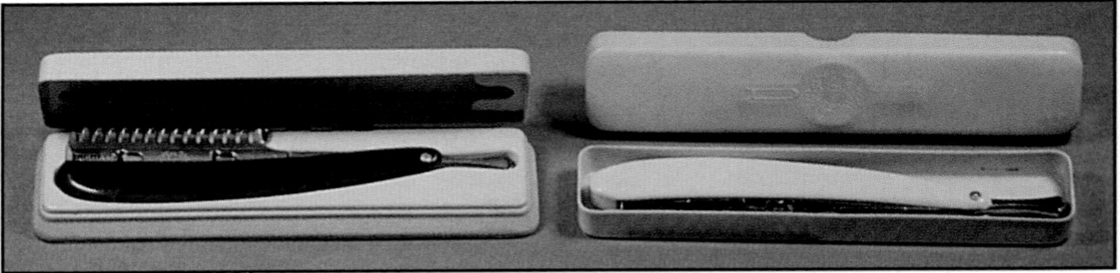

These Durham Duplex razors come complete with an imitation ivory grained celluloid carrying case. $22.00 – $30.00 each.

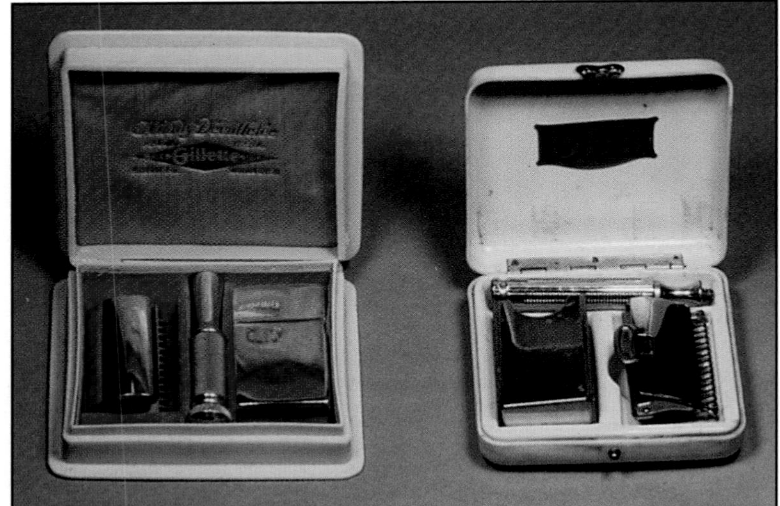

The safety razor was first introduced by King Gillette during WWI when he gave American forces free razors as a means to promote his double edged safety blade. After the war, when dress hems were shortened, women began to shave their legs. This M'Lady Decollete' by Gillette, circa 1924, is gold toned and comes in a sleek celluloid case lined with pink satin. It originally sold for $5.00. Razor and case $30.00. The Gem Safety Razor is housed in an unmarked, thin celluloid case and is valued at approximately $12.00.

This celluloid handled shaving brush and case are nice examples of a style that remained unchanged since the beginning. Continuous manufacture of the plain imitation ivory goods spanned the decades from 1880 through 1929.

This photograph was taken at the DuPont Viscoloid Company, Inc. in Leominster sometime during the 1920s. It shows the packing room where employees assembled the individual components of dresser items into boxed sets. Since dresser sets had so many different components, it became necessary for manufacturing companies to acquire expertise in production of many items such as monogramming, engraving, glass cutting (mirrors were cut into a variety of shapes), metal insert, plush lining, decorating, assembly and brush bristling. Russians staffed the hairbrush department for DuPont Viscoloid, using Siberian hog bristles; workers in the infant brush department used goat hair; and the clothing brush department used select horsehair.

NPCM

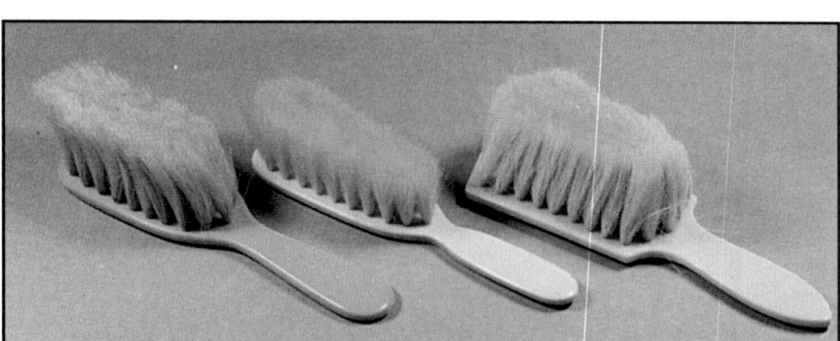

Three celluloid and goat hair baby brushes ranging from 4" to 4¾" long w/1" bristles. $5.00 – $8.00 each.

Rectangular clothing brushes with choice 1" horsehair bristles. $8.00 – $10.00 each.

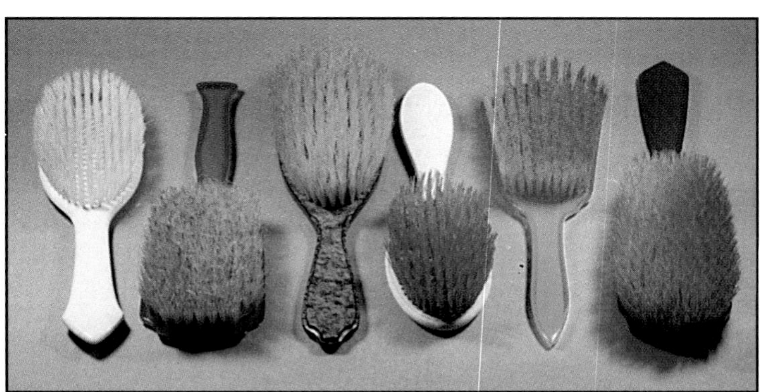

Collection of six various shaped and colored brushes with stiff ¾" hog hair bristles. $10.00 – $12.00 each.

These odd-shaped brushes were designed for a variety of uses. The oblong example was probably for clothing and is marked Travelers, Pat. 7-26-10, France with an "L" inside a six-pointed star. The example with the circular hole was most likely a crumb brush for the table; it is marked EI DuPont and Cie. France, and the long handled brush was commonly known as a "bonnet brush"; it is marked with Keystone-French Ivory, with a cursive "L" inside a clover shape. All unusual and valued at $18.00+ each.

Hand Mirrors

Hand mirrors were manufactured using several construction methods. The higher price mirrors used beveled glass and were made of solid celluloid stock, or laminated two-tone stock. A "sprung" mirror has had the glass plate forced into an opening that has been routed out of the solid back and it is held in place by a pad of felt pushing it tightly toward the edge. A "reed" mirror has the glass plate held in place by a celluloid bezel which surrounds the rim.

Cheaper mirrors were made by assembly of a formed celluloid back with a cardboard filler, glass plate, and a formed front. The front and back each had an outer flange that was sealed together by the application of heat and pressure.

Mirror plates with beveled edges were cut in a variety of shapes including oval, round, rectangular, square, and irregular. Mirrors were classified by the shape of the handle: millinery, ring handle, and easel, which permitted the use of both hands.

Shoe Horns

The great variety of shoe horns manufactured in both functional and novelty forms covered a wide range of colors and styles. The photograph below gives one a good idea of what is available, should one decide to assemble a collection. The functional examples are relatively inexpensive, and the novelty forms are more costly.

Various mirrors.

Shoe horns were first made from the material that gave them their name – horn. First introduced in the late 1870s, the earliest celluloid examples were of plain "white" celluloid then later of ivory grained celluloid. This exceptional 7" long imitation grained ivory shoe horn w/engraved design, filled with black paint is marked "1880 Brig Rose." Made in England. $25.00.

Various shoe horns.

Novelty Items

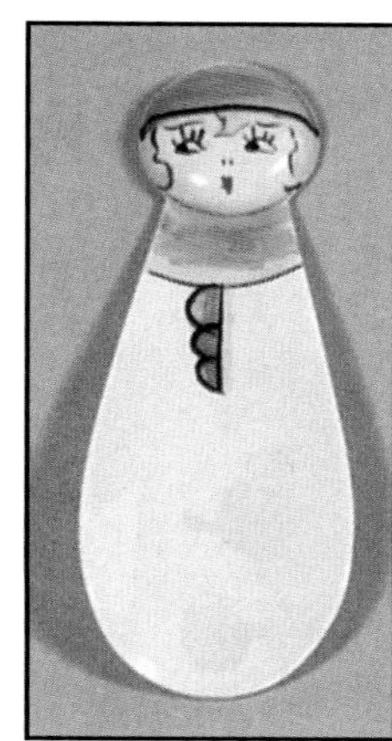

This tiny novelty shoe horn would have been suitable for a child. It is fashioned from cream colored celluloid and hand painted to look like a girl with an adorable expression. $18.00 – $22.00.

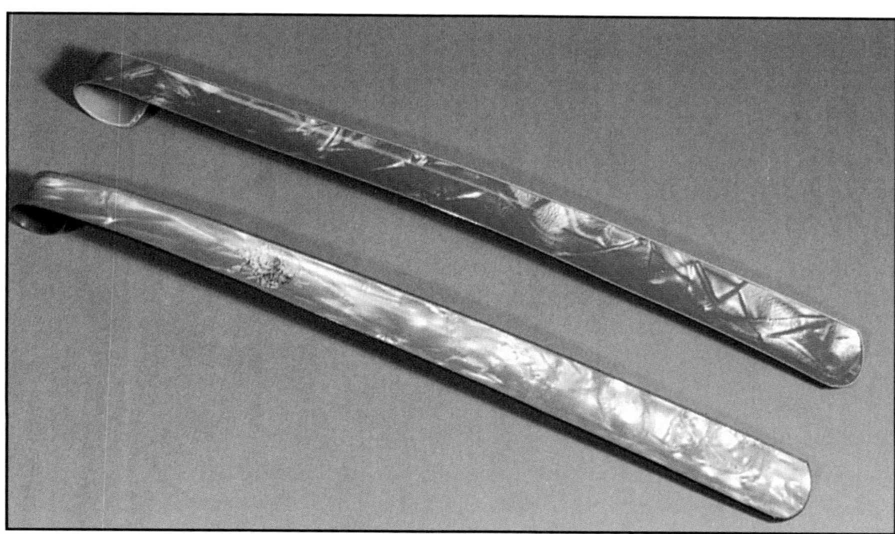

These two 20" long pearlescent laminated shoe horns were just the thing for those who had a hard time bending over. $18.00+.

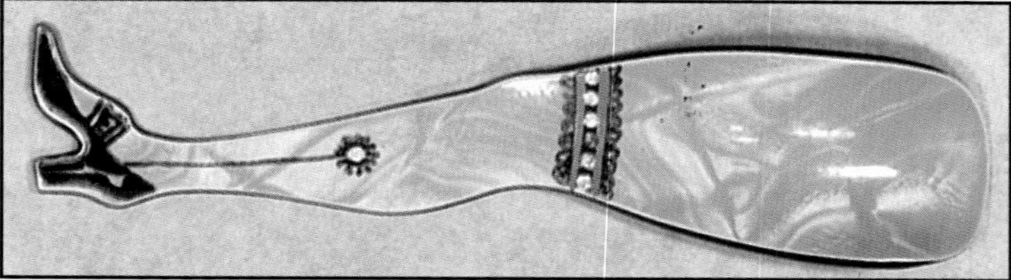

This pink pearlescent laminated shoe horn is fashioned into a shapely leg and accented with paint and rhinestones. A wonderfully naughty novelty. $35.00.

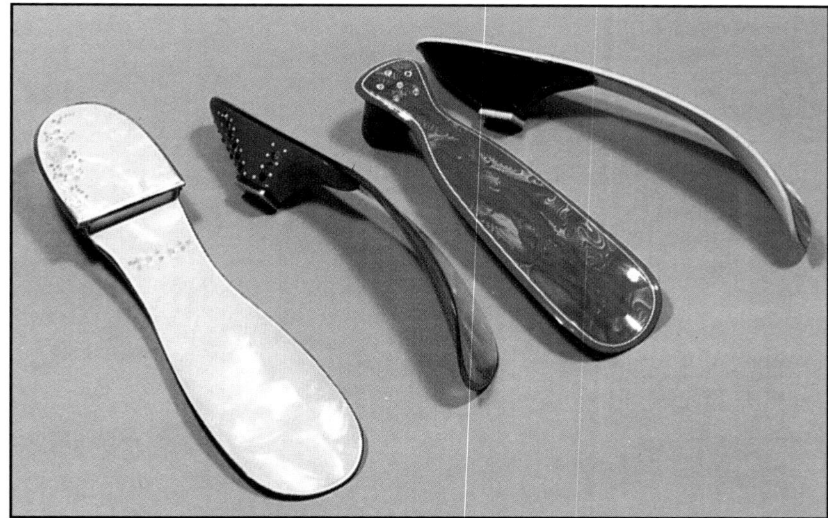

The four novelty shoe horns shown were manufactured in the late 1920s of pearlescent celluloid laminate. Each one is in the shape of a lady's shoe. The largest pale amber/pink example opens at the heel. Each is decorated with either painted flowers or studded with rhinestones. $18.00+ each.

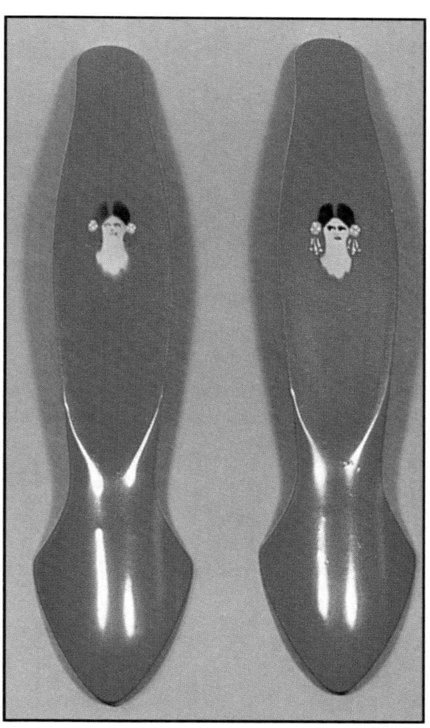

These bold red shoe forms are molded of thick, slightly curved celluloid with a spray painted female image. An unusual item. $20.00.

The toothbrush case shown here is fashioned from imitation ivory and decorated with the solid molded head of an elephant. Unmarked. $18.00.

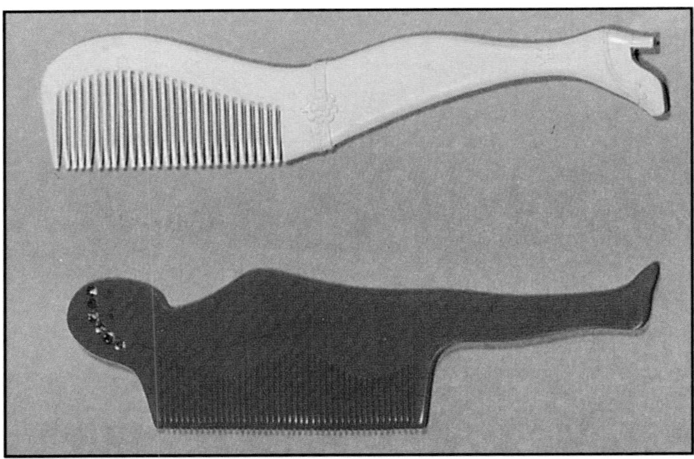

Two novelty combs fashioned from red and cream colored celluloid. The female form measures 5⅛" tall and is molded in striated opaque and translucent celluloid, further decorated with blue rhinestones and scored features. The leg comb is 5" tall and marked Germany with a star. Red, $45, rare color; white, $30.00.

This cream colored collapsible cup is fashioned from four separate rings of celluloid and topped off with a lid which fits tightly together to form a sealed case. Marked Germany. $35.00.

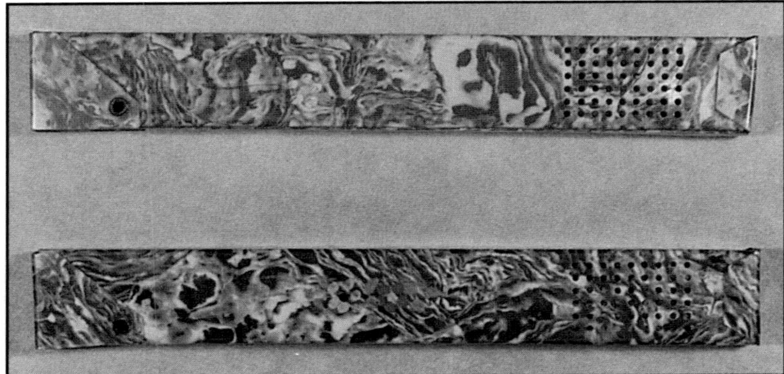

The rectangular toothbrush cases shown here are molded from swirled green and cream/brown and cream celluloid and decorated with hand painted flowers. The average price for such an item in 1925 was 65¢. $6.00 – $8.00 each.

First advertised in the 1886 Celluloid Novelty catalog, the backscratcher – a molded hand on the end of a 12" rod – was a popular seller throughout the history of the company. The item, design unchanged, was also featured throughout the 1920s. $18.00.

The following is a list of the major dresserware producers, known patterns, and year of dresserware introduction.

Celluloid Corporation
1925 – Introduces Arch Amerith patterns: Priscilla, Carleton, Chilton, Beverly, Royalton, Laurelton, Haddon, Windsor
1928 – Hepplewhite, Hampton, Stratford
1929 – Lotus, Orleans, Brinkley, Shelburne, Berkley, Carree, Rond, Vinoy, Travel, LaVerne, and Avalon.
19?? – Versailles, Monticello, Marquise, Savoia, Broadmore, Eton, Kingston, Carlyle, Normandie, Fairmont, Sherlain, Kingsly, Barclay, Geneva, Bermuda, LaReine, Claridge, Alviene.

Arlington Co.
1915 – Introduces DuBarry pattern
1923 – Nemours pattern, LaBelle pattern
1925 – Mayflower pattern
1927 – Sheraton Pattern, Lido pattern
1929 – Introduction of Lucite with 10 patterns: Sonya, Navarre, Crystal, Ming, Empore, Orchis, Wedgewood, Watteau, Diane, and Venetia
1930 – Lucite Introduces Adam, Fleuret, Trianon, Montacello, Pyralin Lustris, and Madelon
1931 – Lucille, Ebonette, and Camille

Fiberloid Corporation
1924 – Cleopatra, Fairfax, Berkshire, and Ivory
1925 – Diane, Patricia, Juliet, Deauville, and Princess

Decorative Boxes and Albums

Decorative Celluloid Boxes

The beautiful decorative boxes that were so popular around the turn of the twentieth century are among the most desirable of celluloid collectibles. Attractive and practical, they were fashioned in an array of shapes and sizes from pasteboard and thin wood, then covered with decorative sheets of embossed, printed, and colored celluloid. Most boxes were designed for a specific purpose as storage containers for gloves, jewelry, fans, neckties, hankies, cuffs, and collars. Some boxes were fitted with manicure implements, shaving sets, and vanity items. Early celluloid boxes were pretty accessories, as well as useful and necessary items for storing the many adornments that were part of late Victorian and Edwardian era fashions.

The first decorative celluloid boxes appeared sometime in the early 1890s. Alfred Hafely of New York patented a method of making celluloid covered box tops, USP #488,630, issued December 27, 1892. The following year Hafely and an associate, Jens Redlefsen, made application and received a patent for improvement in the method of manufacturing celluloid covered boxes, USP #505, 462, issued Sept. 26, 1893.

Hafely was known to have worked for the Koch and Sons Company of Brooklyn, New York. This firm is listed in the 1906 Thomas Register as being a manufacturer of decorative celluloid boxes.

The improved process of manufacturing decorative boxes involved covering the entire pasteboard or wood frame with a thin sheet of decorative celluloid instead of just the lid. A special machine was designed to press the box base, together with an adhesive and the celluloid sheet, into a heated compartment. This made the plastic pliable enough to conform to the sides and edges of the box.

A variety of decorating techniques were used to manufacture these beautiful accessories. Celluloid was embossed, reverse painted, layered over prints, lithographed, and printed upon. The decorative treatments were often used in pleasing combinations of color and texture.

It should be understood that these lovely accessories are in high demand and as supply diminishes, the cost increases. Pricing therefore is difficult to establish. Those listed are considered to be the fair starting price to the current selling prices of similar boxes. Any box in excellent condition for under $85.00 is a real bargain.

The first boxes were manufactured with paper sides and celluloid only upon the lids. However, just because an item is assembled in this fashion does not mean that it is an early example, but rather that it was a less expensive item.

Two boxes on the following page feature a decorative image of a pretty lady draped in yellow lace and identical paper sides. It can therefore be assumed that they were made by the same manufacturer. A similarly decorated box was advertised by Butler Brothers for $10.65 per dozen in 1906.

Andra Behrendt. Photograph by Harry Rinker, Jr.

The box shown here features a print entitled "Alone" that is covered with clear celluloid. The side are printed green, blue, and white floral motif paper. Originally the box advertised in Butler Brothers 1906 catalog came fitted with an array of manicure implements. It sold for $1.00 then but today a box in such excellent condition would bring between $100.00 – $150.00+.

Andra Behrendt. Photograph by Harry Rinker, Jr.

This beautifully decorated shaped box was originally fitted with a shaving set, mug, brush, and razor. Like items cost approximately $1.39 from Sears, Roebuck Co. Today such a fine example would sell for between $150.00 – $225.00.

Andra Behrendt. Photograph by Harry Rinker, Jr.

This 3" tall, 5" x 5" hankie box with rounded front corners features the image of a pretty lady draped in yellow lace. A carnation and violet border surrounds the image. Sides are covered with a green and white floral paper. Excellent condition. On the bottom is written "Friday May 5, 1911" in pencil. $75.00 – $125.00.

The 6" tall collar and cuff box shown here features lid in cream celluloid that has a water scene, forget-me-nots, and decorative curlicues printed right onto the celluloid. The sides are finished in a honeysuckle printed paper that has been covered with clear celluloid. $110.00 – $165.00.

The 5" tall x 5¾" square collar box shown here has a sloping top which is covered with a printed and embossed celluloid sheet. The pretty woman in a yellow lace shawl was a common theme repeated on several boxes. Celluloid in greenish yellow also covers the front of the box, however the sides and back are covered in a green and white floral printed paper. Slight lifting of celluloid along embossed edge. $65.00 –$75.00.

This collar box measures 6" x 7" and 6¼" tall and has a pull-out drawer on the bottom for storage of cuff links and collar studs. Lined with pink satin, it features a celluloid printed lid in cream with printed pansy and ivy decorations. $65.00 – $75.00.

The 2" tall x 10" x 5" shaped Christmas theme box was advertised in the 1906 Butler Brothers catalog for 87¢. The lid features two vignettes, one a house scene and the other a small child with a dove, which are secured to a paper background and covered with clear celluloid sheet; the background paper for the entire box is silver with green and red holly sprays and bells. Only the lid is covered with celluloid.

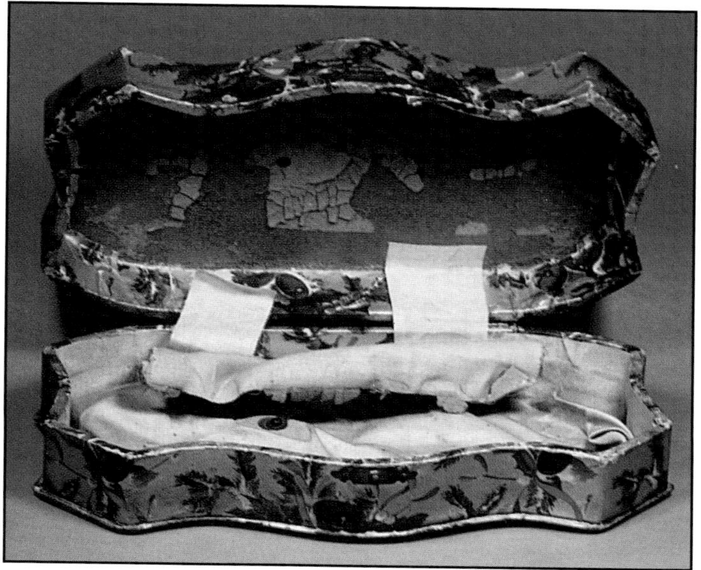

Upon first glance the Christmas box appears to be in pretty good shape, but this close-up photograph reveals several problems. The celluloid covered paper on the top has chipped away leaving the pasteboard visible. Secondly, when the box is opened, a real mess unfolds. No serious collector would consider adding such an example to their collection. Nevertheless, it is a good example of a bad example; the poor quality of this box, inside and out, was reason for the selling price of $8.00.

Odd-shaped boxes, like the one shown here, are very desirable if they are in good condition. Unfortunately sometimes the curves and bends of such items cause the celluloid to lift and separate from the box base. This three-tiered shaped collar box lid is in excellent condition and features a variety of decorative techniques including colored, reverse painted embossing and clear celluloid. Another interesting aspect of the box is the decoration, a female dressed in male clothing with a mandolin. 4" tall x 7" x 7¾". $155.00 – $225.00.

This paper covered wooden hankie box measures 7" square and 3" tall. It is finished off in embossed clear celluloid with a Greek Key design along the bottom and a reverse painted circular embossed rim for the illustration of a pretty girl picking red and white flowers. $95.00 – $165.00.

Dottie Maust

6" tall round collar box is covered with gold paper with a pink, green, and yellow floral motif. Entirely covered with clear celluloid, the top is finished with an embossed circle reverse painted gold with a print of a pretty girl. $165.00+.

Andra Behrendt. Photograph by Harry Rinker, Jr.

Shaped collar box measures 8½" x 6" finished in ivy printed paper over a wooden base. It is covered over all with clear celluloid. The oval center decorations feature a couple playing the violin and piano and the celluloid is embossed around the outer edge. Separate lift lid compartment and drawer compartment for cuff links and other small accessories enhance this exceptional box. $175.00 – $225.00.

A pale green shaving box that features embossed green and clear celluloid over a nicely printed fountain scene. Front is decorated with two embossed trimmed scenes of cherubs. Originally fitted with a shaving mug, brush, and razor. Approximately 4" tall by 9" x 7". $155.00 – $200.00.

5" x 7" x 2" tall rectangular manicure box with manicure items, cream colored embossed and printed celluloid w/house in snow scene. Blue satin lining. $85.00 – $125.00.

The hankie box shown here resembles the popular English Wedgwood look. The wooden box is covered with embossed celluloid that has a reverse painted white design. Shows a pretty classical lady feeding a small dog. $95.00 – $165.00.

5" tall and 5¾" square collar box with a sloped and shaped top, this box is finished in a green and yellow printed paper that has been covered with embossed and reverse painted celluloid. Embossing trim is painted gold. $75.00 – $95.00.

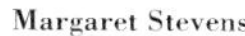
Margaret Stevens

12" x 4" x 2" tall fan box; sides are covered in embossed cream colored celluloid, top is clear celluloid with the outline of a fan printed on it. The fan is reverse painted with green, gold, and amber. The bottom of the box is covered with a floral motif beige paper and stamped patent dates Dec. 27, 1892 and Sept. 26, 1893. These dates coincide with the Redlefsen and Hafely patents. A small round sticker that says Pierson's Pharmacy, Hornellsville, indicates that the box was purchased in that small New York town near Buffalo. $165.00 – $225.00.

This 14" x 4" x 3" tall oblong box features pointed edges, a marbleized paper covered lid with scene of courting couple, reverse painted embossing, and heavily embossed sides in a red and green floral motif. A nice unusually shaped example. $100.00 – $145.00.

John and Gail Dunn

The oblong glove box is finished in a garish plaid green, red and orange paper, and features a beautifully feminine picture of three lovely ladies under clear celluloid. $65.00+.

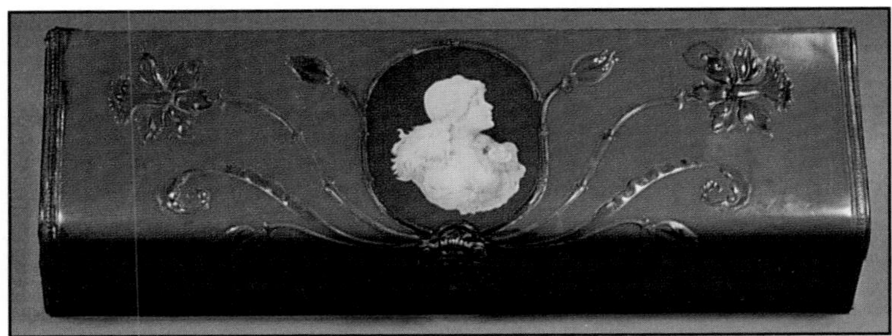

This embossed brown oblong box features an Art Nouveau theme in the flowing vines and flowers. The center motif of a pretty lady has been damaged as a result of some type of solvent which was spilled on the celluloid. Take care when using perfume, cologne, or cosmetics around these lovely antique items as the result of an accidental spill is irreversible. In such condition a box is only worth a few dollars.

A beautiful example of an embossed necktie box measuring 4" x 13" x 3" tall. It features a floral motif and the word "Neckties" that is reverse painted in cream, pink, and yellow while the ground is done in varied shade of green. A beautiful box. $100.00 – $175.00, as high as $245.00.

A common type of decoration was plain cream celluloid embossed with words and decorative designs. This necktie box measures 4⅝" x 13" and is 3" tall. The circular design on lid and body of box match up exactly. $85.00 – $125.00.

The color combinations on the next two accessory boxes seem less than compatible. The fan-shaped collar box is covered with a printed simulated wood grain pattern in brown and gold-tan, embossed top with a lovely yellow and pink rose motif. Lined in pink satin with compartments for cuffs and collars. $75.00+.

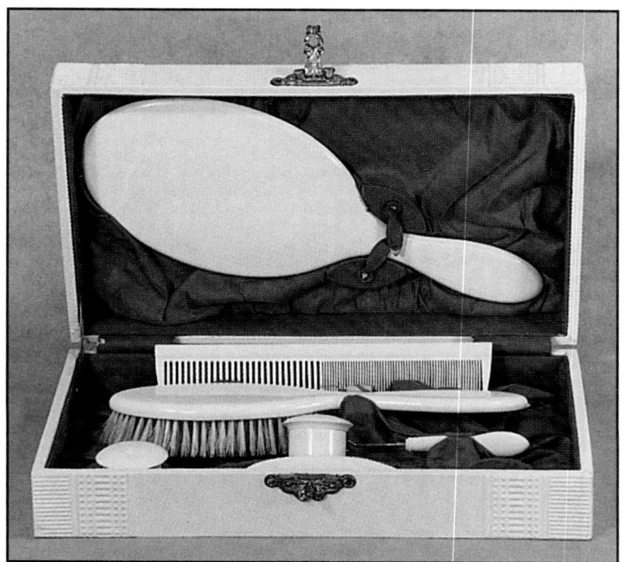

A 10" x 6¼" embossed cream colored celluloid box with reeded edging and a cornflower motif in the center is lined with maroon satin and includes a complete dresser set. Included are a brush, comb, mirror, two suave containers, nail buffer, button hook, and cuticle tool. Each implement is marked with the word "Celluloid." Completely fitted, excellent condition with original price of $4.25 on the bottom. $195.00 – $250.00.

Sally Block

The three-way mirror shown here is an article that would have been displayed on one's vanity table, much like a celluloid box. It is fashioned from embossed and reverse painted celluloid and features a cherub motif. The paint is beginning to flake away from the inside of the angel's head. The framework is brass, with three exceptionally clear mirrors. Trademark on back, "Celluloid – Pat. Date 1888." $150.00.

Photograph and Autograph Albums

Generally photograph albums are priced slightly higher than decorative boxes. The smaller autograph albums are more expensive because they are now quite scarce. Some fancy albums were made with music boxes built into an enclosed base, but these are becoming difficult to find, especially in good condition, because they were handled so much.

Andra Behrendt

This 16" x 7" photograph album is commonly called a "Longfellow." The variety of decorative motifs includes embossing, celluloid covered prints, and lithographed celluloid. This example, showing a beautiful woman with embossed iris along the edge, is backed with maroon velour. $375.00+.

Andra Behrendt.

Typical decorative motifs for large photograph albums that measure 8" x 10" are children and beautiful women. This example shows a pretty gal in pink plumed bonnet, corners are embossed. Backed with deep blue velour. $225.00 – $250.00.

Hollsopple Auctioneers

The 9" x 13" album illustrated here shows a beautiful child embracing a huge bouquet of purple lilacs. The back is finished in purple floral print velour. Unfortunately the item was probably placed in the sun as the image appears faded. $95.00.

Mishler's Auction House

An 8" x 10" album with a cream ground and printed violet motif, printed child holding a kitten, purple velvet backing w/music box in base. Unfortunately the music box device was replaced and the newer model plays "Sunrise Sunset" from *Fiddler on the Roof*. $150.00 – $200.00.

This 6" x 4" autograph album features embossed decorated covers. It is reverse painted gold and green floral motif with the word "Album" in script. Backed with maroon velour, it is valued at $75.00 – $85.00.

Conemaugh Township Area Historical Society, Davidsville, PA.

This 6" x 4" autograph album features embossed decorated covers. Embossed floral motif in clear celluloid, reverse painted, and placed over a paper printed background with a center vignette of pretty Gibson Girl. Maroon velvet backing. $125.00.

Evelyn Robinson

This 6" x 4" autograph album shown here belonged to Julie Jensen of Grand Forks, N.D., between 1905 – 1911. It featured a printed celluloid cover in a pastoral scene; the title of the painting of the famous couple is called "Giving Thanks." $75.00 – $85.00.

While religious theme items are not among the most desired of collectible celluloid, some of the early articles manufactured are beautiful. This lovely 5¼" x 4" embossed New Testament has an inset lithographed oval of Jesus and a lamb; the front and back are embossed cream celluloid. Printed 1889. $45.00.

The three religious articles shown here feature two celluloid covered New Testaments; the smaller example is believed to be Polish and is also dated in pencil "1889" while the larger example is German and dated 1901. The ivory grained rosary box and beads complete the photograph. Both testaments printed celluloid, $25.00 – $35.00; Rosary box and beads, $45.00 set.

Household Accessories

Utensils and Dining Items

Napkin Rings and Eating Utensils

Napkin rings have been popular table accessories since the late Victorian era. The most desired types of napkin rings were made with figural forms a trend not found in celluloid. However, filigree with monogrammed initials, basket weave, applied decorative motifs, and hand painting were all methods of embellishment for napkin rings that can be found today.

A variety of utilitarian items was made from celluloid beginning in 1874 when the Meriden Cutlery Co., of Meriden, Connecticut, began to manufacture knives and forks with imitation ivory grained handles.

Two filigree celluloid napkin rings (2" x 1¾"), thick die cut, embossed celluloid sheet, oval, scalloped center surface suitable for monogramming or painting, $12.00 – $15.00; Simple 1" wide rings, cream and amber w/applied metal "L", $16.00 – $18.00 ; 1¼" tall cream napkin ring w/applied Indian head, painted "1000 Islands", $12.00 – $15.00; 1¼" thick imitation ivory ring w/etched monogrammed name "Agnes E. Wallin," $18.00; 1 " wide examples in cream and light green can be found for as little as $4.00 each; two thin imitation ivory grained rings; round is 1" dia., oval is 2", $2.00 – $4.00.

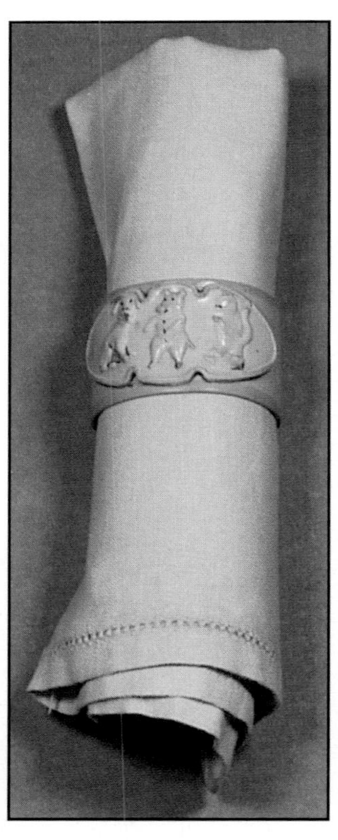

Napkin ring, 15/16" wide, 1" dia. Cream napkin ring w/pink trimming; attached scalloped edge decoration; embossed and painted in pink and blue, showing a dog, pig, and cat. $8.00 – $10.00.

1" tall basket weave napkin ring of thin ivory grained celluloid strips. $18.00 – $20.00. The knife and fork shown in this photograph were manufactured by the Royal Cutlery Company; a set for 10 was purchased in the original cardboard box for $30.00 at auction. Because most people used their cutlery on a daily basis, not many complete sets have survived and there is no established market price for these types of utilitarian items. Spoons with celluloid handles are scarce. Other companies known to market celluloid handled cutlery were Meriden and Standard.

Dining Room Accessories

Crumb trays were popular dining room accessories; the small tray was used for the purpose of pushing crumbs off the tablecloth and into the larger tray. The three examples here show a very plain Fuller Brush Company example; a set with fancy border molded into the celluloid; and a lovely imitation ivory set w/monogrammed T and decorative border which would have made a fine wedding gift.

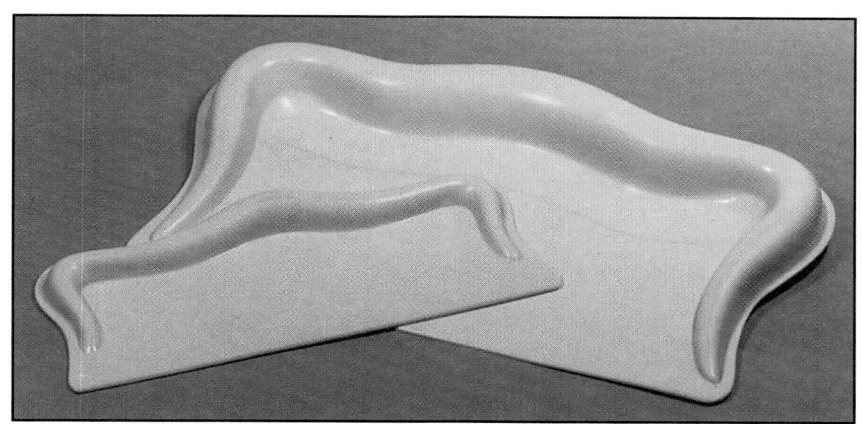

Plain set, Fuller logo. $18.00 – $20.00.

Molded border set. $35.00.

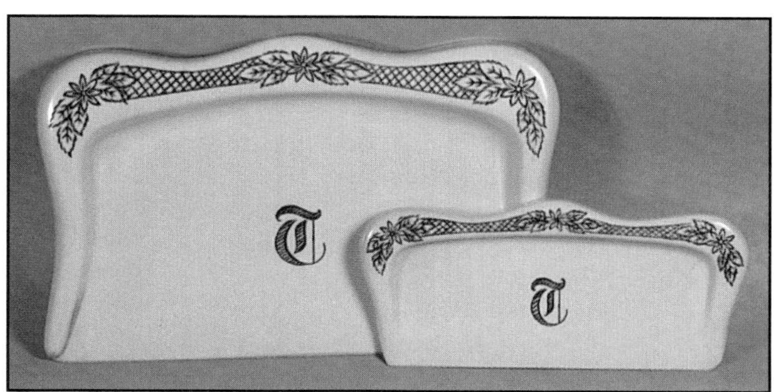

Monogrammed set. $45.00+.

Decorative Accessories

Although it is hard to believe, the items shown here are actually candle stick holders. Considering celluloid's highly flammable nature, it seems absurd that any manufacturer would have produced articles that were intended to be used in close proximity to an open flame. These examples surely would have been used for decorative purposes. 5" tall round pair with weighted base and flared tube holders, unmarked, $35.00 – $40.00. 7" tall round weighted base with tapered ring center and cup shaped holders, marked Tuskeloid in diamond shape, $45.00 – $50.00. 5¼" tall square shaped holders with square weighted base and top, $35.00 – $40.00.

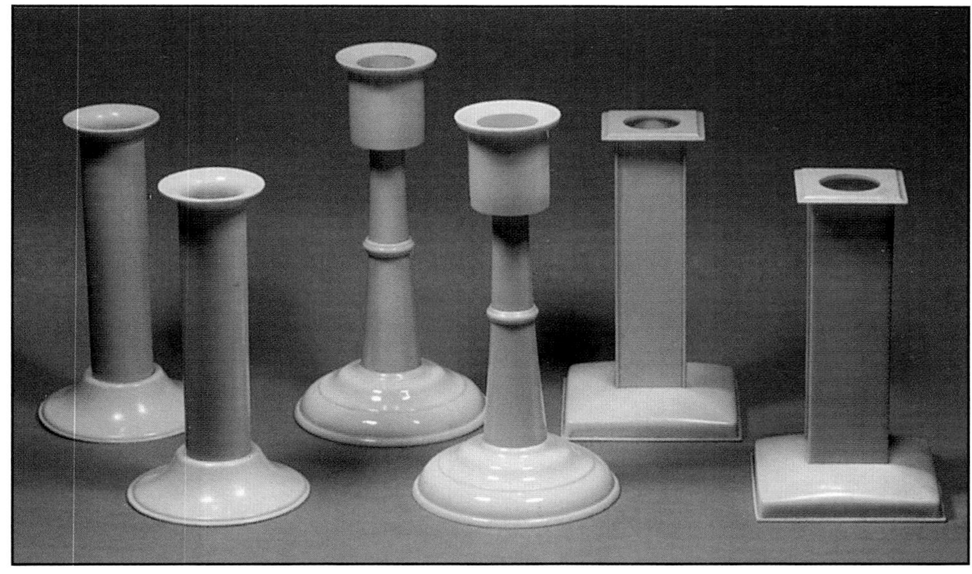

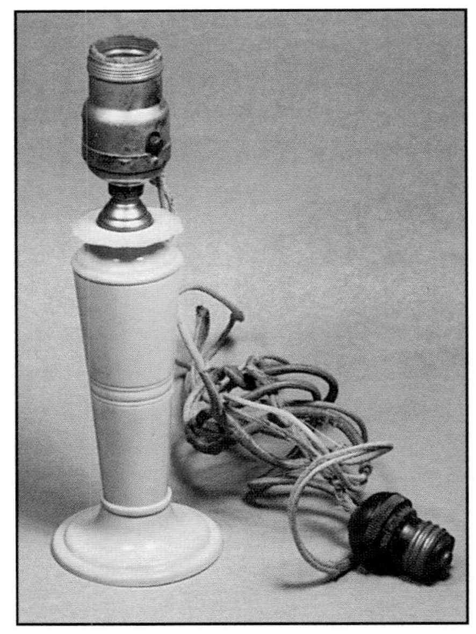

No trademark can be found on this old electric lamp base. It is made of imitation grained ivory with a scalloped flange around the base of the socket. The entire base is filled with plaster to make it heavy so it won't tip over. Note the electrical cord is not the type with a plug, but rather a fixture that was designed to be screwed into a light bulb socket. $40.00.

A variety of vases can be found in celluloid. The different sizes, styles, and colors are represented here nicely with a tall 10" opaque amber round bottom vase with pink and blue hand painted flowers; 8" imitation tortoise vase with scalloped weighted base; 7¾" translucent amber and pearlized cream laminated base vase; and a 6" imitation ivory example with scalloped weighted base. Prices range from $15.00 to $30.00, the tortoise shell example being the hardest to find.

Mr. and Mrs. Barry Bonnevie

Frames are both decorative and utilitarian and were manufactured in a wide variety of styles and sizes. The ruffled edge rectangular frame w/oval opening was patented in 1884. The pretty nurse is Julie's grandmother Elizabeth, (to read about Elizabeth's unforgettable experience with burning celluloid see the section on fire hazards). 7" x 6", Celluloid Co. $30.00 +. A beautifully molded filigree frame fashioned from embossed die cut celluloid with a solid pocket back and easel. 4" x 2¾", unmarked. $18.00 – $25.00.

This wonderful sturdy filigree frame has a center bottom shield with a monogrammed "G". The family is Keith Lauer's grandparents and his father, circa 1900. 6¼" x 7" w/easel back. $35.00.

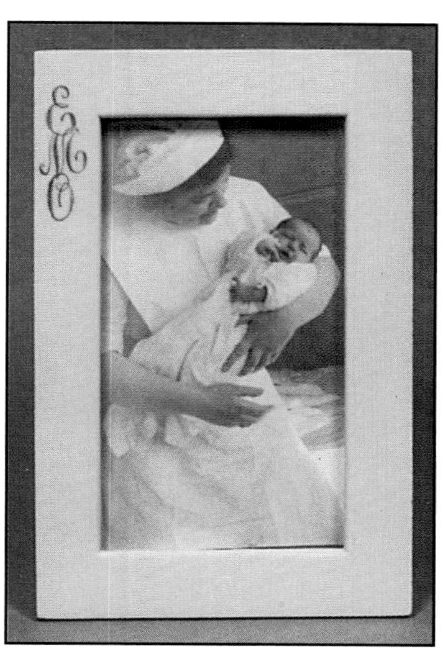

This 4¼" x 3" monogrammed frame is fashioned from Ivory Pyralin and engraved with baby Evelyn Marjorie Olson's initials. She is seen here on March 17, 1916, in her nurse's arms. $15.00.

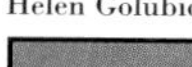

Helen Golubic

4¾" x 6¾" peach celluloid frame, circa 1930, with black enameled oval decoration on top center. Unmarked, felt easel back. $20.00.

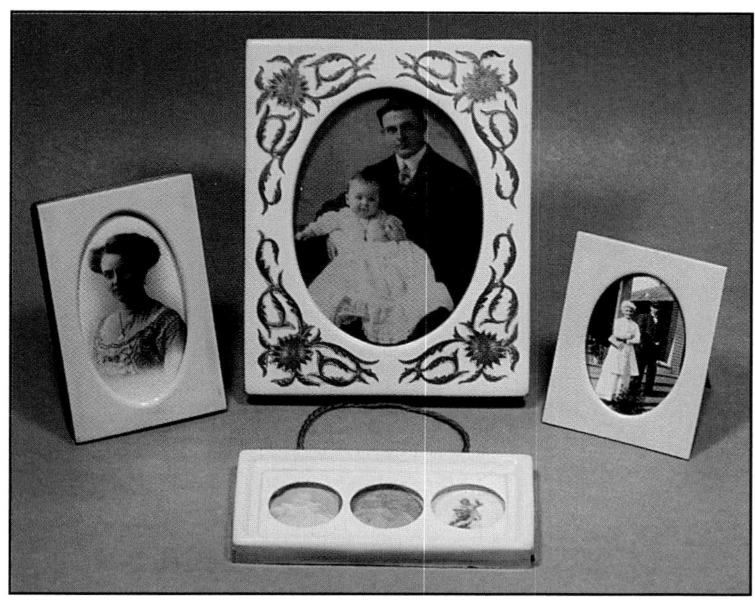

Four rectangular frames with round or oval openings. Smallest easel back measures 3" x 2¾" w/oval opening; medium frame measures 4" x 2¾" w/oval opening; largest frame measures 6" x 5" w/gold floral motif; and 2" x 5" frame w/three circles for photographs. Prices range from $6.00 for the smallest, $8.00 – $12.00 for medium, and $25.00 for large w/decorations.

Two rectangular frames with rectangular openings measure 5" x 4" and 4" x 2¾", both include glass photo covering. $12.00 – $15.00. Small 4" dia, circle frame of cream ivory grained celluloid and photo of a baby. No glass insert but an unusual shape. $15.00.

Plain oval frames in imitation ivory grained celluloid with glass. Large oval frame 9" x 7¼" w/round pegs on bottom, $30.00. Medium oval frame 6¼" x 4", round pegs on base, $20.00. Small oval frame 3" x 2", $6.00 – $10.00.

Gail and John Dunn

Butterfly frame. This unusual pearlescent amber frame, circa 1925, features a cut-out floral motif further embellished with ivory colored hand painted celluloid butterflies in each corner. The amber and gray pearlescent is fastened to a wooden frame. $35.00.

Desk Accessories

The variety of decorative and utilitarian items made from celluloid seems endless. Examples of desk accessories seen here include a square ink well holder w/glass insert and square celluloid cover, $35.00; a letter holder w/handle center $15.00 – $20.00; round string holder on a pedestal base, $60.00; stamp box, $15.00 – $18.00; and gray pearlescent fountain pen, $15.00.

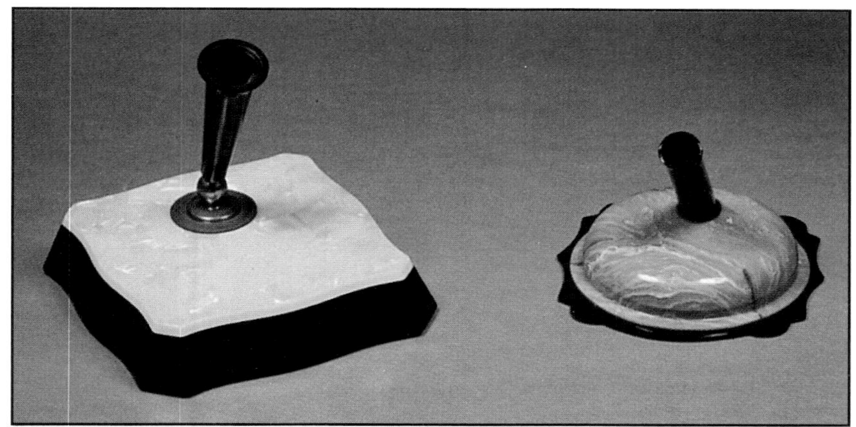

These penholders are fashioned from black celluloid bases with variegated and/or pearlized laminated tops. Unmarked, circa 1930. $15.00 – $18.00 each.

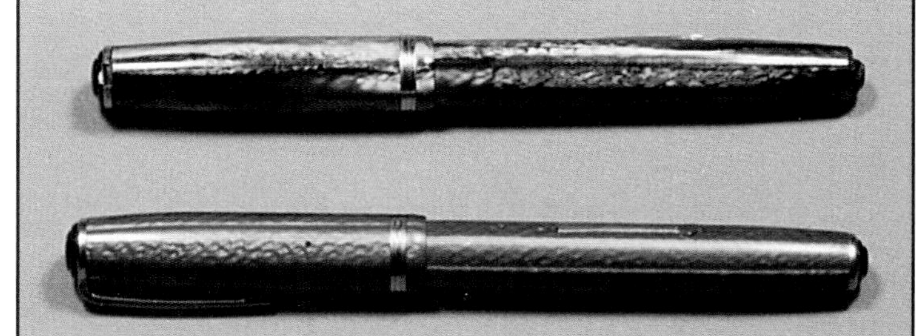

Fountain pen barrels were made of celluloid until the late 1940s in America; however some manufacturers in France and Italy are known to still be using cellulose nitrate plastic as a base material for their pens. The two examples shown here date to the 1930s after pearlescence had been popularized. Both the gray and rust colored pens are Esterbrook. Thousands of pens were manufactured from celluloid yearly including the best known brands like Parker, Sheaffer, Waterman, and Esterbrook. Since pen collecting is well established and many fine resource books available, it is suggested those who are interested in collecting within this category consult the popular published works on the subject.

Measuring 4¼" tall x 3¼" wide x 2¼" deep, this pair of plaster-weighted book ends is made from mottled pink celluloid embossed with an ornamental gold drape. Unmarked, circa 1930. $35.00 – $40.00 per pair.

Clocks and Watch Holders

Most of the old celluloid clocks available today are not in working order. They are collected more for their decorative appeal than that as reliable time pieces. Prior to the 1920s, black celluloid veneer was used to cover wooden clock frames and imitation marble or brass columns of celluloid were used to further enhance a clock's appeal. After the turn of the century, ivory colored clocks in Gothic and neoclassical styles began to appear.

Plain ivory neoclassical clocks were used on dressers, desks, and mantles. This example measures 6" tall x 7" wide. "Made in USA" on face of clock. It runs but does not keep good time. $55.00.

Pearlescent pink and cream neoclassical shelf/alarm clock, 9" wide, 6" tall. Made in USA, clock works are marked Patented Apr. 27, 1920. $45.00+.

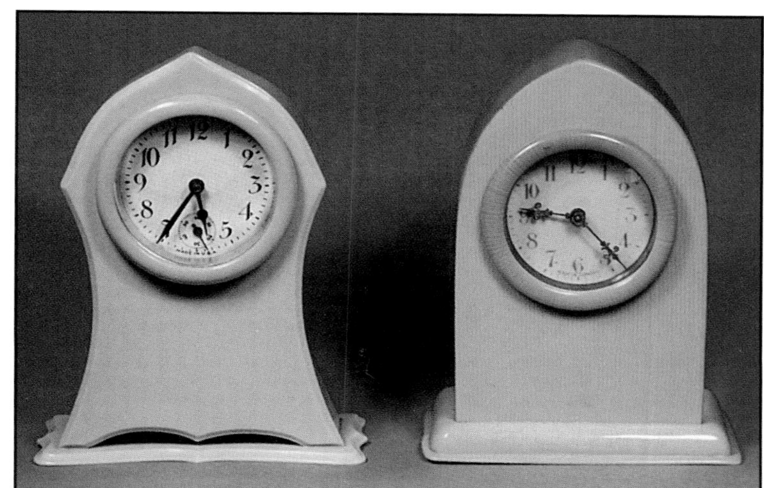

Gothic cathedral-shaped alarm clocks were popular bedside accessories. The scalloped edge example is of small grained ivory celluloid with "Made in USA" on the clock face; it measures 5¼" tall x 3" wide. The 5" x 3" dark yellow grained clock is German made. Both have a key wind and alarm setting mechanisms on the back. $28.00 + each, not in working order.

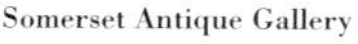
Somerset Antique Gallery

A small Greek Revival alarm clock in gray pearlescence with translucent amber accents. Actual size, 4" wide x 3" tall. Made in USA. $18.00 – $22.00.

The cream colored desk clock illustrated here measures 3" high and 7" wide and is marked "Made by Lux Clock Mfg. Waterbury, Ct. USA" on the clock face. Working order, $25.00+.

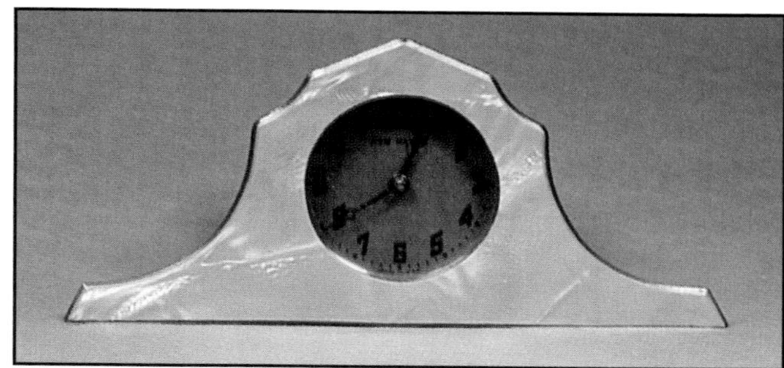

This type of small clock usually accompanied a matching dresser set. The small pearlescent green and translucent amber clock measures 2¾" tall x 6¼" wide, marked on the clock face "New Haven Clock Co. Made in USA." Only the front is made of strong laminated sheet stock; the metal clock is behind the celluloid facade. $15.00 – $18.00.

Pearlescent pink laminated amber celluloid, fold-out 3" square case, 1¼" deep, opens to 4¼" tall clock. New Haven Clock Co. Made in USA. $22.00.

Manufactured of ivory grained celluloid, this unmarked travel alarm folds into a compact 4"x4"x1" deep box. Manufactured in USA, the clock face includes a second hand. Ticks when wound and keeps time by minutes and seconds. $35.00.

Pocket watch holders have been around since the late 1880s and were made from imitation ivory grained celluloid in both round and square shapes. Round two-piece watch holder, 2" diameter, w/round ball feet. $15.00 – $18.00.

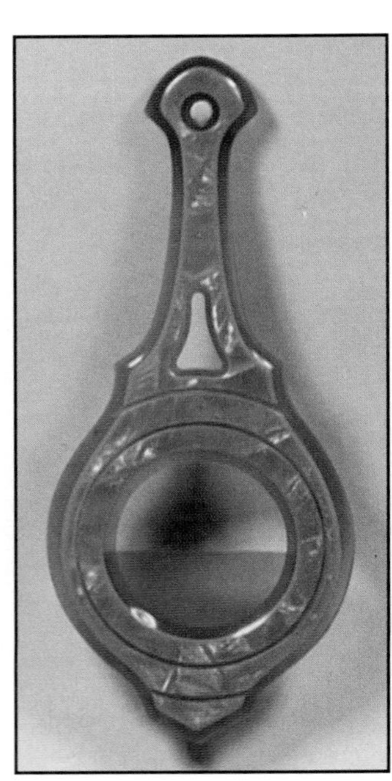

6" long pearlescent blue green and amber Banjo Clock style watch holder w/Wilcox trademark on back. Designed to hang on a wall and hold a pocket watch. Late 1920s. $22.00.

Late 1920s watch holder in laminated amber and pearlescent colors. The standing 2¾" tall x 2" wide example features a grayish/pink pearlized effect. $12.00 – $18.00.

Square two-piece watch holder, 2" x 2". $12.00 – $18.00.

Advertising, Keepsakes, and Souvenirs

Product advertising was big business in the early days before radio made its debut. Every year, manufacturers spent thousands of dollars to promote their merchandise in a colorful and useful way. Celluloid provided an advertising medium that was unparalled to all other materials for this purpose.

Between the years 1886 and 1930, thousands of different celluloid advertising novelties, keepsake items, and souvenirs were mass produced in order to promote businesses, organizations, and a wide variety of consumer products.

Among the best known manufacturers of celluloid advertising and keepsake novelties are those trademarked by the following companies: American Artworks, Coshocton, Ohio; American Badge Co., Chicago, Ill.; Baldwin and Gleason Co., N.Y.; Bastian Brothers, Rochester, N.Y.; Brown and Bigelow, St. Paul, Minn.; Cruver Mfg. Co., Chicago; St. Louis Button Company; Parisian Novelty Co., Chicago; Peacock Co., Providence, R.I.; and Whitehead and Hoag Co., Newark, N.J.

The most prolific manufacturer of engraved celluloid items was the Baldwin and Gleason Company. Their intricately detailed designs were produced on sheet stock supplied by the Celluloid Manufacturing Company of Newark. Although a countless number of celluloid advertising products was manufactured every year using the engraving process, it is the least plentiful to come by.

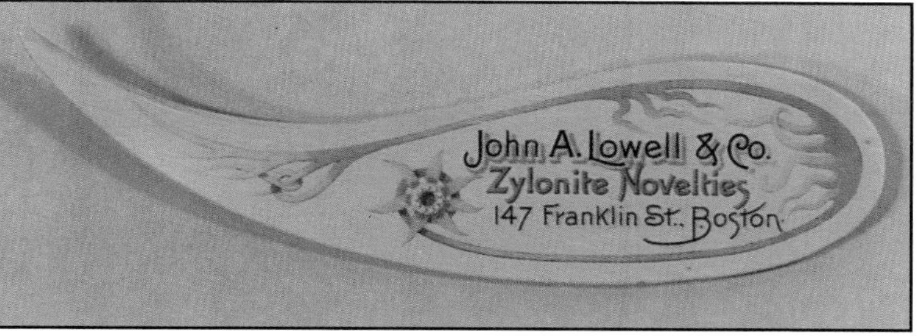

Engraving technique: an equally important piece of advertising is this Zylonite letter opener, a coveted example of advertising among plastics collectors and historians because of the tradename. Since the American Zylonite Company only marketed their brand of pyroxylin plastic, Zylonite, between the years 1883 and 1890, anything bearing its trademark or name is of special significance. 5" long sickle-shaped letter opener/shoe horn, "Zylonite Novelties; John A Lowell and CO. 147 Franklin St. Boston." Engraved floral design. Rare, $150.00+.

Printed celluloid/transfer: this advertising mirror measures 2¾" in diameter and is made of cream celluloid printed with blue ink. It is highly collectible because it represents a manufacturer of celluloid novelties. $95.00+.

Coated paper/laminating: 3" diameter clothing brush, printed paper coated with Fiberloid, "Parisian Novelty Co. Chicago, USA, Supplies for making Fiberloid Novelties and Advertising Specialties." Rare, $125.00+.

Printing Methods

The development of sheet celluloid in 1878 ("Hyatt's Sheeting Method" USP #199,908) provided an exciting new possibility for makers of advertising goods. Celluloid sheet was pliable, water resistant, and much more durable than paper or cardboard. However, before the advertising industry could benefit from this new product, successful printing techniques had to be fully developed, and this challenge took nearly a decade to achieve.

There were three methods of printing on celluloid: engraving, transferring, and laminating. It was the discovery of these three decorating methods that escalated the medium of celluloid to the forefront of the advertising industry.

The first method of producing images on sheet celluloid involved a time consuming, hand operated engraving technique. The engraving method of decorating sheet celluloid involved pressing a design into the surface of the plastic by means of a heated metal stamp, then rubbing colored metal powder, wax, or dye into the impression. This technique was in use as early as the mid 1880s, however the process wasn't perfected until several years later. The introduction of stamping machines, steam heated presses and a dipping/polishing method made the operation more efficient by 1886 (USP #417,727 – granted).

4¾" x 3" keepsake card, "A Joyous Season," engraved ivory grained card with lake scene, Baldwin and Gleason. $25.00 – $35.00.

3¹⁄₁₆" x 2" keepsake greeting, "With best wishes." This engraved card features a detailed floral design colored with a variety of blue inks. A lovely item. $25.00 – $35.00.

This wonderful novelty item would have probably been presented to the employees of Krupps Steel Works. The 1¾" dia. straight pin holder with "F Krupps Steel Works; Thos. Prosser and Son, NY." is most likely one of the earliest forms of celluloid advertising novelties. The front shows advertising; obverse pictures a small child, an appealing decoration for ladies. Engraved ivory grained celluloid set in metal framework, Baldwin and Gleason. $45.00 – $55.00.

4⅛" x 2⅞" ink blotter with 1890 calendar, "Black Diamond File Works, Philadelphia, Pa." Two engraved ivory grained celluloid sheets with thick blotter attached by a rivet, Baldwin and Gleason. $35.00 – $40.00.

The second technique involved decorating celluloid with ink in single color and multicolor printing processes.

Transferring an image onto celluloid was a challenge for advertising manufacturers because traditional printer's ink would not adhere to its slippery surface and the design would smudge off. As early as 1880, a method of coating imprinted objects with a clear layer of pyroxylin varnish was attempted (USP# 233,851) but proved to be unsuccessful when it caused the sharpness of the printed image to distort.

It wasn't until 1882 that success in developing an ink for celluloid was achieved. Peter Reid and John Eastwood, assignors to the Celluloid Manufacturing Company, developed a pyroxylin based solution containing acid (USP#256,597) that quickly adhered to the surface of celluloid. While this was clearly a giant step in the right direction, there was one major drawback; the solvent in the ink evaporated too rapidly, making it difficult to work with for extended periods of time. The method was improved upon in 1885 (USP# 348,222) by John W. Hyatt and Marshall Lefferts, assignors to the Celluloid Mfg. Co., when they introduced heat and pressure to the imprinting process.

The two PyroPrints illustrated in the next few photographs show the technique in use on advertising which was large and suitable for framing as art. They are nicely detailed and date to about 1891.

8" x $5\frac{5}{16}$" PyroPrint with lovers embracing in a kiss. Dark blue ink on ivory grained celluloid sheet; Smoke Mellow Mixture; Pyro Photo Co., NY on lower left of picture. $85.00+.

3" dia. mechanical calculating disc, "Cleveland Twist Drill Co." copyright 1928. Three revolving ivory grained discs printed with black ink. $30.00 – $35.00.

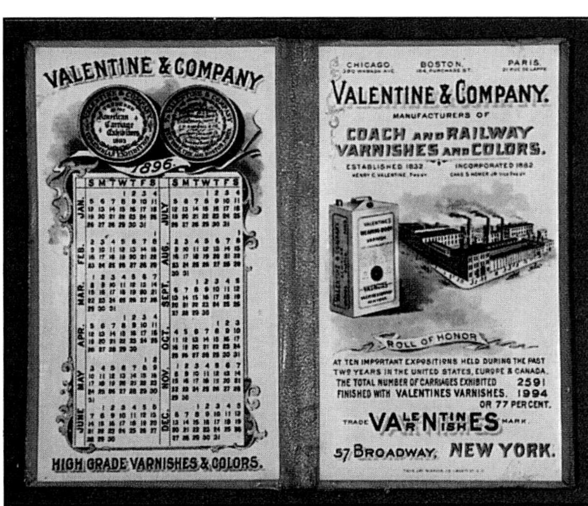

$5\frac{5}{8}$" x $3\frac{1}{4}$" Leather bound folding pocket wallet, "Valentine and Company – Coach and Railway Varnishes and Colors." Obverse, 1896 Calendar, printed on ivory grained sheet celluloid. Thomas Jay Gleason Co. N.Y. $35.00 – $45.00.

$7\frac{7}{8}$" x $5\frac{5}{16}$" PyroPrint, black ink on ivory grained sheet, image: boy and girl at water's edge. "Smoke Mellow Mixture", Pyro Photo Company, NY. Impressed patent date, Aug. 11, 1891. On edge of sheet printed in gray,"Stock 44y10110, Dec. 4, 91." $85.00+.

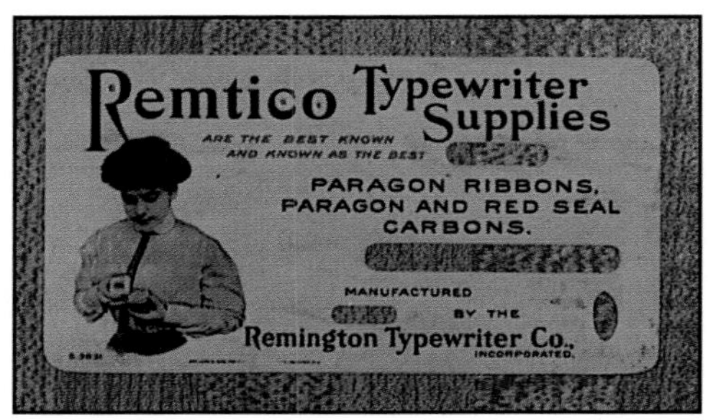

3 7/16" x 1 13/16" typewriter correction template, "Remtico Typewriter Supplies" Remington Typewriter Co. Whitehead and Hoag. $35.00+.

Dottie Maust

2" x 1¼" toothpick holder; political advertising premium, "Pick Samuel Lemmon Reed for Orphan's Court of Cambria Co. Pa." American Art Works, Coshocton, Ohio. Ivory Grained celluloid w/transparent reverse, holder. $35.00 – $40.00.

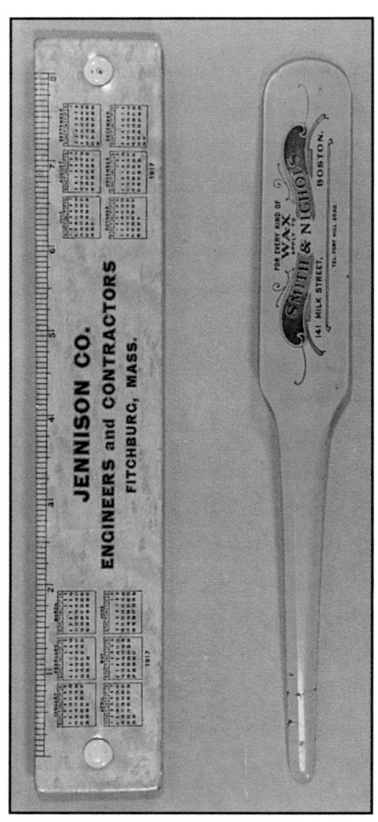

8¾" x 1" combination ruler, ink blotter, and 1917 calendar, "Jennison Co. Engineers and Contractors" Brown and Bigelow, St. Paul. $25.00 – $35.00; solid molded letter opener advertising Smith and Nichols Wax Co. of Boston, $45.00+.

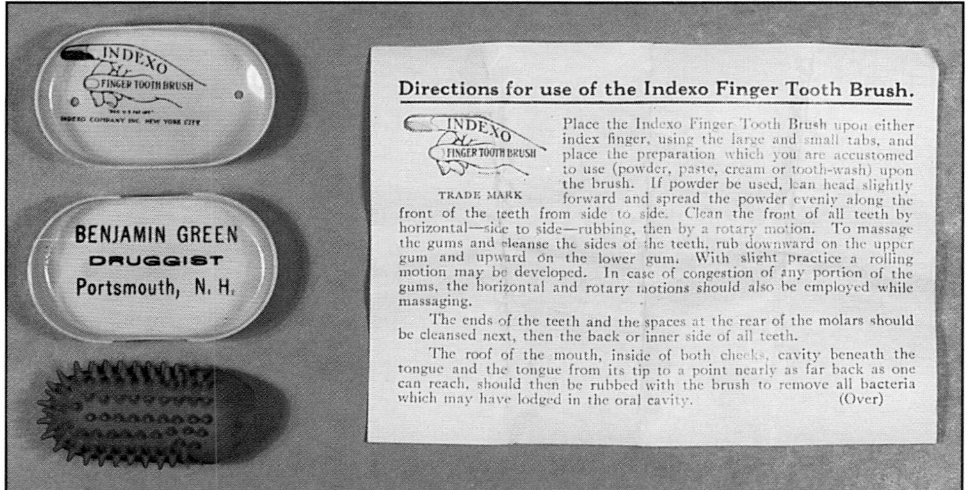

Directions for use of the Indexo Finger Tooth Brush.

INDEXO FINGER TOOTH BRUSH
TRADE MARK

Place the Indexo Finger Tooth Brush upon either index finger, using the large and small tabs, and place the preparation which you are accustomed to use (powder, paste, cream or tooth-wash) upon the brush. If powder be used, lean head slightly forward and spread the powder evenly along the front of the teeth from side to side. Clean the front of all teeth by horizontal—side to side—rubbing, then by a rotary motion. To massage the gums and cleanse the sides of the teeth, rub downward on the upper gum and upward on the lower gum. With slight practice a rolling motion may be developed. In case of congestion of any portion of the gums, the horizontal and rotary motions should also be employed while massaging.

The ends of the teeth and the spaces at the rear of the molars should be cleansed next, then the back or inner side of all teeth.

The roof of the mouth, inside of both cheeks, cavity beneath the tongue and the tongue from its tip to a point nearly as far back as one can reach, should then be rubbed with the brush to remove all bacteria which may have lodged in the oral cavity. (Over)

This molded sheet celluloid carrying case is printed with INDEXO finger toothbrush logo and the name of Druggist Benjamin Green of Portsmouth, N.H. Complete with rubber finger brush and instructions, this dental collectible is valued in this excellent condition at $65.00 – $85.00.

2¾" x 1" baseball game counter, Peter Doelger Bottled Beer. Ivory grained celluloid w/printed advertising; eight rotating wheels inside for keeping score. $40.00 – $55.00.

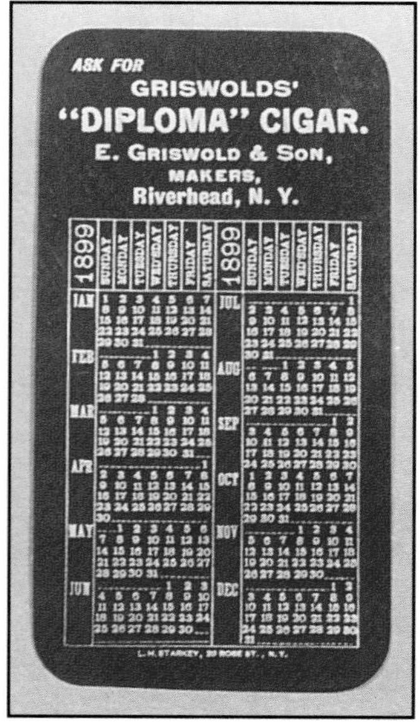

The unusual thing about the 1899 advertising calender is the color. It is very uncommon to find true red transparent celluloid, and this example with the white lettering advertising Diploma Cigars is a rarity. Printed by L.M. Starkey, Rose St., N.Y. $45.00+.

Printing multicolored pictures on celluloid involved a process first patented by Adolph Bensinger in 1888 (USP#383,272). The method involved painting a multicolored picture on paper or textile, then transferring the image to celluloid by means of pressure in the presence of a solvent. A variety of finishing techniques was then employed:

1.) The imprinted sheet could be passed through heated rollers to further press the image into the celluloid.

2.) A liquid coat of pyroxylin varnish could be applied to the printed image to seal it.

3.) A second sheet of thin transparent celluloid was applied over the printed image and subjected to heat and pressure.

Bookmarks made from celluloid come in several styles. The most common variety is die cut from ivory grained sheet stock, then printed with advertising and a variety of decorative motifs. The embossed 5¼" bookmark has a silk fringed chord, hand painted embossed roses and perforated embroidered "Amitié." $25.00 – $35.00; die cut heart w/grape motif and picture of Christ, from the Brooklyn Tabernacle; and 3¼" "Greetings" bookmark w/floral motif and verse on folded top, David C. Cook Publishing Co. $18.00 – $22.00 each.

This ivory grained card measures 5" x 7" and dates from the late 1890s. The verse on the front says, "We are happy little faces, Made to brighten lonely places and to bring you in our way, Peace and joy this Xmas Day." Multi colored ink in blue, brown and yellow, with gold lettering. $35.00+.

Bookmarks: 4¾" butterfly w/1st Psalm, grained celluloid, by Westminster Press; 4" rose motif on grained celluloid, advertising Bair and Lane of Greensburg, Pa., the Meek Co., Coshocton, Ohio; 4¾" poinsettia bookmark with Footpath to Peace by Henry Van Dyke, unmarked. A nice Christmas cross-over collectible, $25.00 – $30.00 each.

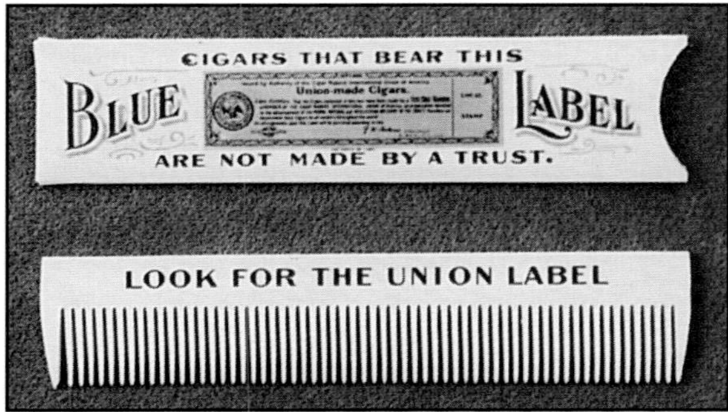

These wonderful advertising items feature novelties made with ivory grained celluloid and decorated with black and blue inks. Matchsafe and comb. $45.00 – $50.00.

"New England Made Cigars" by Whitehead and Hoag, circa 1908. $45.00 – $50.00 each.

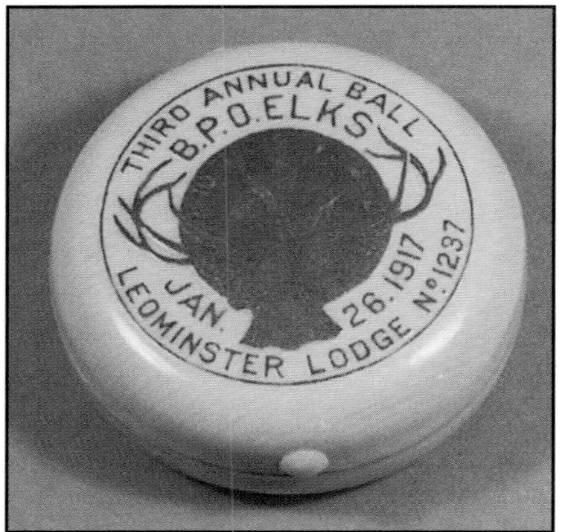

Fraternal organizations used celluloid as an advertising medium for pin back buttons, badges, souvenirs, and other novelties. The examples shown here are but a few of the many items available in celluloid. BPOE souvenir celluloid compact from Leominster Lodge 1917 Annual Ball, powder box with gold lettering and Elk logo. Lid pops open when button is pushed; although unmarked, it is most likely this item was made of Viscoloid since that compnay was also a Leominster pyroxylin plastics manufacturer. $45.00+.

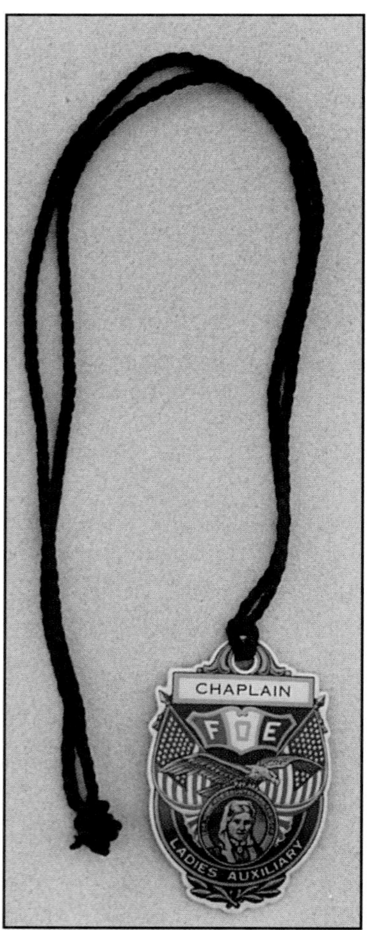

2⅞" fraternal badge, Chaplain, Ladies Auxiliary, FOE. Thick multiple layered celluloid, embossed on back Whitehead and Hoag, Newark, N.J. $18.00 – $22.00.

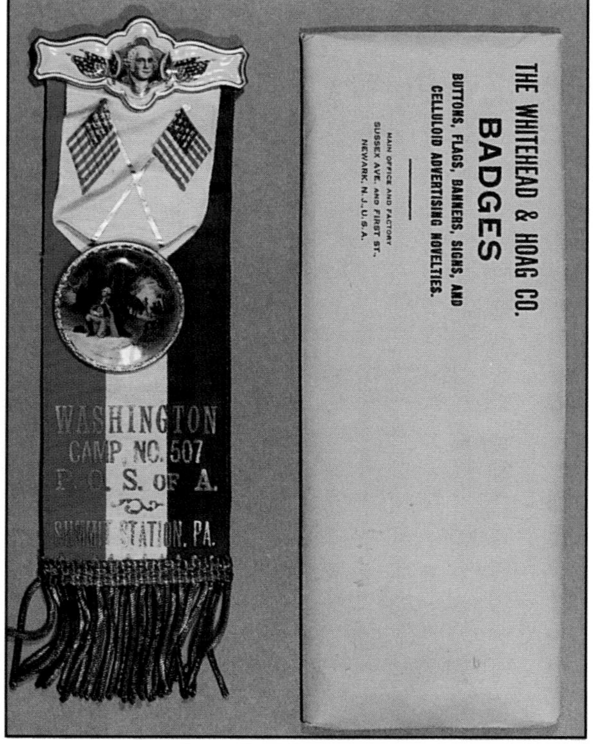

9" fraternal pin, Patriotic Sons of America, Washington Camp, Summit Station, Pa. Includes celluloid pin back and medallion with image of George Washington, Pat. Nov. 7, 1897. Complete with envelope from Whitehead and Hoag Co. $150.00 – $175.00.

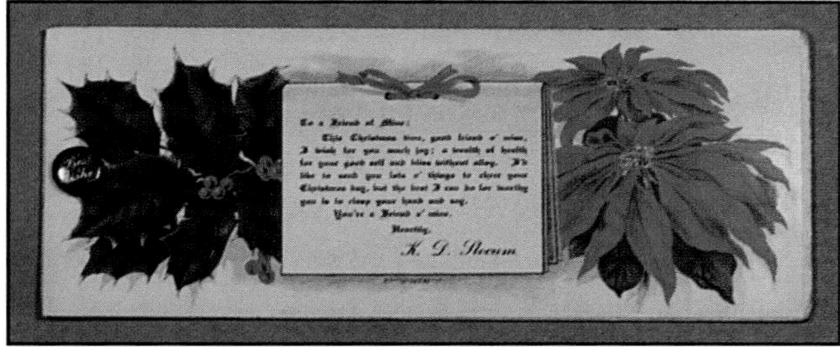

Christmas and New Year were opportunities for business owners to promote their wares through advertising premiums. These ink blotter packets with colorfully printed celluloid covers date from 1908 through 1929. Note the decorative fasteners on several of the blotter packets. All measure 7¾" x 3" and include a bunch of pastel colored blotters. $40.00 – $65.00 each.

Terry Leffler and Penny Lane Antiques

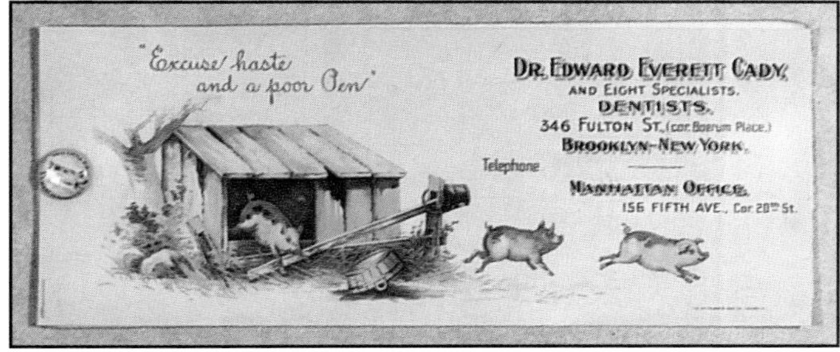

This advertising ink blotter features three little pigs escaping from their pen. Printed by Whitehead and Hoag Co., the ivory grained celluloid sheet stock undoubtedly came from the Celluloid Manufacturing Co. Probably given as a premium to patients, this advertising ink blotter is from the office of Dr. Edward Cady of N.Y. $95.00+.

The image of a pretty girl has always been a sure way to attract attention. Lovely ladies can be found gracing the covers of these memo booklets. 4¾" x 3" booklet, combination memo, calendar, and advertising. Beautiful girl on ivory grained celluloid, "Season's Greetings, 1906," from Alphonse Judas Co.; Thomas Pl Moore of Reading, Pa. $45.00+ each.

4¾" x 3" colorful memo booklet from Metropolitan Life Insurance Co. Woman in red cape with colorful leaves printed on ivory grained celluloid. Both Whitehead and Hoag. $45.00+ each.

This leatherbound diary shows a New Year's baby with banner and cymbals. Reverse features a 1929 calendar. Bright and colorful, but no specific advertising. $30.00+.

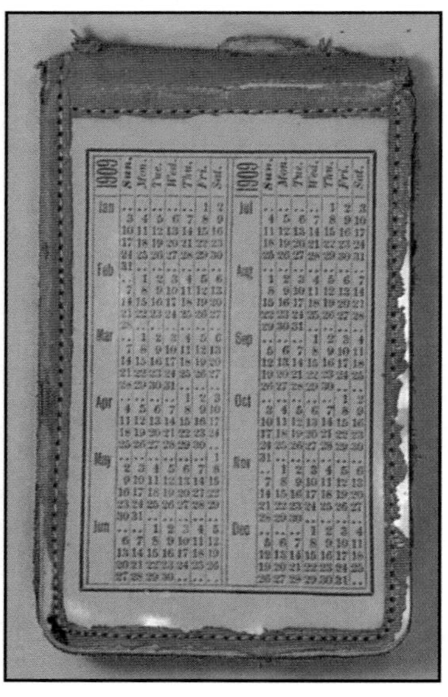

4¾" x 3" leatherbound memo with celluloid front and back, ornate medallion of pretty girl on front, circa 1909 from Germania Savings Bank, Pittsburgh. $45.00+ each.

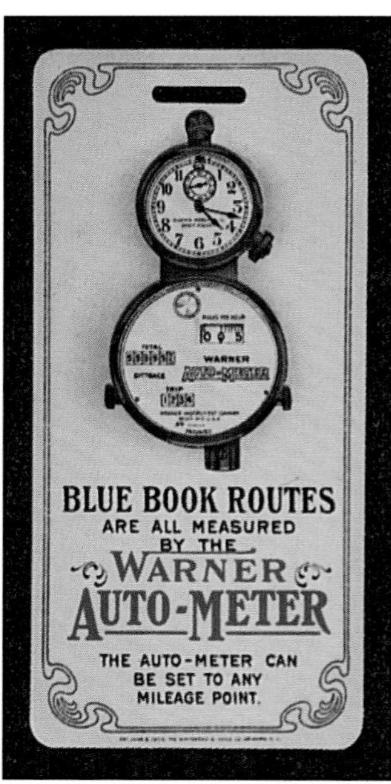

This 3" x 1⅝" memo advertises Warner Auto Meter's, printed by Whitehead and Hoag in Newark. Reverse has area for calculating mileage in pencil. Three tone red, black, and gold on cream sheet stock. $15.00 – $20.00.

Keepsakes and Souvenirs

Delicate lace edge, floral motif embossed greeting card with hand painted yellow rose decorations. Glued paper insert. $20.00+.

Bicycle greetings of embossed and die cut ivory grained celluloid with roses; hand painted detailing with paper card tacked to celluloid. Fragile spokes are subject to breaking, note the missing piece. $45.00+.

The following variety of small novel greeting cards includes die cutting, embossing, and decorative painting. These small keepsakes feature ornamental sheet celluloid covers which are glued, brad fastened, or sewn onto paper inserts. They date to the turn of the century. This selection of novel cards features inserts that have been sewn in place. The various decorative motifs often relate to other collectibles – the horseshoe, cruise ship, and sailboat; however they are still reasonably priced when found. $12.00 – $18.00.

In 1890 the third method of protecting mulitcolored pictures with celluoid was developed by Joseph France, assignor to the Arlington Company of Arlington, N.J., manufacturers of "Pyralin." France's process (USP #458,020) involved laminating printed paper between two thin sheets of transparent pyroxylin plastic and applying heat and pressure. The resulting product was an indelible, yet pliable image that could be applied over any dry surface, or housed in a framework. The process became widely used in the manufacture of postcards, advertising mirrors and pinback buttons.

Three early twentieth century 5" x 3" embossed celluloid postcards. Each is embellished with an additional decorative motif; the horseshoe bears a flocked green shamrock and holly with purple/gray velvet; embossed fan has velveteen flock and applied metal words "Many happy Returns," and the embossed "Best Wishes" pansy card, dated 1908, features a felt butterfly. All are glued to a paper backing. $15.00 – $20.00 each.

This turn-of-the-century gold tone metal trinket box is designed as a souvenir item from the nation's capital. The lid features a celluloid laminated print of the Capitol building. $25.00 – $35.00.

This 5" x 3" Christmas postcard, circa 1907, features clear celluloid over an embossed card, "A Happy Christmas" with traditional holly and berry design and vignette of a beautiful child. $15.00 – 18.00 unused.

Diane Saylor

A 2¾" long oval trinket box fashioned from ivory grained celluloid features a fitted lid that has a printed paper picture of the BPOE Home in Johnstown, Pa. As of the writing of the book, the building, complete with majestic looking Elk statue on the roof, is still occupied. $35.00 – $45.00.

When friction strike matches were first invented, they were a hazard to carry loose in one's pockets because they could easily ignite. The solution was to store them in a fireproof metal container. The outer surface could be colorfully decorated with celluloid coated prints or advertising. The only problem associated with this decorative technique is that celluloid is extremely flammable, and the strike surface is on the outside bottom of the match safe. Had the flame gotten too close to the celluloid, it most certainly would have caught fire. Perhaps this is one of the reasons so few match safes with celluloid coverings are available today.

A variety of small metal and celluloid advertising premiums including a Star Shoe pencil clip, Waterman's Fountain Pen tack, and an REO Speed Wagon pencil clip. The thumb tack is somewhat more desirable than the other items because fountain pen collecting is so popular. $25.00 – $35.00 each.

Terry Leffler and Penny Lane Antiques, Schellsburg, PA

This wonderful match holder is fashioned from embossed tin and is designed to hang on the wall. A celluloid advertising oval showing a pretty lady promotes the G.W. Shaffer Stores of Altoona and Juniata, Pa. $110.00 – $125.00.

Helen Golubic

2¾" x 1" match safes, metal with celluloid covered printed paper. Pretty women and colorful consumer products are more appealing and expensive than plain printed celluloid. $85.00 – $115.00 each. The reverse of the pretty lady piece advertises the St. Louis Bar, Pueblo, Colo.

Three 2¼" x 1" match box covers made of celluloid covered paper over metal frame. The C-shaped framework is just the right size to snugly hold a small box of safety matches. These circa 1920 items are much less expensive than the previously shown variety and are more plentiful also. They frequently show scenic tourist sites, as in the case of the Atlantic City, and Gettysburg examples. $18.00 – $25.00.

These two round pencil clips were colorful premium items used by grocery store owners around 1920. Salt pencil clips, Diamond and Colonial Brands. $15.00 each.

While most collectible celluloid tape measures are pocket sized, this example produced by Whitehead and Hoag is quite an exception. Note its size in comparison to the smaller one. 3" dia. advertising tape measure, "The GM Parks Co. Fitchburg, Mass." Whitehead and Hoag. $35.00 – $40.00. 1" dia. advertising tape measure, "JR Kramer Inc. Butter, NY." J.B. Carroll Co. of Chicago. $12.00 – $15.00.

Advertising and souvenir tape measures are especially collectible today because they are plentiful, easy to display, and provide colorful advertising from days gone by. In addition they were useful tools for both men and women, as well as a handy reminder to patronize a favorite business or product. Six 1" diameter celluloid tape measures with various decorative treatments. Souvenir of Johnstown, Pa. w/Indian and landscape, no ID, $25.00; pretty child w/flowers and advertising for First National Bank of Boswell Co. Pat. 7-10-17, Chicago, on curl and side, $35.00; Fab Soap by Colgate Co., G. Felthenstall and Son Chicago, $35.00 – $45.00; green and mother-of-pearl surface and branded ivory grained sides w/Pat. 7-10-17, PN Co. (Parisian Novelty Co.) $15.00; J.R. Kramer, Inc. Butter white w/black lettering, Pat. Pending, B. Carroll Co. Chicago, $20.00; Michigan Central Depot, Detroit, unmarked, $20.00.

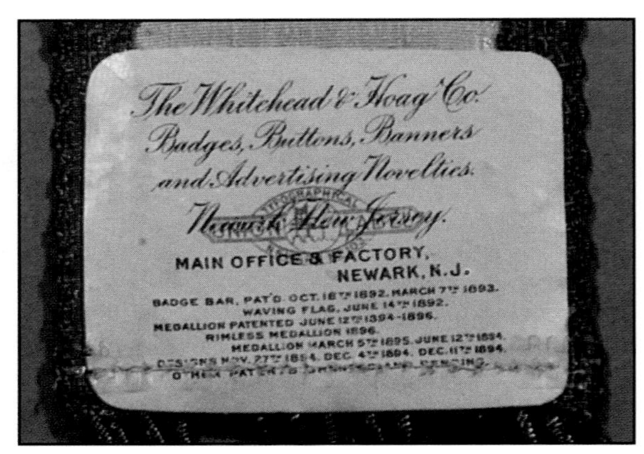

Whitehead and Hoag Company of Newark was the most prolific manufacturer of pinback celluloid buttons. Made from stock supplied by the Celluloid Manufacturing Co., the buttons became immediately popular because of their appealing decorations which allowed them to be worn as a new kind of personal adornment.

3" dia. celluloid covered paper over tin disk, "American Bulb Co. of Chicago and New York," Easter lily on a green ground w/dark blue trim and white lettering. Parisian Novelty Co. on curl. 6" long wire hook for bills. $45.00 – $65.00.

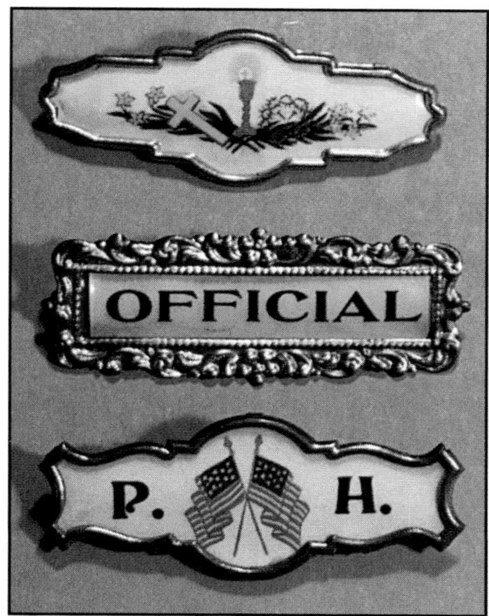

By the turn of the twentieth century, pinback buttons had come to represent political, fraternal, and religious affiliations, as well as popular consumer products. The examples shown here are of the generic type; none are highly collectible and are therefore inexpensive. The smaller buttons can usually be picked up for a dollar or two while the larger more colorful variety could sell for about $5.00 – $8.00. The most expensive types of pinback buttons are those which advertise colorful consumer products around the turn of the century; these are valued between $45.00 – $85.00 each depending on graphics. Political buttons can sell for hundreds of dollars if the image is that of a president.

Trademarks can be found on the "curl" of the pin, the edge where the plastic wraps around the framework. Look for the names listed in the beginning of this section. Most common are Whitehead and Hoag; Bastian Brothers; Cruver Mfg.; and Parisian Novelty Co. The photo illustration shown here also shows a few unknown manufacturers.

Another identifying part of the pinback button is the back paper, which is pressed into the back behind the pin stem. These circular pieces of paper are printed with company identification. Although many of these back papers have since fallen out and been lost, when present they offer important information pertaining to age and origin.

Pocket mirrors touted everything from patent medicines to clothing. Many were used as promotional premiums and will state specific directions on the curl about obtaining duplicate mirrors. In good condition these are more valued then most pinback buttons because they suffered more handling.

When purchasing pinback buttons or pocket mirrors, examine closely to determine authenticity. Beware of reproductions which do not exhibit the telltale signs of age: wear, patina, quality printed images and manufacturers trademark.

Watch for broken mirrors; missing pin stems; and damaged surfaces. Scratches, dents, cracking, and foxed paper under transparent celluloid are all factors which reduce collector value.

Souvenir mirrors; Niagara Falls, Grand Forks, N.D., and advertising for Foot-Schulze-Glove of St. Paul, Mn. $45.00 – $65.00.

2" dia. mirror advertising Mifflin County Jewelry Co. of Lewistown, Pa., shows the birthstone and virtue for every month, on ivory grained celluloid and printed by Kemper – Thomas Co. of Cincinnati, Ohio, $45.00. 1" dia. pocket mirror advertising Duffy's Pure Malt Whiskey, Makes The Weak Strong, P.P. Pulver Mfg. Co. Rochester, N.Y. on curl. $85.00+.

The image seen on the pocket mirror shown here can be changed by turning the mirror upside down. Advertising from Hager's Store in Frostburg, Md. $110.00.

Large 2" diameter pocket mirror is printed celluloid over tin framework; pretty lady with roses but no advertising, a nice keepsake. $65.00.

By the turn of the twentieth century, manufacturers began reproducing photographs on celluloid novelties. The method became widely used by politicians who had their likeness reproduced in mass quantities on small inexpensive pinback buttons. This example measures ⅝" in diameter, with J. Fred. C. Talbott For Congress; back paper states, "Made by HYATT MFG. CO., Baltimore, MD." Complete with original box. $18.00 – $25.00.

5" fraternal ribbon with celluloid bar pin saying "Member" and photographic image of Robert Davis. "11th Annual Outing of the Robert Davis Association, Hudson Co. N.J., Sept. 14, 1898." Whitehead and Hoag Co.; many fraternal organizations remain a mystery today. $30.00 – $40.00.

When photographic keepsakes were introduced to the general public, the popularity of such personalized novelties soared. Thousands of celluloid photographic images are available today in the form of pocket mirrors, pinback buttons, stick pins, and easel back discs; the most collectible and expensive items in this category are those that feature the likeness of a famous person, while generic images are less collectible and therefore quite reasonably priced.

Helen Golubic

The colorized photo of a bathing beauty was probably a souvenir item from someplace like Atlantic City, N.J., while the 2¾" sepia oval mirror showing two girls in white dresses bears no identification $18.00 – $22.00. Bathing beauty, 2¼" dia. pocket mirror with colorized picture of an ocean scene, featuring a bathing suit clad beauty next to a wicker booth. $35.00 – $40.00.

6" dia. easel back picture showing little boy in U.S. Navy suit, small print: "July – Birth flower, Pond Lily or Waterlily, Birthstone – July, Ruby." Decorative motif includes water lilies and red gemstone. \$25.00 – \$30.00. 2¼" pocket mirror, girl looking down, small print: "February, Birthstone, Amethyst, Birth flower, Carnation." Depicts winter scene with pink and red carnations and purple gemstone. \$25.00 – \$30.00. Both items copy written by the Cruver Mfg. Co. of Chicago.

A variety of souvenir items showing photographs of famous sites, all produced by the Cruver Mfg. Co. with the exception of the pocket mirror. 2¼" x 1" match safe with scenes from Atlantic City, N.J., \$15.00 – \$25.00. 2¼" salt and pepper shakers, metal with applied celluloid scenes of Washington, D.C., \$25.00+. 3" dia. clothing brush showing Pennsylvania State Memorial of Gettysburg, Pa. \$25.00+. 2" dia. pocket mirror showing Eiffel Tower; regular photograph covered by a clear celluloid disc, both fitted into mirror framework. \$15.00 – \$25.00.

Novelties

Game Items

A variety of games and game pieces was made from celluloid throughout the years. The earliest game related items known are score keeping devices manufactured from celluloid sheet with rotating discs that display numbers. Advertised as game markers, these counters have been useful since the Celluloid Novelty Co. in Newark began marketing them in the late 1870s. To find examples in the original box is a rare occasion; it is obvious these counters were never used. Red is an unusual color, especially for such early celluloid items.

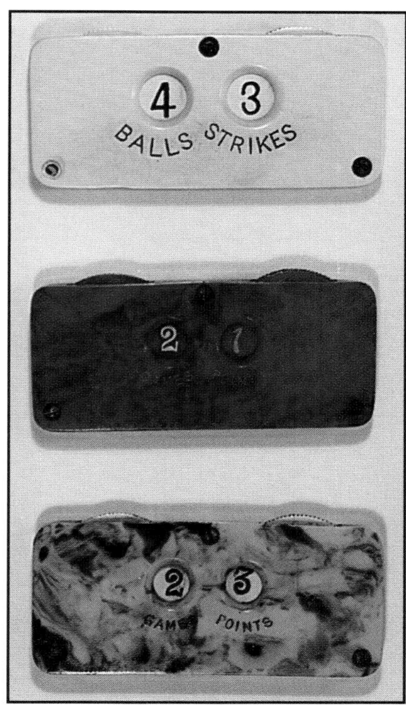

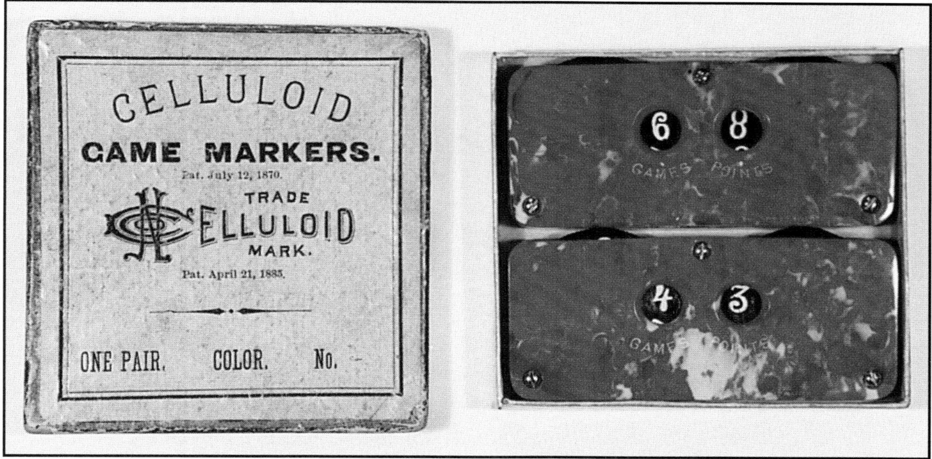

The baseball game counters shown here were manufactured in three colors, cream, mottled red, and variegated cream and brown. They are sturdy rectangular boxes ⅛" thick and fastened together at the lower corners and center top; although they are not marked, their design is so similar to those manufactured by the Celluloid Novelty Co. They are presumed to be a product of theirs. $15.00 each.

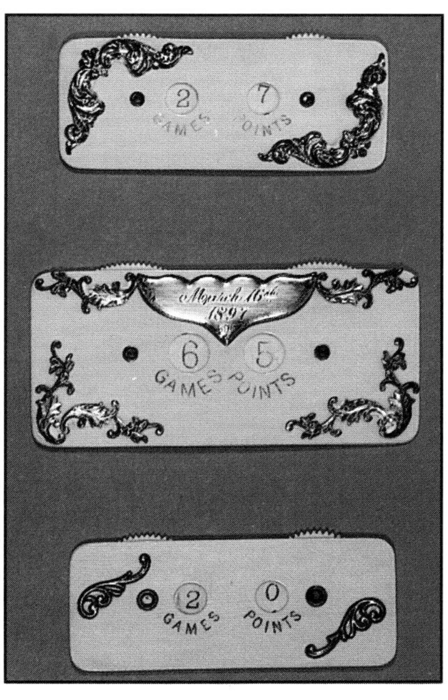

Three cream colored game counters embellished with sterling silver ornamentation. The smaller examples would sell for $25.00 – $30.00 each and the center item, which is dated March 16, 1891, would start at $35.00. Unmarked.

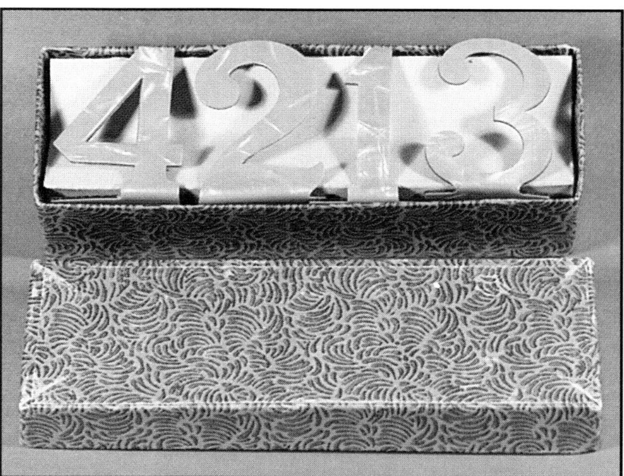

Bridge table markers. Original box with numbers 1,2,3,4, in pale green pearlescent celluloid. Each table marker has a flat base upon which it would balance. Set $25.00.

Bridge trump indicator. 2" sq. scallop edge pearlescent green base w/translucent amber and cream flipping suit display. $18.00 – $25.00. Combination pencil holder and trump indicator, 3¼" x 2" mottled green pencil holder w/revolving circular suit display, hand painted floral decoration, circa 1930. $25.00 – $30.00.

The card case shown here is made from laminated amber and pearlescent celluloid and features a red and black decoration showing a bob haired gal and the four suits: hearts, spades, clubs, and diamonds. Circa 1930. $20.00.

The 2" tall red trump indicator here probably dates to the mid 1920s. $25.00. The ivory grained card case has been a popular item since the Celluloid Company introduced it in their 1892 catalog. The same item was carried by the firm until well into the 1920s. Card case, $22.00 – $24.00. The "Hyatt" playing cards advertise Hyatt Roller Bearings and show a picture of a Model A car from the rear. This was another of J.W. Hyatt's inventions.

4" x 2" tablet with pearlescent cream front marked BRIDGE and a mechanical pencil covered with a thin sheet of pearlescent celluloid decorated with the red and black clubs, diamonds, spades, and hearts. Pad, $12.00 – $18.00; Pencil, $18.00 – $22.00.

These wonderful celluloid dreidels were used by Jewish children to play games during Hanukkah. Spun like a top, the symbols on the sides are traditional Hebrew and represent numbers, much like dice. (These examples have the numbers underneath the symbols.) Large, $35.00; small, $25.00 – $30.00.

Celluloid playing cards have been popular since the turn of the century because they are resistant to wear and are also waterproof; however their flammable nature is a problem for card players who smoke. The example shown here was manufactured by Kem. Cruver, a major supplier of celluloid advertising items, and Permanite also produced playing cards. Decks generally came in some sort of plastic playing case, often made of celluloid, sometimes Bakelite. Alone, a deck would be valued at about $12.00, more if it has an interesting decoration or the name of a particular manufacturer known to produce celluloid items.

1" dia. cream colored celluloid table markers w/applied imitation tortoise shell numbers; storage box; Fuller trademark. $18.00 – $25.00.

The card set shown here features a green and pearlescent celluloid box, two decks of celluloid playing cards, and a variety of round red, blue, and black poker chips. $40.00+.

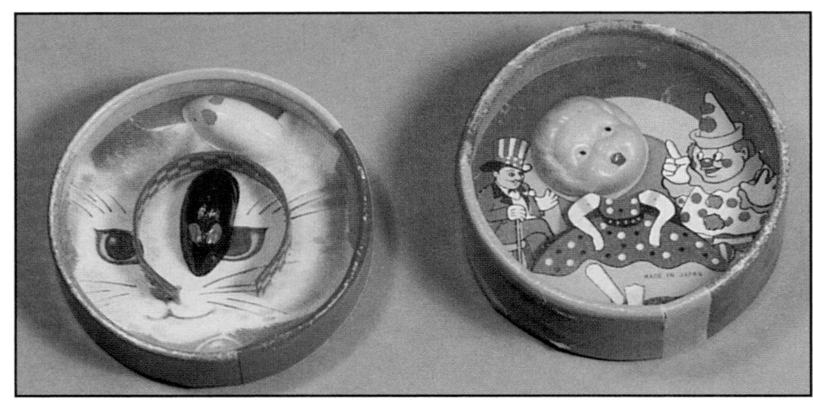

Japanese maze games have small celluloid objects inside a shallow cardboard and glass cylinder, 3" diameter. Circa 1950. $22.00 each.

Poker chips of celluloid could have been a dangerous item since someone was usually smoking during a poker game. Perhaps this is why so few exist. Poker chips, thin celluloid in black, red, and blue. $15.00 – $20.00.

In his quest to invent celluloid, John W. Hyatt produced a wood-based composition material from which dominoes were prolifically manufactured for many years, beginning in 1868 at the Hyatt Mfg. Co. in Albany, N.Y. Most of the boxed sets around today were manufactured from this composition material, Hyatt's first successful moldable substance. It is unusual to find a complete set of Celluloid dominoes in the original box; circa 1891, The Celluloid Company of Newark, $45.00+.

This solid celluloid box measures $7\frac{1}{4}$" x $2\frac{3}{4}$" and is made in swirled gray, orange, and aqua. The top slides open to reveal a collection of $1\frac{1}{4}$" sq. poker chips in thick orange, green, and grained ivory. Made by E.B. Kingman Company of Leominster, Massachusetts. $45.00 – $50.00.

3" tall x 2" dia. cream and ivory grained dice shaker cup and poker dice. Cup was first marketed in the Celluloid Novelty Co. 1889 catalog, as were the poker dice. $15.00 – $20.00 each.

Among celluloid items still available on the market today are ping pong balls. This collection has been accumulated from various sources, as ping pong is a popular pastime for players of all skill levels. The early vintage ball from the 1950s can be found at thrift shops and yard sales for a few cents and the new brightly mottled Chinese balls can be purchased in a set from sporting good and department stores for a few dollars. The countries represented in this assortment include China, Japan, England, Sweden, and the U.S.

A turn-of-the-century Parker Brother's Mah Jongg Game in original wooden box. All game pieces are bamboo with celluloid laminated tops, colorfully decorated. Complete set, $125.00+.

Letter Openers, Foam Flippers, and Page Turners

Letter openers, foam flippers, and page turners are a nice collectible category because they came in such a wide variety of styles and designs. The purely functional items which display no molded designs or painted decorations are not as desirable to collectors as the decorated variety and therefore sell for only a few dollars when found.

The most collectible types fall into two categories: advertising and novelty. Advertising pieces may also include souvenir type items featured elsewhere in this book. This section features novelty items which have handles in the shapes of animals, people, or things.

Letter openers, foam flippers and page turners were made by a variety of methods; die cut from embossed sheet celluloid then decorated with advertising or paint; blow molded in celluloid, with hollow handles in the image of an animal or flower; and solid molded with metal embellishments.

The Celluloid Novelty Company was the first manufacturer of letter openers. The three fine examples below left are found in a company catalog from the turn of the twentieth century and are listed as "light antique" in color. They were manufactured from solid celluloid and have wonderful detailing.

Consider yourself fortunate if you are able to add such examples to a collection for under $85.00.

Novelty letter openers that are designed for multi-purpose use generally command higher prices than one-piece openers. Interesting decorative motifs, ethnic depiction, and removable parts all enhance the collectibility and value of this category.

A variety of both advertising and novelty letter openers.

9⅝" solid figural bull head with glass eyes; 9" solid figural lighthouse; 8¼" solid sword with fern motif. Starting, $85.00+.

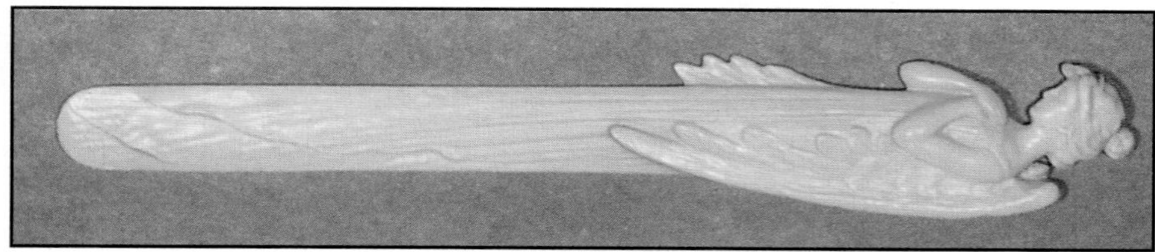

Not to be confused with the letter openers are foam flippers and page turners. The latter types are generally longer and blunt on the end. This 10¼" seraph page turner is molded from solid cream colored celluloid and because of the angel motif is highly collectible. These types of articles were used to skim the foam off a glass of beer or to turn the pages of sheet music and cookbooks. $100.00 – $125.00.

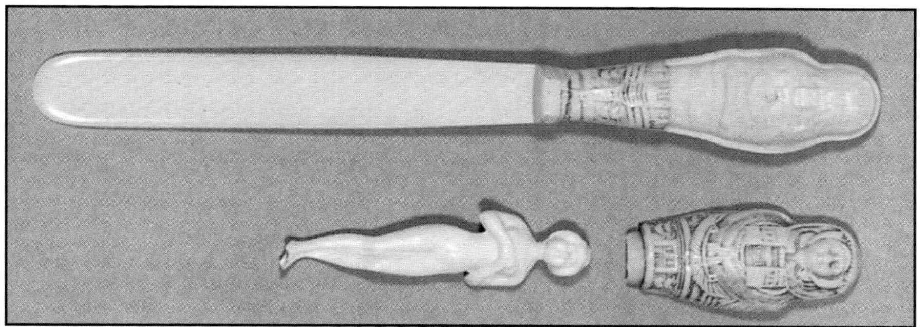

This wonderfully detailed Egyptian styled novelty piece could be used as a foam flipper or page turner, although it is commonly mistaken for a letter opener. It measures 9⅝" with a handle in the shape of a sarcophagus and features a removable front and naked woman inside. Originally the nude figure was a mummy, wrapped in a long cotton string. $100.00 – $145.00.

Floral motifs are especially popular with the nicest examples featuring distinct flora and fauna. 7⅝" edelweiss flower figural paper knife. $45.00 – $50.00.

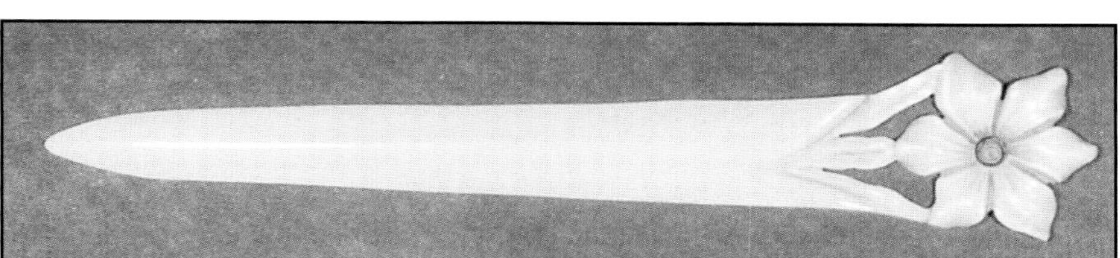

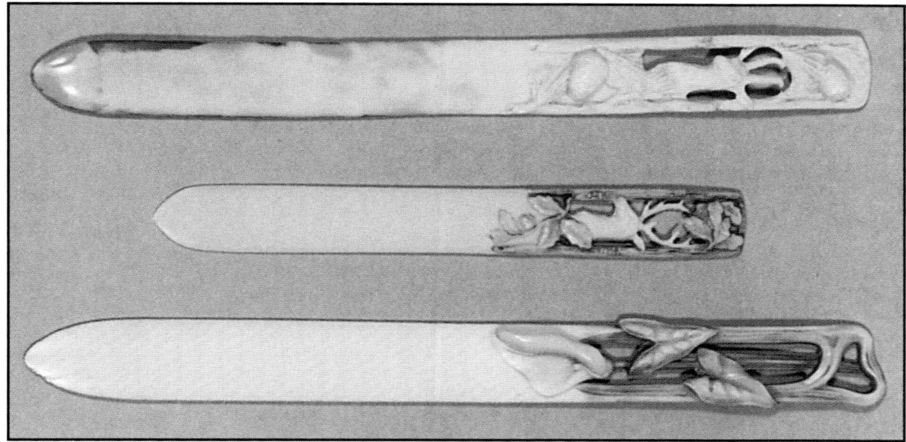

The type of open work seen on the three letter openers here makes very attractive decorations. Two 10¼" openers with deer and acorns; arrow leaf plant, $55.00 – $75.00; the smaller 7" has very nicely detailed decorations. $55.00.

Some celluloid letter openers serve a dual purpose or have applied embellishments of another material. This 7⅜" brown and ivory grained opener w/magnifier and coiled metal snake w/red glass eyes is a fine example. $75.00 – $95.00.

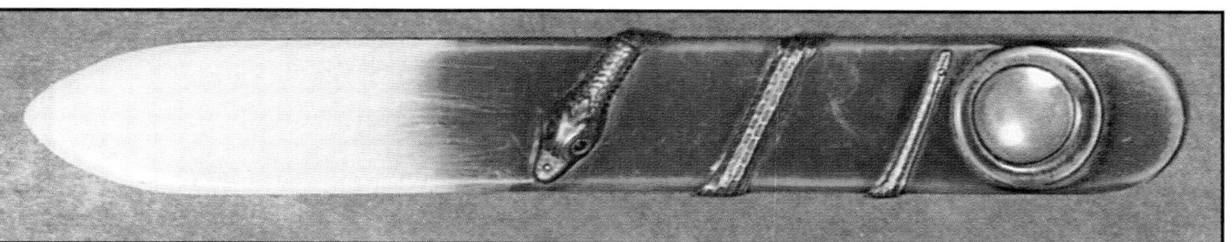

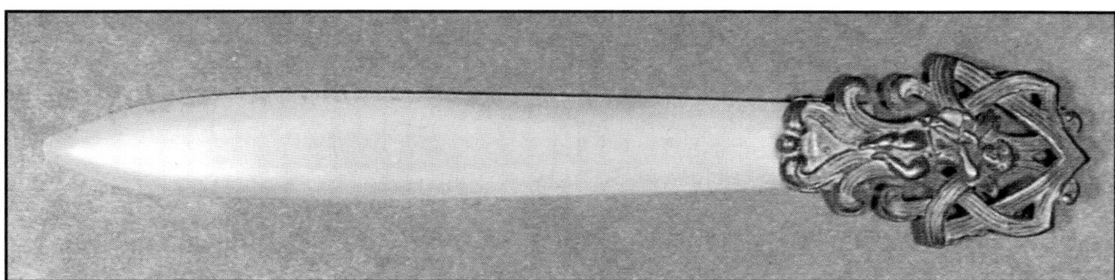

A lovely 7" example featuring a bronze Art Nouveau cupid handle and a mellow cream colored celluloid paper knife. Since angels are highly collectible today, the value of this particular letter opener could start between $65.00 – $75.00.

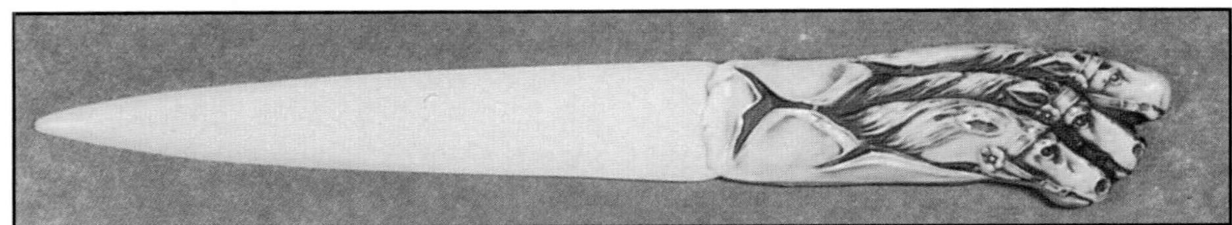

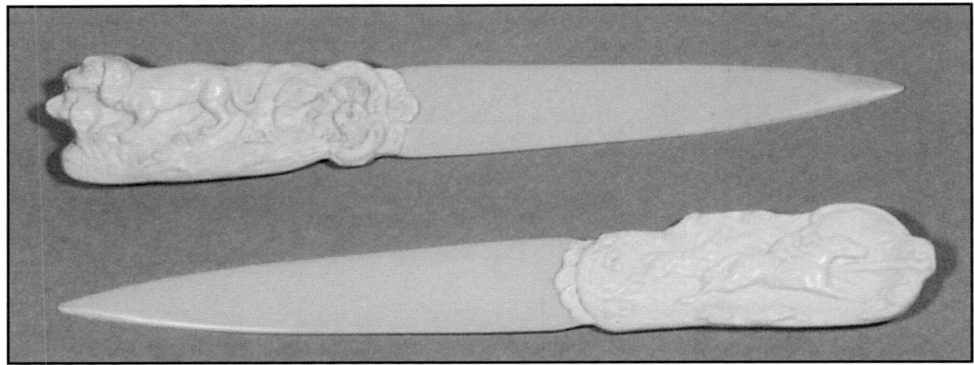

Animal images have always been popular with the horse and dog among the most desired. The examples shown here have hollow handles and solid paper blades, and all measure 7⅝". At top, three horse heads; below hounds hunting; rider on horse w/hounds. $35.00+ each.

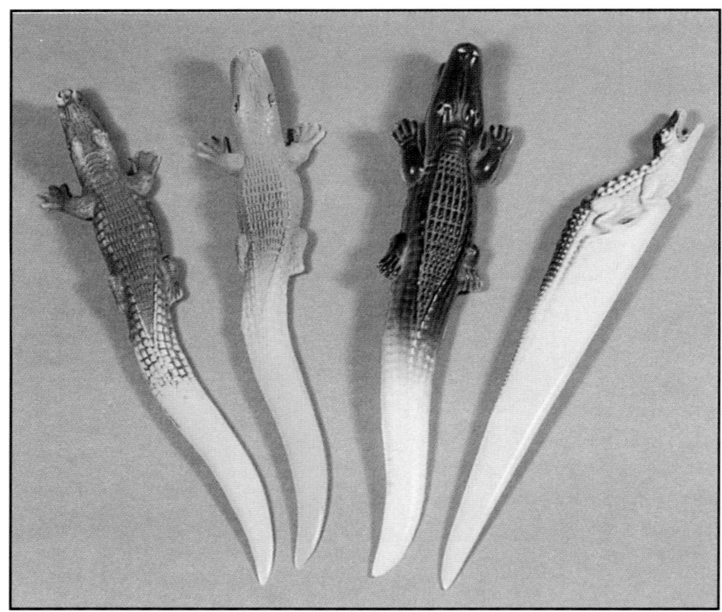

The alligator openers shown here were manufactured, left to right, VCO/USA; VCO/USA; Japan; and Germany. The first three examples could be confused as toys, but when comparing them to the toy examples, it is obvious their tails were designed for a different purpose. Blow molded of cream celluloid with painted highlights. $12.00 – $18.00 each.

Figural Tape Measures

Figural tape measures are quickly becoming scarce as collectors snatch them up at antique shops and auctions. Although the prices here may seem high, the celluloid collector should be aware that this is an established collecting category and competition is stiff.

Styles of tape measures shown here include flowers, fruits, and character themes. Animal tape measures can be found in the section on Animal Novelties. Thanks to John and Gail Dunn for use of their collection.

1" strawberry, \$200.00 – \$245.00. 2" plum w/fly pull, \$225.00 – \$235.00. 2¼" pear w/ladybug pull, \$200.00 – \$225.00.

1¾" chariot w/horses and driver, imitation bronze. \$225.00 – \$250.00.

2" t. girl w/basket of flowers and dog. Blue and maroon highlights; Japan Circle T trademark. \$125.00 – \$145.00.

2" t. handled basket w/flowers, marked Made In Japan. \$125.00 – \$150.00. 2" t. silver handled basket w/fruit; made in Germany. \$100.00 – \$125.00. 1" dia. basket w/fruit; unmarked. \$100.00 – \$120.00. 1¼" dia. basket w/flowers; Made In Germany. \$145.00 – \$155.00.

Dottie Maust

2" Billiken in cream celluloid w/applied brown highlights. Trademarked JAPAN on tape. $175.00 – $200.00.

1¾" t. Turkish bandit head, sword pull, unmarked. $250.00. 1¼" t. smoking Indian head, cigar pull, Japan. $250.00 – $285.00.

1⅛" sq. dice, ivory w/black dots, $200.00 – $250.00. 1⅛" sq. bridge marker, ivory w/suits, $200.00 – $250.00.

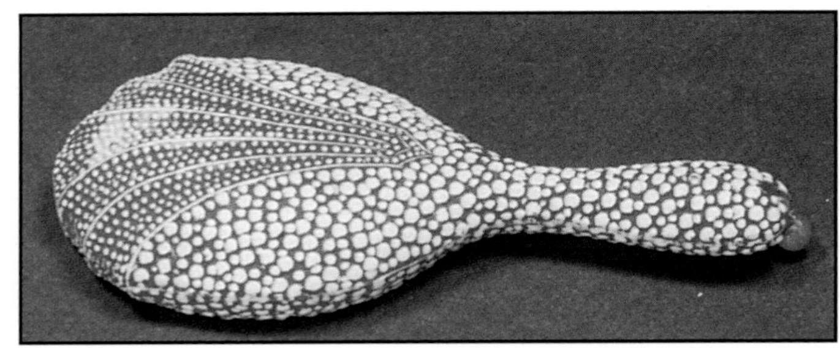

3¼" t. mirror, red and white polka dot, shell-shaped back. $250.00 – $265.00.

Souvenir Items

Souvenir novelties can be found throughout this book in many of the other categories. Because they are plentiful and relatively inexpensive, assembling a collection of souvenir novelties would be a good starting place for the beginning collector. The most frequently seen items are letter openers, figurines, figural tape measures, fans, and compacts.

Indian motifs are among the most popular themes found on souvenir novelties. The variety of items decorated with a molded and painted profile of a chief in full head dress is represented here by several of the most common forms.

Key chain souvenirs are usually celluloid items that are found with a small hole for attaching to a chain. 2" palm tree w/attached mailing tag. The flamingo is also believed to be a souvenir of Florida as well. Tree, $12.00; flamingo, $18.00 – $22.00.

2⅛" novelty souvenir bag, "Oh You Bootlegger," Montreal, Canada, complete with glass bottle of scotch. $15.00 – $18.00.

The novelty souvenir pincushion shown here has a 3" blow-molded character figure attached to the base, Lighthouse, CT. $25.00 – $30.00

2" statue/figurine souvenir of Niagara Falls, Indian in canoe, Japan, $8.00 – $12.00.

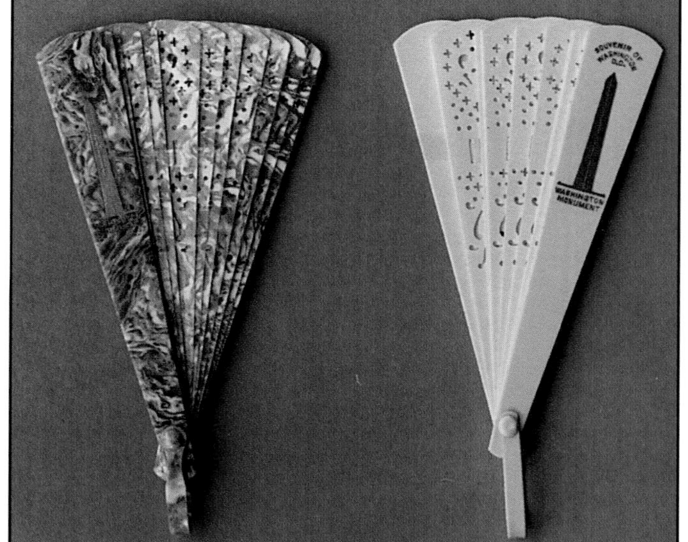

Small brisé fans were often embossed as souvenir items. The two miniature examples shown here measure 3¼" long and are fashioned from mottled green and cream celluloid. Souvenirs of Washington, D.C. $15.00 each.

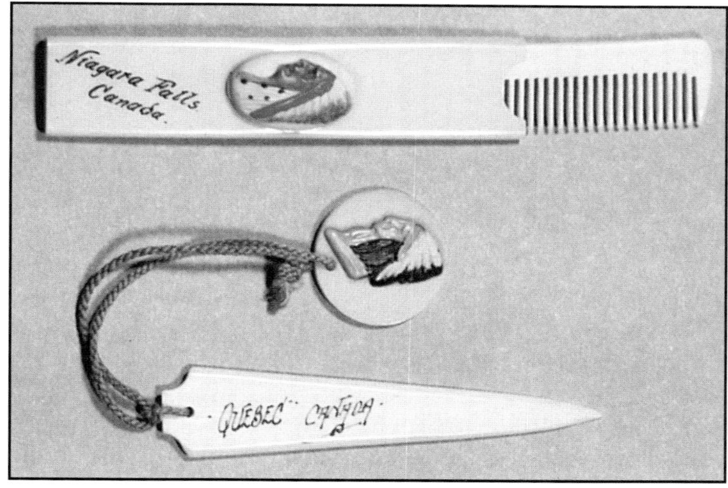

3¼" pocket comb w/case, and combination letter opener/book marker, both souvenirs of Canada. $12.00 each.

Celluloid Toys

About Celluloid Toys

Introduction

Collectors of celluloid often focus on a particular category, with toys being one of the most interesting and popular specialties. The variety of articles classified in this area cover a wide range of items including animal toys, character figures, children's rattles, holiday novelties, knick knacks, whimsical gadgets and playthings.

In choosing this class of collectible, one should be aware of entering a highly competitive field. The supply of good vintage celluloid is beginning to dwindle, while the demand continues to intensify. This perplexing situation, coupled with the popularity of selling items through the Internet, has begun to result in stiff competition among collectors world wide.

As a result, the cost of quality celluloid toys is rapidly escalating, causing a dilemma for the frugal collector. Likewise, these circumstances also make it very difficult for a beginner to enter into the competitive arena. However, with a little luck and a lot of perseverance, bargains can still be found.

Among the more aggressive rivals on the playing field are collectors who seek wind-up tin toys which often have celluloid components; animal collectors with an emphasis on cats, dogs, and horses; toy dish collectors who especially seek miniature examples of food items; doll and character figures collectors and collectors with a particular interest in holiday themes.

This section will focus on the wide array of celluloid toys that fall into animal, character, and novelty categories. While a few of the items featured are fashioned from tube or die cut celluloid, the majority of articles featured here were made by the blow molding process. A simple explanation of this technique provides a better understanding of how these items were assembled.

The Blow-Molding Process

The blow-molding process consists of three steps. First, two halves of a metal mold are coated with soapy water or glycerin, then a thin sheet of celluloid is placed on each side. Next, the mold is clamped shut and steam or heated air is forced between the celluloid sheets, softening the material and causing it to conform to the mold. Finally, the hot mold is immersed in cold water, then opened, and the hollow celluloid object removed.

During the blow-molding process, the application of heat and pressure forces the two pieces of celluloid sheet to expand into the extreme recesses of the mold cavity. A joining seam, or

NPCM.

This early blow molding machine was designed by Charles Burroughs for the manufacture of hollow celluloid objects.

The items shown here are mold making tools. This set of punches would have been used to impress intricate feather markings onto the interior surface of a metal bird mold.

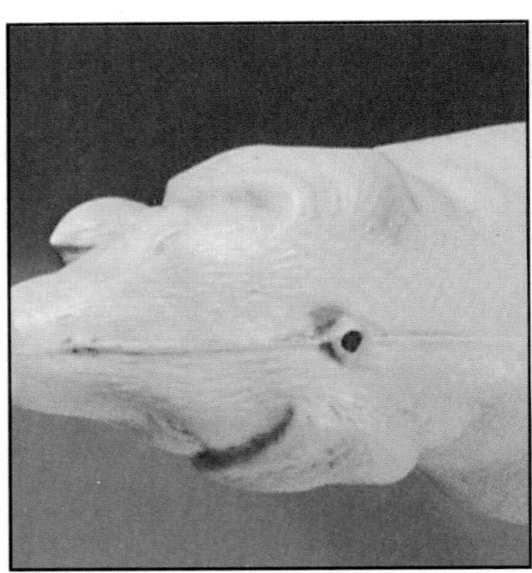

On occasion, an obvious hole, the place at which the forced air was blown in during the molding process, can be found, as seen on the back of this Viscoloid pig.

mating line, forms in the article as the two halves are molded together.

When the blow-molding process was completed and the hollow article removed from the mold, a thin, ragged edge of excess celluloid, called flash, remained on the mating line. It was necessary to trim away this extra material, by hand, with a sharp blade. It was a time consuming, tedious task that required patience and coordination.

Frequently, members of the producing community were hired by the fabricating company to carry out this task on a piecework basis. Untrimmed, blow-molded articles were brought into private homes, and whole families were put to work cleaning the unsightly edges where the seams were joined.

In Leominster where the Viscoloid Company manufactured blow-molded celluloid toys, animals, and novelties, people who did this type of homework called the process of trimming "tickling."

The great variety of articles produced by the Viscoloid Company made them a leader in the manufacture of blow-molded toys and holiday novelties. Their animal figures, both wild and domestic, set the standard for the industry. So popular were Viscoloid articles, at one time the company employed 350 workers in toy production alone. The most notable of toy designers for the company was Paul Kramme, a German born artist who went to work for Viscolid in 1914.

Kramme, born on Jan. 26, 1868 in Bielfeld, Germany, was educated in the local school system and went on to receive his formal art education in Karlsruhe, where he majored in sculpture. He came to America in 1903 to work on the St. Louis Exposition. Later he was commissioned to design stained glass windows in Cincinnati. He moved to Meriden, Connecticut, and worked as a free lance artist on several design projects for International Silver Co., eventually moving on to Brooklyn, New York, where he worked as a designer for various companies. At the age of 46, Paul Kramme came to the Leominster area with his wife Lena and their three daughters. He began work at the Viscoloid Co. designing toys, among them animals, dolls, and holiday novelties. Kramme's St. Nicholas figures, molded in graduated sizes, have a definite German influence and are highly collectible.

Other German designers were also hired by Viscoloid to make the molds and dies for celluloid articles. Among them were Paul Holzhauer, G.Kolb, E. Hechtler, Mr. Sielike and John Schultess and son, who were chemists at the plant.

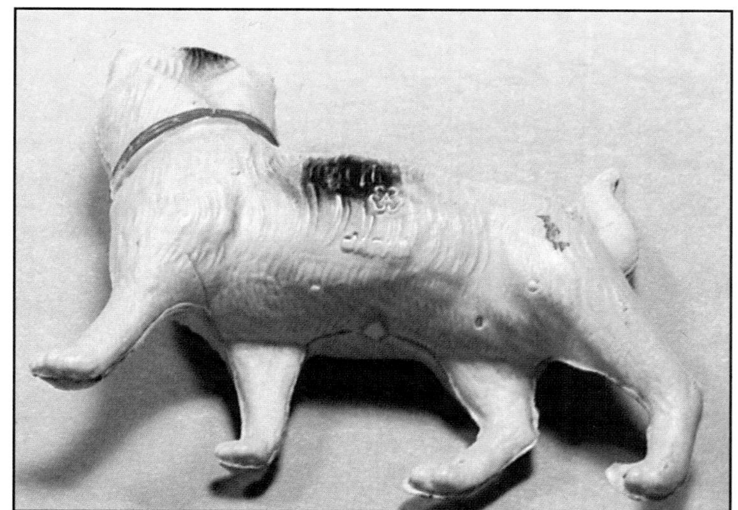

Usually the "blow hole" was sealed up, as seen on the underside (looks like a navel) of this circa 1950 Japanese cat, manufactured by Sekiguchi Co. Ltd. in Tokyo. Note the scalloped three-petal flower logo above the word "Japan" on the cat's side.

After the trimming or "tickling" of the excess material, the product was finally ready to be decorated. This amusing cat is an unpainted salesman sample; note the product number written in black on the base. Accent colors would have been spray painted onto the article through fitted stencils, or masks, while intricate detail work, like the eyes and mouth, would have been hand painted.

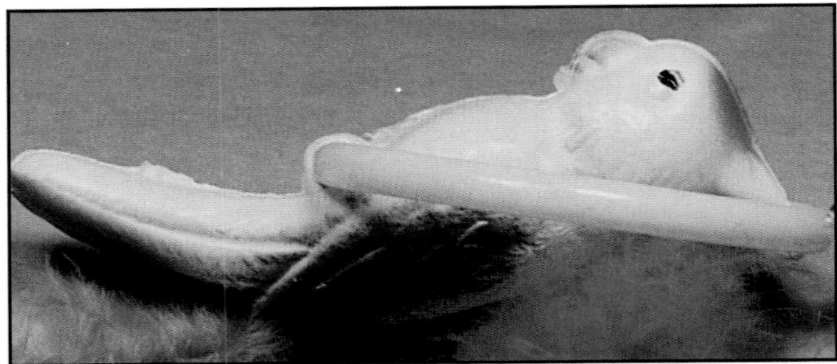

The rough appearance of the belly seam on this toy indicates that little attention was given to detail and finish work. None of the excess celluloid has been "tickled" or trimmed from the mating line near the beak, talon, and underside of the tail feathers. While the toy itself is unmarked, the box which accompanied it was labeled "Made in Occupied Japan."

This elephant appears to be made from brown celluloid with a painted red and cream blanket, but the opposite is true. It is molded from cream colored celluloid, then spray painted brown with red detailing. Viscoloid/USA trademark.

Trademarks and Logos

Several different trademarks were used by Viscoloid Company (see the Mark Identification section of this book). Company logos can usually be found appearing on the underside of the animal or in another inconspicuous location.

The serious collector will carry a magnifying glass and carefully scan for the identifying logo, but be aware that trademarks cannot always be found; sometimes the soft celluloid blurred the mold mark before the piece was thoroughly set.

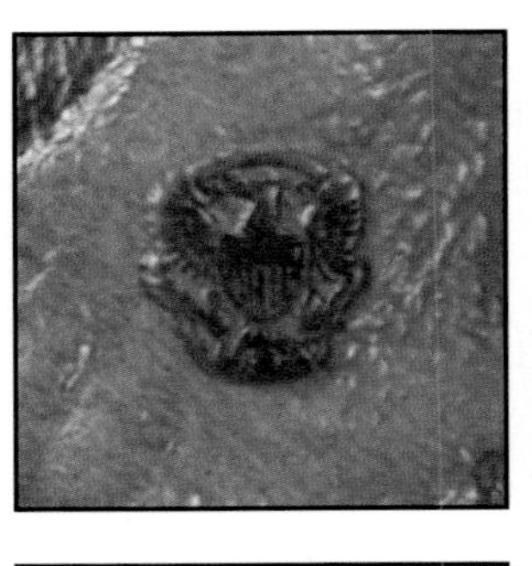

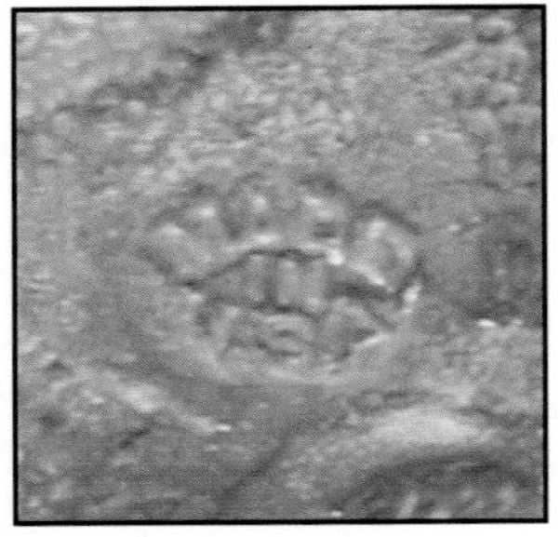

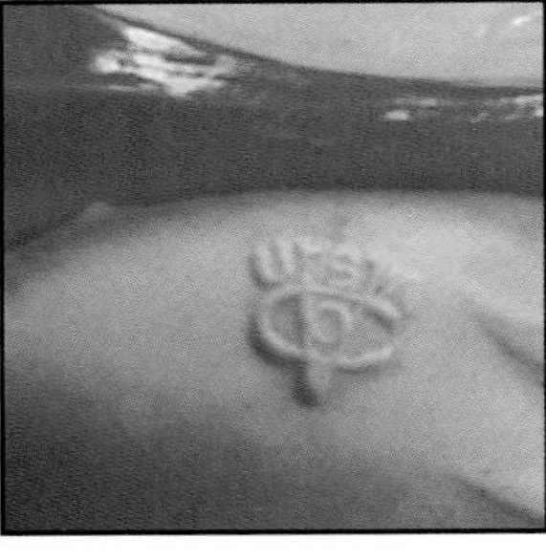

Shielded eagle w/USA; oval Made in USA; intertwined initials VCO w/USA; circled intertwined initials w/USA.

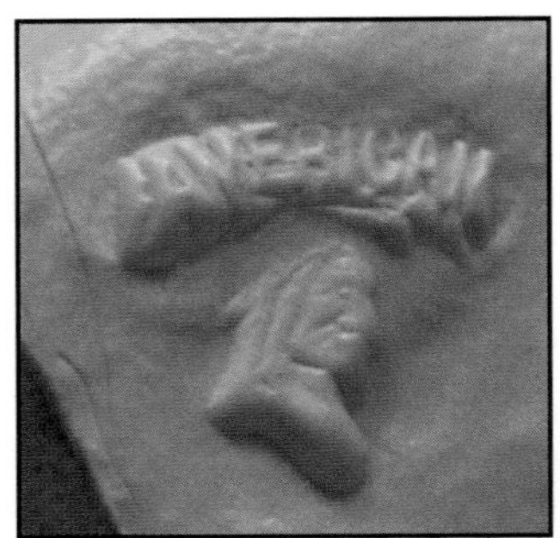

Several other firms also manufactured blow-molded celluloid toys. In America, Louis Sametz of New York manufactured dolls and other articles between the years 1918 and 1924. Sametz's blow-molded animals, marked with the Indian head logo, are the most elusive of American made celluloid toys.

Petitcollin, established in 1914 in Paris, Etain, and Lilas France is well known for its dolls. Although rare, Petitcollin blow-molded figures were also made. Only one example, bearing the Petitcollin eagle head and France logo, is featured in this book, a realistic figure of a giraffe.

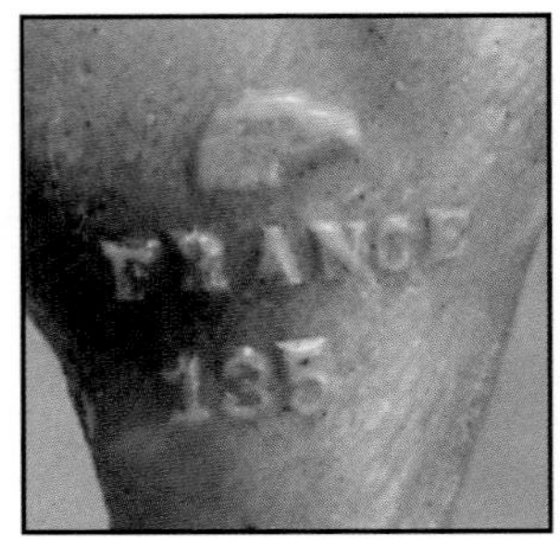

Dr. Paul Hunaeus of Hanover, near Linden, Germany founded a celluloid factory in 1890 to manufacture dolls. An intertwined PH diamond trademark was registered in 1901 and can be seen on several toy animals represented in the wild animal and bird sections. PH toys usually exhibit exceptional craftsmanship and are highly prized. In 1930 the Hunaeus Factory merged with Rheininisch Gummi-und Celluloid-Fabrik.

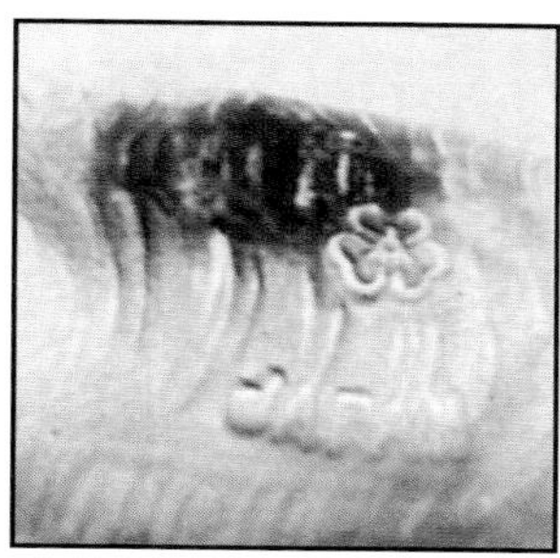

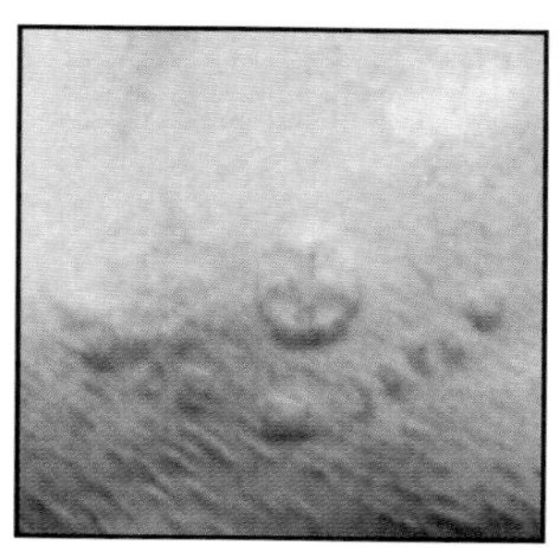

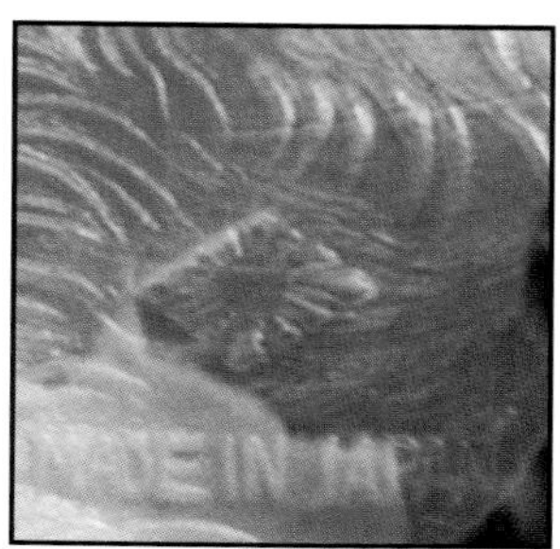

Among the Japanese firms that mass marketed blow-molded toy animals beginning in the 1920s, several have been identified. Known trademarks found on animals, birds, and fish are from Genroku Sagawa, Sekiguchi Co. Ltd.; Royal Co.Ltd.; Ando Togoro Workshop and Tsutsunaka Celluloid Co.

Animals

Domestic Animals

The camel is a large domesticated beast that has served man for over 5,000 years. It is able to carry heavy loads over long stretches of barren land and is invaluable to man for trade, transportation, food, and clothing. African and Arabian camels are called Dromedary and are easily recognized by the large hump on their back. The Central Asian species has two humps and is the bactrain camel. The celluloid interpretations of this interesting animal usually portray the single hump Dromedary, but on occasion a double hump bactrain camel can be found.

Cats have been kept as beloved pets since the days of ancient Egypt and today are the most common of house animals. Over the years cat figurines have grown in popularity, making this subject a favorite among collectors. It should be noted that very few celluloid examples were manufactured; in the many years of collecting, these felines are the only ones ever seen by both authors.

The small examples illustrated here are all nicely detailed, note the middle animal is molded in colored celluloid and features a two hump bactrain camel while the two Dromedary are done in cream colored celluloid and have painted highlights. From left: 2¼" x 1⅝" tall, Dromedary, cream celluloid w/light brownish gray highlights, Made In USA, $15.00. 2¼" x 1⅞" tall, peach double hump bactrain camel, "Made in Japan" on underside, $15.00. 2" x 1¾" Dromedary w/light brown and textured surface, unmarked, $12.00 – $15.00.

3¼" long x 2 " tall Viscoloid Dromedary; the variegated swirled example is the only one ever seen by the authors. The example with ribbon also rattles. Both nicely detailed and colorful; marked VCO/USA. $18.00 – $22.00.

The Japanese example shown here is nicely detailed. Note tail and neck position. 3¼" x 2" cream colored bactrain camel w/brown highlighting; Made in Occupied Japan. $25.00.

The two Dromedary shown here look almost identical, but upon close observation, various small differences are evident: the wave of the hair on the neck, facial structure, details on feet. Both stand 4" wide x 4¾" tall, but the bright orange camel is trademarked with the Dupont oval, while the pink and white example is marked Made in Japan, $35.00 – $40.00 each.

Both the peach and cream colored cats were manufactured by Sekiguchi Kako Co. Ltd. in Tokyo, Japan, during the late 1940s and early 1950s. They measure 3" long x 2¼" tall and both feature black spots, pink bows, ears, and mouth; floral trademark, JAPAN and Made in Occupied Japan $25.00 – $30.00 each.

This playful looking kitty seems ready to pounce upon something, most likely because a small hollow opening between the front paws indicates that another object was attached to it at one time, (perhaps a mouse or ball of yarn). Nevertheless, the cat is nicely detailed with a real bell attached to its blue collar. 2¾" long x 3"; JAPAN, \$45.00 – \$50.00

This beautifully executed Viscoloid cat is 5¼" long x 2¾" tall. It is blow-molded in cream colored celluloid and decorated with peach and black highlighting. The fine detailing, especially evident in the ribbon with bell around its neck, make this a highly desirable item. Made In USA mark on the underside \$55.00 – \$65.00 rare.

Viscoloid Co. also produced celluloid cows in lying positions, although they are quite rare. Collectors who are able to add such examples to their collections should consider themselves fortunate because few were manufactured. 3¼" lying cow, cream and black or tan and black, intertwined VCO/USA, \$45.00+. 2¼" lying calf, tan, cream and black, intertwined VCO/USA, \$45.00+.

Realistic looking Viscoloid cows were made in a variety of different sizes ranging from 2" to 7" long. The examples shown here reflect the assortment of color and size. 7" gray cow, as shown above; marked w/eagle, \$50.00 - \$55.00. 5" cream cow w/gray highlights; marked w/eagle, \$25.00 – \$30.00. 4¼" cream and gray cow; marked w/circle VCO over USA, \$15.00 – \$25.00. 3¼" brown cow; marked w/circle VCO, \$10.00 – \$15.00. 2⅛" cream cow w/pink highlights; marked Made In USA, \$8.00 – \$10.00. 2" brown and cream cow; unmarked, \$5.00 – \$8.00.

Observe the realistic detailing in the design of these animals; slight protrusions on the udders, intricate overall surface hair, precise bone and muscle mass and defined facial structure. This type of precision quality is what made Viscoloid products so successful. 7" cream cow w/orange and black highlights, hand painted facial features; marked w/eagle, \$50.00 – \$55.00; 4" cream and orange cow; intertwined VCO/USA, \$15.00 – \$25.00; 2⅛" cow, Made in USA. \$8.00 – \$12.00.

This is the largest standing cow figure that Viscoloid produced. It measures 7" long and is molded in light gray celluloid with dark gray highlighting; hand painted details include the facial features, hooves, and horns. What is highly unusual about the example shown here is the anatomically correct udder; rather than being a part of the mold design, tiny pieces of celluloid rod were cut into equal lengths and cemented to the underside. Because there is no molded detailing in the protrusions, the effect is somewhat crude in contrast to the excellent workmanship reflected in the molded surface. Eagle and shield. \$55.00.

The popularity of toy dogs during the early part of the twentieth century is clearly reflected in the variety of celluloid breeds available to today's collector. Both realistic and novelty dogs were manufactured in a range of colors, styles, and sizes by Viscoloid Co. and several Japanese firms.

Because toy dogs were so popular, today's collectors benefit greatly from the mass production of yesteryear. A plentiful supply is still available, and a nice assortment can easily be assembled into an impressive collection.

4" Airedale, anatomically correct male; pink celluloid w/orange highlights; trademark, intertwined VCO/USA. \$25.00 – \$30.00.

6" wide, 4" tall Airedale, white w/black highlights, red collar; trademark, Crossed circle and JAPAN/ designed by Ando Togoro. $35.00 – $40.00.

3" wide, 2" tall Airedale, white with pink and dark purple highlights, and hand painted collar. Plaster filled, nice detailing; trademark, Made In Japan w/unidentified semicircle.

These three bulldogs are unusual because the colored celluloid is semi-transparent. All are 4" long and have the intertwined VCO/USA logo on the underside. $25.00 – $30.00 each. Brown w/silver collar; green w/red rhinestone eyes; orange w/green rhinestone eyes.

The largest bulldog made by Viscoloid is 4¾" long and 2" high with a spiked neck collar. Color and painted highlights may vary, but this example is blow molded in cream colored celluloid with black highlights; Intertwined VCO/USA. $25.00 – $30.00.

It is not known which country produced the first bulldogs, but the Japanese industry had a reputation for imitation. This 3¾" long cream colored bulldog is so similar to the Viscoloid examples it could easily be attributed to them; however it bears a Japanese trademark. The blue collar and belly band with a "Y" represents the mascot for YALE University, therefore it is a collectible of greater significance. SK in diamond Made In Japan, attributed to Genroku Sagawa of Tokyo. $25.00 – $30.00.

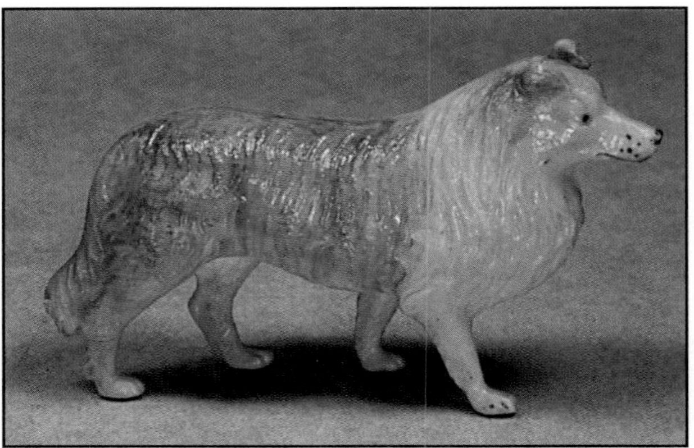

This beautifully molded collie dog is the only known example of the breed executed in celluloid. Blow molded in a shiny cream color w/amber highlighting and hand painted facial features, the dog's most intriguing aspects are its carefully formed ears and snout. 3¼" long, "Noris" trademark (Unidentified but possibly of English origin), rare. $65.00+.

Another unusual dog figure is this 3" tall, sitting German shepherd of Japanese origin. The detailing is so precise on this white plaster-filled example that even the teeth can be seen inside the open mouth. The ears were molded separately and attached to the top of the head. Unidentified trademark, " M inside C", Made In JAPAN, uncommon. $55.00+.

To date, only one size Viscoloid hound has been found, a 5¾" long example w/outstretched tail. This cream colored dog is finely detailed and spray painted with gray/brown highlights; VCO in circle and USA. $30.00+.

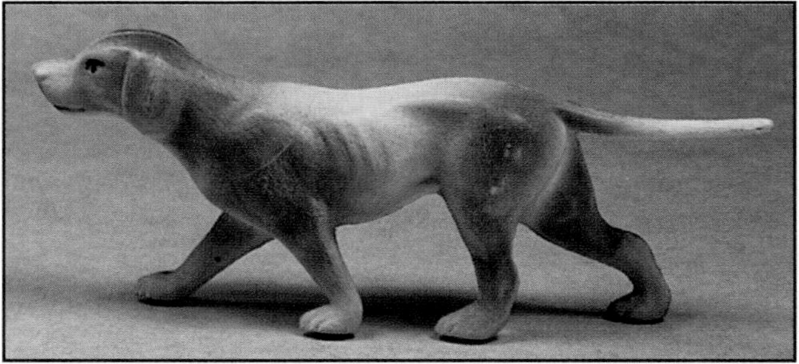

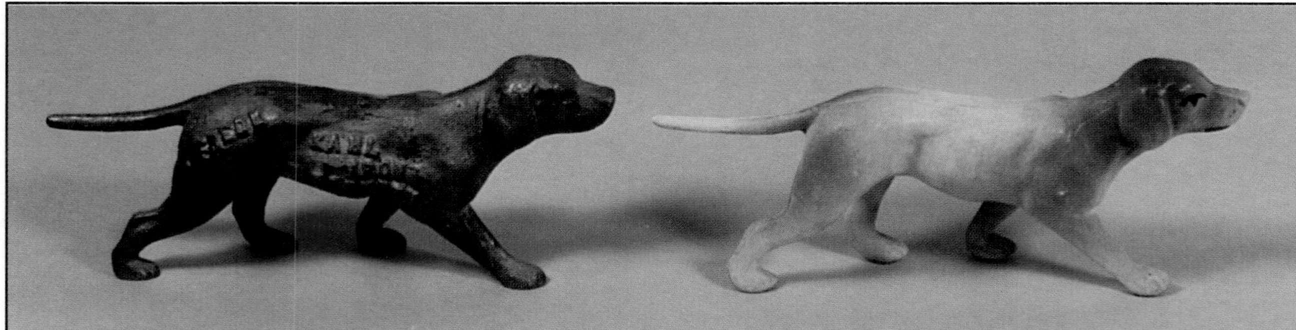

The celluloid hound and cast iron copy shown here are both 2⅜" tall and 5¾" long from nose tip to tail end. Both items bear the Viscoloid "VCO in Circle over USA" trademark, although it is somewhat blurred on the cast iron copy. It appears that the iron dog was made from a sand cast mold that was formed using a Viscoloid dog as the master. The iron copy also bears the additional words "Fredi" on the hip, and "Kahl Iron Foundry" on its side. While the location of the Kahl Iron Foundry is neither indicated on the cast iron copy nor known by either author at this time, it may be assumed that someone named "Fredi" was the craftsman behind this unusual item. It was discovered in New Hampshire at a flea market. Celluloid hound and cast iron copy, quite possibly a one-of-a-kind article. $65.00 set.

4" long hound dog, dark peach/pink celluloid w/brown collar and highlights; manufactured by Ando Togoro, crossed circle trademark and Made in Japan. $20.00 – $25.00.

The St. Bernard must have been a great seller for the Viscoloid company as it has been found in a progression of different sizes ranging from 1" high x 2¼" long, through 7" high x 10" long. All the examples shown here were manufactured in cream colored celluloid and have painted highlights ranging from black/grayish purple to peach/coral. Perhaps another reason for the mass production of this particular canine toy was due to the fact that Bernard Doyle, the president of Viscoloid, favored the St. Bernard above all other breeds for his own personal pet. 10", Made In USA, $45.00 – $50.00; 8", Made In USA. $30.00 – $35.00. 5", VCO in circle over USA. $20.00 – $25.00. 4¼", intertwined VCO/USA. $18.00 – $22.00. 3", intertwined VCO/USA. $15.00 – $20.00. 2¼", Made in USA. $10.00 – $15.00.

This absolutely striking "End Of Day" St. Bernard was actually made of mottled sheet fashioned from scrap celluloid and is the only known example in this color combination. The design is so similar to the Viscoloid dogs shown previously that it could easily be attributed to the company; however upon close observation, a starburst in diamond/ Made In Japan mark can be located on the underside near the rear leg. Manufactured by Tsutsunaka Celluloid Co. Ltd., Sunloid, in Osaka, Japan. 6¼" multicolored End of Day St. Bernard. Very rare. $65.00 – $75.00.

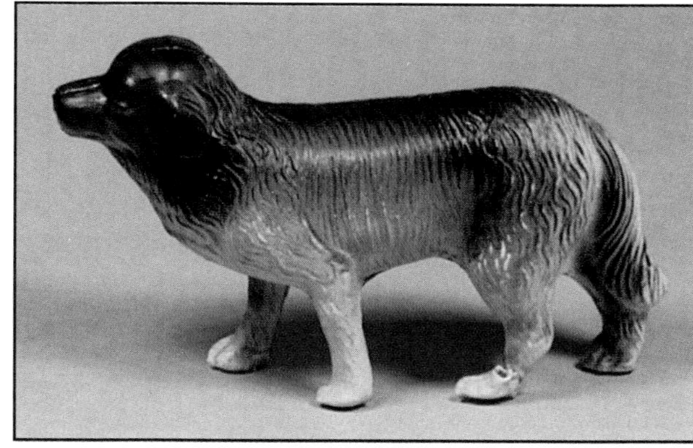

This nicely detailed 4" long x 3" high Newfoundland is molded in white celluloid, then spray painted with black. the proper coloration for the breed. Manufactured by Ando Togoro of Tokyo, it is marked with the crossed circle logo and Made in Japan. $25.00.

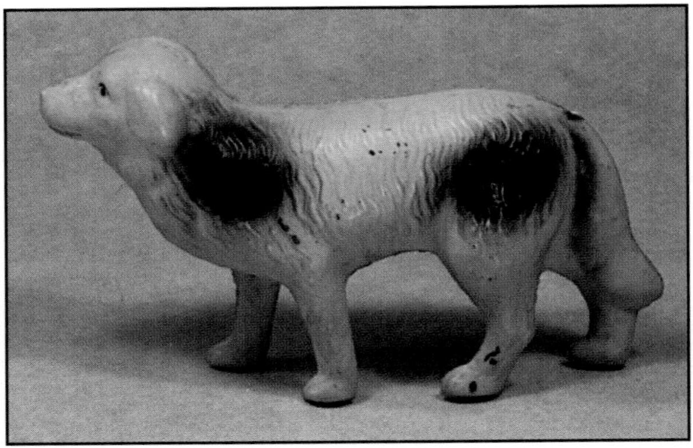

Bearing similar shape and dimensions but poorly detailed, this 4¾" cream colored Newfoundland could have been modeled after the one shown previously. Splattered paint and sloppy highlights leave this dog with much to be desired. Trademarked w/unidentified lantern symbol and Japan. $15.00 – $20.00.

President FDR's dog, Falla, inspired a trend for the Scottie dogs. It has been established as a popular collectible since the 1930s. Viscoloid Scotties were made in one known size and two colors, black and cream, the lighter having various hues of highlighting ranging from brown to orange. In nature, Scottie dogs are either black or dark gray. 4" black male Scottie and 4" cream, male Scottie w/gray highlights; both trademarked w/intertwined VCO/USA. $20.00 – $25.00.

The Japanese Scotch terriers shown in this illustration are nicely detailed with rhinestone eyes. Their upright tails appear to have been separately formed, then applied to the blow-molded body. Both were manufactured by Royal Plastics Ltd. in Osaka and measure 5¾" long x 4" tall. Molded from cream colored celluloid with orange/pink or purple/gray highlighting, both are marked with the fleur-de-lis, Royal Japan logo. $25.00+.

No animal has served man better than the donkey. Domesticated thousands of years ago, it has been used both for transportation and hauling heavy loads in desert and mountain areas. The donkey is sure footed and slow, qualities often attributed to stubbornness, yet well suited for domestic service. Related to the horse, yet possessing three primary differences: stature, ear shape, and a tuft of hair at the end of the tail, donkeys are usually dark gray or grayish brown.

Two realistic donkeys by Viscoloid show precise coloring and fine detailing in stature, ears, and tail. Large 7" long donkey, dark gray with VCO/USA mark $40.00 – $50.00. Small dark gray donkey, 2" long w/Made in USA mark. $15.00 – $20.00.

Standing 1" tall and measuring 2⅛" long, this tiny dark brown donkey bears an intertwined PH trademark. Designed by Dr. Paul Hunaeus and manufactured in Linden, Germany during the early part of the twentieth century, it is a rarity. $45.00+.

Measuring 3" long x 2¼" tall, this whimsical Japanese donkey has long brightly colored pink ears. Blow molded in cream celluloid with grayish/pink highlights, it bears a floral trademark. Manufactured by Sekiguchi Co. Ltd, Tokyo. $15.00 – $20.00.

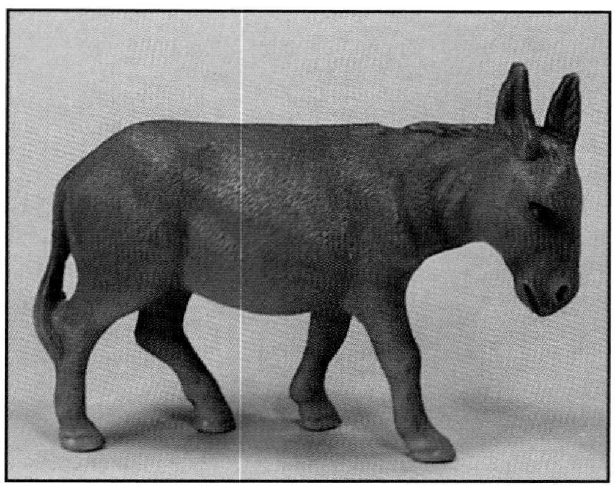

A medium sized 3⅝" long dark brown donkey with the intertwined VCO/USA trademark has a slightly different tail position that its larger counterpart. $25.00 – $30.00.

The realistically molded examples shown in this illustration are also Viscoloid, however they are done in cream celluloid with coral and gray highlighting. The tails and ears are in slightly different positions than the previous ones. Detailing is exceptional however. Medium, 3⅝" long, $25.00 - $30.00. Small, 2" long, $20.00 – $25.00.

The burro is a smaller breed of donkey primarily used as a pack animal in places like Mexico and the American Southwest. The two Viscoloid burros illustrated here measure 4" long x 3¾" tall. They have nicely detailed facial features with charming expressions. The distinctly molded harnesses, saddles, and blankets are carefully painted which adds to their appeal; cream w/tan, greenish blue, and yellow peach highlights and grayish brown w/red and orange highlights. Intertwined VCO/USA. $35.00 – $45.00 each.

3" x 2¾" cream colored burro w/gray highlights, molded saddle, and blanket in pink, untickled ears; manufactured by Sekiguchi Co. Ltd. and bearing a floral trademark, JAPAN. $25.00+.

Horses are among the most popular of collectible celluloid animals. They were mass produced in a variety of colors and sizes by the Viscoloid Company and are readily available for today's collector. Prized among domestic animals for its strength and beauty, the horse has aided man in transportation, farming, and sporting for thousands of years. The range of sizes, colors, and decorative treatments by Viscoloid can be seen in these photographs, which illustrate seven different sizes. Each animal is distinctly unique due to the varying sizes and color combinations. The smallest stands 1⅞" x 2¼", and the largest is 7¾" x 9¼".

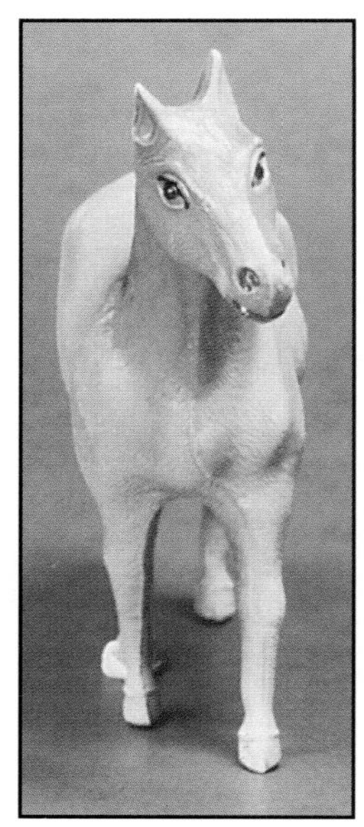

Of the several dozen Viscoloid horses observed by both authors, this is the only example with the head turning to the left. This brings up a question of whether there was a distinct mold for this example or if there is yet another explanation? Perhaps while the celluloid was still pliable and the horse was being removed from the blow molding press, the machine operator accidentally bumped it or purposely twisted it to change the head position. It is an interesting variation that should be noted by the serious collector of celluloid horses.

9¼" x 7¾", Made In USA. $45.00 - $50.00; 7" x 5¾", Made In USA or VCO-USA. $35.00 – $40.00; 6" x 4", oval Dupont. $25.00 – $30.00; 4¾" x 3¾", eagle and shield. $18.00 – $25.00; 4" x 3", Made In USA. $12.00 – $18.00; 3¼" x 2", circle/VCO. $8.00 – $12.00; 2¼" x 2", Made In USA. $5.00 – $10.00.

These four Viscoloid horses are all decorated with the bright peach/pink and gray/purple highlighting over cream colored celluloid. Priced by size according to listing at bottom of facing page.

The two brown horses are shown here for comparison purposes. Note the distinct lines and clear anatomical detailing on the Viscoloid example on the left. The unmarked copy on the right shows a lack of definition with softer curving lines, especially in the areas around the head and legs. It is assumed that the copy is of Japanese origin.

Viscoloid manufactured horses in a progression of sizes, ranging from 9¼" x7¾" to 2¼" x 2". Detailing is exceptional on all examples.

This 5¼" x 3¾" horse was blow molded in cream celluloid, then spray painted with deep pink/purple and black highlights at the Ando Togoro workshop in Tokyo. It displays less detailing than its American-made counterparts, with a slightly fuller body, rounder face, and oval-shaped ears. Crossed circle, JAPAN. $15.00 – $18.00.

This 4" wide white celluloid horse was blow molded by Sekiguchi Co. Ltd. in Tokyo and exhibits pink highlighting, a molded blanket, saddle and harness in shades of red, purple, and gold. It has nice mold detailing, but the application of painted decorations is sloppy and detracts from its value. Floral trademark w/JAPAN. $20.00 – $25.00.

3¾" wide cream horse with pink highlights and 3" wide orange horse, both having hand painted facial features and hooves. The larger example features nice detailing, although not as precise as American design; it is valued at $25.00 because of the detailed mark indicating the location of origin, an intertwined "TS" and words "Made in Tokyo Japan." The smaller orange horse lacks definition and highlighting but still possesses a realistic resemblance. It is trademarked with the unidentified round lantern logo and JAPAN. $6.00 – $8.00.

Goats have been favored domestic animals for thousands of years, prized for their milk, meat, skin, and hair. In nature, goats come in a variety of colors including black, brown, yellow, and pure white. The goat has a short tail and a beard under its chin. Its horns are flat and twist backward at the tips.

Today pigs are regarded as a whimsical collectible, however during the time of production, these animals were probably made to compliment toy sets of barnyard livestock. The Viscoloid company produced solid colored pigs in two sizes: 4" long x 2¼" high and 2¼" high and 1" long. Because the pig was a less desired children's toy, fewer were made, and therefore they are somewhat illusive. Collectors who are able to find any such examples should consider themselves fortunate.

All three goats shown in this illustration are white with grayish brown highlighting. True to form, the goats have short tails, a beard, and flattened curvy horns. The intertwined VCO/USA logo appears on the underside of all three goats. 3¾", $25.00; 2¾", $20.00; 2⅛", $15.00.

The large and small pigs shown here are both molded in pinkish/peach celluloid and have hand painted facial features but no highlighting. Both are trademarked with Viscoloid's Made In USA logo. $30.00 – $35.00+ each.

This illustration covers the extent of Viscoloid's color schemes for their toy pigs. A multicolored example would be of more desirability than a solid colored specimen; however, because these were one of the lesser produced toys, any example would be of value to a domestic animal collection. Small, $25.00 - $30.00; large, $35.00 – $45.00.

This nicely formed pig is molded in creamy yellow celluloid with soft hues of brownish purple and peach sprayed on to carefully highlight the ears, back, and neck area. This careful attention to detail increases the value. Also notice the small variation in molding marks along the tail, hooves, and ears. $45.00.

Wild Animals

The producers of celluloid wild animals attempted to make their toys as realistic as possible. While whimsical interpretations do exist, their origins are mainly Japanese. The majority of "wild animals" in the market therefore, seem to be somewhat lifelike. The most prolific manufacturer of realistic articles was the Viscoloid Company; however Louis Sametz, Paul Hunaeus, Petitcollin, and a host of Japanese companies also produced a variety of interesting examples. Bears and elephants seem to be the most commonly found animals and are the least expensive. Some animals, such as the beautifully sculpted boar and giraffe are very uncommon which accounts for the greater value ascribed to them.

The bears produced by the Viscoloid Company all reflect a similar style with those of darker color representing grizzly bears and the white variety being polar bears. They were made in a progression of sizes ranging from 1⅛" high and 2¼" long to the largest at 5" tall and 9" long. The two extremes in size are both marked Made in USA, while medium-sized bears are marked USA/VCO.

The bison is a large American animal belonging to the cattle family. At times it has been referred to as a buffalo, however this term is incorrect as true buffalo only live in Asia and Africa. Bison have a large hump on the shoulders and the head hangs low. The horns are curved and hollow, a thick shaggy mane covers the head and neck, and under its chin the bison has a beard.

This photograph shows the extremes in size for both varieties of bear. 9¾" x 5" and 2¼" x 1⅛" brown grizzlies; Made In USA. Large, $40.00 – $50.00; small, $8.00 – $10.00.

This photograph shows style differences between American and Japanese manufacturers. Left: 4¾" Viscoloid, intertwined VCO/USA mark; right: 4½" pink bear w/black highlights. Ando Togoro, crossed circle/Japan. $15.00 – $20.00 each. Photo may not reflect the undercolors of these items as they are heavily painted.

Graduated sizes of bears. Prices range from $8.00 to $25.00. 5" x 2" Viscoloid bear, cream celluloid with peach and black highlighting, $18.00 – $25.00; 3¾" x 2", gray bear, circle VCO/USA, $15.00 – $20.00; 3¼" x 1¼", white or tan bear, circle VCO/USA, $10.00 – $15.00; 3¼" x 1¼", brown bear, intertwined VCO/USA, $12.00 – $15.00; 2¼" x 1¼", polar or colored, Made in USA, $8.00 – $10.00.

Viscoloid produced bison in four different sizes ranging from 2" long to 5" long. 5" x 3" black bison w/painted white eyes and horns, $20.00 – $25.00; 4" x 2", dark brown bison, VCO w/circle and USA, $18.00 – $22.00; 3¼" x 2", dark brown bison, eagle w/shield, $15.00 – $20.00; 2" x 1", cream bison w/brown highlights, Made in USA, $12.00 – $18.00.

Note the detailing on these two tan Viscoloid bison. 3¼" x 2" examples. $18.00 – 20.00.

The caribou is a member of the deer family which lives in northern climates. It is the only type of deer in which both the male and female of the species have antlers. When caribou are domesticated, they are called reindeer and can be ridden or hitched to a sled; the females are often kept in herds and milked like cows.

Elephants have captured the imaginations of young and old alike ever since P.T. Barnum introduced his famous circus attraction "Jumbo" to the world in the early twentieth century. In nature, the elephant is the strongest and largest of animals. They are exceptionally intelligent, and while some female elephants have been trained to serve mankind, most live in the wild. The two species, African and Indian, are both gray colored; however, occasionally a grayish white elephant is born. Many people believe that these "white" elephants bring good luck. Another popular belief is that the upraised trunk is symbolic of good luck.

The large caribou in this photo is 7¼" long and 6¼" tall and made by Viscoloid. It was blow molded in light cream celluloid and spray painted with light brown accents. The antlers were molded separately and then cemented to the head. Domesticated caribou are known as reindeer and for this reason are sought after by collectors of Christmas-related novelties. $35.00. The smaller example measures 5¼" long x 4⅝" tall and is a product of the Ando Togoro workshop in Tokyo. Excellently detailed, it is blow-molded in cream celluloid with deep reddish brown highlighting and red rhinestone eyes. $30.00+.

This beautifully molded caribou is also a product of the Togoro workshop, but it differs from the previous example. The ears protrude from the head and the antlers are much thinner and upright. It also bears the crossed circle and Japan logo. $30.00+.

These 4¼" x 4" long Viscoloid caribou are molded in cream colored celluloid and highlighted with a variety of light peach, brown, and black paints. The antlers are molded separately and cemented in place. $15.00 each.

The wild boar is an ancestor of the domestic pig. It is a fierce animal with razor sharp tusks and a body covered with very short hair called bristles. The gray celluloid boar toy shown here is the only known example. It is 3¼" long and 2" tall. It bears the PH mark of Dr. Paul Hunaeus. Rare. $85.00+.

The largest and the smallest of Viscoloid elephants in white celluloid with brownish gray highlighting. Note the missing tusks on the largest example. Small, $8.00 – $10.00; large, $30.00 – $45.00.

4" x 2¾" tan elephant w/red and cream floral blanket, intertwined VCO/USA, $15.00 – $25.00. 3" x 2¼" white elephant w/red and cream floral blanket; Made In USA, $12.00 – $15.00.

The Viscoloid elephants, illustrated here in progression of size, were molded in dark gray celluloid except for the smallest example, which is highlighted with gray paint. The three largest elephants have separately applied tusks. 7¾" x 5¾", eagle and shield trademark. $45.00+. 6¾" x 4¾", Made In USA. $30.00 – $35.00. 5" x 3¼", eagle and shield. $25.00 – $30.00. 3¼" x 2¼", eagle and shield. $15.00 – $20.00. 2¾" x 1⅞", Made In USA. $12.00 – $18.00. 2⅜" x 1", VCO/USA. $6.00 – $10.00. The elephant that has a metal ring in its back would have been worn at a GOP rally dangling from a pin.

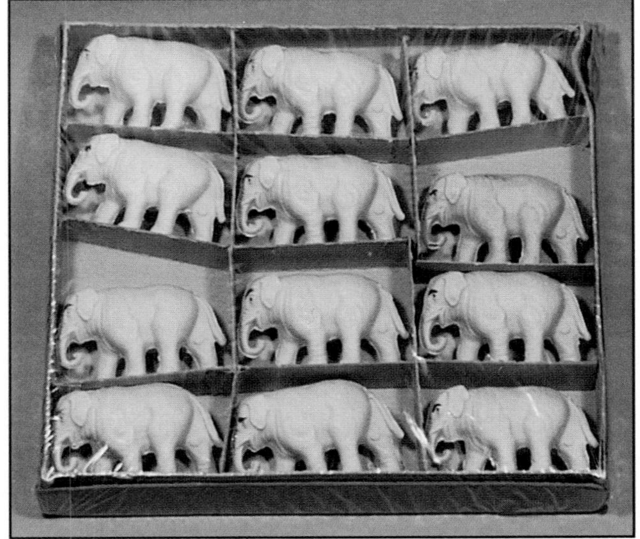

This box of 12 white elephants is sure to bring good luck. Manufactured by Viscoloid Co. The entire unopened package was quite a find. Separately these 2¼" long x 1" tall elephants would sell for about $5.00 each. Made in USA trademark.

Collector Caution
Collectors of toys should be aware that both cellulose nitrate and cellulose acetate were used in the production of blow-molded figural toys.

3" x 2¼" white and gray elephant w/purple ears, Made In Occupied Japan. $18.00 – $25.00.

3¼" x 2" cream colored elephant figurine with raised trunk for good luck, plaster filled, intertwined VCO/USA, $10.00 – $15.00. 3¼" x 2" cream elephant w/raised trunk, lacking detail, trademark, "JAPAN w N-Circle." $5.00 – $8.00.

The African giraffe is the tallest of land animals. It can grow to heights of 18 feet, getting its height from a very long neck and legs. The coat of the giraffe has a random patchwork pattern in nature, quite unlike the spots portrayed on these two celluloid toys. Only two giraffe toys have been seen by the authors, and neither is of American origin.

6" tall x 5" wide, this yellow celluloid giraffe features a realistically shaped head and randomly painted brown spots, trademark can be seen on the rear hind leg, eagle head, FRANCE, 135 - Petitcollin, rare. $85.00+.

3¾" x 3" tan giraffe w/black spots; marked Made In Occupied Japan. $35.00+.

Of all the wild African and Asian cats, the leopard is the most ferocious and savage fighter. In nature it is a beautiful animal with a soft yellowish fur coat with clusters of black spots called rosettes.

The lion is one of the largest members of the cat family and because of its cleverness, terrifying roar, and royal looking appearance, it is called "King of the Beasts." In nature the lion has a tawny yellowish brown coat with red or black highlights.

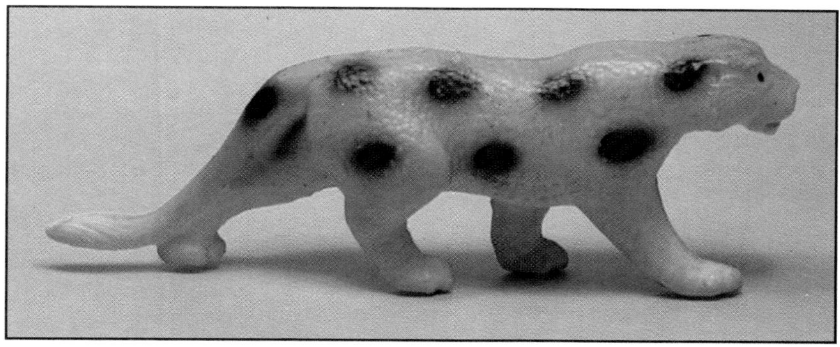

To date, this 4" cream colored celluloid leopard w/orange highlights and black spots is the only known example, Made in Occupied Japan. $35.00 – $40.00.

5" cream lion w/pink highlights, oval DuPont (after 1925). $25.00 – $30.00.

4¼" cream lion w/tan and purple highlights; Made In Occupied Japan. $25.00 – $30.00.

3¾" tan lion w/brown highlights, TS - Made In Japan. $18.00 – $22.00. 3¾" pink lion; Ando Togoro crossed circle, Japan. $18.00 – $25.00. 3" cream and brown lion, unmarked. $15.00.

In nature, gorillas are either black or gray, but in Occupied Japan, they were manufactured of light purple celluloid and sprayed with brownish purple paint.

Hippos are native to Africa. They spend most of their time in rivers, streams, and lakes. (Hippopotamus actually means river horse.) Hippos are large, shy animals that are naturally dark gray in color.

The rhinoceros is a fierce, clumsy beast that has a hide one-half to three-quarters of an inch thick. There are several species within the rhinoceros family: the white rhino, the largest; the Indian rhino that has one horn and a hide that is folded into plates that look like armor; and the African black rhino with two horns on its snout.

This opened mouth ape is the only known example. 3" purple gorilla w/open red mouth, Made In Occupied Japan. $35.00+.

3" peach hippo w/open mouth, trademark TS, Made In Tokyo Japan. $20.00 – $25.00; 2" peach hippo w/purple highlights, open mouth, unmarked. $15.00 – $20.00.

3¼" white and purple hippo w/open mouth, Made In Occupied Japan. $25.00 – $35.00.

5" gray African rhinoceros, spray painted over cream celluloid, great hand painted detail, PH, Paul Hunaeus trademark. $55.00+.

These two Indian rhinos are fabulously designed with accurate, realistic features and coloring. The larger example is marked PH and was designed by Dr. Paul Hunaeus. The smaller example was manufactured by Viscoloid and bears the Made in USA trademark. $65.00+ each.

4" rhino of cream colored celluloid, detailed nicely, smiling, with floppy almond-shaped ears, Made in Occupied Japan. $25.00 – $35.00. This smaller rhino has detailing similar to the smaller example in the previous photo.

The type of animal portrayed here is a species of wild sheep known as the bighorn, native to the American Rocky Mountains. They have long curving horns that form almost a complete circle. The male is called a ram and the female, a ewe. Viscoloid Company made sheep in a series of graduated sizes. All were produced in cream colored celluloid with dark gray highlights and marked with the Made in USA logo.

This 4" Viscoloid sheep is molded in cream celluloid and highlighted in light brown. An intertwined VCO/USA logo is barely visible, hidden among the wavy lines of the sheep's coat. $20.00.

Bighorn sheep in progression of sizes: 8", $35.00 $40.00; 5¾", $25.00 – $30.00; 4", $15.00 – $20.00. 3¼", $10.00 – $15.00; 2¼" and 2", $5.00 – $10.00.

This smiling bighorn sheep is the only item bearing the Sametz logo. It measures 4¼" long and is blow molded of shiny cream colored celluloid, Indian Head/AMERICAN, Louis Sametz trademark. $45.00+.

The squirrel is a small animal belonging to the rodent family. The species shown here is one that lives in trees, thriving on nuts. The squirrel has a big bushy tail that helps it keep its balance.

The largest and fiercest of all wild cats is the tiger, which inhabits Asia and India, but not Africa. Several species exist including the Indian or Bengal tiger which is a tannish yellow with long narrow black stripes, the Caucasian tiger which has brown stripes, and the Siberian tiger which is the largest and has a lighter shaded soft, thick coat.

The variety of realistic bird species represented in blow-molded celluloid toys range from domestic barnyard chickens and ducks to the exotic parrot and ostrich. Because so many manufacturers, Viscoloid as well as German and Japanese, produced birds, the species, color combinations, and sizes seem almost endless. A varied flock can be easily assembled as bird forms are plentiful and reasonably priced.

2⅞" brown squirrel w/nut, Made In USA, uncommon. $40.00+.

These two Viscoloid tigers could represent the Bengal and Caucasian tigers. 4" orange tiger w/black stripes, Made In USA. $25.00 – $30.00. 2" cream tiger w/orange highlights and black stripes, Made In USA. $18.00 – $22.00.

This photograph illustrates the sizes and colors Viscoloid used in producing their tigers. Large, $25.00 – $30.00; small, $18.00 – $22.00.

4¼" white tiger w/tan highlights and black stripes, open mouth, Made in Occupied Japan. $25.00 – $35.00.

4" tan tiger w/orange highlights and hand painted black stripes and facial details, unidentified trademark of two stick men, Made in Japan. $25.00 – $30.00.

3" gray or tan hens w/black tail feathers, hand painted beaks and combs, made in USA. $18.00 – $20.00 each.

2¾" hen w/metal feet, double diamond w/Made in Japan. $12.00 – $15.00.

3" standing hen in grass, cream or tan with gray highlights, yellow feet and red combs, intertwined VCO/USA. $20.00 – $25.00.
3" standing brown rooster in grass, black highlights and hand painted details, intertwined VCO/USA. $20.00 – $25.00.

⅞" yellow chick, black eyes and beak, unmarked. $3.00 – $5.00.

Two Viscoloid ducks molded of cream colored celluloid and painted with a striking variety of deep teal, blue, pink, and purple tones. 3¼" cream duck w/teal blue and gray highlights, Made in USA, $12.00 – $15.00. 2" cream duck w/teal blue and gray highlights, eagle and shield, $8.00 – $12.00.

2¼" standing chicken and duck, cream colored celluloid w/hand painted eyes and bills, original paper label and Made In Japan. $10.00 – $12.00 each.

4" yellow, green and orange duck, PH (Paul Hunaeus) w/25¢ on bottom, $20.00 – $25.00, and 1¾" yellow duck w/green and orange highlights, PH (Paul Hunaeus), $12.00 – $15.00.

Three wonderfully molded Viscoloid ducks in graduated sizes 3¼", 2", and 1". All blow molded in cream colored celluloid with gray, black, and teal blue spray painted highlights and hand applied facial features. All bear a VCO/ USA trademark. Small, $5.00 – $8.00; medium, $8.00 – $12.00; large, $12.00 – $15.00.

The tiniest of blow-molded ducks are these examples, slightly longer than 1". They have "untickled" seams and sloppy painted details. 1¼" white duck w/hand painted green, red, gold, and black details, unmarked, $1.00 – $2.00 each.

The celluloid ducks featured in the next few photographs have a different, less realistic look to them. The molding isn't as detailed, resulting in a shiny painted celluloid surface. The examples shown here look as if they are swimming forward and preparing for take-off. 4" yellow ducks, shiny surface w/red and green highlights, intertwined VCO/USA, $15.00 – $22.00.

4" long shiny duck, unmarked example featuring style unlike the Viscoloid examples. Cream colored celluloid with light yellow and peach highlighting. $20.00.

This tiny 2" tall flamingo was probably used as an attachment to a souvenir key chain from Florida. It is the only celluloid pink flamingo ever seen by the authors. Marked JAPAN. $15.00+.

4" and 2¾" ducks, both large and small are blow molded in cream celluloid w/shiny colorful surface. All bear VCO/USA trademark. Large, $18.00 – $22.00; small, $10.00 – $15.00.

5" standing cream goose, weighted metal feet, various highlights ranging from gray to pink, blue, and yellow; intertwined VCO/USA. $35.00 – $40.00. 3¼" standing cream goose, pink highlights, metal feet, intertwined VCO/USA. $25.00 – $30.00.

4" cream swimming goose, peach details, intertwined VCO/USA. $18.00 – $22.00.

This wonderful standing pelican was manufactured by Viscoloid, the intertwined trademark just in front of the webbed foot. It stands 3" tall and is molded from shiny cream colored celluloid with light brown, green, and peach highlighting. The words "From Florida" can be seen on the neck, which indicates that this particular example was produced for the tourist trade. It is an uncommon bird. $45.00+.

4" white parrot w/bright pink, green, and yellow highlights, fine detailing, CT, Made In JAPAN. $15.00 – $20.00.

6⅜" long cream colored parakeet w/yellow and black highlighting. Marked Germany. $28.00 – $35.00.

This is the only known blow-molded ostrich figure. Measuring 3¼" tall, the standing cream bird has dark pink and blue highlights. Examples with peach, red, and purple highlights have also been seen, Made In Occupied Japan. $25.00 – $35.00.

3¼" balancing sparrow, yellow or teal, tail weighted, oval Made in USA trademark near talon. $10.00 – $12.00.

These two storks were probably used as decorations for a baby shower, as a number of examples were recently seen at a Pennsylvania flea market with the explanation that they had served as table favors for a 1950s celebration. 6¾" standing white stork w/pink legs and beak and black tail feathers, Sekiguchi Co. Ltd, Tokyo "Flower, Made in Japan" trademark, $30.00 – $35.00. 2⅞" standing stork w/pink legs and beak, unmarked. $15.00+.

4" yellow sparrows w/red highlighting. Round head example marked Made in Japan and flatter head marked Made in USA. $15.00 each.

In addition to ducks, swans were the most prolific among the celluloid birds. The variety of styles, colors, and manufacturers represented here are all different and just a sample of what is available on the market today. A nicely molded celluloid toy by German manufacturer Paul Hunaeus. 4" cream swan, orange beak and feet, fine details, PH. $25.00+.

5¼" white swan w/green and red highlights, unmarked, $20.00. 4¼" white swan w/yellow beak and feet, unmarked. $15.00.

4" long mother swan w/her 2¼" babies. Note the precision and consistency in molding and decorating of these cream colored w/black highlight Viscoloid birds. Large, $20.00; small, $8.00 – $10.00.

The slightly elongated wings and necks on these Viscoloid swans are different than most of the others shown here. 3¼" cream swan w/pink, green, and blue highlights, Made In USA. $15.00 and 2¼" cream swan w/pink, green, and blue highlights, Made In USA. $8.00 – $10.00.

These two swans are unusual as they have separately molded wings that have been attached to the body. The smaller one measures 1" and the larger is 3¼" long. Both feature gray highlights, maroon beak and feet; Made In USA on the smaller example. Small, $16.00 – $20.00; large, $18.00 - $22.00.

5" cream swan w/black and pink highlights, smooth shiny surface, intertwined VCO/USA. $18.00 – $25.00. 4 " cream swan w/red beak and feet, shiny smooth surface, intertwined VCO/USA. $15.00 – $18.00.

The pheasant is another bird not often found in celluloid. These two examples are real beauties and collectors able to add them to their collections are fortunate indeed. 2" standing pheasant in grass, cream w/hand painted details, unmarked. $30.00+. 2" standing pheasant, yellow and teal w/orange metal feet, the source of the "Noris" script trademark is still unidentified. $35.00+.

Water Creatures

This section will feature the creatures that thrive in and around fresh and salt water. Because blow molded toys were hollow, and celluloid was water resistant, such creatures were favorite bathtub toys of little children. Note the assortment of Viscoloid articles listed in the B. Shackman and Co. Advertisement from 1924.

4" cream turkey w/pink and blue highlights, green base, unmarked. $35.00 – $40.00.

5¾" tan alligator w/light brown highlighting, facing left, intertwined VCO/USA. $20.00 – $25.00. 4¼" tan alligator, facing forward, intertwined VCO/USA. $15.00 – $20.00.

Two Viscoloid alligators molded in cream colored celluloid and painted with either green or tan highlighting. Both measure 3" and each bears the intertwined VCO/USA logo. $10.00 – $15.00 each.

This standing alligator made by Viscoloid is a ferocious looking beast with its open mouth full of sharp looking teeth. The base, which is fashioned to look like swamp grass, reveals the intertwined VCO/USA mark at the base of the curled tail. This item is marked on the other side, "Souvenir of Florida." An uncommon example. $45.00+.

6¾" large yellow fish w/red, green, and blue highlights, molded scales, Made In USA visible on tail fin. $18.00 – $20.00.

B. SHACKMAN & CO. "THE NAME IS IMPORTANT"

906 BROADWAY At 20th Street, NEW YORK

CELLULOID NOVELTIES (CONTINUED)

CELLULOID FLOATING TOYS

37/579

37/867

50/539

		DOZEN
31/858	Celluloid Battleship. 4 inches	$0.42
50/399	Colored Celluloid Duck. 2 inches	.20
75/943	Colored Celluloid Swan. 2½ inches. (Heavier celluloid)	.35
50/400	Black and White Celluloid Swan. 3¼ inches	.35
37/567	Colored Celluloid Duck. 3¼ inches	.75
50/539	Colored Celluloid Duck. 4¾ inches	.70
37/577	Brown Alligator. 4 inches	.80
37/579	Trick Seal juggling colored ball. 3¾ inches	.65
37/825	Red Lobster. 3¼ inches	.78
37/580	Fish, assorted colors. 3½ inches	.75
37/821	Tiny Green Frog. 1¾ inches	.42
37/822	Green Frog. 3 inches	.78
611	Green Frog. 4½ inches	1.80
37/823	Brown Turtle. 1¾ inches	.42
37/824	Brown Turtle. 3 inches	.78
37/868	Ducks and Swans, assorted. Beautiful bright colors. 3½ inches	.80
37/869	Ducks and Swans, assorted. Beautiful bright colors. 4¼ inches	1.20
37/871	Bright Red Fish. 7½ inches	1.85
37/872	Duck. Nicely colored, and well made of heavy celluloid. 4½ inches	1.85
37/873	Swan. Nicely colored, and well made of heavy celluloid. 4½ inches	1.85
37/865	Duck. Nicely colored, and well made of heavy celluloid. 5½ inches	3.75
37/598	Swan. Nicely colored, and well made of heavy celluloid. 7 inches	8.00
37/884	Swan. Nicely colored and well made of heavy celluloid. 9 inches	14.00

FLOATING SETS

		DOZEN
37/867	Floating Toys. Ducks, Swans, Fish, Frogs and Turtles. Each about 1½ inches. Packed 12 assorted in a box	$0.33
609	Floating Toys. Ducks, Swans, Fish, Frogs. Each about 2 inches. Packed 12, assorted, in a box	.45
610	Floating Toys. Ducks, Swans, Fish, Frogs. Each about 2¾ inches. Packed 12, assorted, in a box	.85
37/832	Floating Toys. Ducks, Swans, Fish, Frogs, Turtles. Each about 4 inches. Packed 12, assorted, in a box	1.10
37/833	Floating Set. Ducks, Swans and Fish. Each about 5 inches. Packed 6, assorted, in a box	1.60
32/390	Floating Duck Set, consisting of two 2-inch celluloid ducks and four 1½-inch ducks and 7-inch net mounted on lithographed card	1.70
		DOZEN SETS
721	Magnet Floating Set, consisting of 14 pieces. Fish, swans, ducks, frogs, seals, turtle, and a metal magnet. Each piece about 2 inches. Each article has a piece of steel in its mouth, and is attracted by the magnet when floating	$9.00

101

No catalogs or printed illustrations of the full range of Viscoloid's toy animals have been discovered, however this 1924 advertisement from B. Shackman and Co. of New York lists a wide range of Celluloid Floating Animals, most of which are featured in the birds and fish shown in this book.

58 PLAYTHINGS *June, 1928*

It's easy to sell Viscoloid Toys!

Appearance—More lifelike than toys of other material, and decorated to suit those who seek dainty colored toys, or those with modernistic taste.

Packing—Attractive and colorful cartons—Viscoloid display fixtures—Cellophane Envelopes—are used in the packing of various numbers. Retail values are 10c. to 25c. each toy. Many other playthings to retail profitably from 5c. to $1.00 and up.

Variety—An advantageous method of featuring the Viscoloid line is in the form of toy assortments, comprising two, three or four dozen. Each assortment contains a large variety of floaters, animals, and other amusing playthings.

50c. and $1.00 gift packages, containing several toys, are attracting marked attention.

If your jobber does not carry the Viscoloid line of toys, write us for information today.

DU PONT VISCOLOID COMPANY

Pacific Novelty Division DU PONT 330 Fifth Ave., Cor. 33rd St., N. Y. Cit

One good turn deserves another—please mention PLAYTHINGS.

1924 advertisement from B. Shackman and Co. of New York.

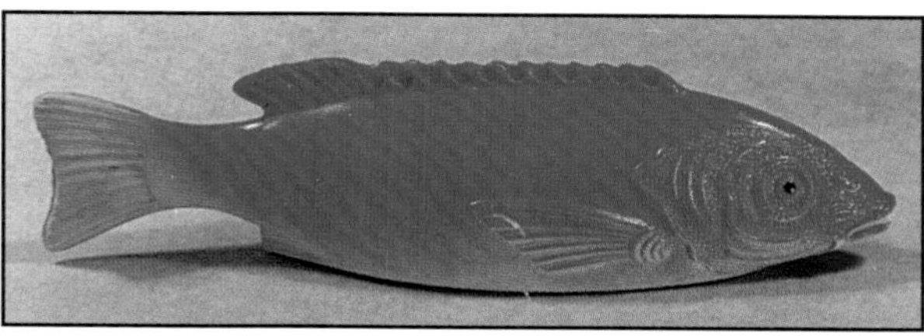

6¾" large white and red fish, smooth surface, molded fin, less common than the other style, intertwined VCO/USA. $18.00 – $22.00.

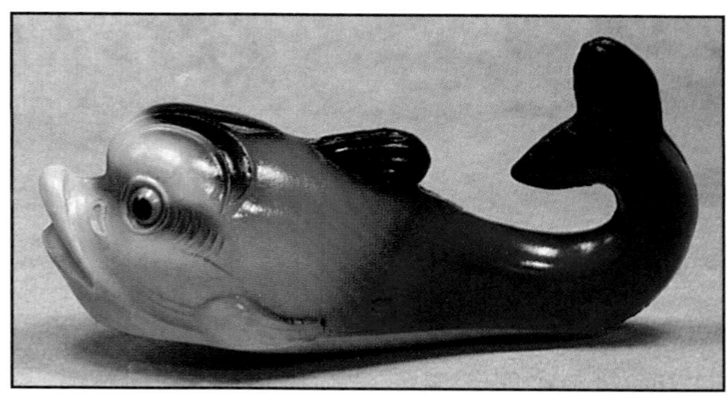

4½" whimsical fish with a curled-up tail, smooth molded details in cream celluloid highlighted with green, red, and yellow, intertwined VCO/USA. Uncommon. $25.00.

This 4½" Viscoloid fish is molded in pale cream celluloid, then highlighted in pink and blue. It is marked with Made in USA on the tail fin. $18.00 – $22.00.

These two Viscoloid fish are of the same design, measuring 5¾" long with curved tail fin and elongated features. The first is molded in cream colored celluloid and features an array of colorful painted highlights while the second is molded in yellow celluloid w/red highlights. Both are marked with the Made In USA logo visible on the tail. $15.00 each.

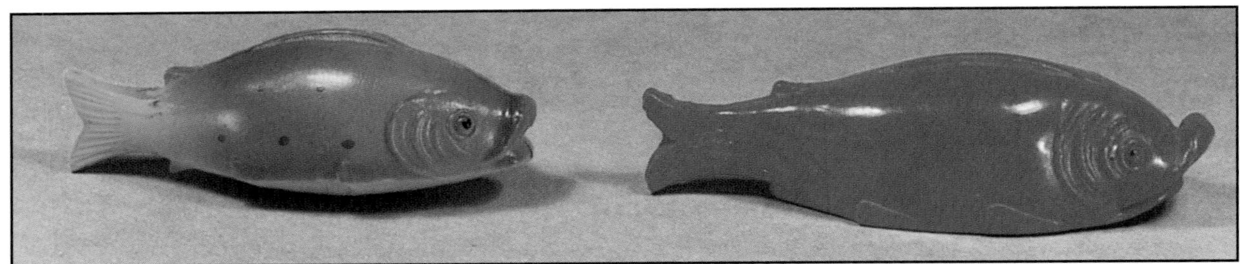

These two smooth shiny fish are both Viscoloid with the smaller example being more uncommon. 3" medium yellow fish, smooth sides, brown highlights w/red spots, molded fins and gills, Made In USA. $12.00 - $18.00. 4" medium red fish, smooth sides, molded fins and gills, Made In USA. $12.00 – $15.00.

These four fish all are shaped like the popular goldfish, although none are orangish colored like the ones found in nature. Nevertheless, they are all nicely molded with intricate detailing. 3" medium reddish-pink fish, molded scales and fins, nicely detailed, Japan. $12.00 – $16.00. 2⅞" small yellow fish w/brown highlights, molded scales, intertwined VCO/Circle. $8.00 – $10.00. 2⅜" small reddish-pink fish, molded scales, fat tail, no trademark. $6.00 – $8.00. 1⅛" small pinkish-peach fish w/yellow, molded scales, JAPAN. $2.00 – $4.00.

Three small Viscoloid fish fashioned after the largest example shown at the beginning of the section. Note the differences in coloring. 1⅞" small red fish, yellow fish, or yellow fish w/red highlights, molded scales, Made In USA. $5.00 each.

This realistic looking whale is the only known example of its kind. It bears no trademark, but the intricate detailing suggests that it may be of German origin. It measures 5¼" long and is blow molded of tan celluloid with brown and pink highlighting, unmarked. Rare. $75.00+.

Frogs are amphibians and were manufactured in celluloid and marketed as floating bathtub toys. Most are shaped as if they are in the sitting position, but on occasion a "swimming" frog with all four legs extended can be found.

The lobster is a member of the crustacean family and is prized as a food delicacy the world over. The shell of a live lobster is dark mottled green and the underside is yellow. It only turns bright red when it has been cooked. The lobster is a decapoda, meaning it has 10 legs. A smaller celluloid example by Viscoloid is known to exist. Size has no bearing on price because these crustaceans are so uncommon, they will command a high price, just like in nature!

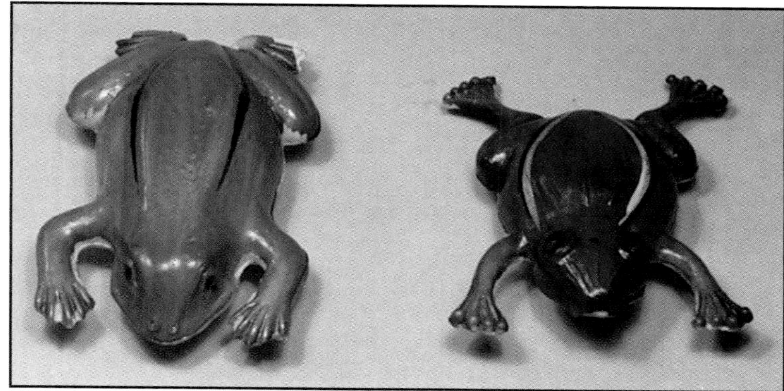

Two frogs with dark green paint and striped backs, the smaller example has extended legs. Both are two-toned with light belly and painted backs. ¾" white celluloid w/painted green top, black stripes, MS in diamond, Made in Japan. $8.00 – $12.00. 2 " yellow celluloid w/green painted top, black and white stripes. Unmarked. $8.00 – $10.00.

The six Viscoloid frogs shown in this illustration are molded from a variety of yellow and green celluloid with green painted highlights. They are made in a progression of five sizes and molded detailing include striped backs, spots, and eyes. 3⅞" yellow celluloid w/green highlights and black spots; VCO in circle over USA. $16.00 – $20.00; 2¾" bright yellow frog w/green highlights and black spots, intertwined VCO/USA. $12.00 – $18.00; 2⅜" green painted frogs, molded from white, yellow, or green celluloid, spotted backs, Made in USA inside circle or VCO in circle over USA. $12.00 – $16.00. 2" yellow frog w/green highlighting, circle VCO trademark. $12.00. 1¼" green or yellow frogs, stripe on back, intertwined VCO/USA. $10.00 – $12.00.

3¼" shiny red lobster, smooth surface, intertwined VCO/USA, rare. $65.00+. 2¾" red and gray lobster, molded rough surface, unmarked. $50.00+.

Turtles are egg laying, air breathing reptiles that have a backbone and a protective shell. Since all the turtles illustrated here have feet instead of flippers, none can be considered marine species, but rather land turtles or fresh water turtles.

The unusual design of this Japanese made turtle is intentional. Never before seen, it is fashioned from peach colored celluloid with brown highlighting on the top and a red painted bottom. The trademark, currently unidentified, is an MS inside diamond and Japan on the underside. $15.00 – $18.00.

Medium and small turtles; the larger is Japanese made, but with a different head position and shell design than previous examples. The smaller turtle is Viscoloid and quite similar to the Oriental style. 4" cream turtle w/pearlescent pink highlights, Made In Japan. $25.00 – $30.00. 2" cream turtle w/pink and dark brown highlights, Made In USA. $15.00 – $20.00.

These large and medium cream colored examples are intricately detailed on the shell and leathery hide of the turtle. Spray painted highlights are ever so pale. 5" cream turtle w/green and orange highlights, Made In Japan. $35.00+. 4" cream turtle w/orange highlights, CC in diamond, Made In Japan. $30.00+.

The turtles illustrated here are two-tone, blow molded from a translucent imitation tortoise shell sheet on the top of the mold and an opaque yellow sheet celluloid on the bottom. The result is a realistic interpretation of the Hawksbill turtle that featured a "mottled and blond" shell used extensively in the manufacture of natural plastic combs during the mid to late nineteenth century. Brown translucent top and opaque yellow bottom, all Viscoloid trademarks. Large, 3", $25.00+; medium, 2", $15.00+; small, 1¾" and 1¼", $10.00 – $12.00.

3½"; 3"; 2½" cream turtles w/gray or brown highlights, Viscoloid trademarks, Made in USA, VCO in circle over USA, eagle and shield. Small, $8.00 – $12.00; medium, $15.00 – $18.00; large, $20.00 – $25.00.

In 1924, B. Shackman advertised 3¾" "trick seals juggling colored balls" for 65¢ per dozen. Today similar Viscoloid examples could sell for as much as $65.00 each if they are found in undamaged condition. Note the detailed front and back flippers. 4 " gray or brown seal w/red or green balancing ball, intertwined VCO/USA. $45.00+.

Animal Novelties

This section will focus on the use of celluloid animals, birds, and fish that were fashioned into useful novelties and children's playthings. Some of the items featured here combine comical or amusing animal shapes with pincushions, letter openers, tape measures, or other small utilitarian objects. Other animals, both whimsical and realistic images, were fashioned into entertaining toys for children; these include rattles, poseable figures, and motion toys.

The variety of celluloid animal novelties marketed during the first half of the twentieth century is quite extensive and in no way can be fully represented in this book; nevertheless, we are pleased to feature a sample of the forms that are currently available to the collectors of today.

Utilitarian novelties are those items which combine some form of animal image with an object of specific purpose; they were not necessarily designed for children as play things. The letter openers, bookmarks, memo pad, and pencil holder shown here fall into this catagory.

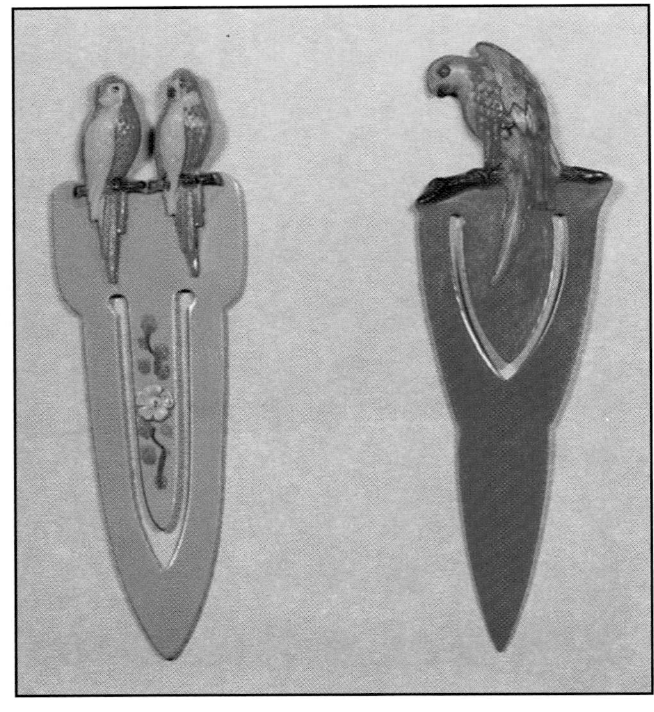

These two colorful red and blue bookmarks feature parrot and lovebird figures. The same type of image is seen on the bright green memo pad with celluloid cover. All items are attributed to the late 1920s, the time period when both parrots and bold colors were all the rage. $15.00 – $18.00 each.

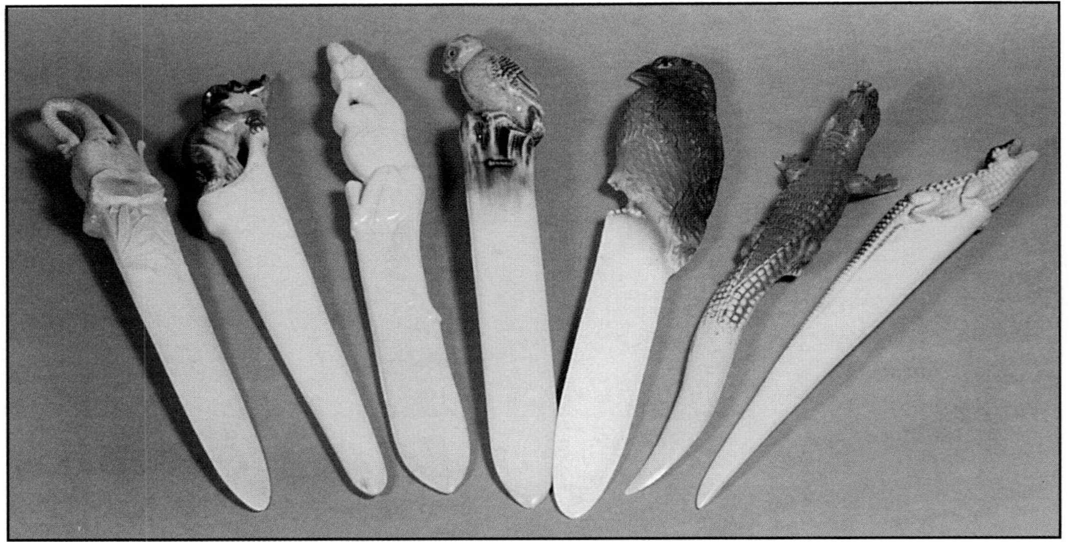

A collection of seven letter openers that feature a variety of bird and animal images. Each is molded in cream celluloid and highlighted with brown or gray paint, with the exception of the hound dog. Examples include two elephants, a hound, an owl, hawk, and two alligators. The owl is marked Germany while the alligator and elephant head are Viscoloid. 7¼" to 8¾" long, price ranges from $25.00 for common paper knives like the alligators and elephant head to $55.00 for the unusual, nicely molded bird items.

3¾" variegated green, black, red, and yellow balancing parrot, Made In USA, $18.00 - $20.00; 4" balancing sparrow, orange w/red highlights, OC trademark. $12.00 – $15.00.

6" light green balancing parrot with pinkish purple highlights, open beak for insert of a name card to use as a table setting novelty or a toy, intertwined VCO/USA. $28.00 – $35.00. 4" cream balancing parrot w/black details, excellently molded, German, PH trademark (Paul Hunaeus). $25.00+.

B. SHACKMAN & CO. "THE NAME IS IMPORTANT" **906 BROADWAY** At 20th Street, NEW YORK

CELLULOID NOVELTIES
(CONTINUED)

CELLULOID BIRDS

BALANCING BIRDS WITH SLITS IN BEAKS TO HOLD CARDS. PLACE CARD HOLDER AND NOVELTY. 1 DOZEN BIRDS IN EACH BOX, INCLUDING CARDS.

719 35/100 35/106

		GROSS
35/100	Yellow Bird. 3 inches....	$4.32
35/101	Pink Bird. 3 inches....	4.32
35/102	Blue Bird. 3 inches....	4.32
35/103	Green Bird 3 inches....	4.32
35/104	Red Bird. 3 inches	$4.32
35/105	White Bird. 3 inches......	4.32
35/106	Parrot, variegated colors..	4.32

		DOZEN
606	Imported Balancing Bird, carefully made and beautifully tinted in natural colors. 4½ inches	$0.85
32/392	Large Balancing Parrot, beautifully colored. No card holder. 5¾ inches	1.20
31/809	Tiny Parrot in variegated colors; on swing perch. 2 inches	.30
31/815	Parrot, 4 inches, in variegated colors. Balances on celluloid ring	.75

		DOZEN
48/444	Celluloid Basket, oval-shaped, 3 inches. Can be had in pink, white, yellow, red or green.	$0.60
48/440	Celluloid Umbrella. Comes in pink, blue, green, yellow, orange or red. Open Umbrella. 1¾ inches	.70
48/441	Celluloid Open Umbrella. Same colors as 48/440. 2½ inches	.85
35/578	Brown Celluloid Alligator with paper cutter tail. 7 inches	1.20
37/861	Brown Celluloid Football with ring for hanging. 2½ inches	.80
37/817	White Platter with fish and dressing. 3½ inches	1.10
713	Comic Celluloid Nude Baby Doll with black high hat. 2½ inches	.70
714	Comic Black Celluloid Nude Baby Doll with white high hat. 2½ inches....	.70
1400	Heart-shaped Mirror with red celluloid back. 2¼ inches	.75
1403	Oblong-shaped Mirror with white celluloid back and metal easel. 2¾ inches	.75
37/860	White Celluloid Comb in leatherette case. 5 inches	.80
37/856	Imitation Tortoise-shell Doll Spectacles, made of celluloid. 2½ inches......	.60
75/1323	Oblong White Celluloid Box with celluloid animal mounted on top, and a good quality celluloid thimble inside. 1¾ inches	2.25
75/1324	Horse with rider, mounted on white celluloid base which is studded with black-headed pins that can be removed. 2¼ inches	2.25
704	White Celluloid Goose with shaking head. 2¾ inches	.80
75/1413	Animal Mounted on white celluloid base. Comes assorted styles. Frogs, seals, swans, etc. 2 inches	.45

Balancing birds were not only popular as toys, but could also be made with a slit in the beak for use as place card holders at the table. They would perch precociously on the edge of a tumbler, holding the name card of the dinner guest in the beak.

Bright green celluloid covered memo pad features a molded parrot like those featured on the bookmarks on the previous page. $15.00

This 1924 Toy Fair advertisement shows a Viscoloid balancing cat that looks so similar to the Japanese example shown on facing page. It is not known where the idea for such a toy originated.

5" pink Viscoloid parrot w/blue and yellow highlights, perching on a light green pencil holder base, intertwined VCO/USA under tail feathers, Viscoloid. $50.00 – $60.00.

3" white parrot w/pink and blue highlights, applied feathers, balancing on ring attached to rubber suction cup, unmarked, original brown box lid, "Made In Occupied Japan." $10.00 – $12.00.

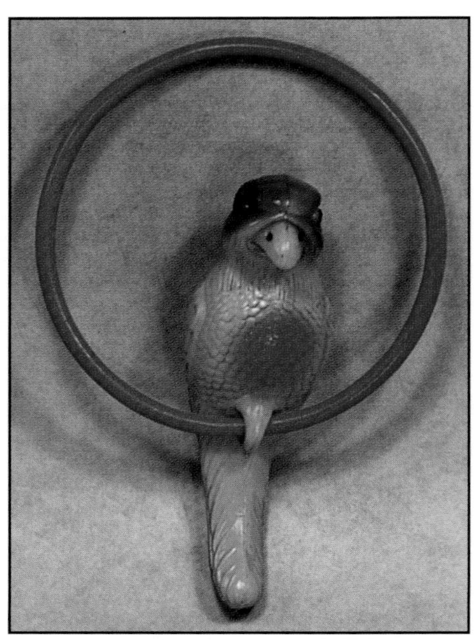

The balancing parrot shown here and the two pictured below were designed as rattles for children as well as whimsical toys or decorations. 4¼" parrot, yellow celluloid w/red and green highlights, balancing on red ring, intertwined VCO/USA trademark near talons. $45.00.

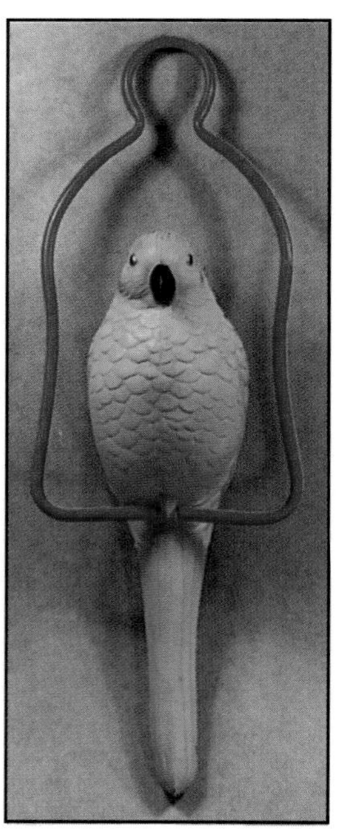

8¾" yellow parrot w/pink and gray highlights, balanced on bright red bell-shaped perch, intertwined VCO/USA. $45.00.

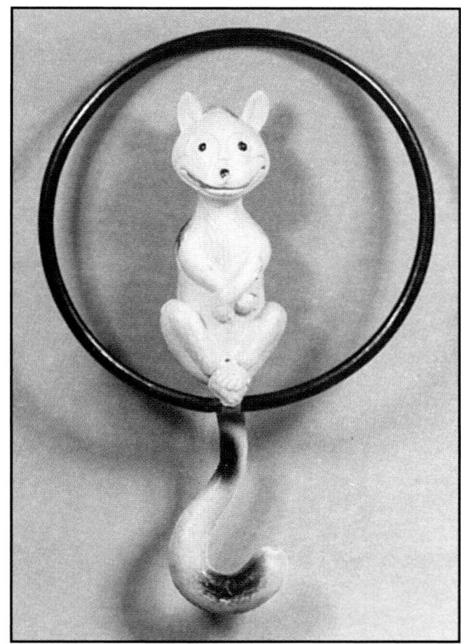

Both the cat and monkey are animal images not frequently seen in celluloid and therefore highly desirable. 5" grinning cat, white w/peach and black highlights, balancing on green ring, JAPAN, K in diamond trademark, F. Kanematsu and Co. $65.00+. 5" smiling monkey, red and yellow swirled celluloid, balancing on green ring, unmarked. $65.00+.

These two illustrations show novelties similar to roly polys but not quite falling into that category. Although this 3" tall novelty looks like a roly poly at first glance, it is stationary with a weighted base. The elephant with upraised trunk balances on a blue and white ball, no trademark. $25.00; 3" x 4" rooster and hen on rocking base; 2⅜" cream hen w/black tail and orange comb and 2⅞" tan rooster w/black tail and orange comb; birds marked with intertwined VCO/USA logo. $50.00 each.

Roly polys are eagerly sought after by collectors who focus primarily on this catagory. Because animal examples often fall into holiday themes they can also be considered cross-over collectibles. The roly polys shown here all feature realistic animal images.

1⅝" cream and gray mongoose, an unusual animal seen here with wonderfully detailed features. Designed and manufactured by Dr. Paul Hunaeus of Germany, intertwined PH trademark. $95.00 – $125.00.

Celluloid cats are one of the most elusive of animal figures. This wonderful 2" tall roly poly example with a hand painted pink coat and black tie is a rarity, unmarked. $75.00 – $100.00.

Two serious roly poly bulldogs. The largest balances on a green base and measures 3¼" tall; unmarked, $75.00 - $125.00. The smaller bulldog is decked out in a blue overcoat with pink trim and formal bow tie; 2" tall and marked with the Viscoloid intertwined VCO/USA logo. $75.00 – $100.00.

While these barnyard bird roly polys are more common than the previous animals, they are becoming increasingly difficult to find, which results in escalating prices. 2¾" rooster and 2" hen, both marked with the intertwined VCO/USA logo. $50.00+ each.

The turkey shown here is only the second realistic looking example known in celluloid. It measures 2" tall from the base up. Gray turkey w/black stripes and red comb, intertwined VCO/USA. $75.00+.

2½" monkey dressed as a bell hop, holding suitcases in both hands and glancing sideways, red hat and coat, blue pants, and black shoes; nicely detailed and balancing on pink roly poly base marked GERMANY in blue ink. $85.00+.

Another Viscoloid roly poly manufactured in cream colored celluloid and painted with primary colors. A 3¼" male chick in top hat and tails, nicely detailed. $85.00+.

This large Viscoloid duck is molded in bright yellow pyroxylin plastic, then spray painted with highlights in bright primary colors. Measuring 5" tall, she wears a detailed scarf and bonnet. VCO/USA in grass. $85.00+.

Two roly poly rabbits, one dressed as a jester and the other in formal top hat and tails. Teal blue and pink highlights on the jester and teal w/red highlights on the top hat bunny. These are frequently collected as holiday novelties for Easter. Because of that, the price is escalated. $75.00 – $110.00+ each.

3⅛" molded roly poly egg has a detailed mother hen with her chicks. Cream colored celluloid, with spray painted highlights of teal blue, green, and yellow. The eyes and red comb are hand painted. Marked VCO/USA. $125.00+.

While rattles are thought of mostly as items for babies, manufacturers of celluloid blow-molded toys often fashioned figural animal items with small pellets inside.

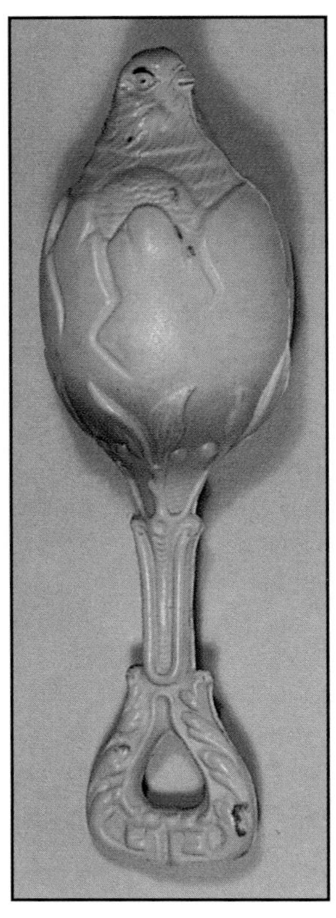

Wonderful Viscoloid figural rattle showing a realistic looking chick hatching from an egg has an ornately molded handle. Such intricate blow-molded toys are difficult to come by in such fine undamaged condition. $75.00+.

This realistic figure was fashioned into a rattle by the addition of small pellets inside. Even though this 2¾" swan with white w/blue highlights has pellets inside, it is still light enough to float. The unusually nice molding is attributed to the Ando Togoro workshop in Tokyo. Crossed circle w/Japan. $20.00 – $25.00.

A wonderfully unusual 4¼" tall nodding penguin, blow molded in white celluloid with black, pink, and blue highlights, circle in diamond trademark, Daihachi Kobayashi, Tokyo, Japan. $55.00 – $75.00.

Birds in shoes can also be considered Easter holiday novelties. Both molded in light cream colored celluloid with painted highlights. $55.00+ each.

Two 4" x 3¼" donkey nodders molded in cream celluloid w/black highlights; unmarked but nicely detailed, $35.00 – $50.00.

Motion Toys

There are several different kinds of toys within this category, but all have one thing in common: they move in some way. The type of motion any given toy makes can be directly related to its shape, as well as the assembly of the article. At times, a particular action is the result of a wind-up mechanism, as illustrated by the Japanese cat and dog. Other times movement is dependent upon interaction, as in the case of novelties like the rooster pull toy or the poseable Bonzo figure. Still other motion is contingent upon balance, such as toys with parts that bob up and down like nodders, or wobble back and forth like roly polys. Most frequently, these types of toys reflect a whimsical nature, even when combined with realistic animal interpretations.

When purchasing toys with wind-up mechanisms, be sure to examine them closely. As a collector of pyroxylin plastic, you may be tempted to purchase an item based solely on its particular design style or the quality of workmanship in the molded celluloid. However keep in mind that a toy in working order is of much more value than a broken toy. If it doesn't do what it is supposed to do, don't pay top dollar. Be sure that the wind-up key is included with the toy since they were frequently lost.

Colorful 5¾" standing elephant has movable arms and legs and also rattles. Molded in white celluloid w/red and orange highlights, unmarked. $45.00 – $65.00.

Viscoloid dog, 5" peach and cream, jointed Boston terrier in cream colored celluloid highlighted with glossy peach paint, intertwined VCO/USA. $45.00 – $50.00.

Bonzo, the English cartoon character, has closed eyes. His legs are strung together so he can be posed. VCO/USA trademark. $65.00.

This wonderful duck dressed in a teal police uniform features poseable jointed legs. Marked with VCO/USA logo, the same item has been reported in a green uniform. Unusual and nicely detailed. $75.00 – $125.00+.

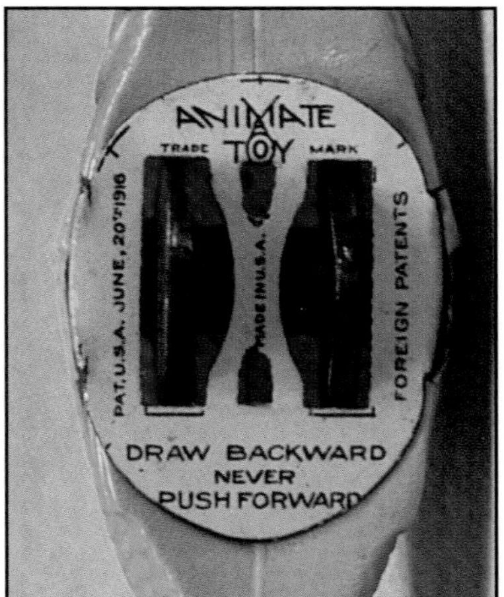

The Viscoloid fish illustrated here is molded of bright yellow celluloid and spray painted with red highlighting. It features the Made In USA logo, visible on tail fin. The bottom of this toy has a mechanism that is activated when the toy is drawn backwards. Marked "Animate Toy, Patent June 30, 1916." A nice example in excellent working condition! $75.00+.

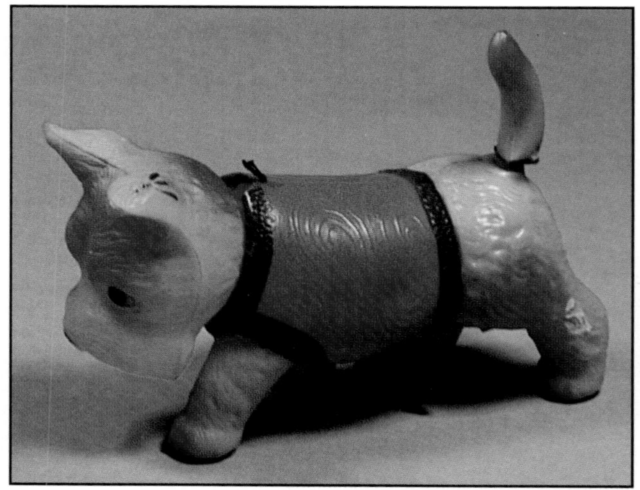

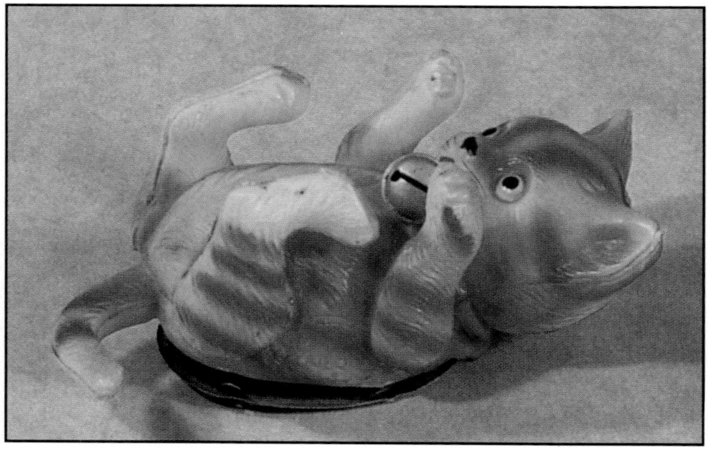

The wind-up cat and dog shown here were both manufactured in Japan between 1945 and 1952. Because they are embossed with these words, "Made in Occupied Japan," they are earnestly sought by collectors whose primary focus is on MIOJ items. Therefore the prices quoted here are competitive for these cross-over collectibles. Kitten, cream colored celluloid with bright pink stripes, jointed limbs, wind-up key missing from center; however the mechanism indicates that the item was wound up, then spins around. Made in Occupied Japan. Present condition, $55.00. Wind-up terrier with a fly on its ear, tail spins around. Molded of semi translucent yellow celluloid with orange red highlights and a bright pink painted sweater w/blue trim. Made in Occupied Japan, wind-up key on underside. Excellent working condition, $75.00+.

These animal pull toys illustrate two types that can be found. The first is the most common, a figure secured to a base that has wheels. The second illustration is less common and features a rooster perching on the cross bar between two wheels. 3" x 2" pull toy, cream donkey w/pink highlights on black celluloid platform w/wooden wheels, intertwined VCO/USA. 2¾" rooster pull toy, cream w/bright pink wheels, black tail feathers, intertwined VCO/USA. $65.00 – $85.00.

Figural tape measures have recently become one of the most sought after collectibles on the current market, and those fashioned from celluloid are no exception. As a result, buyers must be prepared to pay the competitive prices these novelties are currently fetching. The prices listed here may seem somewhat vague, however they are meant to reflect both the low end and the high end of this category. Anything selling for less than the listed low price is sure to be a deal. Keep in mind that these wonderful little novelties are also crossover collectibles, which increases their value.

A playful family of Airedale terriers fashioned into figural tape measures. The 2" tall mother w/puppy is molded in cream celluloid and hand painted with brown details. The second, slightly larger example, straddles a round suitcase, its handle being the pull tab for the measuring tape. All were made in Japan and range in price $150.00 – $200.00 each.

Helen Golubic

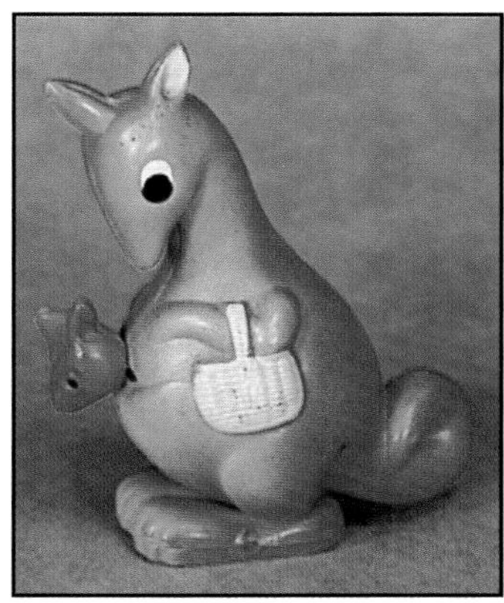

Common, Mother Kangaroo, holding hand painted white basket, looks down at her Joey, whose head is peeking out of her pouch. Tape extends by pulling the baby's head. Measuring 3¾" tall, fashioned from peach/pink celluloid, marked Made In Occupied Japan. $55.00 – $70.00.

4¼" fish tape measure, on backside the words, "I was caught at Aquamarine of Cape Cod." can be found. Manufactured by the Royal Co. Ltd. of Tokyo, it is trademarked with the word "Japan" w/fleur-de-lis logo. $45.00 – $60.00.

Figural Characters

The use of celluloid in children's toys can be traced back to early 1880 when William B. Carpenter, an employee of the Celluloid Novelty Company, filed application for a method of coloring celluloid doll heads to imitate the appearance of flesh. Since the patent states that doll heads made of celluloid had a certain glossy appearance, it is therefore reasonable to assume that such items were being manufactured during the late 1870s. Later, Marshall Lefferts joined Carpenter in filing an additional patent in Jan. 1881 for a Celluloid doll. (Pat. #237,559, Feb. 8, 1881.)

The most common type of celluloid dolls and toys available for today's collector is the blow-molded figural character. These were manufactured from thin sheet celluloid which was placed in a mold that had hot air forced between the two halves of plastic. Blow-molded toys are thin and hollow, rendering them somewhat fragile; for this reason many toys of this type are cracked or dented.

The most prolific production era for these toys where the years following WWI; it was during this time that the American toy industry developed more fully, as trade with European countries had ceased during the war. Many of the figural toys in this section were manufactured by Viscoloid Co., of Leominster, and others were imported into the United States from Germany, England, and France. During the 1920s through the 1930s, millions of Japanese blow-molded toys flooded the market as Japan's natural resource of camphor and low labor costs made the plastic inexpensive to produce. For identification on the various trademarks found on these toys, see the section at the end of the book.

These three figurines were manufactured by Kintaro Aiba of Tokyo. Marugane also used the same trademark during the 1930s. The items were most definitely manufactured for export as the images are in no way Oriental. 5" cowboy w/pistols, tan, blue, and pink on green base; 6½" beefeater w/British flag, green base; 5" soldier w/brown military uniform and rifle, standing on green base. All items marked on the bottom Made In JAPAN, house in circle. $35.00 – $40.00 each, more for the item w/flag.

Circa 1925 aviators all manufactured in Japan with the exception of the second one, a product of the toy manufacturers of Leominster. Sizes range from the 6½" tall slightly Oriental looking aviator in orange suit with black collar, trademark of Marugane in the 1930s, house in circle w/Japan; 5" Viscoloid aviator, VCO/USA; 4½" aviator, orange/peach flesh tone w/grayish purple highlights, Made In Japan; and 4" aviator, green and orange pink uniform, standing w/plane propeller, Made In Japan. $65.00 – $75.00 each.

Jackie Coogan, 5" newspaper boy, peach celluloid w/blue details, intertwined VCO/USA. $65.00 – $75.00.

The 5¾" cadet is blow molded in white celluloid and features hand painted detailing. Made in Japan. $45.00+.

A Celluloid Limerick
By Keith W. Lauer

The plastics "grandaddy" of all
Developed the Celluloid pool ball.
The products of John W. Hyatt
Induced the public to buy it,
Including many a Celluloid doll.

This "Crawling Soldier" has a friction mechanism on the underside and the barrel of the gun is made of two separate pieces of molded celluloid that are held together by a rubber band. The purpose for the "folding gun" was so that it would fit into a small box for export. Japan. $85.00+.

The three 4" tall football players shown here were manufactured in Japan and have an unidentified CT Japan trademark on the back. The figurines had a dual purpose; during the 1950s they were worn dangling from the attached pinback buttons at college football games to show team support. Later the pins were removed and a string attached to the loop on the helmet, and they were used for Christmas tree ornaments. Button and ribbon attached with a rubber band to the neck. Complete, $25.00+.

Figural toys which portray a sporting activity are more collectible. This nicely detailed 6" tall boy is blow molded of peach celluloid and features hand painted features and clothing. He holds a fishing pole in one hand and a bright red fish in the other. Intertwined YS and Made in Japan. $75.00+.

This 4¾" mail delivery boy is blow molded in flesh tone celluloid then painted with blue, gray, red, and black highlights. Nice detailing, holding a mail pouch and letter, mfg. by Rheinische Gummi und Celluloid Fabrik Co., Schutz, mark, diamond turtle, Germany. $75.00+.

A commonly found fellow from the 1950s, this 4" cowboy is blow molded in flesh tone celluloid and decorated with bright primary colors, movable arms w/pistol and rope, manufactured by Nagamine Co., club shaped trademark w/JAPAN. $35.00+.

This wonderfully detailed 4¾" clown has hand painted highlights and rattles when shaken, a feature that increases its collectibility. Although there is no trademark, the original price tag from John Wanamaker, 15¢, Philadelphia, is on the back. $65.00+.

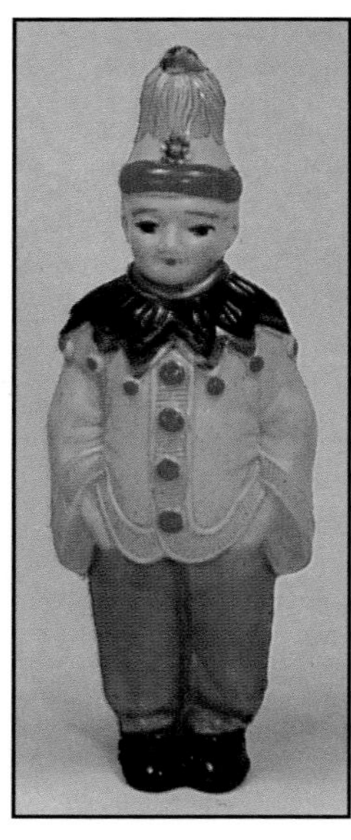

This 6½" cream clown bears no identifying trademarks but has nicely molded detailing although the painted features are quite sloppy. Attached to the top of the hat is a child's teething ring. The clown also rattles but with a dangerous element; when peering down into the toy from a hole in the top of the hat, a number of small finishing nails can be seen! It seems totally absurd that a toy manufacturer could have used such dangerous components when making a rattle for a baby. Perhaps someone improvised when the original noise makers were lost; we may never know. $55.00+.

Two clown theme roly polys. The 4" balancing full body figure is perched on red and white ball base and features green, red, and brown highlights, the ball of feather on the top of the hat is missing, imprinted GERMANY; 3" clown w/pink and white base, attached feather, unmarked, nice detailing. $45.00+ each.

The 2½" tall Buster Brown roly poly illustrated here is a fine example of the craftsmanship of Dr. Paul Hunaeus of Hanover, Germany. The image of Buster Brown was introduced as a comic strip character, along with his dog Tige around the turn of the century; later he became even more famous as an emblem for a shoe company. $150.00 – $200.00.

These small roly polys were sold as penny toys around the turn of the twentieth century. Dr. Paul Hunaeus of Germany was one of the known manufacturer of the finely molded figures and his trademark, an intertwined PH, can often be found if examined closely. 2½" unmarked black man w/straw hat, flower on lapel; 2½" unmarked lady w/straw bonnet, fan, gray coat and orange bow; 2½" commodore w/Navy suit and white hat, intertwined PH; 2" unmarked man w/hat, flesh tone, black bow tie, brown jacket; 2" bald man w/spectacles, blue suit, orange tie, intertwined PH. Prices for these small, finely detailed items begin around $125.00 and can go as high as $250.00 for the items that represent special collecting categories.

This circa 1920, 3" Viscoloid roly poly WWI era soldier boy is molded in cream colored celluloid w/brown highlighting, Made In USA. $150.00+. 3" man w/spectacles blown in gray celluloid with black and white highlights on pink base, embossed, Palitoy, Made In England by Cascelloid Ltd. $70.00+.

Dolls

Kewpies were first introduced in *The Ladies' Home Journal* as illustrations by Rose O'Neill. Original Kewpies have tiny blue wings sprouting from their shoulders. Dolls in the image of Kewpies began to appear in bisque around 1913; blow-molded celluloid Kewpies and Kewpie types were mass marketed in Germany, America, and Japan prolifically during the 1920s. Because Kewpie dolls are highly collectible, prices for these tiny examples may seem expensive, but the competition from serious collectors is stiff.

Collection of Kewpie and Kewpie types. Left to right: 3½" Japanese example, CT trademark, w/wings; 2⅜" Viscoloid w/Made in USA, w/brown wings and painted orange shield on chest; 3½" Japan soldier Kewpie; 2½" Viscoloid Kewpie, blond hair and blue wings, Made in USA; ¾" sitting unmarked Kewpie w/movable arms and legs. $35.00 – $50.00 each.

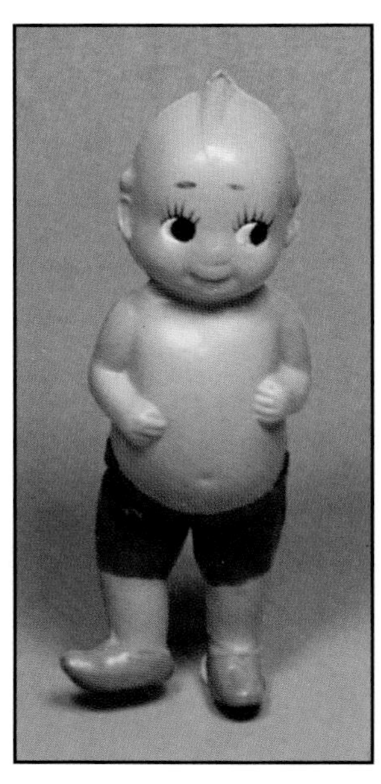

This adorable little 4" tall Kewpie type figure has green painted trousers and yellow shoes, only one leg is movable. Unidentified SS in Diamond trademark. No wings. $35.00 – $45.00.

Matching couples are always a nice addition to one's collection. While bride and groom figures are quite common, the other examples shown are more difficult to finds. Consider yourself fortunate if you come across companion dolls they are becoming increasingly elusive.

Circa 1925 bridal couple, Kewpies with wings, but no trademarks are visible because the ribbon, net, and crepe clothing is glued onto the dolls' bodies. They could have been used for wedding shower favors, cake toppers, or toys and sold for only pennies each. $65.00+ set.

Commonly referred to as George and Martha Washington, this charming couple was designed and blow molded by the Ando Togoro workshop of Tokyo. The gentleman is dressed in colonial era knickers with vest, ruffled shirt, and formal overcoat; the female has a corseted hourglass shape and is elaborately dressed. Blow molded in peach celluloid with painted highlights, crossed circle w/Japan trademark. $125.00 pair.

This pair of matching Viscoloid dolls could double as Easter toys because the little girl is holding a chick and the boy is holding a rabbit. The figures also rattle when shaken, making them cross-over collectibles as well. Both measure 4" tall and are blow molded in cream celluloid with blue and red detailing, intertwined VCO/USA. $100.00+ pair.

Blow molded entirely of red celluloid then painted with deep brown and black paint, these babies are especially desired by collectors of black memorabilia. The clothing is molded and the arms are strung. 2⅜" Marugane, 1930s house in circle trademark; 3½" doll w/strung arms and legs, unidentified lantern trademark, Made in Japan. $35.00 – $55.00 each.

Three little babies in molded pajamas and night caps, the sitting dolls measure 3" and are marked with a rising sun – Japan trademark; the standing doll is 4⅛" tall and holding an unidentified object, Made in Japan. All are Kewpie type dolls. $25.00 – $30.00 each.

These one-piece molded figures are unmovable. The 2" example is similar to a Kewpie type doll. Advertised as "Cute Negro Babies" in a 1924 B. Shackman Co. catalog, they originally sold for $5.40 per gross. $30.00 – $55.00 each.

Dottie Maust

Although these two blow-molded toys are not a companion set, they were both manufactured in Japan. The 5½" long Indian with full head dress, paddling a canoe, is strung together and has movable arms and head, Unidentified CT trademark w/Made In Japan. $65.00+. The Indian maiden, complete with yarn braids and an imitation leather dress, was purchased as a souvenir during the 1950s by Dottie Maust at Idlewild Park in Ligonier, Pa. Marked Japan. $20.00.

The Indian squaw and papoose are tightly wrapped together in a woolen blanket. The body of this item seems to be made of wood because it is very sturdy. It appears that only the heads are celluloid. Unmarked. $40.00.

Dotty Maust

3¾" toddler in pink snowsuit, yellow and red trim, F in diamond, Made In JAPAN. $15.00 – $20.00. 5" girl w/flowers, white w/bright pink hat and dress, mfg. by Gonzoburo Takeda w/star in circle, JAPAN trademark. $15.00 – $20.00.

The three dolls shown here all wear hats and have molded dresses. 5¾" Dutch girl w/green, pink, yellow, and black details, manufactured by Yoshino Sangyo Co. Ltd. Tokyo, butterfly trademark, Made In JAPAN. $30.00 – $35.00. 4⅛" girl doll, movable arms, bright pink and green clothing and cloche hat, Made In JAPAN. $15.00 – $25.00. 3" peach blow-molded doll w/strung arms, matching hat and dress in red and teal, unmarked. $15.00 – $25.00.

Helen Golubic

This figural toy is among the most desirable type because of the many images it represents; both doll and dog collectors would find it of special interest. The standing girl measures 6¾" tall and is molded in peach colored celluloid. She holds a baby doll and a cute little dog is peering out between her feet. Painted with pink, green, gray, and purple highlights, the article was designed and manufactured by Ando Togoro of Tokyo. It bears the crossed circle w/Japan trademark. $75.00+.

Advertised as Becky Thatcher from *Tom Sawyer*, this little 5½" Viscoloid girl is a charming example of the detail put into the American made figural toys that were marketed during the 1920s. The designer of this particular item cleverly reflects the female attitude of bashful flirtatiousness in her childlike expression. Peach celluloid w/pink and green clothes. Intertwined VCO/USA. $65.00 – $75.00.

Bathing beauty dolls are highly collectible and eagerly sought by collectors of ladies' vanity items. These Japanese examples in celluloid are no exception. The 8¾" bathing beauty in green swimsuit w/umbrella also rattles; she is circa 1925 and originally sold for $2 per dozen, marked with SS in diamond, Made In Japan. $65.00 – $85.00.

The 6" flesh tone doll shown here with curly gold hair is actually a boudoir accessory which retailed for about 89 cents during the 1920s. Holes in the top of the head indicate this was a novelty powder shaker. Such items were popular during the 1920s. A small hole is opened in the back for filling with powder. Lined butterfly trademark, Yoshino Sangyo Co. Ltd. $45.00 – $65.00.

This 12" tall googlie-eyed powder shaker doll has movable arms and satin bloomers. Trademarked with the star in circle, this novelty doll was manufactured by Gonzoburo Takeda. $75.00 – $85.00.

Referred to as "carnival dolls" because they were won as prizes from the game booths that lined the midway at fairs and carnivals. These dolls are usually half naked except for the application of glitter, ribbon and feathers. They frequently held canes and wore top hats, earrings, and necklaces of glass beads. These dolls came in a variety of sizes ranging from 6" to 12" and were manufactured by a number of companies in Japan as "Papoose Dolls." 8" doll w/glitter and feathers, top hat and cane, gold shoes marked on back Made in Japan. Hideo Iwai Sangyo, Tokyo Japan, $30.00. 12" doll w/pink and white feathers, silver top hat, earrings and bracelet, red shoes w/white socks. Intertwined COH, Made in Japan. $45.00 – $50.00.

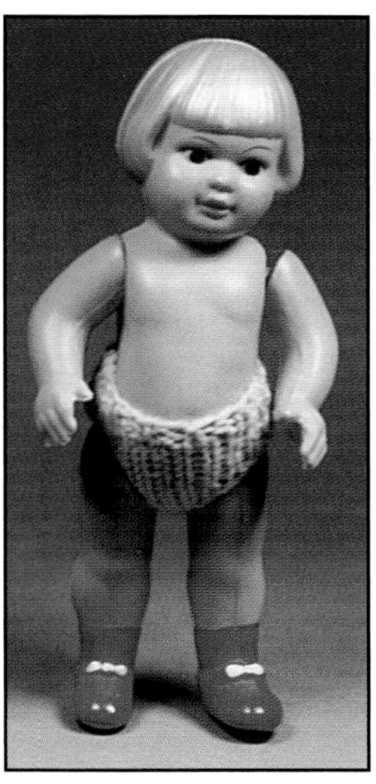

An adorable little girl with the short blond bob hair cut, movable arms and legs. Manufactured from thick blow-molded celluloid. Stands 5¾" tall and bears an unidentified shell trademark. Original ethnic costume included purple and black blouse, skirt and bonnet; tag attached to wrist by string said "Denmark." $65.00 – $75.00.

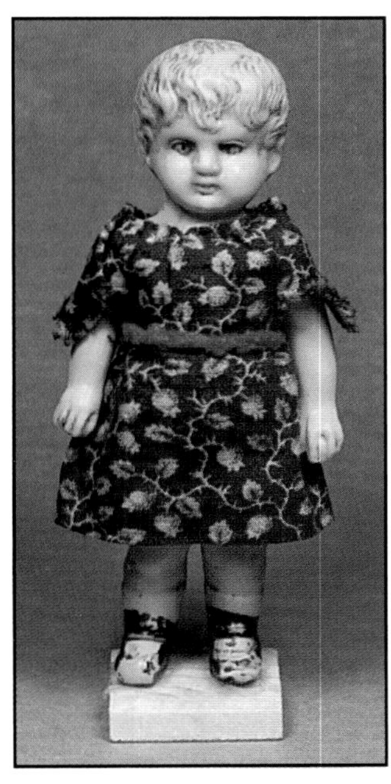

This doll figurine, measuring 5" standing on a square base, has very poorly painted details, making the baby appear to be cross-eyed. Nevertheless, it is included because this is an example of the solid celluloid items manufactured by Rheinische Gummi und Celluloid Fabrik Co. of Germany. It bears the turtle, Schutz-marke – Germany. $35.00 – $45.00.

This little 7¾" baby doll has wonderfully detailed realistic looking features. A crochet sweater and bonnet complete the outfit, trademark on the back is a star inside diamond w/Made in Occupied Japan. $45.00+.

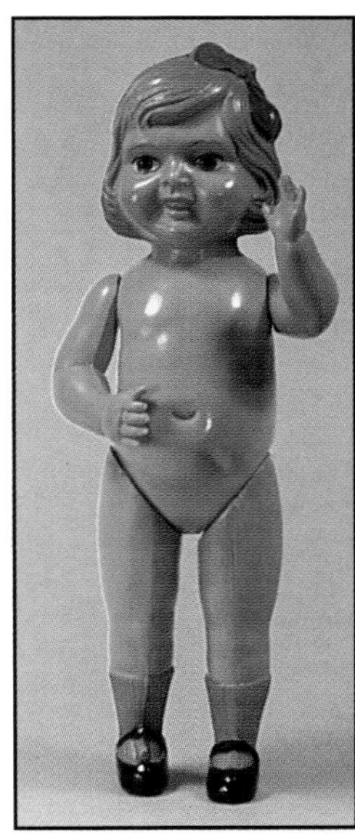

7" doll, girl w/bobbed hair and blue bow, black shoes, movable arms and legs, unmarked but believed to be Viscoloid, circa 1927. $50.00 – $65.00.

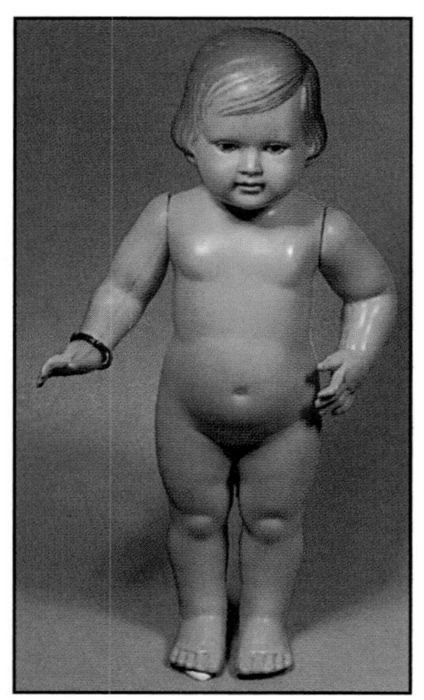

7" tall German made doll with movable arms, nicely molded hair, realistic facial features, and molded bracelet on right wrist. Marked with Cellba, Celluloidwarenfabrik Co., mermaid trademark in shield and DRP, Germany. $65.00 – $80.00.

Lucille Mauro

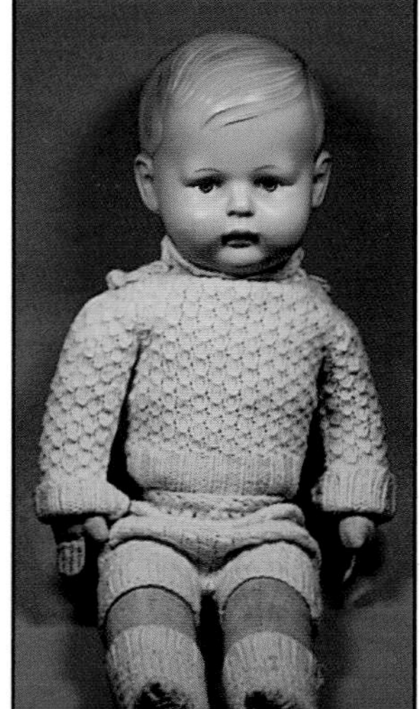

Realistic baby doll, 18" long, features stuffed textile body with nicely detailed celluloid head. Manufactured by Minerva, Buschow and Beck, helmet-shaped trademark registered in 1888. A wonderful example of fine German design. Trademark, helmet, No. 7, 42, Germany. $185.00+.

The two Viscoloid dolls shown here are both manufactured from sturdy blow-molded celluloid in flesh tone. The 11" baby doll with movable arms and legs is wearing socks and is marked with the Made in USA logo and #6 on back. $95.00 – $150.00. The larger doll baby measures 16½" and has red hair and bright blue eyes; celluloid is slightly thinner and glossier than the smaller doll, marked with USA logo and #9. $150.00 – $175.00.

Novelty Toys

Toys for Little Girls

Betty Clawson

Dottie Maust

These two boxed items are small dolls with accessories that were imported from Japan between the Occupation years. Unmarked. In original boxes with all accessories, they range from $25.00 – $35.00.

The doll carriage seen here is marked with Ando Togoro's crossed circle trademark. It is assembled from embossed and die cut sheet celluloid with a thin metal frame. The doll is not original to the piece and is manufactured from hard plastic, not celluloid. Carriage alone, $65.00 – $85.00.

This 17-piece tea set comes complete with 4 plates, 4 cups and saucers, tea pot, sugar, creamer, and lids. It is made from plain cream celluloid sheet stock that is die cut and molded. Although it is a plain set with no decorative motifs and no trademark, it is a highly unusual item. $65.00+.

The small platters of food items shown here were all manufactured by the Viscoloid Company of Leominster. Each is marked with the intertwined VCO/USA trademark. The oval fish, goose, and ham measure 2¾" long and are nicely detailed and colored. The cake on round plate is 2" in diameter. $85.00 – $125.00 each.

Toys for Little Boys

The blow-molded toy boats seen here were intended to be bath time toys. They are becoming increasingly difficult to find and prices have escalated because of their rarity. While little girls most certainly played with these toys, they were geared toward the little boy market. During the years following WWI, the American and foreign toy markets were in competition with one another. It is impossible to determine which manufacturer designed certain articles, however the item with the finest quality detailing is probably the original.

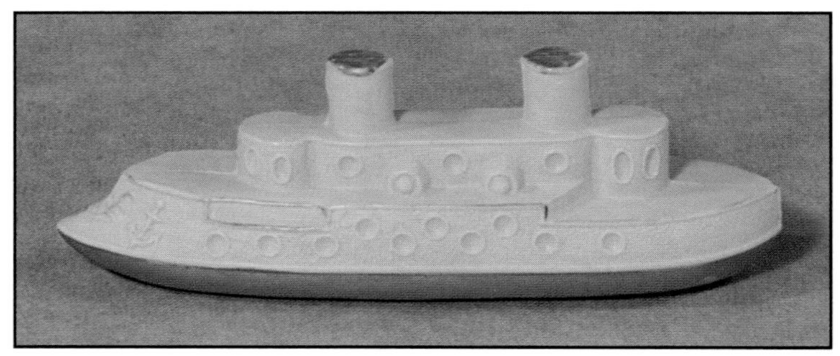

Possibly inspired by the Maine, this 4½" steamer has double stacks, cream and red detailing, and intertwined VCO/USA. $28.00 – $35.00.

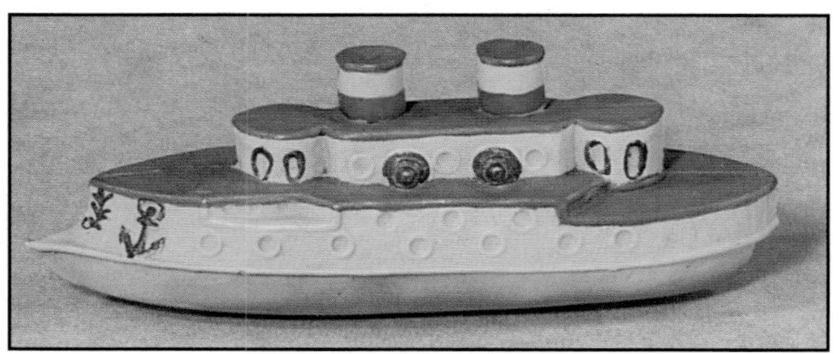

5" cream steamer w/gray, pink, and gold details, unmarked. $28.00 – $32.00.

5" gray battle ship w/gold anchor, Made In USA. $30.00 – $35.00.

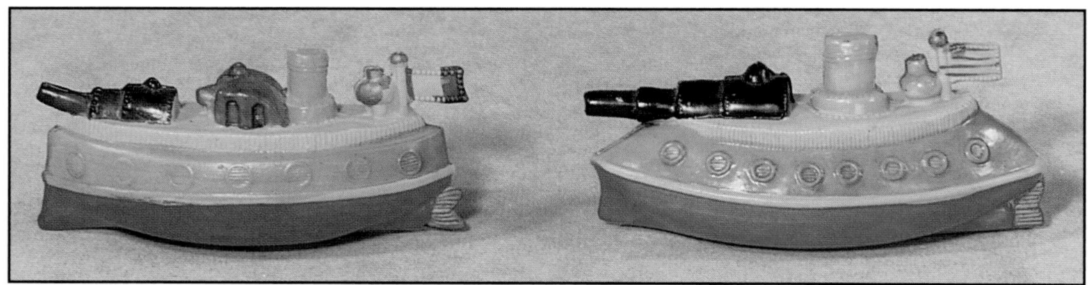

3¾" gun boat, purple, cream, and pink flag, bow trademark, Made In Japan, $25.00 – $28.00.
3⅞" gun boat, American flag, unmarked. $25.00 – $30.00.

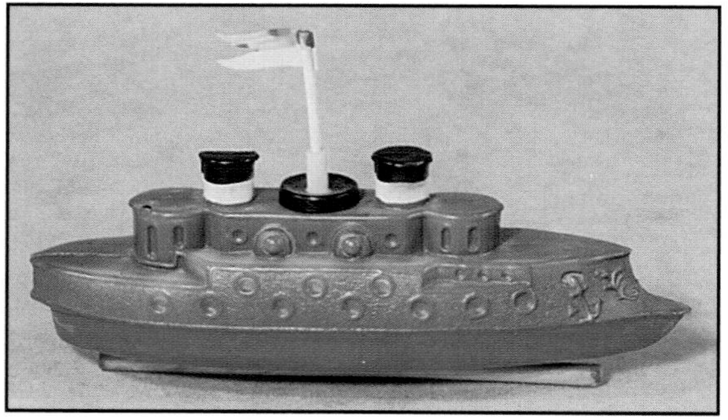

These two steamers were imported from Germany and are marked with the intertwined PH, which indicates that they were made in Linden at the Paul Hunaeus factory. 5" cream steamer, orange bottom, black details and flag, intertwined PH. 5" gray and red steamer w/flag, intertwined PH. $40.00 – $50.00 each.

Whistles

Whistles, especially those which were manufactured in novel designs or those that could be played like a musical instrument producing varying tones and pitches, were great fun for children.

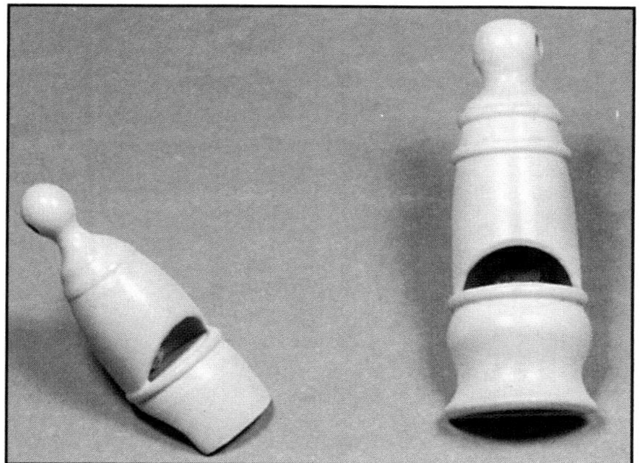

Cream colored whistles manufactured by the Celluloid Novelty Co. This type of whistle was advertised in the 1883 catalog. Both whistles have an opening in the top for a lanyard. 2¾" and 2" whistles. Small, $10.00 – $12.00; large, $15.00 – $20.00.

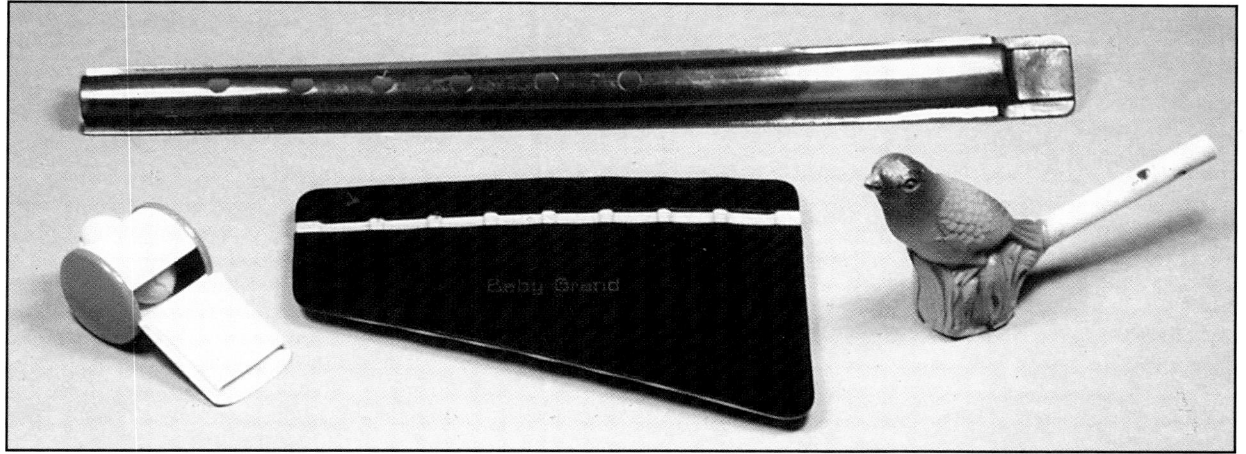

9" x ¾" recorder whistle in transparent teal celluloid. Molded mouthpiece and 6 holes for playing notes. $20.00. 4" long, 1" and 3½" ends, black and cream graduated pipe whistle, "Baby Grand". $25.00. 3½" long and 2½" tall, nightingale bird whistle, yellow celluloid w/green and red highlights, VCO/USA. $20.00 – $25.00. 2⅛" green and ivory standard whistle, lanyard attachment on round end, unmarked. $12.00 – $15.00.

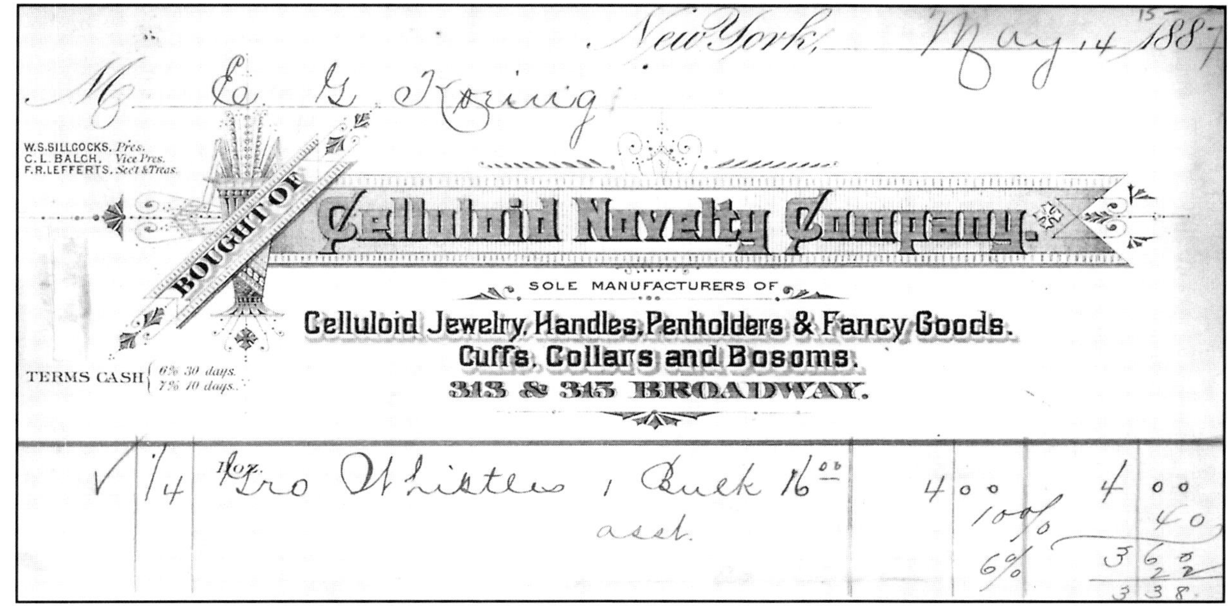

New York, May 14 1887

W.S. SILLCOCKS, Pres.
C.L. BALCH, Vice Pres.
F.R. LEFFERTS, Sec'y & Treas.

BOUGHT OF Celluloid Novelty Company.

SOLE MANUFACTURERS OF

Celluloid Jewelry, Handles, Penholders & Fancy Goods.
Cuffs, Collars and Bosoms.
313 & 315 BROADWAY.

TERMS CASH { 6% 30 days. 7% 10 days.

✓	1/4	Gro Whistles 1 Buck 16 asst.	4 00 / 10% / 6%	4 00 / 40 / 3 60 / 22 / 3 38

Celluloid Co. invoice for a whistle order.

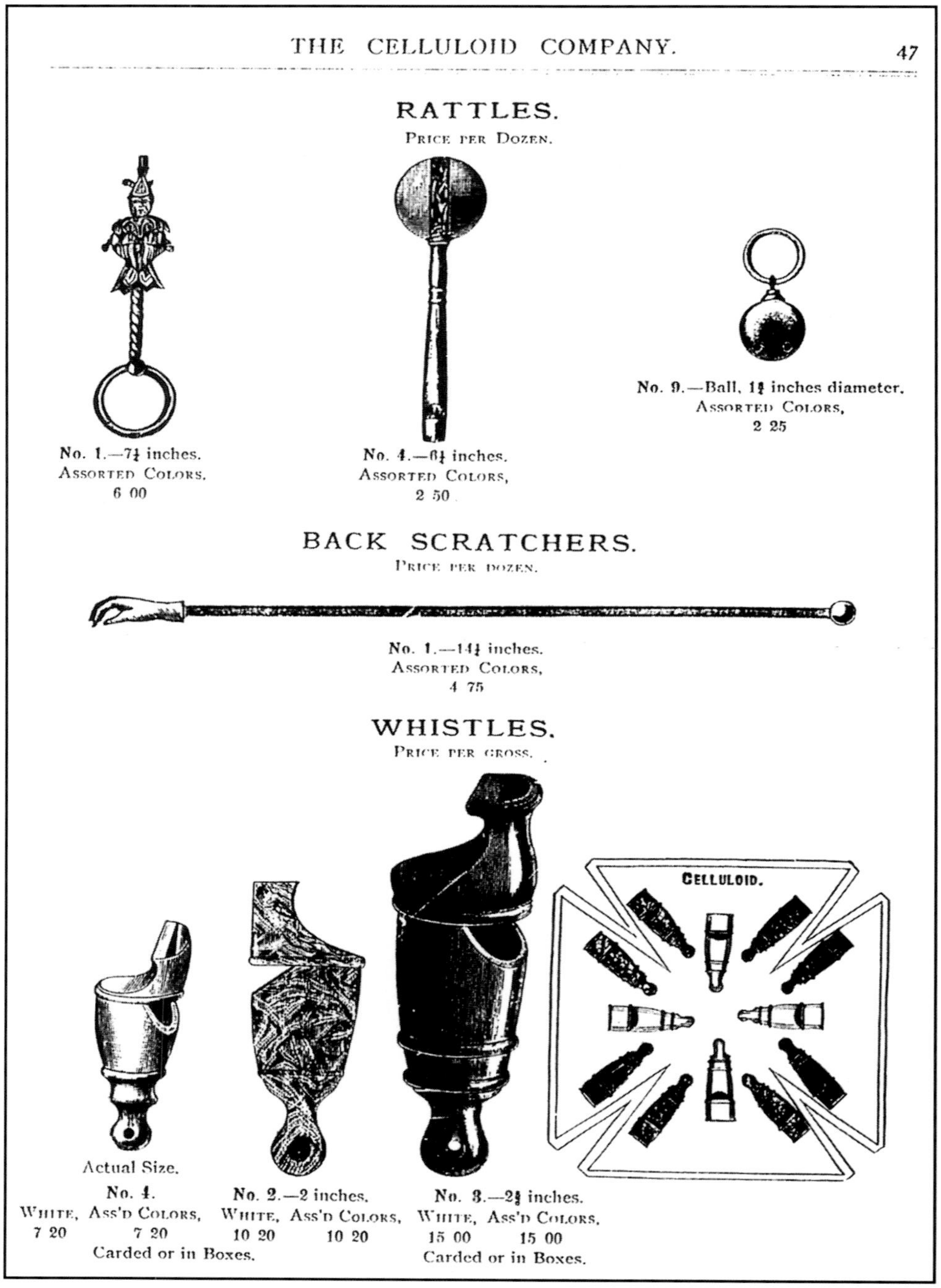

THE CELLULOID COMPANY. 47

RATTLES.

PRICE PER DOZEN.

No. 1.—7½ inches.
ASSORTED COLORS,
6 00

No. 4.—6½ inches.
ASSORTED COLORS,
2 50

No. 9.—Ball, 1¾ inches diameter.
ASSORTED COLORS,
2 25

BACK SCRATCHERS.

PRICE PER DOZEN.

No. 1.—14½ inches.
ASSORTED COLORS,
4 75

WHISTLES.

PRICE PER GROSS.

CELLULOID.

Actual Size.
No. 4.
WHITE, ASS'D COLORS,
7 20 7 20

No. 2.—2 inches.
WHITE, ASS'D COLORS,
10 20 10 20

Carded or in Boxes.

No. 3.—2⅜ inches.
WHITE, ASS'D COLORS,
15 00 15 00
Carded or in Boxes.

Original advertising for Celluloid Company whistles, 1887.

Novelty Items

This small trinket box has a full figured male on top of the lid, painted highlights. Unmarked. $25.00+.

12" tall celluloid die cut bell hop, flat weighted base, w/painted features, red dome top for holding a hat. $85.00+.

2" novelty flower w/face, leaves and black base, original sticker on bottom, 10¢. $10.00 – $12.00.

Two VCO/USA novelty toothbrush holders, circa 1920, 4½" orange boy figurine on cream base and 4½" peach girl figural on cream base. Rings attached at elbow hold toothbrushes. Uncommon. $85.00 – $125.00 each.

Holiday Collectibles

Among the most sought-after celluloid toys are those that represent a holiday theme. Viscoloid Company was the most prolific manufacturer of these items, employing 360 workers in their toy department alone.

The company's novel designs frequently combine traditional holiday characters engaged in whimsical activities. Although some figural toys can be found in colored celluloid, they were most often blow molded in ivory, then embellished with painted decorations.

Christmas Collectibles

Probably the most plentiful novelties available in celluloid represent the Christmas holiday. Beginning in 1914, German born artist Paul Kramme designed molds for the Viscoloid Co. Kramme's St. Nicholas figures exhibit a definite German influence and are highly collectible.

All four of these Santa figures were manufactured by Viscoloid Co. Each features a sack over the shoulder with a baby doll stuffed into it, and a basket full of fruits and nuts or flowers. The 9" tall undecorated Santa may have been a salesman's sample or work in progress; nevertheless it is highly unusual to find an example with so little decoration. $95.00+. The 7" VCO/USA marked Santa is almost identical in design to the undecorated example; both exhibit the same features. $65.00 – $70.00. 5" VCO/USA Santa with a basket of roses and a fur trimmed suit. $55.00 – $60.00. 4" Santa w/Made in USA. $40.00 – $45.00.

Roly polys are cross-over collectibles with holiday themes being among the most desirable. The 3" cream colored celluloid Santa w/hand painted facial features is probably a Paul Kramme design, VCO/USA trademark. $85.00 – $125.00.

Three Japanese Santa figures. All blow molded in peach colored celluloid with applied red, white, and black details. 3¾" tall Santa w/horn and sack, hole in back for Christmas light bulb, trademarked S in circle and Made in Japan. 3" Santa holding sack and canteen, "Made in Japan" and diamond. 4¼" waving Santa w/lantern, Japan. $35.00 – $45.00 each.

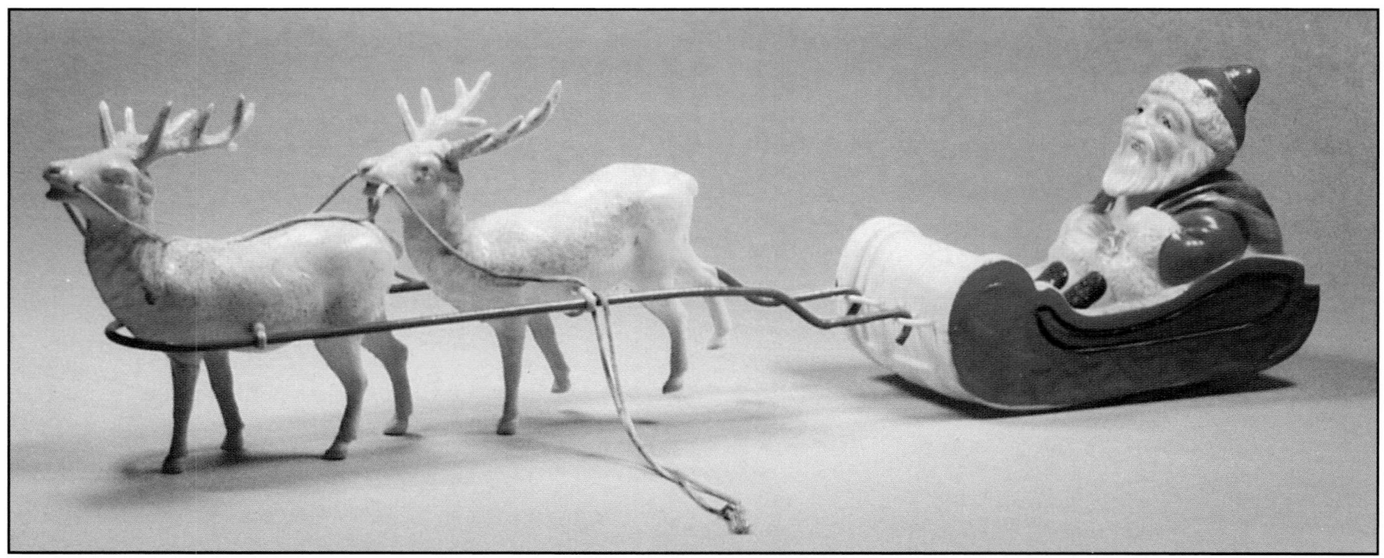

This unusual looking Santa and sleigh figural with a team of two reindeer is blow molded of white celluloid with hand painted detailing. Marked VCO/USA. $85.00 – $100.00.

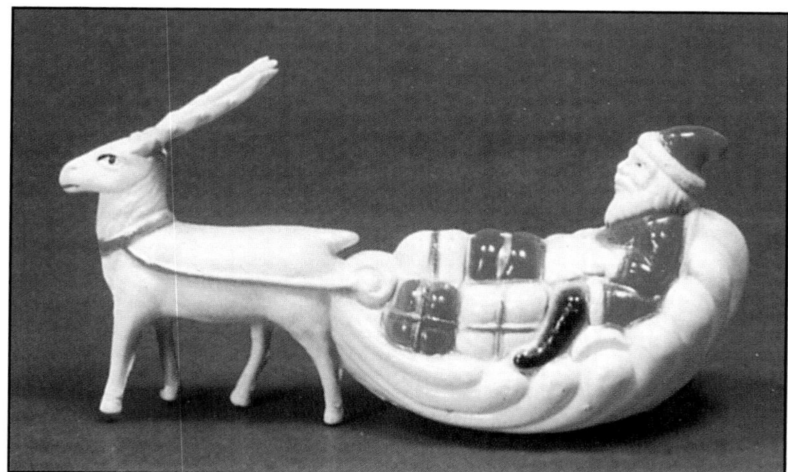

Blow-molded holiday novelties showing Santa Claus in a sleigh laden with gifts and a team of reindeer were especially popular as is evident by the different designs seen here. Prices for the items shown here continue to escalate as the supply cannot meet the demand. Consider anything under $75.00 a real bargain and expect to pay at least $110.00 for a toy in nice condition. 4" x 2⅛" reindeer pulling sleigh w/Santa and packages, VCO/USA. 3" x 1" figural toy, reindeer pulling Santa in sleigh. Cream celluloid w/red and black detailing, VCO/USA trademark. 4" x 3" reindeer pulling loaded sleigh w/Santa, cream celluloid w/hand painted green, gold, and red detailing, VCO/USA.

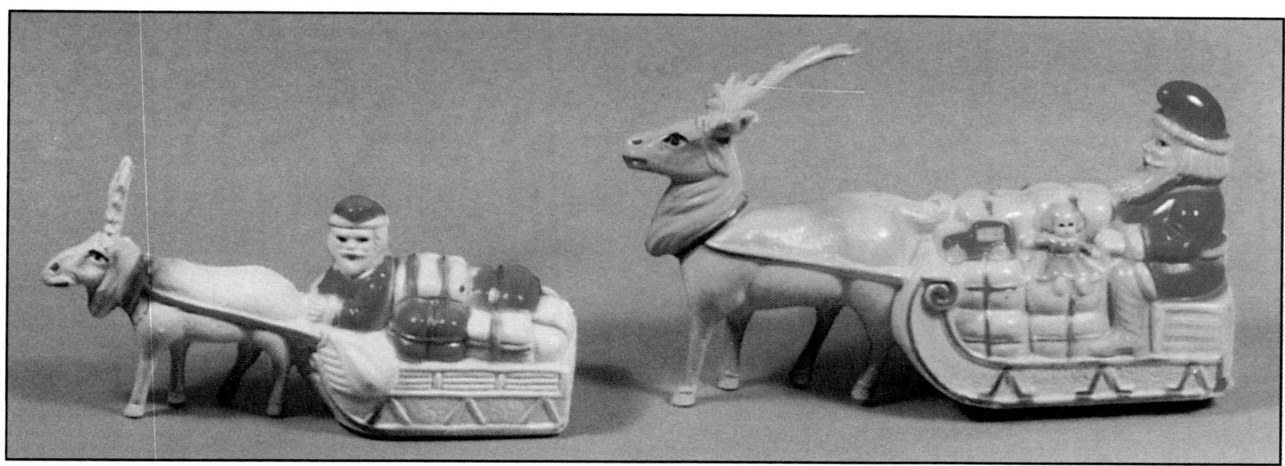

A mechanical wind-up tin sled with celluloid Santa and reindeer figures, marked Made in Occupied Japan on sled, Japan on deer. $135.00+.

Santa Express, 5⅜" x 2". Santa riding on a train laden w/holiday decorations and gifts including a doll, puppy, and rocking horse. Greatly detailed cream celluloid w/red and green highlights, VCO/USA on Santa. (Buyer beware: this item has also been produced in cellulose acetate and bears an Irwin trademark over the old VCO/USA.) $85.00 – $165.00.

3⅝" x 2" Santa driving house-shaped automobile, white w/applied red, yellow and green painted highlights, VCO/USA trademark. $110.00 – $155.00. 3⅝" house ornament w/Santa approaching door, white w/red, green, and gold hand painted details, VCO trademark, roly poly bottom. $110.00 – $150.00.

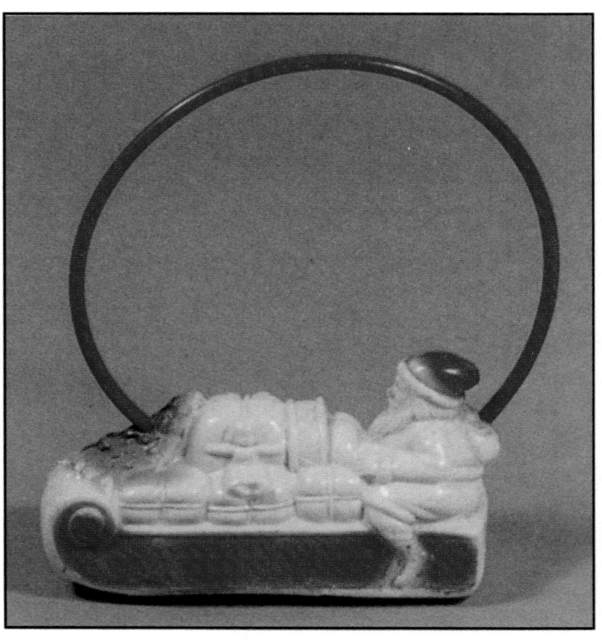

3⅓" dia. ornament w/3¾" Santa on sled, white w/applied highlights in red and green, VCO/USA. $95.00 – $125.00.

6" Christmas horn ornament, no mark on this particular horn, however others have been identified with Japanese marks. Red, pink, and yellow. $45.00 – $65.00.

This little unmarked boy is seen swinging from the boughs of an evergreen tree. It is a highly desirable novelty because the child is engaged in activity and the piece also has a small light bulb attached into the back for use as a Christmas ornament. $125.00 – $165.00.

Two 3" x 4" religious ornaments showing Madonna w/child and Joseph. Embossed sheet celluloid w/applied highlights. Germany. $30.00 – $35.00 pair.

9" x 7" and 7" white stylized reindeer w/pink and brown hand painted detail, Made in Japan, Patent #97,485 on larger example, Floral Sekiguchi trademark on smaller. These are featured as photographic illustrations in the Japanese publication on nitro-cellulose manufacturers of Japan, *Celluloid of Japan*, c. 1957. $35.00 – $45.00 each.

4" white deer w/molded ears and applied antlers, red nose and eyes. $15.00 – $20.00 each. 4¾" cream colored deer w/red eyes and mouth, gold glitter over entire article, Japan. $15.00 – $20.00 each.

St. Patrick's Day Collectibles

"Paddy and the Pig" is known as a St. Patrick's day collectible figure. This Japanese example features Paddy riding a pink pig with adjustable legs. The unidentified "Stickmen" trademark is located on the pig's side. $125.00.

Easter

Traditional Easter characters like bunny rabbits, chicks, ducks, and eggs were represented in a wide variety of blow-molded novelties made by Viscoloid Co. The most desirable toys and figurines are those which show more than one character engaged in an activity. Since no catalog showing the extent of Viscoloid toy items was ever published, the chance of a collector finding an unknown example is a distinct possibility.

The whimsical nature of these collectible figurals makes them especially desirable. They are becoming increasingly difficult to find which of course is increasing their value. Bargains can start as low as $65.00, but expect to pay up to $125.00 per item if condition is pristine.

Viscoloid Company was most prolific in the production of ducks, chickens, and swans as can be seen in the section on bird toys. Crossing over into the Easter holiday realm by combining bird figures dressed in fancy clothing or engaged in whimsical activity was a profitable venture for the company.

3" girl rabbit, pink stripe dress, holding chicken, intertwined VCO/USA. 3" boy rabbit, yellow tie, holding basket of eggs, intertwined VCO/USA. $65.00 – $75.00.

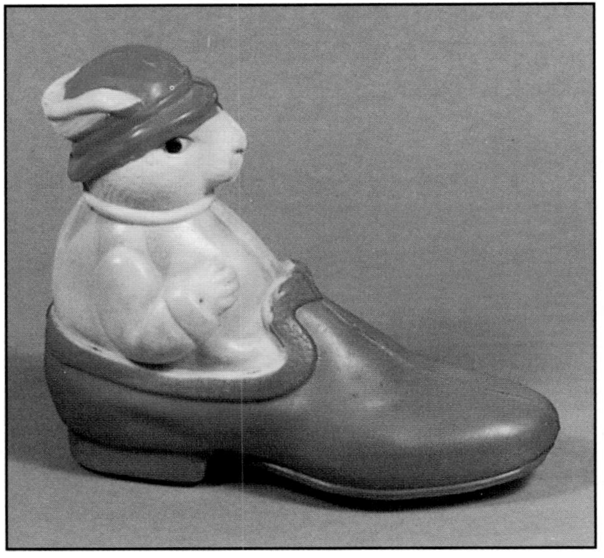

Viscoloid bunny sitting in a shoe, blow molded of cream celluloid and highlighted with subtle yellow on the rabbit and bright pink on shoe and hat. A charming expression on the face. $65.00 – $85.00.

4" white rabbit w/pink and blue highlights, top coat and purse, unmarked. $25.00 – $35.00.

3¾" rabbit in red jacket pushing chick in egg carriage, intertwined VCO/USA. 3¾" cream rabbit pulling egg shell carriage w/yellow chick, intertwined VCO/USA. $85.00+.

3¾" rabbit driving chick in egg shell car, yellow, red and green, intertwined VCO/USA, inscribed on bottom "Baby Kudd, 1st car, Aunt Evangeline." 3¾" rabbit driving green and yellow car, eggs in back, red jacket, intertwined VCO/USA. 3¼" rabbit driving egg shell car, yellow w/green wheels, rattle, intertwined VCO/USA, 10¢ on bottom. $110.00 – $135.00 each.

3¾" roly poly rabbit w/light blue sailor suit; 3" roly poly jester rabbit; 3" roly poly rabbit w/dark blue top hat and jacket; 3" roly poly rabbit inside dark blue eggshell. All items marked with Viscoloid's intertwined VCO/USA logo. $125.00 – $175.00 each.

4" white standing duck, blue hat, and red bow, intertwined VCO/USA. 4¾" standing duck w/red top hat and coat, intertwined VCO/USA. $55.00 – $65.00 each.

4" x 3" duck boat w/chicken in top hat, coat and full figured chick facing larger; this has also been seen with garish red, purple, and green details. VCO/USA. $85.00 – $125.00.

Figural Easter toys with ducks pulling other animals are much less common than those that feature the traditional chickens and bunnies. 3¾" cream duck pulling swan in egg cart, blue and red highlights, intertwined VCO/USA. 4¼" cream duck pulling standing rabbit in egg shell, intertwined VCO/USA. $85.00 – $125.00.

4¼" colorful rooster pulling rabbit and chick in eggshell cart, intertwined VCO/USA. 3¾" rooster pulling egg shell w/sitting rabbit. Intertwined VCO/USA. $85.00 – $125.00.

3" figural swan in cream and yellow w/chick in eggshell molded into back, intertwined VCO/USA. Three 3¾" figures are shown here, the swan boat, a dressed rabbit, and a little chick in an eggshell, intertwined VCO/USA. $125.00 each.

1" red woven basket, lid w/blue painted bunny and egg; unmarked. (Red is an unusual Easter color.) $45.00 – $60.00.

Independence Day Collectibles

These two Viscoloid Uncle Sam figures are appealing to both holiday and political memorabilia collectors. Circa 1920. 5¼" and 8⅞" tall Uncle Sam figures; blue top hat and vest, red coat and tails, striped pants w/gold watch fob. Made in USA. $150.00 – $175.00 each.

Halloween Collectibles

Perhaps the most coveted of holiday collectibles are Halloween articles. Since few were made, the supply and demand has caused prices to escalate rapidly. The chances of finding such novelties for under $100.00 today are slim. Recently the figure showing the witch and black cat sold for over $250.00.

3¾" standing black cat w/orange bow, on grass, rattle, intertwined VCO/USA. 3" black cat w/white face and red bow, crossed paws, intertwined VCO/USA, $145.00 – $165.00.

3" figural toy, black cat pushing a witch in a pumpkin carriage, intertwined VCO/USA. 3" figural toy, scarecrow pulling a ghost in black cart, intertwined VCO/USA. $250.00 – $350.00 each.

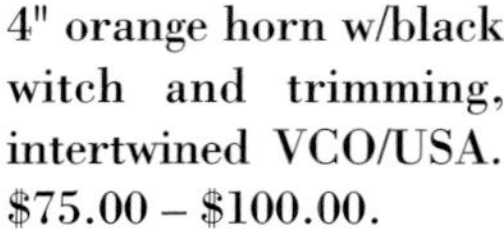

4" orange horn w/black witch and trimming, intertwined VCO/USA. $75.00 – $100.00.

This molding tool, called a "hardened punch," was used in detailing the mold for the Halloween horn at left.

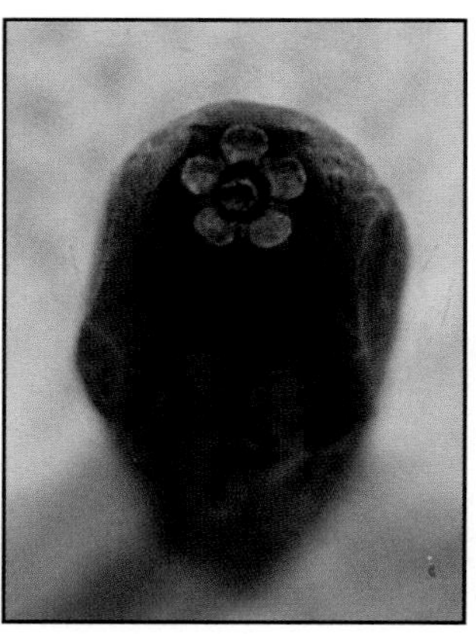

1$\frac{3}{4}$" dia. and 1" tall novelty container, yellow sides w/imitation tortoise shell bottom and lid. Applied celluloid witch riding a broom on lid. $110.00.

4" yellow roly poly owl w/orange and black highlights, intertwined VCO/USA. 3$\frac{1}{4}$" black cat on orange pumpkin, roly poly, intertwined VCO/USA. $200.00 – $250.00.

Baby Rattles and Other Baby Items

The first baby rattles were manufactured by the Celluloid Novelty Company beginning in the late 1870s. Early catalogs show a selection of eight different styles, which came in a color choice of amber, ivory, pink, and blue. Prices ranged from $1.50 to $8.00 per dozen.

The first rattles were made of thick sturdy celluloid, making them resistant to damage under normal use. Up to nine individual pieces were used to make a single rattle. The ball was fashioned from two molded halves, one of which had holes. A single brass bell was placed inside, and the halves were glued tightly together. A coupling was then joined to the round ball and the handle attached. Some rattles had a long molded handle with a whistle in the end, while others employed a solid celluloid teething ring as a grip.

As technology advanced and the blow-molding press was perfected, rattles took on a different form. Figural shapes with molded handles were introduced and quickly became popular. The Viscoloid Company was a leading manufacturer of this type of rattle, and their identifying trademarks can often be found embossed on the back.

When collecting rattles, condition should be the greatest consideration. The thin lightweight celluloid used in their manufacture damaged easily, therefore it is difficult to find them in fine condition without split seams, cracks, or dents. Look for fine detailing in the design, manufacturers' trademarks, and neatly painted features.

National Archives, Washington, DC

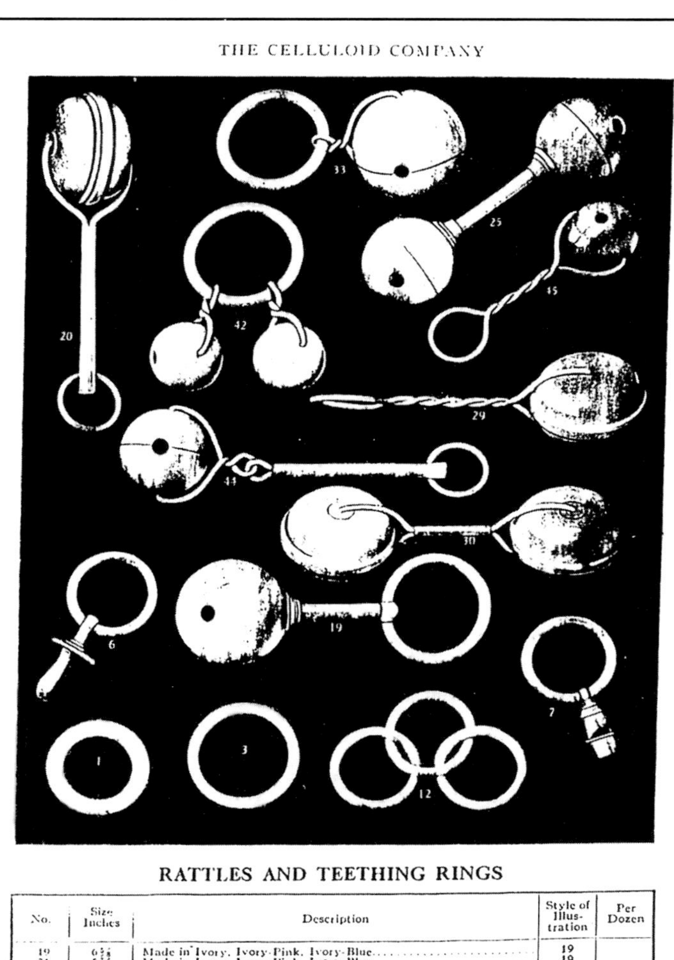

THE CELLULOID COMPANY

RATTLES AND TEETHING RINGS

No.	Size Inches	Description	Style of Illustration	Per Dozen
19	6 5/8	Made in Ivory, Ivory-Pink, Ivory-Blue	19	
21	5 7/8	Made in Ivory, Ivory-Pink, Ivory-Blue	19	
20	7	Made in Ivory, Ivory-Pink, Ivory-Blue	20	
25	6 1/4	Made in Ivory, Ivory-Pink, Ivory-Blue	25	
29	6 3/4	Made in Ivory, Ivory-Pink, Ivory-Blue	29	
30	6 3/8	Made in Ivory, Ivory-Pink, Ivory-Blue	30	
33	5 1/4	Made in Ivory, Ivory-Pink, Ivory-Blue	33	
42	4 1/2	Made in Ivory, Ivory-Pink, Ivory-Blue	42	
44	7 1/2	Made in Ivory, Ivory-Pink, Ivory-Blue	44	
45	4 3/4	Made in Ivory, Ivory-Pink, Ivory-Blue	45	
1	2 1/8	Made in Ivory, Pink, Blue	1	
3	2 1/4	Made in Ivory, Pink, Blue	3	
10	1 3/8	Made in Ivory, Pink, Blue	3	
6	3 1/2x1 3/8	Made in Ivory, Pink, Blue	6	
7	3 3/8x1 3/8	Made in Ivory, Ivory-Pink, Ivory-Blue	7	
12	4 5/8	Made in Ivory, Ivory-Pink, Ivory-Blue	12	

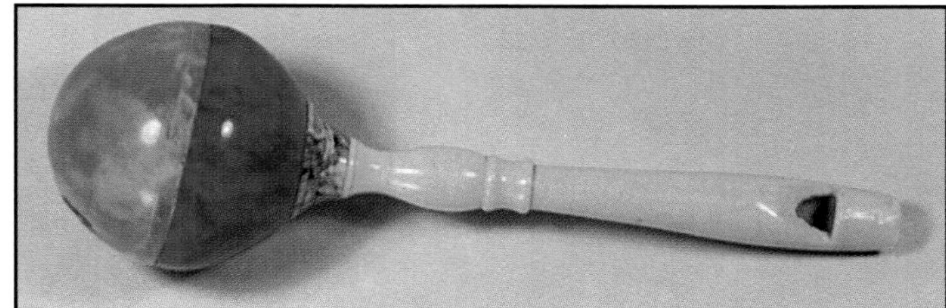

6¼" Celluloid Company rattle. Amber and red sphere, variegated coupling and ivory grained whistle handle. $45.00+.

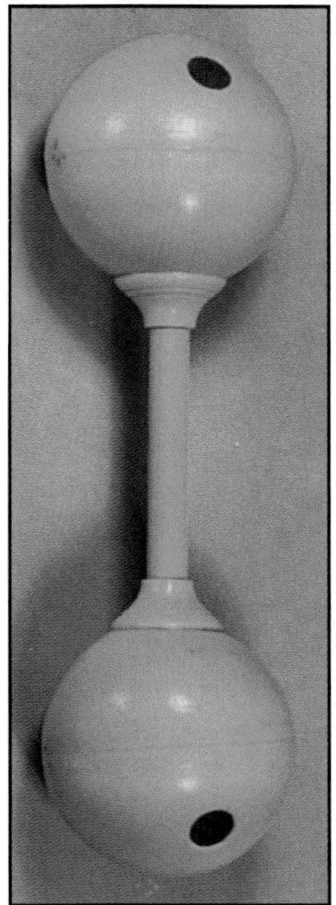

6" ivory grained dumbbell rattle w/ remnants of blue paint in a floral design. $28.00 – $35.00.

5¾" pink girl playing lute, w/ dark pink highlights. Intertwined VCO/USA trademark. In very good conditon, $55.00 – $75.00.

The clown is a desirable image, therefore this 6" ivory figural rattle w/ pink and blue highlights would start at about $50.00 – $55.00.

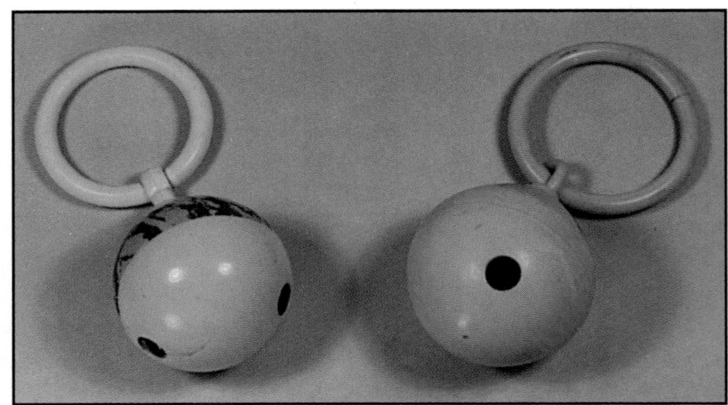

4" ivory ball rattle with attached teething ring. $24.00+.

4½" white clown with pink and brown highlights playing lute. Intertwined "VCO/USA" trademark on back. Bright orange-red clown with lute, no evident trademark, but attributed to Viscoloid. $35.00 – $45.00 each.

Most rattles have tiny metal pellets inside that make a noise when the toy is shaken. On occasion, however, a rattle can be found that has a bell or ball attached to the handle, as is shown in this fine Viscoloid example.7" blue boy with guitar, amber ring w/attached blue and white rattle ball. Intertwined VCO mark on back of leg. $55.00 – $65.00.

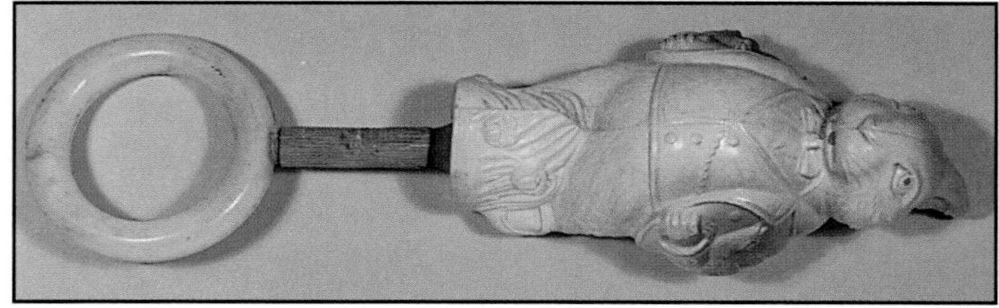

Standing figural toys, animals, and birds were also filled with tiny metal balls to produce a vast array of novelty rattles. Occasionally a handle was attached to one of these flat bottom toys. This example is probably an Easter figural that was converted into a baby rattle. ¾" white rabbit carrying birds with pink and blue highlights. Flat bottom indicates a figural toy with attached handle. Intertwined "VCO/USA." $65.00 – $70.00.

Lucille Mauro

6¼" pear w/brown twig stem. Blow molded of yellow celluloid and highllighted with orange/red paint. $55.00 – $65.00.

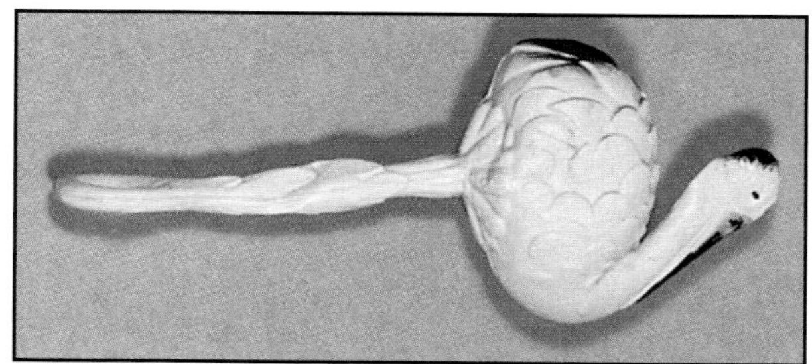

6¼" white stork with black highlights, trademark shows a sitting rabbit next to the word "JAPAN." $55.00 – $65.00.

The rattles illustrated below were assembled using two pieces of embossed and shaped sheet celluloid and handles that are fashioned from celluloid covered wire.

4½" pink and cream rattle with pink teething ring. Hand written ink lettering on top "FOR BABY Elmer." A celluloid coated wire links a pink teething ring to the rattle. $18.00 – $25.00.

Helen Golubic

5¼" face rattle of painted cream celluloid and reverse in dark pink. Handle is celluloid covered wire. $55.00 – $65.00.

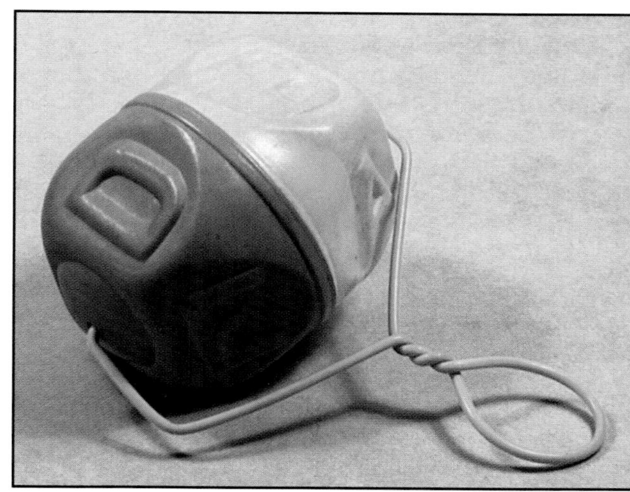

5" rattle, green and cream embossed w/letters that spell BABY DEAR, celluloid covered wire handle, $15.00 – $18.00.

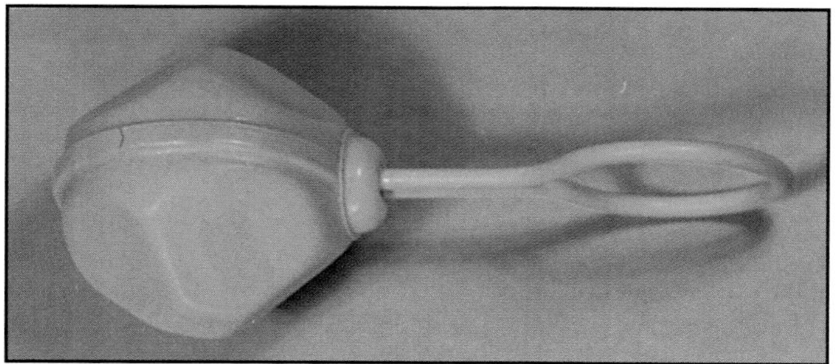

5" rattle, pink and cream embossed w/letters that spell BABY DEAR, celluloid covered wire handle, $12.00 – $15.00.

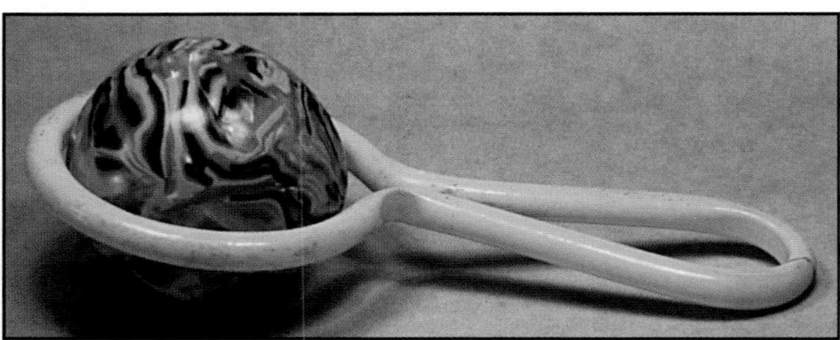

The illustrations on this page show hollow handles that wrap around the central rattling element of the rattle. 9" multi-colored, pink, black, and green pearlescent ball set within cream frame. $25.00 – $35.00.

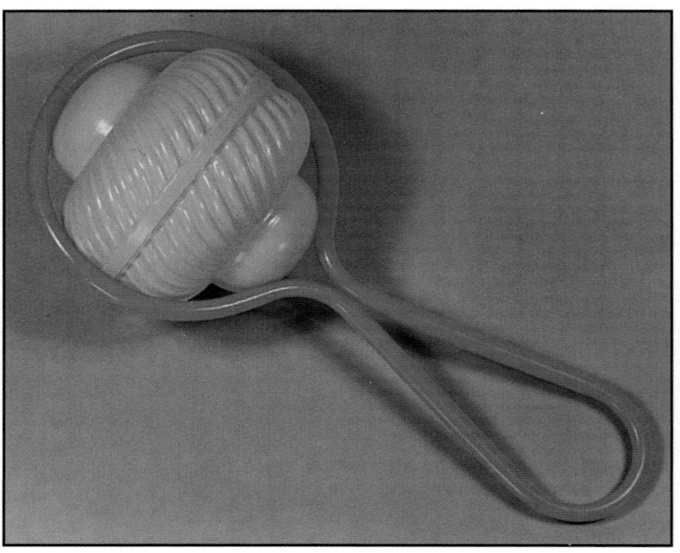

7" light pink embossed swirl design rattle set in dark pink frame handle. $25.00 – $35.00.

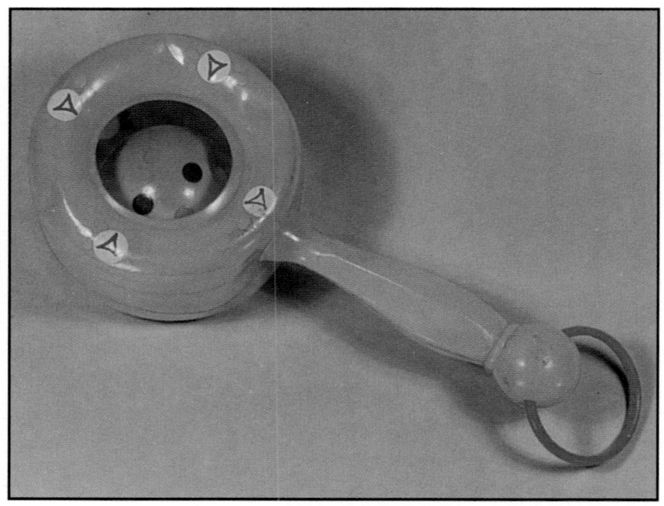

7" pink hollow rattle with blue polka dot ball. Hand painted polka dot decorations. Flower trademark Sekiguchi, "Made in Japan" on bottom of handle. $30.00 – $35.00.

Dottie Maust

Boxed infant set: 5½" cream colored rattle, celluloid covered wire handle with rattling ball; 4" comb and 4¾" brush; 3" dia. x 1⅞" tall powder box. Original box w/75¢ written in pencil on the bottom. $45.00 – $60.00.

Two pairs of pearlescent finish blanket clips with painted floral detail. $10.00 pair.

Helen Golubic

2" x 2⅝" dia. bank, ivory grained w/blue ribbons and hand painted blue birds. Ribbons attach lid to bank by slipping through tiny holes in rim. $18.00 – $22.00.

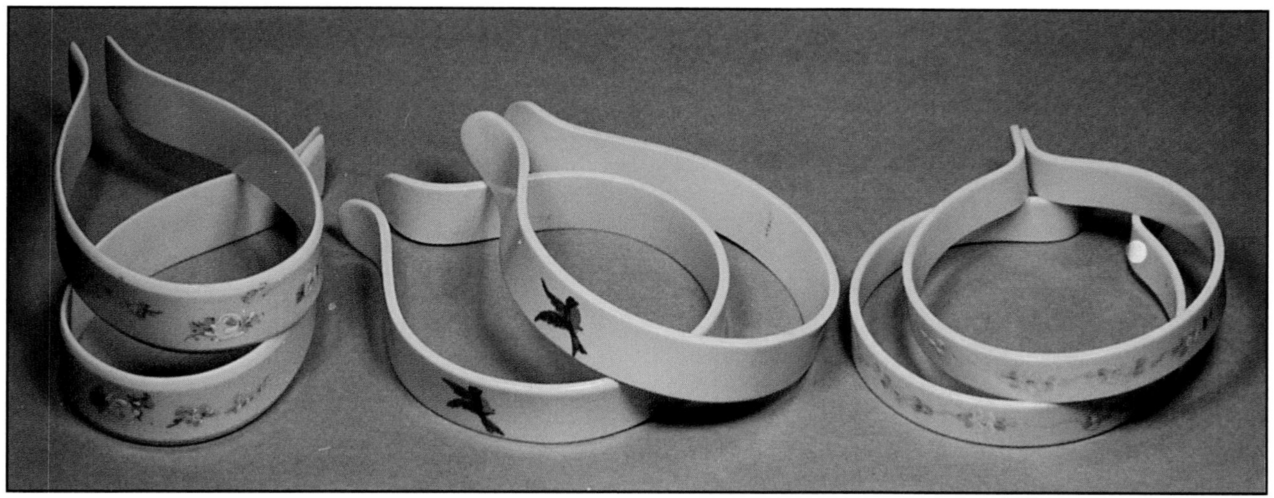

The three sets of blanket clips shown here were designed to secure a baby blanket snugly in place while in a carriage or crib. These items have been mistaken for bracelets and even identified as French cuff holders. $8.00 – $10.00 pair.

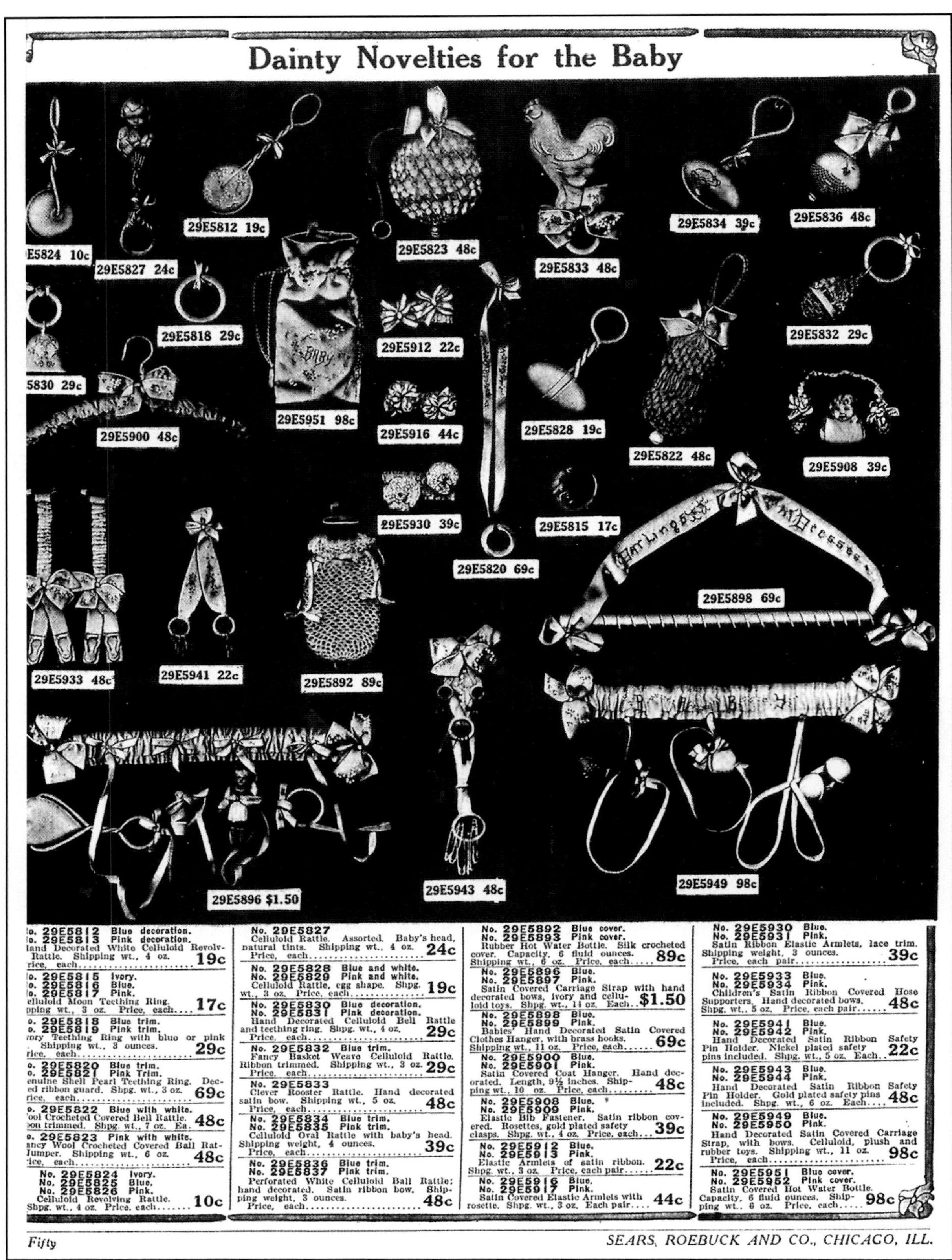

Dainty Novelties for the Baby

lo. 29E5812 Blue decoration.
lo. 29E5813 Pink decoration.
Hand Decorated White Celluloid Revolv- Rattle. Shipping wt., 4 oz. rice, each 19c

lo. 29E5815 Ivory.
lo. 29E5816 Blue.
lo. 29E5817 Pink.
elluloid Moon Teething Ring. pping wt., 3 oz. Price, each.... 17c

o. 29E5818 Blue trim.
o. 29E5819 Pink trim.
vory Teething Ring with blue or pink . Shipping wt., 3 ounces. rice, each 29c

o. 29E5820 Blue trim.
o. 29E5821 Pink Trim.
enuine Shell Pearl Teething Ring. Dec- ed ribbon guard. Shpg. wt., 3 oz. rice, each 69c

o. 29E5822 Blue with white.
ool Crocheted Covered Bell Rattle. bon trimmed. Shpg. wt., 7 oz. Ea. 48c

o. 29E5823 Pink with white.
ancy Wool Crocheted Covered Ball Rat- Jumper. Shipping wt., 6 oz. ice, each 48c

No. 29E5824 Ivory.
No. 29E5825 Blue.
No. 29E5826 Pink.
Celluloid Revolving Rattle. Shpg. wt., 4 oz. Price, each...... 10c

No. 29E5827
Celluloid Rattle. Assorted. Baby's head, natural tints. Shipping wt., 4 oz. Price, each 24c

No. 29E5828 Blue and white.
No. 29E5829 Pink and white.
Celluloid Rattle, egg shape. Shpg. wt., 3 oz. Price, each 19c

No. 29E5830 Blue decoration.
No. 29E5831 Pink decoration.
Hand Decorated Celluloid Bell Rattle and teething ring. Shpg. wt., 4 oz. Price, each 29c

No. 29E5832 Blue trim.
Fancy Basket Weave Celluloid Rattle. Ribbon trimmed. Shipping wt., 3 oz. Price, each 29c

No. 29E5833
Clever Rooster Rattle. Hand decorated satin bow. Shipping wt., 5 oz. Price, each 48c

No. 29E5834 Blue trim.
No. 29E5835 Pink trim.
Celluloid Oval Rattle with baby's head. Shipping weight, 4 ounces. Price, each 39c

No. 29E5836 Blue trim.
No. 29E5837 Pink trim.
Perforated White Celluloid Ball Rattle; hand decorated. Satin ribbon bow. Shipping weight, 3 ounces. Price, each 48c

No. 29E5892 Blue cover.
No. 29E5893 Pink cover.
Rubber Hot Water Bottle. Silk crocheted cover. Capacity, 6 fluid ounces. Shipping wt., 6 oz. Price, each..... 89c

No. 29E5896 Blue.
No. 29E5897 Pink.
Satin Covered Carriage Strap with hand decorated bows, ivory and celluloid toys. Shpg. wt., 14 oz. Each.. $1.50

No. 29E5898 Blue.
No. 29E5899 Pink.
Babies' Hand Decorated Satin Covered Clothes Hanger, with brass hooks. Shipping wt., 11 oz. Price, each...... 69c

No. 29E5900 Blue.
No. 29E5901 Pink.
Satin Covered Coat Hanger. Hand decorated. Length, 9½ inches. Shipping wt., 10 oz. Price, each......... 48c

No. 29E5908 Blue.
No. 29E5909 Pink.
Elastic Bib Fastener. Satin ribbon covered. Rosettes, gold plated safety clasps. Shpg. wt., 4 oz. Price, each... 39c

No. 29E5912 Blue.
No. 29E5913 Pink.
Elastic Armlets of satin ribbon. Shpg. wt., 3 oz. Price, each pair...... 22c

No. 29E5916 Blue.
No. 29E5917 Pink.
Satin Covered Elastic Armlets with rosette. Shpg. wt., 3 oz. Each pair.... 44c

No. 29E5930 Blue.
No. 29E5931 Pink.
Satin Ribbon Elastic Armlets, lace trim. Shipping weight, 3 ounces. Price, each pair 39c

No. 29E5933 Blue.
No. 29E5934 Pink.
Children's Satin Ribbon Covered Hose Supporters, Hand decorated bows. Shpg. wt., 5 oz. Price, each pair...... 48c

No. 29E5941 Blue.
No. 29E5942 Pink.
Hand Decorated Satin Ribbon Safety Pin Holder. Nickel plated safety pins included. Shpg. wt., 5 oz. Each.. 22c

No. 29E5943 Blue.
No. 29E5944 Pink.
Hand Decorated Satin Ribbon Safety Pin Holder. Gold plated safety pins included. Shpg. wt., 6 oz. Each.... 48c

No. 29E5949 Blue.
No. 29E5950 Pink.
Hand Decorated Satin Covered Carriage Strap, with bows. Celluloid, plush and rubber toys. Shipping wt., 11 oz. Price, each 98c

No. 29E5951 Blue cover.
No. 29E5952 Pink cover.
Satin Covered Hot Water Bottle. Capacity, 6 fluid ounces. Shipping wt., 6 oz. Price, each..... 98c

Fifty *SEARS, ROEBUCK AND CO., CHICAGO, ILL.*

Sears, Roebuck and Co. catalog page, circa 1920.

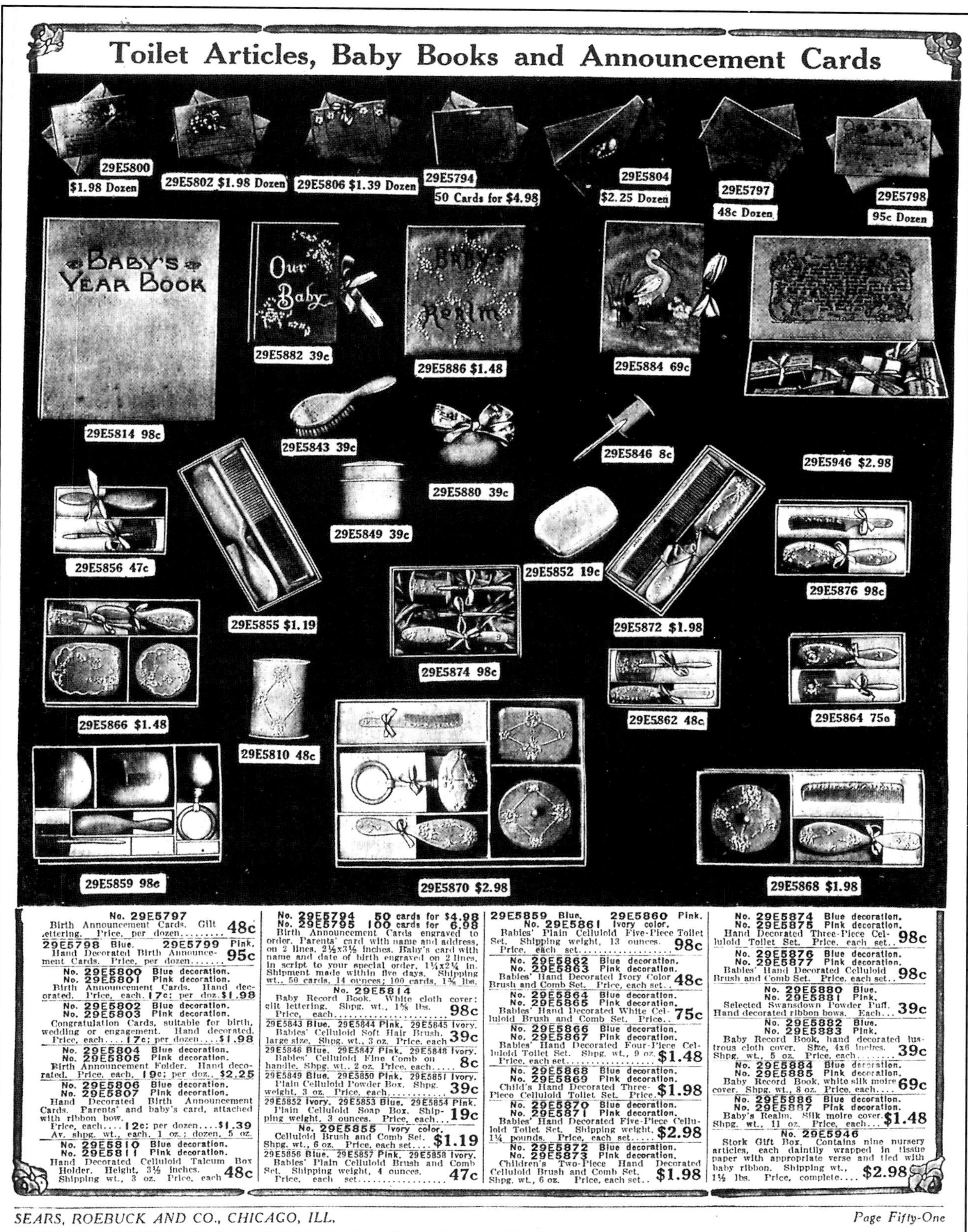

Toilet Articles, Baby Books and Announcement Cards

No. 29E5797
Birth Announcement Cards. Gilt lettering. Price, per dozen......... **48c**

29E5798 Blue. **29E5799** Pink.
Hand Decorated Birth Announcement Cards. Price, per dozen....... **95c**

No. 29E5800 Blue decoration.
No. 29E5801 Pink decoration.
Birth Announcement Cards. Hand decorated. Price, each. **17c**; per doz. **$1.98**

No. 29E5802 Blue decoration.
No. 29E5803 Pink decoration.
Congratulation Cards, suitable for birth, wedding or engagement. Hand decorated. Price, each.... **17c**; per dozen.... **$1.98**

No. 29E5804 Blue decoration.
No. 29E5805 Pink decoration.
Birth Announcement Folder. Hand decorated. Price, each, **19c**; per doz., **$2.25**

No. 29E5806 Blue decoration.
No. 29E5807 Pink decoration.
Hand Decorated Birth Announcement Cards. Parents' and baby's card, attached with ribbon bow.
Price, each.... **12c**; per dozen.... **$1.39**
Av. shpg. wt., each, 1 oz.; dozen, 5 oz.

No. 29E5810 Blue decoration.
No. 29E5811 Pink decoration.
Hand Decorated Celluloid Talcum Box Holder. Height, 3½ inches. Shipping wt., 3 oz. Price, each **48c**

No. 29E5794 50 cards for **$4.98**
No. 29E5795 100 cards for **6.98**
Birth Announcement Cards engraved to order. Parents' card with name and address, on 2 lines, 2½x3½ inches. Baby's card with name and date of birth engraved on 2 lines, in script to your special order, 1¼x2¼ in. Shipment made within five days. Shipping wt., 50 cards, 14 ounces; 100 cards, 1⅜ lbs.

No. 29E5814
Baby Record Book. White cloth cover; gilt lettering. Shpg. wt., 1⅝ lbs. Price, each........................ **98c**

29E5843 Blue. **29E5844** Pink. **29E5845** Ivory.
Babies' Celluloid Soft Hair Brush, large size. Shpg. wt., 3 oz. Price, each **39c**

29E5846 Blue. **29E5847** Pink. **29E5848** Ivory.
Babies' Celluloid Fine Comb on handle. Shpg. wt., 2 oz. Price, each..... **8c**

29E5849 Blue. **29E5850** Pink. **29E5851** Ivory.
Plain Celluloid Powder Box. Shpg. weight, 3 oz. Price, each........... **39c**

29E5852 Ivory. **29E5853** Blue. **29E5854** Pink.
Plain Celluloid Soap Box. Shipping weight, 3 ounces. Price, each... **19c**

No. 29E5855 Ivory color.
Celluloid Brush and Comb Set. Shpg. wt., 6 oz. Price, each set.... **$1.19**

29E5856 Blue. **29E5857** Pink. **29E5858** Ivory.
Babies' Plain Celluloid Brush and Comb Set. Shipping weight, 4 ounces. Price, each set.................. **47c**

29E5859 Blue. **29E5860** Pink.
No. 29E5861 Ivory color.
Babies' Plain Celluloid Five-Piece Toilet Set. Shipping weight, 13 ounces. Price, each set.................... **98c**

No. 29E5862 Blue decoration.
No. 29E5863 Pink decoration.
Babies' Hand Decorated Ivory Color Brush and Comb Set. Price, each set.. **48c**

No. 29E5864 Blue decoration.
No. 29E5865 Pink decoration.
Babies' Hand Decorated White Celluloid Brush and Comb Set. Price.. **75c**

No. 29E5866 Blue decoration.
No. 29E5867 Pink decoration.
Babies' Hand Decorated Four-Piece Celluloid Toilet Set. Shpg. wt., 9 oz. Price, each set................. **$1.48**

No. 29E5868 Blue decoration.
No. 29E5869 Pink decoration.
Child's Hand Decorated Three-Piece Celluloid Toilet Set. Price. **$1.98**

No. 29E5870 Blue decoration.
No. 29E5871 Pink decoration.
Babies' Hand Decorated Five-Piece Celluloid Toilet Set. Shipping weight, 1¼ pounds. Price, each set..... **$2.98**

No. 29E5872 Blue decoration.
No. 29E5873 Pink decoration.
Children's Two-Piece Hand Decorated Celluloid Brush and Comb Set. Shpg. wt., 6 oz. Price, each set.. **$1.98**

No. 29E5874 Blue decoration.
No. 29E5875 Pink decoration.
Hand Decorated Three-Piece Celluloid Toilet Set. Price, each set.. **98c**

No. 29E5876 Blue decoration.
No. 29E5877 Pink decoration.
Babies' Hand Decorated Celluloid Brush and Comb Set. Price, each set.. **98c**

No. 29E5880 Blue.
No. 29E5881 Pink.
Selected Swansdown Powder Puff. Hand decorated ribbon bows. Each... **39c**

No. 29E5882 Blue.
No. 29E5883 Pink.
Baby Record Book, hand decorated lustrous cloth cover. Size, 4x6 inches. Shpg. wt., 5 oz. Price, each....... **39c**

No. 29E5884 Blue decoration.
No. 29E5885 Pink decoration.
Baby Record Book, white silk moire cover. Shpg. wt., 8 oz. Price, each.... **69c**

No. 29E5886 Blue decoration.
No. 29E5887 Pink decoration.
Baby's Realm. Silk moire cover. Shpg. wt., 11 oz. Price, each... **$1.48**

No. 29E5946
Stork Gift Box. Contains nine nursery articles, each daintily wrapped in tissue paper with appropriate verse and tied with baby ribbon. Shipping wt., 1½ lbs. Price, complete.... **$2.98**

SEARS, ROEBUCK AND CO., CHICAGO, ILL. — Page Fifty-One

Sears, Roebuck and Co. catalog page, circa 1920.

Celluloid in Musical Instruments

Pyroxylin plastics have been used in musical instruments ever since the Celluloid Manufacturing Company licensed the Celluloid Piano Key Company Limited on December 12, 1878, only two days after John W. Hyatt was granted a patent for an Improvement in Piano Keys, USP #210,780. Shortly thereafter the manufacturing company licensed Denison Brothers of Deep River, Conn., for the production of celluloid organ stop knobs.

Eventually celluloid keyboards on pianos and organs became just as popular as true ivory. Surprisingly there was little or no difference in the cost between the two substances and as a result both inexpensive and fine instruments utilized celluloid keys.

Other uses for celluloid in musical instruments included the keyboards for concertinas and accordions as well as the entire cases of the instruments. Celluloid was used extensively as trimming in the manufacture of stringed instruments; the variety of applications included tuning pegs for stringed instruments, pick guards on guitars and mandolins, plectrums, inlay material for fingerboards, and chin rests.

Entire 20" x 12" sheets of nitrocellulose plastic can also be purchased for the Luthier (instrument maker) who prefers to design a custom pick guard. The cost ranges from about $30.00 for tortoise shell to $45.00 for pearloid. However, it is important to ask if the plastic is actually "nitrocellulose" because there are many look-alike products.

Perhaps some of the most common celluloid items in circulation are the picks musicians use to strum their stringed instruments. Viscoloid manufactured picks for D'Andrea and Herco. Many vintage picks were also imported from Japan and are marked. Simply run hot tap water over a pick for 10 seconds and smell; if the odor of camphor is detected, your pick is celluloid.

The variety of new and vintage celluloid guitar, mandolin, and banjo finger picks seems endless. The most desirable among collectors are ivory grained, odd-shaped imitation tortoise shell, and brightly colored flat picks. The first book on vintage celluloid picks has recently been written for the musician/collector. It is a practice among musicians to trade picks, and many have accumulated massive collections.

Helen D. Golubic

This wonderfully detailed Florentina was made by the New York Accordion Manufacturing Company, Moreschi and Sons. The decorative panel adjacent to the keyboard is fashioned from three pieces of die cut celluloid in pearlized gray, black, yellow, and white; inlaid crystal, topaz, and green rhinestones accent the item. Circa 1930. $135.00+.

Detail of the Florentina accordion.

Pastor Charles Kelly, Boswell Christian Community Church

Imitation ivory pick guard on Gibson Deluxe 6 string acoustic electric guitar; pick guards can be purchased through a guitar supply company.

Leominster Historical Society

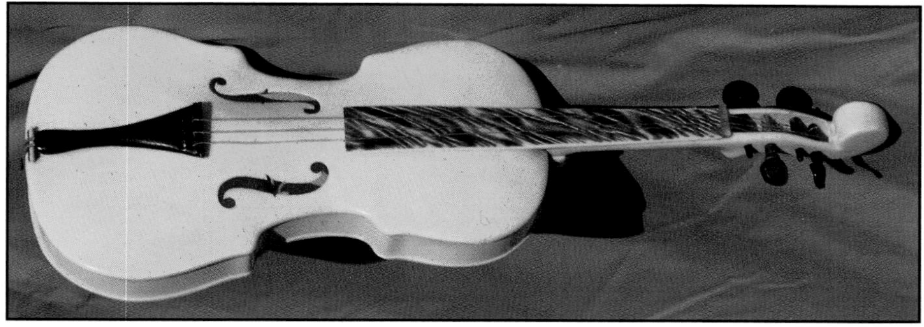

This all-celluloid violin is a one-of-a-kind beauty. Manufactured from cream, black, and imitation tortoise shell, it is a rarity, the only known one to exist. It was designed and made by Joseph Ouellette, a plastics sample maker in Leominster, Mass., and is currently housed at the Leominster Historical Society.

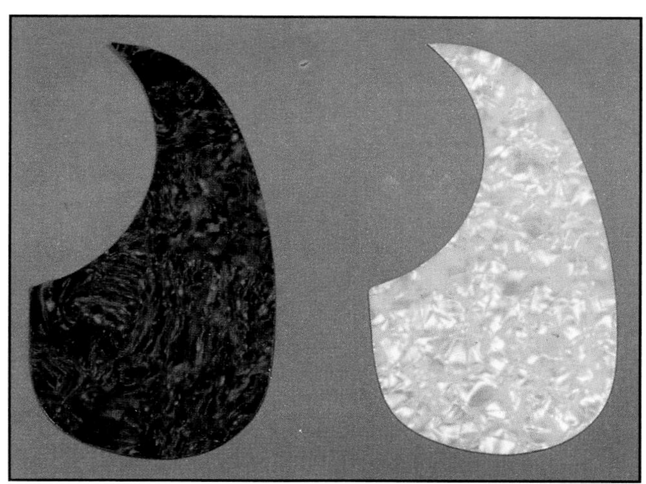

Two brand new cellulose nitrate pick guards, available in pearlescent white and imitation tortoise shell from Stewart Macdonald's Guitar Shop Supply. Tortoise $5.00; Pearloid $8.00.

Photograph by Rebecca B. Pelletier

Instrument maker Dick Pelletier with a sheet of vintage "Mother of Toilet Seat" for use in the repair of antique musical instruments.

Celluloid strips, known as "bindings" to instrument makers, are available in 4' lengths in the following colors: rippled ivoroid, tortoise, grained ivoroid, black, and white. Bindings can be stacked together using acetone, then filed smooth. The cost per strip varies according to color and thickness, but the general price range per strip is \$2.00 – \$5.00.

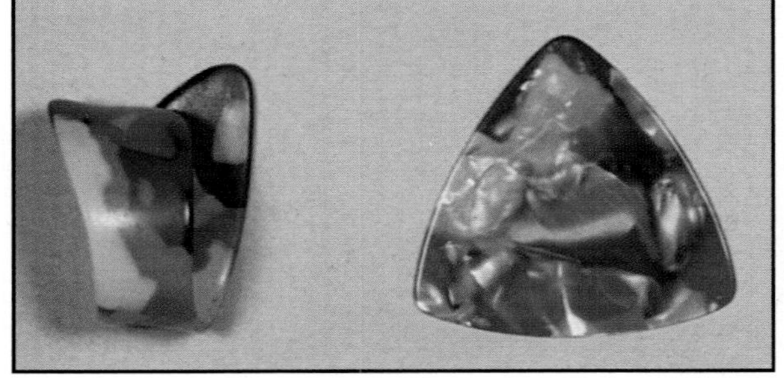

Two colorful vintage picks in mosaic colors. D'Andrea #346 mosaic pick, circa 1950. \$2.00 – \$6.00 each.

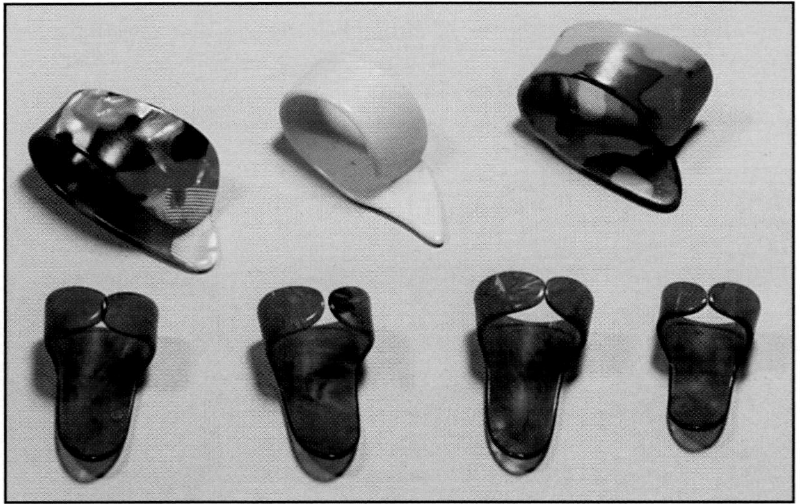

Assortment of finger picks in pearlescent mosaic, imitation grained ivory, mosaic, and imitation tortoise shell. Mosaic and ivory are less common than tortoise and therefore more expensive. \$2.00 – \$6.00 each; tortoise set of 4 (thumb pick is missing), \$10.00.

Celluloid advertising picks are usually available from most music supply stores and are fun to trade with musicians. They can be found imprinted with a variety of brand names imprints as well as personalized messages. 50¢ each.

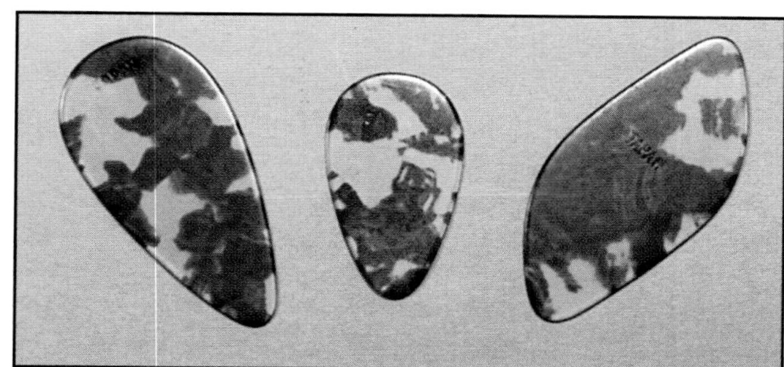

The three picks shown in this photograph include a small mandolin plectrum, a two-point trapezoid, and a long oval. All of the sizes, shapes, and colors look like Herco products, however each one is marked Japan. $1.00 each.

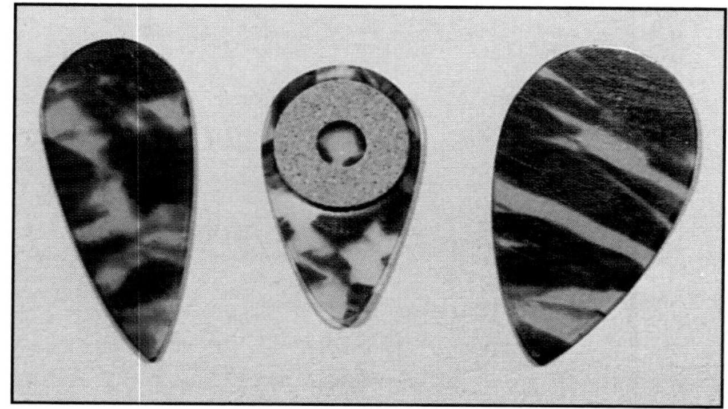

Three long oval picks of varied tortoise celluloid. The center pick is a Herco medium oval with a cork grip. $1.00 – $3.00.

The four imitation tortoise shell picks illustrated here include at top center a Gretsch thin guitar plectrum; clockwise: a small D'Andrea thin mandolin plectrum (both of these picks were manufactured by D'Andrea – note the similarity in the pattern of the imitation shell); H-F mandolin pick; and a Guild medium mandolin pick. Various manufacturers used different patterns of celluloid. $1.00 – $2.00 each.

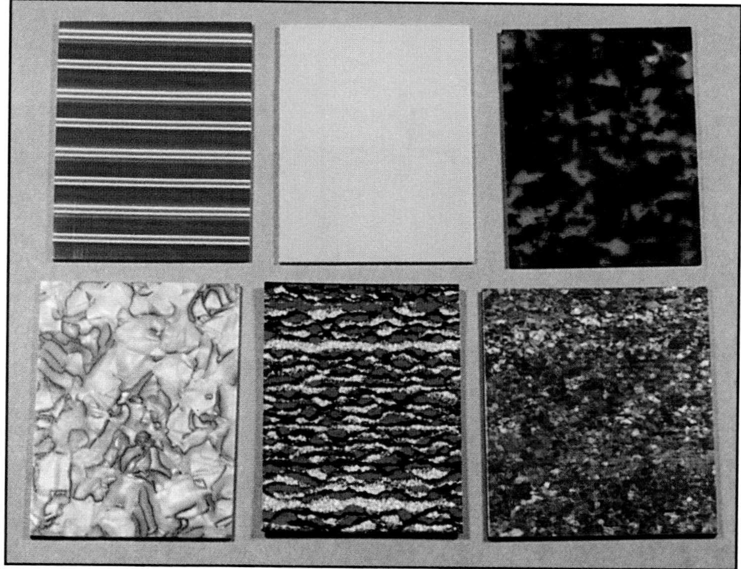

A sampling of six different celluloid patterns manufactured in Italy. 3" x 4" slabs cost approximately $7.00 each from Masecraft Supply Co. Luthier's could use this celluloid to fashion custom-made plectrums and inlay.

Chemistry, Care, and Preservation

Chemistry

Introduction

Since celluloid is made up of both natural and synthetic substances, certain precautions should be taken when collecting, cleaning, repairing, and storing celluloid articles. In order to better do this, a fundamental understanding of celluloid's chemical make up is essential.

Basic Recipe for Celluloid

After cellulose fiber has been treated with nitric and sulfuric acids, it is cleansed repeatedly with alcohol and water. Once the nitrated cellulose pulp is free of all acid residue, the resulting compound (CN) is combined with camphor and thoroughly mixed. As the particles of camphor and CN come into contact with each other, a chemical change begins to takes place. The separate molecules begin to link together, forming a totally new structure that looks something like a chain. This chemical reaction is called "polymerization."

Dyes are added to the compound, resulting in raw celluloid which is ready to be formed into blocks, tubes, rods, or sheets by the application of heat and pressure. Once fabricated, the celluloid stock is placed in a warm seasoning room where evaporation of residual alcohol takes place. After sufficient curing, the celluloid is ready to be fabricated into finished articles.

Cellulose Nitrate - CN

Cellulose nitrate, CN, is a gelatinous pulp-like substance produced by the action of sulfuric and nitric acids upon cellulose fiber. The chief sources of cellulose used in the production of CN for the manufacture of celluloid include cotton linters, cloth scraps, and tissue paper.

Nitrocellulose is created when the molecules in cellulose are chemically modified by nitration, the action of nitric acid on the cellulose fibers. The compound which is formed is dangerously flammable and has been used to produce a wide variety of materials including explosives, adhesives, photographic film, collodion, lacquer, nail polish, and solid plastics.

Cellulose nitrate is soluble in water, methanol, ethylene, alcohols, acetone, acetic, and sulfuric acids, amyl acetone, and ether. Because of this, caution should be exercised when using cleaning solutions on celluloid.

Camphor

Camphor is a white crystalline resin that is derived from the Cinnamomum camphora tree, which is indigenous to Japan and Asia. The trunks, roots, and branches of the camphor tree are steam distilled to yield the resin. Other types of camphor are derived from trees which have a solid mass of the crystallized substance in the center.

Camphor has a strong, mentholated odor and has, for centuries, been used for medicinal purposes. In the production of celluloid, camphor is used as a cellulose nitrate plastizer.

Camphor is soluble in methanol, ethylene, alcohols, acetone, turpentine, mineral spirits, naphtha, acetic, sulfuric and nitrate acids, and benzene. Again, caution should be exercised when attempting to clean celluloid.

Additives and Colorants

Various dyes and pigments, including zinc oxide and zinc carbonate, have been used to color celluloid. Antacids are used to produce translucent celluloid. The combination and quality of additives may affect the stability of finished celluloid.

During the 1890s, the best supply of camphor came from Formosa, which is now known as Taiwan. Raw camphor had to be purified, so it was brought to Kobe, Japan, the camphor refining center of the world. The two camphor tins illustrated here were imported into the United States from Kobe. The plain embossed tin, valued at $15.00 – $22.00, still has a bit of the pungent smelling substance inside. The colored tin is valued between $25.00 – $30.00.

This 1-lb. DuPont camphor tin originally held 32-½ oz. tablets of refined camphor. It was manufactured by E.I. DuPont De Nemours and Co., Inc., Wilmington, Delaware. Note the DuPont oval trademark on the upper left front of the tin; it is the same mark seen on several of the DuPont/Viscoloid toys manufactured in Leominster, Mass., during the late 1920s.

Flammability and Industrial Hazards

Flammability

Because celluloid is made up of 65% cellulose nitrate, it is highly inflammable. However, contrary to popular belief, celluloid is not explosive; the degree of nitration in celluloid is simply too weak to support spontaneous combustion. (A stronger form of cellulose nitrate is used in the manufacture of plastic explosives.) Most likely the misconception is linked to the story of the exploding billiard ball, a story that is simply not true. Hyatt himself addressed the problem in his Perkin Medal acceptance speech in May of 1914.

He explained that during the early days of their production the billiard balls, which were coated with a thin film of highly concentrated cellulose nitrate, sometimes made a loud bang (much like that of a percussion gun cap) when they collided during play. However, the most serious problem related to the balls involved the carelessness of carousing men in saloons and billiard parlors. It seemed that on several occasions serious fires were started when the glowing tips of lit cigars unintentionally came in contact with the billiard balls.

Industrial Hazards

In the early days of the pyroxylin plastic industry, factory fires were a constant threat. Many facilities in America and abroad experienced numerous fires, including Arlington, which lost over a million pounds of celluloid in a 1916 blaze; Fiberloid, which rebuilt an entire facility in Indian Orchard with an established fire department; and the Celluloid Manufacturing Company which suffered 39 fires resulting in nine deaths and countless injuries.

In spite of all the safety precautions exercised, celluloid fires were still common events. Perhaps the most bizarre industrial accident on record is listed in a 1928 volume of *Industrial Fire Hazards* by Gorham Dana and William Milne. It states that a backfire from an automobile ignited a scrap pile of celluloid.

It should also be noted that other hazards were associated with the celluloid industry that did not involve fire. Acid burns on skin were common; nitric acid and wood alcohol fumes sickened many and caused breathing problems; and on occasion a hand was trapped in machinery and severed.

Celluloid Related Fires

Celluloid fabricators also took necessary precautions to protect against the dangers of fire. In the comb factories of Leominster, workers were required to cut the heat-softened celluloid under a steady stream of water. Prevention was of utmost importance because celluloid burned so rapidly; it was nearly impossible to contain a blaze once a fire had started.

Some of the most unfortunate fires happened in businesses and hospitals were celluloid articles were improperly used or stored. One such disaster is recorded by Sam Robinowitz in *Atwood's Catalog of United States and Canadian Transportation Tokens* and deals with the destruction of the car barns and offices of the Sioux City Street Railway Co. of Iowa in the early 1890s. Reportedly, the celluloid tokens used by the trolley company were stored in an office safe that became excessively hot. The result was an explosive fire which completely destroyed the entire facility.

Movie houses were especially susceptible to raging fires since cinema film was made of celluloid. Between the years 1914 – 1936, 197 cinema fires were recorded. The method of projecting movies involved passing the film by a bright light, which inevitably generated heat; the result was all too often disastrous. Among the worst fires was that of stored motion picture film at the Ferguson Building in downtown Pittsburgh. The destruction of the building prompted an extensive investigation of the combustion of celluloid, resulting in the first thorough analysis of the gases emitted from burning pyroxylin plastic.

Perhaps the most famous and tragic of celluloid fires was that of the Cleveland Clinic on May 15, 1929. The disaster was due to the ignition of x-ray film stored in a small improperly vented room in the basement of the fireproof building. The fire damage by itself was contained in a relatively small area, but the poisonous gases given off by the burning celluloid per-

Unfortunately, fires were sometimes the result of employee carelessness. Therefore, a set of strict guidelines was adopted and enforced.

1. The entire factory facility was to be kept scrupulously clean with each worker responsible for the cleanliness of the area around him.
2. Foremen in all departments were to understand and observe specific rules for safe operations, perform careful routine inspections of machinery and maintain all safety and protective appliances.
3. Smoking or the carrying of any matches was forbidden. Any worker found in possession of such items within the vicinity of the factory would be terminated.
4. Employees who worked in the nitration process building were restricted from entering other parts of the factory for fear that inflammable nitric acid residue may be carried into the area.
5. Avoid danger from defective electric wiring, drop cords or lamps. Avoid the use of high temperature heating appliances. Avoid the use of high speed machines, pulleys, and shafting which may create an accumulation of static charges which could ignite the inflammable vapors associated with cellulose nitrate.
6. Install sprinkler systems throughout the facility and emergency fire hoses with unlimited supply of water.
7. Remove scrap celluloid promptly from the building, avoiding the build-up of huge scrap piles. One such 32,000 pound scrap pile burned with such fury the entire mountain of material was consumed within 16 minutes.
8. Seasoning and storage rooms were located in a separate fire proof buildings on the plant facility.

meated throughout the entire structure; of the 250 people in the building at the time of the blaze, 122 lost their lives. From that time forward, x-ray film was stored in a small room on the roof of the hospital or at a separate facility altogether.

In addition to these tragic incidences, there were many bizarre fires that began with individual carelessness and ended in disaster. In the early 1880s, C.V. Boys of the *London Times* warned of a danger to women who wore celluloid buttons. One such case involved a lady who was standing too close to a bright fire and her dress button ignited.

Even more unusual is that of the farmer who had an artificial leg made of celluloid. The story goes that while working one hot summer day, the sun's radiant heat reflected off the shovel he was using and ignited his leg!

Many fires were the result of careless smokers. An incident involving a guest at the Chateau Laurier Hotel in Ottawa, Canada, who was smoking while using the bathroom ended in destruction. He carelessly discarded his smoldering cigarette butt which came into contact with a toilet seat covered in celluloid sheet.

Although there was widespread knowledge of celluloid's flammability, tragedies still occurred; even as late as 1948 two incidents involving celluloid toys killed one child and seriously burned another.

Proper Handling

As a result of celluloid's extreme flammability, the proper handling of objects in the collection is very important. Celluloid should never be placed in close proximity to open flame. It seems rather absurd that some fabricators actually produced such articles as candle stick and cigarette holders, especially considering celluloid's dangerous nature! Nevertheless, these types of articles were produced and on occasion can still be found today. It is strongly recommended therefore, that if such items are part of a collection, they not

The Hazards of Smoking

Another cigarette related fire was unintentionally started by Julie Robinson's grandmother when, as a teenager in the 1920s, she decided to try smoking:

Smoking of any sort was forbidden in the grand old Victorian house in Lyndonville, Vermont, where Grammie grew up. Because her father suffered from severe asthma and her mother was a religious woman, the daughter of an evangelist who didn't believe in smoking, anyone who broke the rule would surely suffer the consequences.

One day while my great-grandparents had gone for a leisurely automobile ride, Grammie and her girifriends decided to sneak a cigarette on the back porch of the house. Because there were no ashtrays around, they found a small celluloid dresser tray, which seemed just about the right size for the job.

Placing it on the window sill, the girls lit their cigarette and began to puff away, but within moments of using the tray, the celluloid blew up, scaring the girls half to death! While it burned furiously, they scurried into action and soon the fire was extinguished, but the damage was done; a hole had been burned into the window sill and the celluloid dresser tray destroyed.

Panic set in, for smoking was expressly forbidden in the home; it was decided the best solution to the problem would be to hide the evidence. The remains of the celluloid tray were wrapped in old newspaper and buried deep in the trash. Soon after, her girlfriends disappeared and my teen-aged grandmother was left alone to fix the burned window sill.

She quickly found an empty glass jar, then got on her bicycle and frantically peddled through the small town, across the railroad tracks past Lyndon Corner, to Ruth Duke's house in East Lyndon. She explained the situation and secured an emergency supply of fresh paint with which to repair the damage. Carefully balancing the glass jar of paint in one hand and maneuvering the bicycle with the other, she hastened home in hopes of arriving before her parents returned from their afternoon drive. But unfortunately while crossing over the railroad tracks, the jar slipped free, fell to the ground, and shattered. Anxiously, Grammie gathered up the pieces of broken glass that were still covered with paint and urgently continued home.

Fortunately her parents had not yet returned, and since there was enough paint still clinging to the pieces retrieved from the broken jar, she carefully camouflaged the charred hole in the window sill. Her repair job was good enough so that neither of my great-grandparents was aware of the fire, and surprisingly, noone ever mentioned the missing dresser tray. Needless to say, that experience cured my grandmother and her girlfriends from ever sneaking cigarettes in the Eaton household again.

The most tragic fires were those that involved children playing with celluloid toys which somehow ignited. This circa 1938 photograph reveals that celluloid was a known fire hazard. The display illustrated here was set up during Fire Prevention Week, Oct. 1938, around Fountain Square in Cincinnati, Ohio.

be used for their intended purpose but remain solely decorative.

In short, the combustion of celluloid is extremely rapid. In a series of tests conducted between 1913 and 1915, results found that 1,900 pounds of the material burned in three minutes time.

The combustion of celluloid is attended by rapid evolution of explosive and inflammable gases which ignite and burn like a violent blowtorch. The combination includes carbon dioxide, carbon monoxide, nitrous oxide, hydrocarbons, nitrogen, hydrogen, and oxygen.

Tests proved that 1,000 pounds of celluloid will form 3,000 to 8,500 cubic feet of this highly flammable gas and that 1,000 pounds of burning celluloid project a blast of flame 70 feet long; furthermore a sample piece of celluloid cinema film six feet long projected a flame measuring 120 feet long as it was rapidly consumed!

To prevent the accumulation of invisible but highly dangerous gases, keep celluloid objects in a well-ventilated area to promote circulation of air. If at all possible, do not store celluloid in tightly closed containers which may accelerate deterioration and the formation of harmful vapors.

Cleaning Tips

It is the authors' opinion that no harsh household cleansers should ever be used to clean celluloid! Window cleaner, nail polish removers, alcohol, ammonia, and concentrated cleansers are all solutions that contain harmful ingredients. With a little patience and a gentle touch, celluloid can be cleaned successfully by using the purest vegetable oil, mild soap, and little water. The following guidelines are suggested for cleaning dirty celluloid objects.

1. Use a bit of plain vegetable oil on a soft cloth or tissue to soften and remove sticky price tag residue on solid celluloid objects. Gently wipe the entire surface with a light coat of oil; after all adhesive has been removed, buff dry.

2. Take care when applying pressure to hollow blow-molded articles while cleaning. Old celluloid often becomes brittle and is susceptible to breakage. Rather than rubbing away sticky price tag residue, try using a piece of cellophane tape to remove the substance; simply apply the tape to the area that needs cleaning and quickly but gently lift away, repeating the process until all the adhesive has been removed.

3. It is safe to clean solid celluloid objects with warm soapy water and a soft cloth or toothbrush on the condition that the piece has no metal parts, monogramming, painted decorations, rhinestones, or laminated paper decorations that could be damaged. Generally solid dresser trays, powder boxes, and hair receivers will not be harmed if they are quickly washed and immediately dried. If celluloid is allowed to soak in water for an extended period of time, the cellulose nitrate will absorb water and begin to break down.

4. Surface dirt should be carefully removed from objects such as decorative boxes, pinback buttons, advertising and jewelry items which may have decorative elements such as laminated paper, photographs, and exterior embellishments or reverse painting under the celluloid.

5. Pieces that include rhinestones or metal parts should not be immersed in water as the deterioration process will be rapidly accelerated. When moisture is trapped between celluloid and metal or the foil backing of rhinestones, degradation is inevitable. Rhinestones become dull and colorless as the backing corrodes, and metal findings may begin to rust. Within time, the celluloid itself will react to the chemical changes and begin to show irreversible signs of degeneration.

6. Some collectors of decorative celluloid boxes and albums have been known to wax their items as a way to protect them from dirt. To date, no adverse effects caused by this practice are known. However, once again caution should be exercised if you plan to treat your collection in this manner; it is suggested that ingredient labels be carefully examined and the owner be absolutely sure there are no harmful ingredients in the wax or cleaning compounds being used.

Special note

When raw celluloid was prepared for fabrication, the manufacturers used a liquid solution to coat the molds to keep the material from sticking. The variety of solutions found to work successfully included pure oil, glycerin, and soapy water. Even today, manufacturers in the Orient still swab their molds with soapy water before the celluloid is inserted for forming. This age-old practice has proven to have had no adverse effects on the celluloid objects, fabricated over 100 years ago, which are still available today.

Decomposition

There are four main processes that have proven to be sources of degeneration in celluloid: thermal, chemical, photochemical, and physical. For the sake of simplifying matters, these processes will be treated as either internal or external problems.

Internal Sources of Deterioration

These are several sources of deterioration which are inherent in the material of celluloid itself. In the early days before quality control guidelines were strictly enforced, there were sometimes variations in the manufacturing process that related to certain types of deterioration. Impure water, unbleached cellulose, unrefined camphor, contaminated additives and colorants were all sources for potential discoloration or spotting.

Another concern for the manufacturers of this material involved the incomplete nitration of cellulose fiber or the incomplete blending of basic ingredients which in the early days could result in a product that was potentially unstable and susceptible to brittleness. In addition, the fabrication of insufficiently cured celluloid was cause for warping, splitting, and deformation of finished products. The seasoning process was essential for the evaporation of residual alcohol. Eventually the variations in manufacturing processes were overcome, and quality control standards enforced.

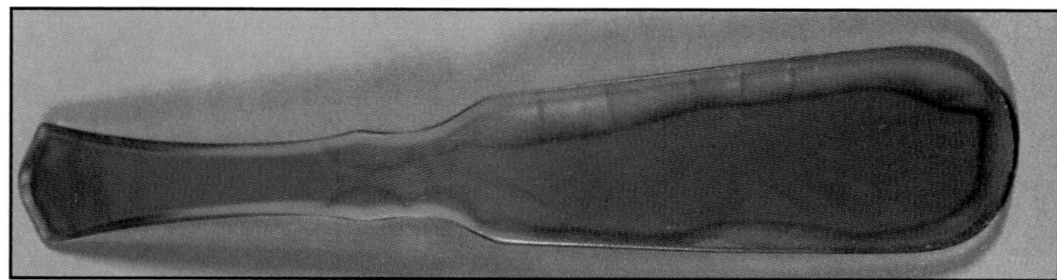

This photograph of a circa 1925 shoe horn illustrates the problem sometimes associated with combining two different batches of celluloid. The lamination process fused contrasting colors of celluloid under heat and pressure. Because the chemical composition of the various celluloid used in fabrication of multicolored objects differed slightly, articles fabricated in this way may warp, split, or separate into layers. The underside of the amber and pearlescent cream article is illustrated here in order to give a full view of the deterioration. The shoe horn is badly warped, although this is not evident in the photograph. What is clear however are the cracks along the edge and an obvious problem of discoloration, most definitely a chemical reaction, where the two different batches of plastic were joined.

This circa 1925 Celluloid Company trinket box is fashioned from a combination of solid ivory grained celluloid with laminates. The imitation ivory sides have become discolored with a slight orangish tinge around the bottom where it is attached to the glittery laminated base. The presence of a greenish color suggests verdigris, the corrosion of copper or brass in the glitter material. Cracks are also evident along the base. When this box was purchased in 1995, only a tiny crack was evident along the bottom lamination with a very small tinge of discoloration. Within two years time, the discoloration had spread throughout the entire bottom and is now affecting the ivory grained sides. The stability of the entire piece is now at risk. A piece of paper that was inside the box since purchase had absorbed the escaping gases, was slightly oily to the touch, and had discolored to a semi-translucent yellowish green. The paper has become nitrated and is highly flammable.

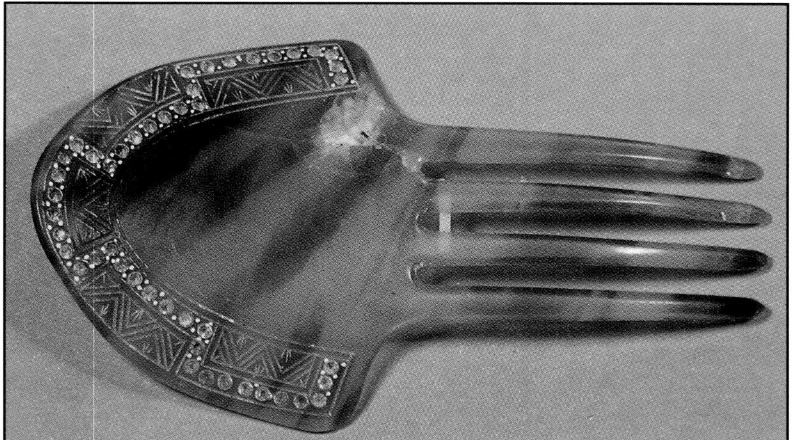

At times, a combination of deterioration processes happens at once. The crystallization of this comb is the most obvious, but in addition there is a thin oily film covering the entire surface; the once translucent imitation tortoise is now cloudy in appearance; the texture of the celluloid itself seems to have been affected by the surface acid and no longer feels dry and hard. This comb was purchased in July 1995 and had a 1⁄16" crack in the celluloid. Within three months, the formation of crystals had become evident around the crack, and a slight cloudy discoloration was beginning to spread around the edges. As an experiment, the deteriorating comb was wrapped in an airtight plastic bag and put away from October 1995 to October 1996, then observation was recorded. The entire surface was coated with a thin film of acid, and crystal formation had begun on the tips of the prongs. The comb was rewrapped and set away for another year and in October 1997 retrieved for observation and photography. By this time formation of cracks and crystallization had spread into a large area, a prong had separated completely along the crystal fault line and the entire comb was cloudy. No longer hard, the texture of the comb had become soft and slightly mushy. This was probably due to the fact that the item had been in an airtight environment and the release of nitrogen dioxide gas was not allowed to dissipate.

NPCM

This disintegrated comb measured 14" from top to bottom and was a product of E.B. Kingman Co. of Leominster, Mass. The pale amber article is completely consumed with disease. Items that show signs of crystal formation should be removed from the collection as the escape of nitrogen dioxide gas will affect the stability of all celluloid it comes in contact with. Keep good articles in a well-ventilated place to avoid contamination.

The brittle, crumbling buttons shown here are in a rapid and advanced state of degeneration. The crystallized formation is commonly called "disease" among collectors of celluloid articles. It has been suggested that the camphor molecules sublime (evaporate), and the remaining cellulose nitrate molecules begin to crystallize. When this occurs, the release of nitrogen dioxide results, causing the eventual complete disintegration of the affected article. Such diseased pieces are terminal and should be quarantined. The button findings and metal embellishments on the examples shown have become rusted due to the chemical reaction of the nitrogen dioxide gases given off by the diseased celluloid. Note the slight trace of verdigris on the left button from the corroded metal button shank.

The combination of metallic substances, such as the goldtone glitter, with cellulose nitrate plastics causes a complex interaction of chemicals during decomposition. The greenish white residue along the seam of this particular piece is believed to be nitric and sulfuric acid residue, combined with verdigris, the greenish corrosion from brass- or copper-based metals.

The formation of a thin film of acid droplets can be seen on this ivory grained box lid. It is as if the celluloid was "sweating" nitric and sulfuric acid residue. The oily film can be removed with a soft cloth dampened with a mild soap and water solution; the cleaned piece should be dried thoroughly. Skin which comes in contact with the acid should be washed promptly and thoroughly. Again, proper ventilation is essential; this item was stored away in a tight box in the back of a dark closet for an unknown period of time. Several other similar articles in the box were affected with the same condition.

External Sources of Deterioration

The external sources of deterioration in celluloid are environmental conditions. Fortunately, these can be adjusted to slow the degeneration of cellulose nitrate plastics, but it should be understood that even under strict environmental control, chemical breakdown cannot be altogether prevented. The aging process is inevitable for all things, and celluloid in no exception.

The external factors relating to the deterioration of celluloid include exposure to heat, light, moisture, solvents, and stress.

When celluloid is exposed to temperatures higher than 140 degrees Fahrenheit, the structure of the cellulose nitrate and camphor molecules begins to change. The evaporation of camphor molecules is believed to leave CN molecules in concentrated sites, and this accelerates crystal formation.

Since celluloid is a thermoplastic, the shape of finished articles is affected by extreme temperature. If exposed to temperatures above 140 degrees, it will begin to lose form. A hole quicky burns in celluloid after a hot pin test (see caption at right). When exposed to flame, celluloid will burn rapidly.

The results of a hot pin test are damaging to thermoplastics. Celluloid cannot resist the effects of heat and pressure. A hot pin sinks into this slab of imitation ivory with no effort at all. The odor of camphor and a slight puff of smoke are evident upon contact with the pin.

Celluloid is affected by the absorption of ultraviolet light which reduces the chain length of cellulose nitrate molecules. The result of strong light can be seen as yellowing or discoloration. The effect of light degradation can be seen on the lid of this imitation ivory grained hair receiver lid. The article was exposed to intense sunlight at an outdoor flea market for an extended and unknown length of time. When the price tag was removed, the original color of the celluloid was revealed. This should be enough evidence to convince collectors and dealers to protect celluloid articles from constant sunlight.

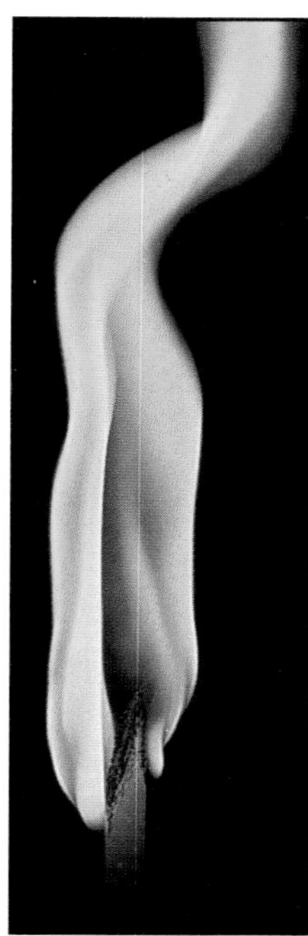

This 4' long strip of cellulose nitrate instrument inlay burned 6" in 18 seconds. Notice the bright, long flame that results from burning the material and inflammable gases that are emitted during combustion.

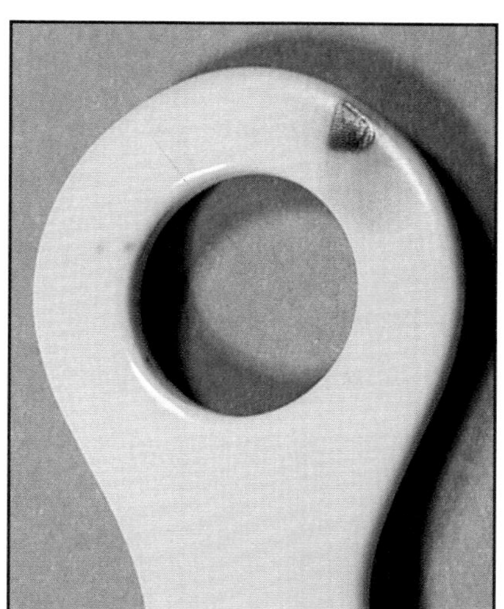

The scorch mark shown on the handle of a shoe horn was probably the result of a smoker who was holding a cigarette while attempting to dress. Before the celluloid began to burn, the person seems to have touched the scorch mark because his fingerprint is embedded in the darkened celluloid.

Due to the normal escape of gases in aging celluloid, its ability to absorb moisture increases. Therefore, it is very important not to soak dirty celluloid items in water. Also, celluloid items that include metal components, rhinestones, or paper should be kept from moisture in order to delay corrosion of metal parts and accelerated deterioration.

The corner of this celluloid covered necktie box is in bad shape. Notice the discoloration under the surface of the celluloid. It appears to be the result of moisture seeping between the plastic laminated cardboard lining.

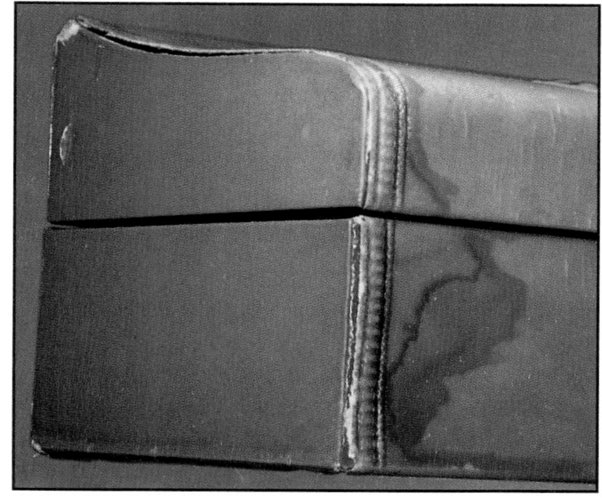

The surface of celluloid objects can be irreversibly marred by a variety of chemical solvents found in common household cleansers. Beware of using hair spray, perfume, nail polish remover, and make-up cleansers around celluloid vanity items. Unfortunately many dresser items have been spotted and discolored when they came into contact with such products. There is no way to clean the stains from items that have been damaged in this manner.

The lovely decoration on the center top of the necktie box shown here has been damaged by some sort of solvent that ate a hole through the celluloid and seeped into the surrounding paper and cardboard causing discoloration. Because perfume, cologne, and nail polish remover all include celluloid solvents, it is important to keep even a small drop from contact with celluloid or irreversible damage will result.

The chemical reaction of the adhesive or dye on the back of the price tag stuck to this item has darkened the color of the celluloid. Buyers should request that sellers carefully remove the price tag before purchasing an expensive item, as the celluloid may be damaged underneath.

One of the most common types of celluloid-related damage is due to stress. Often small blow-molded toys were dented from children dropping them or playing with them. Note the difference in the two rabbits shown here. The only way to repair such damage is to carefully split the item open along the seam, soften the damaged area in hot water, and gently reform the dented area. The seam can be rejoined by the application of a tiny bit of nitrocellulose-based glue or acetone. It should be understood that this method does not always work and the surface paint could be removed or marred.

Sometimes the housing or method of manufacture of a particular celluloid item is responsible for damage, as in the case of this round advertising brush from the Parisian Novelty Co. The paper laminated celluloid was formed over a slightly curved tin disc. Over time, the paper covered celluloid became dry and brittle, then cracked along the slight curve of the housing. The effect is much like the crazing of glaze on china. Once splits form in the surface, environmental factors like heat and humidity have a means to further accelerate the deterioration. Such damage cannot be mended.

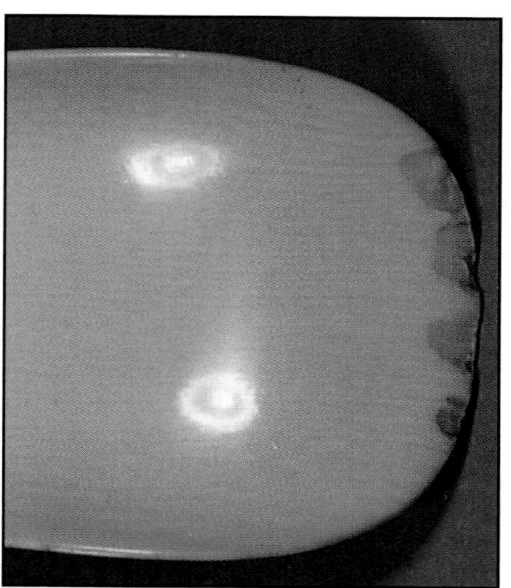

The chipping along the bottom edge of this shoe horn is most likely due to the repeated use of the item. This is an uncommon type of deterioration as most celluloid articles were not used in a consistently aggressive manner.

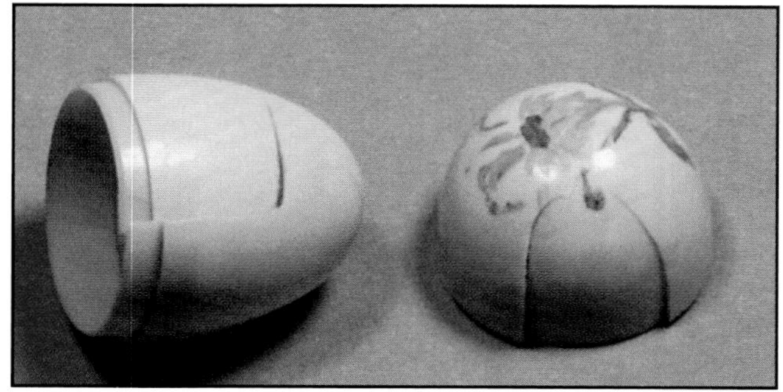

The shape of this tiny egg and the thinness of the celluloid make it susceptible to damage. In order to open the egg, which once held a thimble, one must apply pressure and twist the two halves apart. The stress was just too much for this particular item, and it split in several places.

The solid celluloid wolf head shown here was manufactured in the 1880s by the Celluloid Novelty Co. Note the tiny crack that has appeared along the curved jaw line on the lower center. Over extended periods of time, thick celluloid articles have a tendency to become brittle as the acids and camphor seek to sublime. Also notice the white powdery accumulation in the teeth area, evidence of nitric acid residue that has escaped.

Preservation of Celluloid

Many articles have been written on methods of preserving celluloid items. The best advice that can be given is to carefully inspect items before purchasing them to be sure they are in good condition. Avoid adding diseased pieces to the collection as they will contaminate good articles.

1.) Keep celluloid in a well-ventilated area to avoid the build-up of harmful nitrogen dioxide. In addition to accelerating the deterioration of objects within the vicinity, these gases are highly inflammable.

2.) Refrain from using chemicals, solvents, and detergents to clean celluloid articles. Mild soap and water are all that is needed to remove surface dirt, and a light application of pure vegetable oil is usually sufficient to soften adhesive residue.

3.) Avoid submerging in water items that have metal findings, paper, paint, or other potential areas of decomposition. Likewise, avoid placing celluloid objects in sunlight, high humidity areas, and near flame.

4.) Do not store objects tightly wrapped in plastic wrap but rather use an acid free tissue if possible. Understand that any cellulose based material used for storage (paper, cardboard) has the potential to absorb the acid gases and become nitrated. This poses a serious fire hazard and collectors should keep all high heat and flame from the proximity.

5.) Handle blow-molded articles gently and with care. At times the plastic is so brittle it will shatter into many pieces with the slightest pressure.

Timeline of Celluloid Development 1813 – 1950

1813 Alexander Parkes born on Dec. 29 in Birmingham, England

1832 Daniel Spill born in Gloucestershire on Feb. 11

1837 John Wesley Hyatt, Jr. born Nov. 27, in Starkey, NY

1845 First nitration of cellulose using nitric and sulfuric acids, accomplished by Christian Frederik Schonbein.

1847 Boston chemist, Waldo Maynard discovered that pyroxylin was soluble in a mixture of ether and ethyl alcohol forming a substance he called "collodion."

1862 Alexander Parkes, an Englishman, displayed items made from Parkesine, a cellulose nitrate plastic, at the International Exhibition. Parkes receives a bronze medal for "Excellence of Product."

1863 Phelan and Collender, the leading billiards manufacturer, offers $10,000 reward for the development of a substitute material for ivory in billiard balls. John Wesley Hyatt begins to experiment with various materials in hopes of developing artificial ivory.

1865 Parkesine patented and exhibited at Royal Society of Arts.

1866 Hyatt invents a moldable composition material and along with friend Peter Kinear, begins production of billiard balls at the Hyatt Billiard Ball Co. in Albany, NY.

1866 The Parkesine Co. Ltd. is established at Hackney Wick, London, under the direction of Daniel Spill and Alexander Parkes. Parkes begins to use inferior raw materials in his pyroxylin plastic as a way to lower consumer costs.

1867 Parkesine exhibited at Paris Universal Exhibition.

1868 Parkesine is a commercial failure due to the use of inferior raw materials. The company is liquidated.

1868 Hyatt begins experimentation with solid collodion after accidently discovering a hardened slab of the material one morning in the print shop where he worked. Liquid collodion was used to protect the hands of printers from paper cuts.

1869 John and Isaiah Hyatt of Albany, NY, patent the fundamental invention of pyroxylin plastic and call their material Celluloid, a contraction for the words "cellulose" and "oid," a Greek word meaning "like." (A second explanation states that the word "celluloid" is derived from the combination of the words "collodion" and cellulose.)

1869 The Burroughs Co. is established by Charles Burroughs for the purpose of developing machinery for the manufacture of Hyatt's Celluloid.

1869 Daniel Spill modifies the Parkesine formula and establishes the Xylonite Company in the abandoned Parkesine Works at Hackney Wick.

1870 Hyatt brothers issued patent #105,338 on July 12, 1870 for invention of Celluloid.

1870 The Albany Dental Co. is established at the suggestion of Charles A. Seeley of the American Rubber Co.

1871 The Celluloid Manufacturing Company is formed in Albany, NY, on January 28.

1872 The Celluloid Mfg. Co. moves to a 5-story brick building on Mechanic St. in Newark, NJ. The first injection molding machine for plastics is patented this year.

1873 Celluloid becomes a registered trade name with exclusive rights for use awarded to Hyatt and his company.

1874 Xylonite factory at Hackney Wick in London closes. Daniel Spill relocates to Homerton, London, and establishes Daniel Spill's Ivoride Works to produce pyroxylin plastic.

1874 Imitation coral for use in jewelry patented by Daniel Smith of Syracuse, NY. USP # 150,722

1874 Imitation tortoise shell and amber developed at the Celluloid Mfg. Co.

1874 First use of celluloid in grooming implements by Isaiah and John Hyatt.

1874 Celluloid Novelty Co. licensed to make jewelry items, personal accessories, and novelties from pyroxylin plastic supplied by the Celluloid Mfg. Co.

1875 Devastating fire in September at the Celluloid Mfg. Co. plant in Newark forces relocation to Ferry Street.

1875 First Celluloid plant in England established by Amasa Mason.

1878 Development of sheet celluloid.

1878 License of the Celluloid Hat and Trimming Co.

1878 The Celluloid Shoe Protector Co.

1878 The Celluloid Piano Key Co. USP# 210,780

1878 Celluloid Fancy Goods Co. licensed by Celluloid Mfg. Co.

1878 Joseph R. France of Plainfield, NJ, begins work with nitrocellulose.

1878 Lignoid Fancy Article Co. formed in Newark, NJ.

1878 First German celluloid factory at Offenbach on the Main was Schreiner and Sievers. This was followed by the Berlin firm of Dobler Brothers.

1878 Hyatt patents first multicavity injection mold and also receives a patent for the extrusion method.

1879 Celluloid Veneer Co. established.

1879 Francis Shaw developed the first commercial screw extruder in England.

1880 Inlay of color pigments in Celluloid.

1880 Lignoid Fancy Article Co. of Newark moves to Newburyport, MA, and begins production of pyroxylin plastic.

1880 First German producer of raw celluloid material, Rheinischen Hartgummiwaaren Fabrik, is located in Rheinau.

1880 Celluloid Surgical Instrument Co. formed. John Royle introduced first screw extruder in U.S.

1881 American Zylonite Co. formed by L. L. Brown in North Adams, MA, under license of the British Xylonite Co. Brown, owner of Greylock Paper Mills, hires G. M. Mowbray as chemist to nitrate cellulose from paper.

1881 Merchants Mfg. Co. of Newark, NJ, introduces pyroxylin plastic, trade name Pasbosene.

1881 Patent of celluloid stays for corsets, bustles, hoop skirts and expanders by Marshall C. Lefferts. USP# 238,927

1882 John Henry Stevens, chemist at the Celluloid Co., discovers amyl acetate (banana oil) as a solvent for nitrocellulose.

1882 First celluloid motion picture film produced.

1882 Inlay of color pigments for production of celluloid jewelry.

1883 Development of imitation ivory graining in celluloid. Alternating layers of cream and translucent sheet are compressed into a block, then cut across the grain to produce simulated ivory pattern.

1883 Process of veneering articles with celluloid patented by J.A. McClelland. USP# 271,494

1883 Merchants Mfg. Co. hired Joseph R. France of Plainfield, NJ, and reorganized as the Cellonite Co., moving their pyroxylin plastic works from Newark to Arlington, NJ. The name of Pasbosene was change to Cellonite.

1883 L.L. Brown's pyroxylin plastic works in North Adams, MA, becomes known as the village of Zylonite, complete with a post office. First American Zylonite products are manufactured and marketed by the Zylonite Brush and Comb Co.

1884 Zylonite Collar and Cuff Co., the United Zylonite Co., and Zylonite Novelty Co. are established.

1884 George M. Mowbray of North Adams, MA, is issued U.S. Patent #294,661 for a method of creating pearlescent effects on celluloid by use of ground or flaked mica and soluble pyroxylin (patent filed in Oct. 1883). Prior to this, ground fishscale was used for such effects.

1884 Merging of two MA pyroxylin plastic producers: United Mfg. Co. of Springfield, manufacturer of waterproof cuffs and collars, and the Solid Fiber Co. of Newburyport, makers of sheet celluloid for use in cuffs, collars, and piano keys. The new enterprise is known as Lithoid Corp. and their product is called Fiberlithoid, Lignoid, and Lithoid.

Timeline of Celluloid Development

1885 Cellonite Co. (formerly Merchants Mfg. Co.) of Newark, NJ, reorganizes as the Arlington Mfg. Co. of Arlington, NJ, and renames their pyroxylin plastic Pyralin.

1886 Arlington Collar and Cuff Company is established to manufacture waterproof linen goods from Pyralin.

1887 Daniel Spill dies of diabetes at the age of 55. British Xylonite Co. Ltd. is organized by Amasa Mason and L.P. Merriam and the pyroxylin plastic formula is modified using Hyatt's formulations.

1887 Explosion and fire destroy the Arlington Manufacturing plant, makers of Pyralin.

1887 Printing technique patented for using colored ink on pyroxylin plastics, perfected by Frenchman Albert Roy of La Compagnie Francaise Du Celluloid in Paris. USP #370,546.

1887 Beginning of ornamental comb production in nitrocellulose.

1887 Patent for nitrocellulose photographic film applied for by Reverend Hannibal Goodwin, rector of the House of Prayer in Newark, NJ.

1888 Lithoid Corporation of Newburyport, MA, is taken over by Silas Kenyon and George Tapley and renamed the Fiberloid Corporation of Maine.

1888 Arlington Manufacturing Co. plant is rebuilt and production of Pyralin resumed.

1888 First celluloid eyeglass rims in imitation tortoise, jet, and amber produced.

1888 Process of print transfer on celluloid using pyroxylin solvent; patented by Adolph Bensinger of Mannheim, Germany. USP# 383,272.

1889 Embossing techniques and coating printed paper with translucent sheet celluloid are patented.

1889 Transparent film is introduced by George Eastman and roll cellulose nitrate film replaces glass plates used in photography. Henry Reichenback, employee of Eastman, is issued a patent for nitrocellulose photographic film.

1890 Alexander Parkes dies at the age of 77 on June 29, 1890, in Penrhyn Villa, West Dulwich, England.

1890 American Zylonite Company experiences difficulty due to patent litigation with Hyatt. Over 500 pyroxylin workers lose their jobs and Celluloid becomes known as "the souless Newark concern."

1891 The Celluloid Company of Newark is organized on Jan. 1st by absorbing American Zylonite Co. of North Adams, MA, as well as the Celluloid Mfg. Co.; Celluloid Novelty Co.; Celluloid Brush and Comb Co.; and Celluloid Cuff and Collar Co.

1891 Artificial horn is developed in celluloid.

1891 Arlington Company acquires workers from failed Zylonite Co. and becomes Celluloid's major competitor.

1893 Arlington Mfg. Co. merges with Arlington Collar and Cuff Co. to become the Arlington Company of NJ.

1893 Imitation onyx developed.

1893 Lithoid Corporation of Newburyport reorganized as the Fiberloid Corporation of Maine.

1893 Manufacture of decorative celluloid boxes patented Sept. 26, USP.#505,462 issued to A.C.Hafely and J. Redlefsen.

1894 Cross and Bevan of England issued patent for cellulose acetate.

1898 Fire damages the Arlington Company and plant was rebuilt.

1898 Patent# 610,861 issued to Rev. Hannibal Goodwin for cellulose nitrate photographic film; application had been made in 1887.

1898 Imitation marble developed.

1899 Japanese Camphor Monopoly; camphor, an essential ingredient in the manufacture of celluloid, came from the island of Formosa, which was under Japanese rule. The government of Japan established a monopoly and began to raise the price of export camphor to American pyroxylin plastic manufacturing plants. Aug. 1899, 43.5¢/lb.; Dec. 1899, 51¢/lb.; Jan., 1903, 55 – 60¢/lb.

1899 The first continuous cellulose nitrate photographic film produced by casting pyroxylin on a polished brass roll.

1899 Imitation mosaic, cloisonné and champlevé developed.

1901 Viscoloid Company established by the merger of the Sterling Comb Company and the Harvard Novelty Co., both of Leominster, MA. Founders were Bernard W. Doyle and Alexander Paton, both of Leominster; Paul Rie of Paris and Ludwig Strass of NY. The first sheet of pyroxylin plastic was produced on Dec. 20, 1901. Viscoloid began to produce combs of celluloid.

1902 Patent for setting rhinestones in celluloid is issued to Martin H.Brown of Meriden, CT. USP#714,447

1904 Camphor becomes scarce and expensive in America due to the camphor monopoly becoming an official Japanese entity.

1904 John Chantler of Toronto, Canada, is granted the Canadian agency of the Arlington Company, which later became the Arlington Company of Canada.

1905 Fiberloid Corporation of Newburyport destroyed by fire and a factory rebuilt at Indian Orchard, MA.

1905 Monsanto Chemical Co. of St. Louis, MO incorporated.

1907 F.C. Axtell, former Celluloid Mfg. Co. employee, is commissioned to design and construct a plant to manufacture celluloid at Sakai, Japan, the Sakai Celluloid Company, at a cost of $1,000,000,000.

1908 Due to the Japanese camphor monopoly, the Celluloid Company purchases 5,000 acres of land in Satsuma, FL, to establish a camphor plantation.

1908 Arlington Cuff and Collar Company business peaked.

1911 Fiberloid Corporation becomes the Fiberloid Company of MA, located in Indian Orchard, near Springfield.

1912 Hercules Powder Co. takes over part of E.I. DuPont and produces cellulose nitrate and other pyroxylin products.

1913 Arlington Company of NJ builds a branch factory in Poughkeepsie, NY, to manufacture Pyralin combs, collars, and cuffs.

1913 Arlington Co. formed the Florida Essential Oils Company to raise camphor trees on 12,000 acres of land near Waller, FL. Approximately 5,000 acres of trees were planted and growing when they were attacked by hordes of the thrip insect. The plantation project was abandoned, along with the effort to develop a source of camphor, which was essential to the manufacture of celluloid.

1913 French Ivory dresserware is imported into the U.S. by the French Ivory Products, Ltd. of Toronto, Canada. This Canadian manufacturing company was originally called the Smith d'Entremont Co. and their grained pyroxylin plastic, which was imported from France, carried the trade name Ivoris.

1914 John Wesley Hyatt is awarded the Perkin gold medal by the Society of Chemical Industry.

1914 Fiberloid plant capacity doubled and was responsible for 25% of US production of pyroxyline plastic.

1915 E.I.DuPont acquires the Norwich Paper Co. of Connecticut and the Arlington Company of NJ. DuPont enlarges the plastics manufacturing plant.

1915 Method of fusing two colors of celluloid was developed.

1916 In July a raging fire consumed more than a million pounds of cellulose nitrate scrap at the Arlington plant.

1916 DuPont acquires the celluloid collar manufacturer, A.B. Mitchell of Toronto, Canada.

1917 The Arlington Company is dissolved and their production transferred to E.I.DuPont departments.

1917 Russian artist Naum Gabo constructs modern sculpture Construction Head #3, " Head of a Woman," from Celluloid and metal on wood.

1918 Swiss brothers Henri and Camille Dreyfuss incorporate the American Cellulose and Chemical Manufacturing Co. while working in England. At the request of the American government, a plant for manufacturing cellulose acetate dope to coat the wings of airplanes, is built in Cumberland, MD. The factory is called Amcell.

1919 Pyroxylin Plastics Manufacturing Association formed. Original group consisted of E.I. DuPont Pyralin Department, the Fiberloid Co., the Viscoloid Co., and Celluloid Corporation. Nixon Nitration Works of NJ later joined the association.

1919 The Canadian Explosives Ltd. took over Arlington of Canada from E.I. DuPont.

1920 Celluloid and DuPont abandoned their Florida camphor plantations because of the leaf eating thrip.

1920 John Wesley Hyatt dies of heart failure May 25th in Short Hills, NJ.

1921 Dr. Arthur Eichengruen and Hermann Bucholtz of Germany work together to devise a hand-operated vertical injection molding machine.

1922 Grotelite Co. of IN imports 12 Bucholz injection molding machines from Germany to become the first U.S.A injection molder since J.W. Hyatt.

1922 Irwin Corporation founded in Leominster by Irwin Cohn.

1923 Antoine Pausner, brother of constructionist artist Naum Gabo, creates a second celluloid sculpture, also entitled "Head of a Woman." It is exhibited at the Museum of Modern Art until severe deterioration caused it to be removed.

1924 William Lindsey, chemist with the Celluloid Corporation develops a synthetic pearlescence by applying warm mercury to the surface of celluloid. The technique replaces the ground mica (1884) and fishscale method of pearlizing and is called H-Scale (Hg = Mercury + Scale)

1924 Celluloid x-ray film developed.

1925 Arch-Amerith trademark introduced in dresserware by Celluloid. DuPont purchases the Viscoloid Company in Leominster, MA, and the name changed to DuPont Viscoloid Co., Inc.

1925 Cellulose nitrate lacquers are introduced.

1926 DuPont's Poughkeepsie, NY plant closes with cuff, collar, and rattle production transferred to the Viscoloid plant in MA. DuPont purchases the Pacific Novelty Company of NYC, marketing agents for Viscoloid Company products.

1926 Celanese Corp. acquires controlling stock in Celluloid Corp. and the Celanese Plastics Division is founded. Manufacture of Celluloid in sheet, rod, and tube form continues.

1926 Celanese/Celluloid Corporation develops "Lumarith," a nonflammable cellulose acetate molding material, suitable as an alternative to celluloid.

1926 DuPont introduces a new line of cellulose nitrate dresserware with trademark Lucite. (Later, in the 1930s the name was used to describe acrylic plastics.)

1926 Fiberloid Corp of MA includes 40 buildings and has its own fire department.

1934 Celluloid boasts of over 25,000 product applications.

1938 The Fiberloid Corporation is purchased by Monsanto Chemical Co. of St. Louis, MO.

1941 Celluloid Corporation is fully absorbed into Celanese Corporation.

1941 The Eversharp celluloid "Skyliner" fountain pen, designed by Henri Dreyfus of Celanese, is introduced and becomes a bestseller.

1942 French Ivory Products of Canada begins production of celluloid ping-pong balls.

1946 Nixon Nitration Works of Nixon, NJ, begins production of raw cellulose nitrate.

1948 Production and sales of the Eversharp "Skyliner" fountain pen, the last domestic celluloid pen produced in the U.S., peak.

1949 Celanese Corporation ceases production of celluloid at the Newark, NJ, Ferry Street plant where Celluloid had been made continually for 77 years.

1950 Celluloid trademark dropped by Celanese Corporation.

Manufacturers' Trademarks

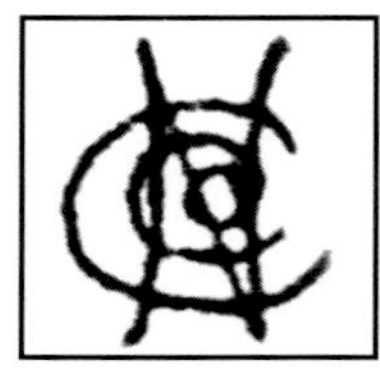

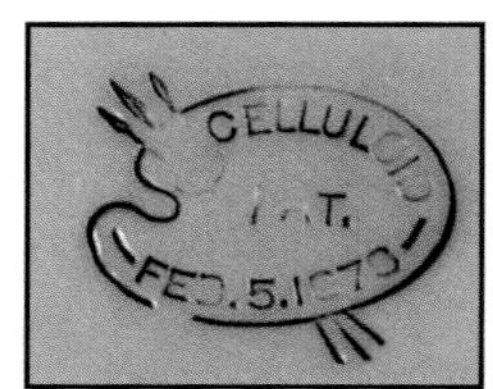

Celluloid Novelty Company, Newark, NJ, 1875 – 1891, intertwined CNCo. artist easel.

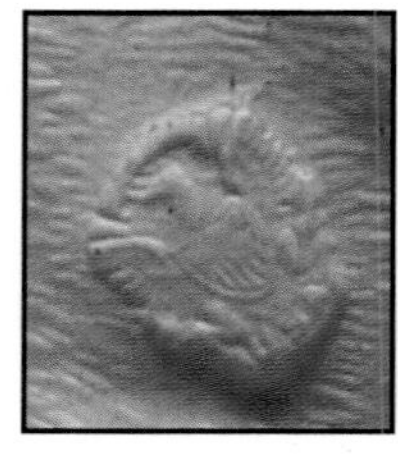

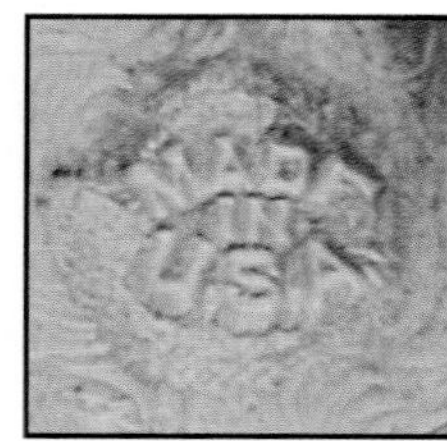

Viscoloid, Leominster, MA 1901 – 1915, spread eagle w/shield; intertwined VCO/USA; VCO/USA in circle w/USA; Made in USA.

American Zylonite, North Adams, MA 1883 – 1889, Arrow Trade Mark.

Celluloid Company, 1920s, Ivaleur; Silvaleur.

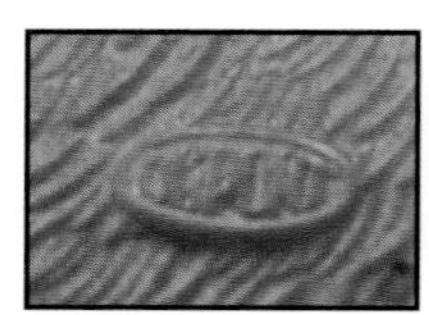

DuPont Viscoloid, Leominster, MA 1915 – 1930s, DuPont oval.

Irwin, Leominster, MA, late 1920s – 1930s, "Irwin" in banner through circle, used on cellulose acetate toys.

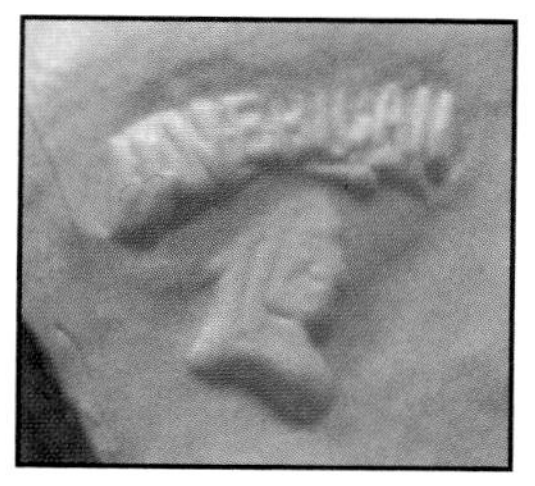

Louis Sametz, New York City, 1918 – 1924, Indian profile w/ "American."

ARLINGTON

"Arlington"

Arlington Manufacturing Company, Arlington, NJ 1881 – 1919, "Arlington;" "Pyralin."

IVORY

FIBERLOID

Fiberloid Corporation, Indian Orchard, MA 1904, "Fiberloid."

Parson-Jackson Co., Cleveland, Ohio, stork trademark.

Dr. Paul Hunaeus, Hanover - Linden, Germany, 1890 – 1930, PH trademark, 1901. "PH" in a diamond after 1901.

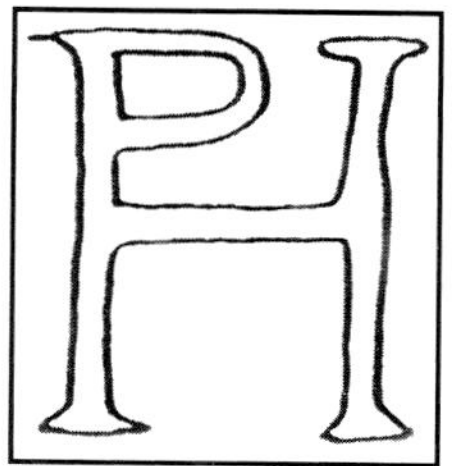

Bushow and Beck, Minerva, Germany 1905 – 1916, Helmet w/"Minerva and Schuttzmarke."

Cellba, Celluloidwarenfabrik, Schoberl and Becker – Badenhausen, Germany, 1923 – 1930, mermaid trademark in shield.

Petitcolin, Paris, Etain and Lilas, France, 1914, eagle head w/"France."

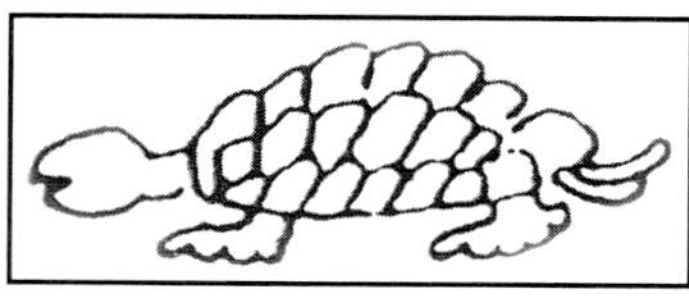

Rheinische Gummi und Cellluloid Fabrik Coi., Germany, turtle; turtle in diamond.

No trademark available

Cascelloid Ltd. England, 1895 – 1940, "Palitoy."

Ando Togoro, Tokyo, Japan, crossed circle trademark

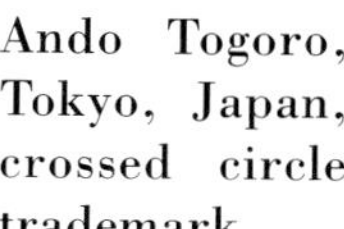

P.R.ZASK, Poland "ASK" in triangle.

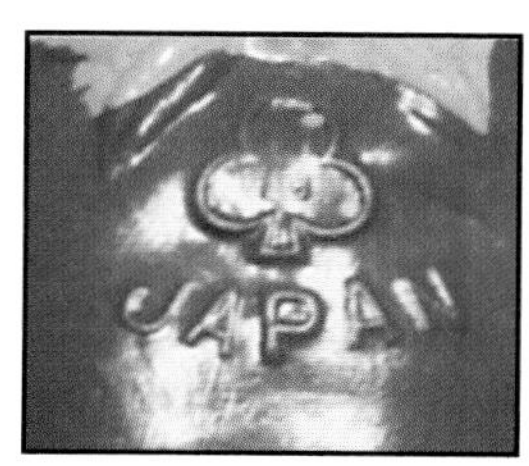

Hasada Minoru, Hasada KK Tokyo, Japan – Club. Nagamine, Japan, club w/no stem; club w/cursive N.

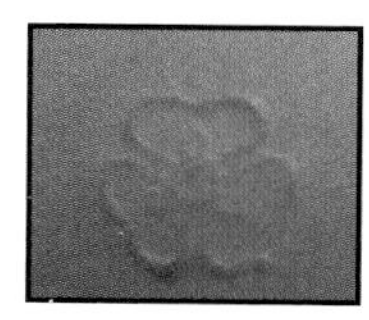

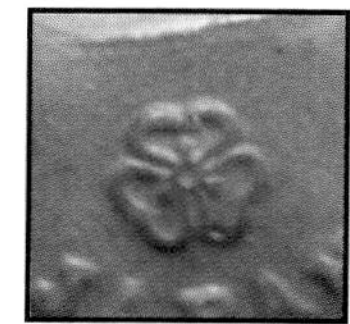

Sekiguchi Co. Ltd., Tokyo, Japan, floral trademark.

Daihachi Kobayashi, Japan, circles in diamond w/top and bottom lines.

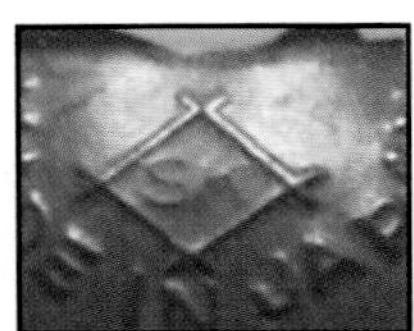

Genroku Sagawa, Tokyo, Japan, SK in diamond w/Made In Japan.

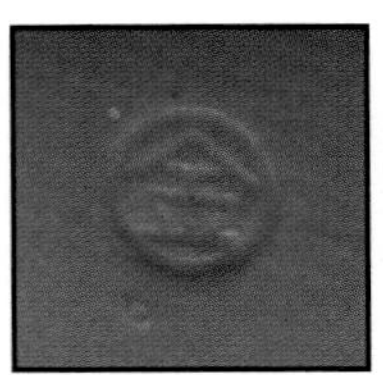

Aiba Kintoro, Marugane, Tokyo, Japan, 1920 – 1930s, house in circle.

Royal Company Ltd., Japan, Fleur-de-lis.

Yoshino Sangyo, Japan, butterfly trademark.

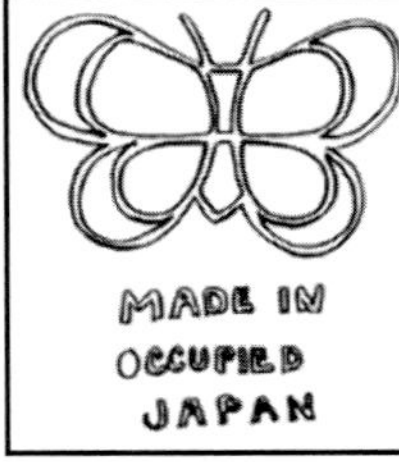

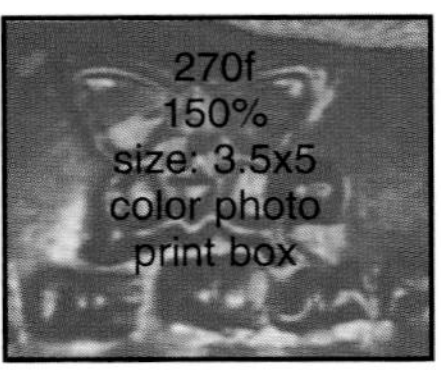

Gonzaburo Takeda, Japan, star in circle.

Daiwazoka Kogyosho Toys, Osaka, Japan, DZK in circle w/flower petals.

Kuramochi, Japan, CK in diamond w/trademark.

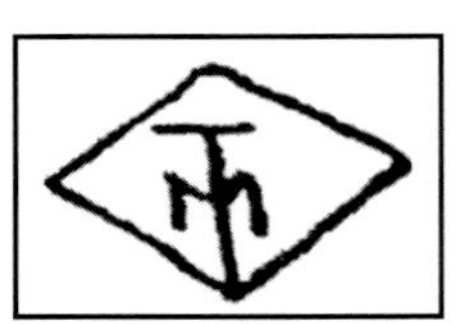

Masudaya, Modern Toys Laboratory, Japan, TM in diamond.

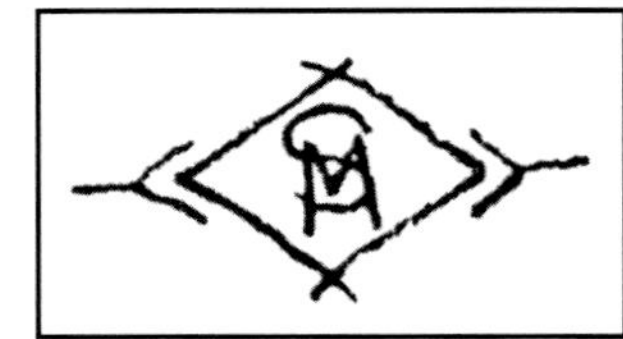

SM Spectacle Co. Ltd., Chiba, Japan, intertwined SM in diamond.

Plastic novelty, Toyo Artificial Flower Mfg. Co. Ltd., intertwined TY in O.

F. Kanematsu and Co., Japan, K in diamond.

Asahi Celluloid, Chori Co. Ltd., intertwined R O in butterfly shape; NKT in keystone; B in circles.

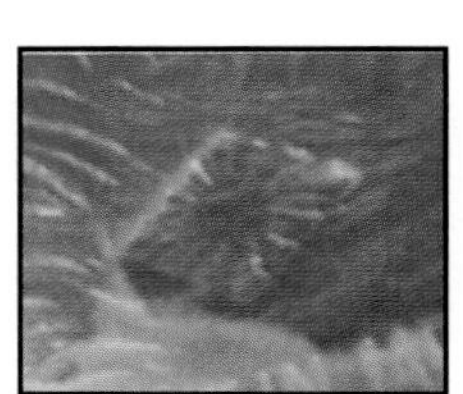

Tsutsunaka Celluloid Co., Ltd., Sunloid, Osaka, Japan, starburst in diamond.

Takigawa Celluloid Co., Ltd, Takicel, Osaka, Japan, stylized figure-8 in circle.

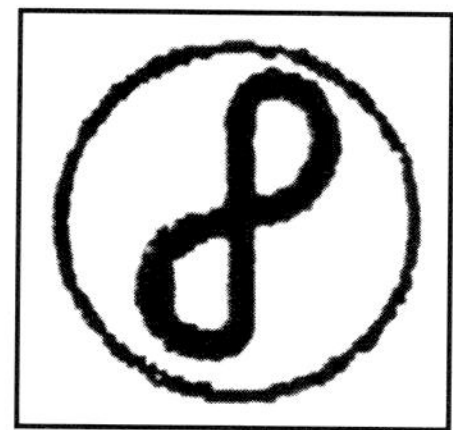

Dainippon Celluloid Co., Ltd., Diacell, Osaka, Japan, KB in pyramid. Iwai Co., Ltd.

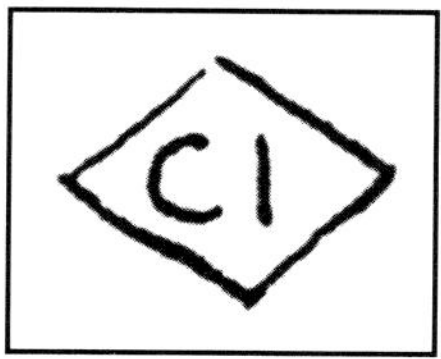

C. Itoh and Co., Ltd., Japan, CI in diamond.

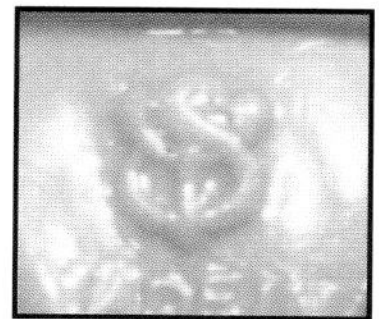

YSP

Togyo Co. Ltd., Tokyo Japan, intertwined YS.

Oriental Celluloid Co. Ltd., Tokyo, Japan.

Onoyoshi Celluloid Co. Ltd., ping-pong balls, script.

TS Industry and Co. Ltd., Osaka, ping-pong balls, TSP.

Nittaku, Japan Table Tennis Ball Co. Ltd., Tokyo, Nittaku NPC.

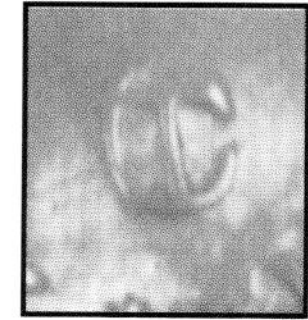

Unidentified Japanese marks.

Taiping Chemical

Unidentified but commonly found mark.

Kogyo Co. Ltd.

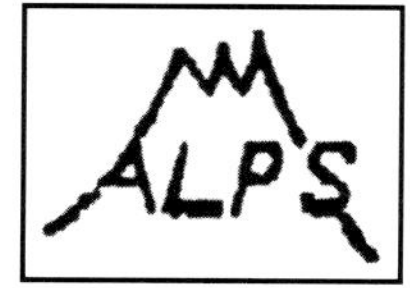

Japan Alps Toy Co., MIOJ.

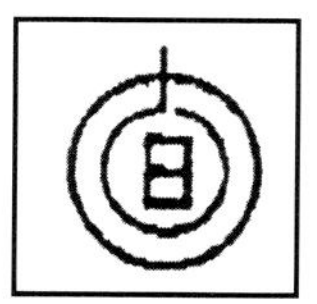

Asahi.

Kokusai Boeki.

Oriental Celluloid Co., Ltd., Tokyo.

Kamematsu.

Manufacturers' Trademarks

Darwa Zoko Kogyosho.

Kuramochi.

F. Kanematsu Co.

Kagyo Co., Ltd.

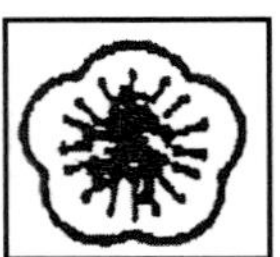

Sekiguchi.

Gonzaburd Takeda.

Asahi Celluloid.

Onoyoshi Celluloid Co.

Towa Optical.

Toyo Menka Kaisha, Ltd., Japan.

Nakatani Celluloid Co.

Miyamoto Optical Co.

Yamomoto Bojin Megane Co.

Sekiguchi Kako.

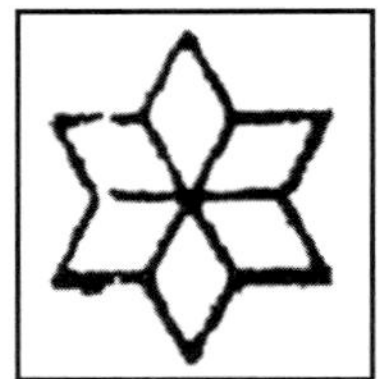

Taiping Chemical.

Marugane.

Masudaya.

Maruni Celluloid Co., Ltd.

Kokusai Bceki, Tokyo.

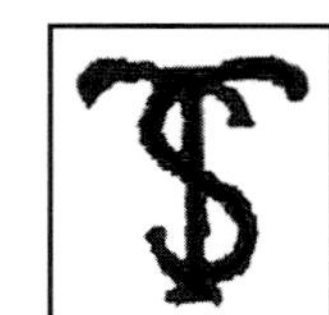

Kokusai Bceki, Tokyo.

Tradenames

for Cellulose Nitrate Plastics

The following list was compiled using information from the National Plastics Center and Museum, the American Plastics History Association, and Celluloid and Nitrocellulose Manufacturers of Japan. The tradenames and manufacturers listed here encompass all areas of cellulose nitrate production including raw pyroxylin plastic material in sheet, rod, and tube form; photographic film; lacquer; and dental products.

Aceloid – American Cellulose
Amerith – Celluloid Corporation, Newark, NJ
Agalyn – J.D.White, Pittsburgh
Alcolite – Alcolite Dental Inc., Pittsburgh
Alino – R.Strauss, Frankfurt, Germany
Artyzan – Celluloid Corporation
Athrombit – FandM Lautenschlager, Munich, Germany
Bexoid – BX Plastics, United Kingdom
Bellaphu – Kalle and Co., Germany
Celastoid – British Celanese
Celastic – Celastic Corporation
Cellobase – Raymond Boisde, Paris, France
Cellon – Germany
Cellonite – Merchant's Mfg. Co.
Celltid – Rheinische Gummi and Celluloid, Germany
Celluloid – The Celluloid Co., Newark, NJ
Celtid – Rhenish Rubber and Celluloid Co., Germany
Celutex – American Celutex Corp.
DiaNippon – Japan
Dentaglene – Canadian Industries Ltd.
Dumold – E.I. DuPont
Exonite – Dover Ltd., UK
Enameloid – Gemloid Corporation
Fiberloid – Fiberloid Corp. Indian Orchard, MA
French Ivory – Canadian
Gemloid – Gemloid Corporation
H-Scale – Celluloid Corporation
Herculoid – Hercules Powder Co.
Hycoloid – Celluplastic Corp.
Ivaleur – Celanese Corp.
Ivoride – Daniel Spill Ivoride Works, Hackney Wick, England
Kodaloid – Eastman Kodak Co.
Lithoid – Lithoid Corporation
Lignoid – Lithoid Corporation
Lusteroid – Lusteroid Container Co.
Lucite – E.I. Dupont Co.
Monsanto CN – Monsanto Chemical Co.
Macoid – Detroit Macoid
Nacara – Fiberloid Corp.
Nixonoid – Nixon Nitration Works, U.S.
Nitron – Monsanto Chemical Company
Novaflex – Belgium
Oralite – Oralite Co. United Kingdom
Parkesine – Alexander Parkes and Daniel Spill, Parkesine Co. Ltd.
Pasbosene – Merchants Mfg. Co.
Pearloid – Joseph H. Meyer Bros., U.S.
Permanite – Parker Pen Co.
Pentex – United Kingdom Plastics Ltd.
Phoenixite – Netherlands
Piroxloid – Piroxloid Products Corp.
Plastine – Miller Co., U.S.
Pyoxyl – Lee S. Smith and Son Mfg. Co.
Pyradiolin – E.I. DuPont
Pyra shell – Shoeform Co.
Pyralin – DuPont Corp., U.S.
Pyrantin – Cellonite Co.
Radite – Schaeffer Pen Co.
Resisto – Cellanese Celluloid Corp.
Rexine – ICI Ltd., United Kingdom
Reliance – Reliance Ltd., United Kingdom
Sunloid – Tsutsunaka Celluloid Co., Osaka, Japan
Viscoloid – Viscoloid Co. Leominster, MA
Venite – Brumel Brothers, United Kingdom
Xylonite – British Xylonite Co.
Zylonite – American Zylonite Co., Adams, MA

Bibliography

Amato, Ivan. *Stuff*, Basic Books: NY, 1997.
Antonelli, Paola. *Mutant Materials in Contemporary Design*, The Museum of Modern Art: NY, 1995.
Becker, Vivienne. *Antique and 20th Century Jewelry*, Van Nostrand Reinhold Co. Inc.: NY, 1982.
Bucholz, Shirley. *A Century of Celluloid Dolls* Hobby House Press, Inc.: Cumberland, MD, 1983.
Dana, Gorham and William D. Milne. *Industrial Fire Hazards* Lakeview Press: Framingham, MA, 1928.
DiNoto. *Art Plastic*, Abbeville Press: NY, 1984.
DuBois, J.Harry. *Plastics History, USA*, Cahners Books: Boston, 1972.
DuBois, J.Harry and Frederic W. Johns. *Plastics*, Reinhold Publishing Corp: NY 1967.
Emerson, Donald W. *Canadian Inventors and Innovators*, Canadian Plastics Pioneers: Toronto, 1978.
Fenichell, Stephan. *Plastics Harper Business*: NY, 1996.
Friedel, Robert. *Pioneer Plastics*, University of Wisconsin Press: Madison, Wisconsin, 1983.
Gerber, Morris. *Old Albany – Vol. 3*, Manufacturing Interest of Albany: Albany, NY, 1971.
Haynes, William. *Cellulose*, Doubleday and Co., Inc.: NY, 1953.
Hoover, Will. *Picks*, Miller Freeman Books: San Francisco, 1995.
Katz, Sylvia. *Plastics, Common Objects, Classic Designs*, Harry Abrams, Inc.: NY, 1944.
_______. *Plastic Designs and Material*, Studio Vista: London, England, 1978.
_______. *Early Plastics*, Shire Publications Ltd.: Aylesbury, England, 1986.
_______. *Classic Plastics*, Thames and Hudson: London, England, 1984.
Kaufman, M. *The First Century of Plastics*, The Plastics Institute: London, England, 1966.
Landmarks of the Plastics Industry, Imperial Chemical Industries: Ltd. England.
McEnery, John J. *Albany Capital City on the Hudson:* 1981.
Meikle, Jeffery I. *American Plastic*, Rutgers University: New Brunswick, NJ, 1995.
Merriam, John. *Pioneering in Plastics*, East Anglian Magazine: Ipswich, Suffolk, England 1976.
Masselon, Roberts, and Cillard. *Celluloid*, translated from the French by Hodgson, Herbert, H.; Charles Griffin and Co. Ltd.: London, England, 1912.
Morgan, John. *Conservation of Plastics*, Plastics Historical Society: London, 1991.
Mossman, Susan, T.I. and P.J.T. Morris. *The Development of Plastics*, The Royal Society of Chemistry: Cambridge, England, 1994.
Mossman, Susan. *Early Plastics*, Leicester University Press: London, England 1997.
Slosson, Edwin E. *Creative Chemistry*, Garden City Publishing: Garden City, NY, 1919.
Smithsonian Institution. *The Smithsonian Book of Invention*, W.W. Norton and Co.: NY, NY, 1978.
Sparke, Penny. *The Plastics Age*, The Overlook Press: Woodstock, NY, 1992.
Wakeman, Reginald L. *The Chemistry of Commercial Plastics*, Reinhold Publishing Corp.: NY, 1947.
Worden, Edward Chauncey. *The Nitro-Cellulose Industry*, D.Van Nostrand Co.: NY, 1911, two volumes.

Catalogs and Magazines

B. Shackman catalog, 1924
Sears, Roebuck and Co. catalog, 1897 and 1900
Charles Williams Store catalog, 1922
Munsey's Magazine, 1897, 1901, 1911
Cosmopolitan, 1898
Hampton's Magazine, 1904
Hearth and Home, 1918
McClure's Magazine, 1899, 1903
Harper's Weekly, 1881
Scientific American, 1912
Plastics Magazine, various articles
Arlington, Celluloid, and Fiberloid dresserware catalogs, 1915 – 1933

Other Publications (not used for this book):

Celluloid Collectibles, ID and Value Guide, Shirley Dunn.
Victorian Treasures, Joan Van Patten.

Index

COLLECTOR BOOKS

Informing Today's Collector

For over two decades we have been keeping collectors informed on trends and values in all fields of antiques and collectibles.

DOLLS, FIGURES & TEDDY BEARS

4707 A Decade of **Barbie** Dolls & Collectibles, 1981–1991, Summers $19.95
4631 **Barbie** Doll Boom, 1986–1995, Augustyniak $18.95
2079 **Barbie** Doll Fashion, Volume I, Eames $24.95
4846 **Barbie** Doll Fashion, Volume II, Eames $24.95
3957 **Barbie** Exclusives, Rana $18.95
4632 **Barbie** Exclusives, Book II, Rana $18.95
4557 **Barbie,** The First 30 Years, Deutsch $24.95
4847 **Barbie** Years, 1959–1995, 2nd Ed., Olds $17.95
3310 **Black Dolls,** 1820–1991, Perkins $17.95
3873 **Black Dolls,** Book II, Perkins $17.95
3810 **Chatty Cathy Dolls,** Lewis $15.95
1529 Collector's Encyclopedia of **Barbie** Dolls, DeWein $19.95
4882 Collector's Encyclopedia of **Barbie** Doll Exclusives and More, Augustyniak $19.95
2211 Collector's Encyclopedia of **Madame Alexander Dolls,** Smith $24.95
4863 Collector's Encyclopedia of **Vogue Dolls,** Izen/Stover $29.95
3967 Collector's Guide to **Trolls,** Peterson $19.95
4571 **Liddle Kiddles,** Identification & Value Guide, Langford $18.95
3826 Story of **Barbie,** Westenhouser $19.95
1513 **Teddy Bears & Steiff** Animals, Mandel $9.95
1817 **Teddy Bears & Steiff** Animals, 2nd Series, Mandel $19.95
2084 **Teddy Bears, Annalee's & Steiff** Animals, 3rd Series, Mandel $19.95
1808 Wonder of **Barbie,** Manos $9.95
1430 World of **Barbie** Dolls, Manos $9.95
4880 World of **Raggedy Ann** Collectibles, Avery $24.95

TOYS, MARBLES & CHRISTMAS COLLECTIBLES

3427 **Advertising Character** Collectibles, Dotz $17.95
2333 Antique & Collector's **Marbles,** 3rd Ed., Grist $9.95
3827 Antique & Collector's **Toys,** 1870–1950, Longest $24.95
3956 Baby Boomer **Games,** Identification & Value Guide, Polizzi $24.95
4934 **Breyer Animal** Collector's Guide, Identification and Values, Browell $19.95
3717 **Christmas** Collectibles, 2nd Edition, Whitmyer $24.95
4976 **Christmas** Ornaments, Lights & Decorations, Johnson $24.95
4737 **Christmas** Ornaments, Lights & Decorations, Vol. II, Johnson $24.95
4739 **Christmas** Ornaments, Lights & Decorations, Vol. III, Johnson $24.95
4649 Classic Plastic **Model Kits,** Polizzi $24.95
4559 Collectible **Action Figures,** 2nd Ed., Manos $17.95
3874 Collectible Coca-Cola Toy **Trucks,** deCourtivron $24.95
2338 Collector's Encyclopedia of **Disneyana,** Longest, Stern $24.95
4958 Collector's Guide to **Battery Toys,** Hultzman $19.95
4639 Collector's Guide to **Diecast Toys & Scale Models,** Johnson $19.95
4651 Collector's Guide to **Tinker Toys,** Strange $18.95
4566 Collector's Guide to **Tootsietoys,** 2nd Ed., Richter $19.95
4720 The Golden Age of **Automotive Toys,** 1925–1941, Hutchison/Johnson $24.95
3436 Grist's Big Book of **Marbles** $19.95
3970 Grist's Machine-Made & Contemporary **Marbles,** 2nd Ed. $9.95
4723 **Matchbox** Toys, 1947 to 1996, 2nd Ed., Johnson $18.95
4871 **McDonald's Collectibles,** Henriques/DuVall $19.95
1540 **Modern Toys** 1930–1980, Baker $19.95
3888 **Motorcycle** Toys, Antique & Contemporary, Gentry/Downs $18.95
4953 Schroeder's Collectible **Toys,** Antique to Modern Price Guide, 4th Ed. $17.95
1886 Stern's Guide to **Disney** Collectibles $14.95
2139 Stern's Guide to **Disney** Collectibles, 2nd Series $14.95
3975 Stern's Guide to **Disney** Collectibles, 3rd Series $18.95
2028 **Toys,** Antique & Collectible, Longest $14.95
3979 **Zany Characters** of the Ad World, Lamphier $16.95

FURNITURE

1457 American **Oak** Furniture, McNerney $9.95
3716 American **Oak** Furniture, Book II, McNerney $12.95
1118 Antique **Oak** Furniture, Hill $7.95
2271 Collector's Encyclopedia of **American** Furniture, Vol. II, Swedberg $24.95
3720 Collector's Encyclopedia of **American** Furniture, Vol. III, Swedberg $24.95
3878 Collector's Guide to **Oak** Furniture, George $12.95
1755 Furniture of the **Depression Era,** Swedberg $19.95
3906 **Heywood-Wakefield** Modern Furniture, Rouland $18.95
1885 **Victorian** Furniture, Our American Heritage, McNerney $9.95
3829 **Victorian** Furniture, Our American Heritage, Book II, McNerney $9.95

JEWELRY, HATPINS, WATCHES & PURSES

1712 Antique & Collector's **Thimbles** & Accessories, Mathis $19.95
1748 Antique **Purses,** Revised Second Ed., Holiner $19.95
1278 Art Nouveau & Art Deco **Jewelry,** Baker $9.95
4850 Collectible **Costume Jewelry,** Simonds $24.95
3875 Collecting Antique **Stickpins,** Kerins $16.95
3722 Collector's Ency. of **Compacts, Carryalls & Face Powder Boxes,** Mueller ..$24.95
4854 Collector's Ency. of **Compacts, Carryalls & Face Powder Boxes,** Vol. II $24.95
4940 **Costume Jewelry,** A Practical Handbook & Value Guide, Rezazadeh $24.95
1716 Fifty Years of Collectible **Fashion Jewelry,** 1925–1975, Baker $19.95
1424 **Hatpins** & Hatpin Holders, Baker $9.95
4570 Ladies' **Compacts,** Gerson $24.95
1181 100 Years of Collectible **Jewelry,** 1850–1950, Baker $9.95
4729 **Sewing Tools** & Trinkets, Thompson $24.95
2348 20th Century Fashionable Plastic **Jewelry,** Baker $19.95
4878 Vintage & Contemporary **Purse Accessories,** Gerson $24.95
3830 Vintage **Vanity Bags & Purses,** Gerson $24.95

INDIANS, GUNS, KNIVES, TOOLS, PRIMITIVES

1868 Antique **Tools,** Our American Heritage, McNerney $9.95
1426 **Arrowheads** & Projectile Points, Hothem $7.95
4943 Field Guide to **Flint Arrowheads & Knives** of the North American Indian $9.95
2279 **Indian Artifacts** of the Midwest, Hothem $14.95
3885 **Indian Artifacts** of the Midwest, Book II, Hothem $16.95
4870 **Indian Artifacts** of the Midwest, Book III, Hothem $18.95
1964 **Indian Axes** & Related Stone Artifacts, Hothem $14.95
2023 **Keen Kutter** Collectibles, Heuring $14.95
4724 Modern **Guns,** Identification & Values, 11th Ed., Quertermous $12.95
2164 **Primitives,** Our American Heritage, McNerney $9.95
1759 **Primitives,** Our American Heritage, 2nd Series, McNerney $14.95
4730 Standard **Knife** Collector's Guide, 3rd Ed., Ritchie & Stewart $12.95

PAPER COLLECTIBLES & BOOKS

4633 **Big Little Books,** Jacobs $18.95
4710 Collector's Guide to **Children's Books,** Jones $18.95
1441 Collector's Guide to **Post Cards,** Wood $9.95
2081 Guide to Collecting **Cookbooks,** Allen $14.95
2080 Price Guide to **Cookbooks & Recipe Leaflets,** Dickinson $9.95
3973 **Sheet Music** Reference & Price Guide, 2nd Ed., Pafik & Guiheen $19.95
4654 **Victorian Trade Cards,** Historical Reference & Value Guide, Cheadle $19.95
4733 **Whitman Juvenile Books,** Brown $17.95

GLASSWARE

4561 Collectible **Drinking Glasses,** Chase & Kelly $17.95
4642 Collectible **Glass Shoes,** Wheatley $19.95
4937 Coll. **Glassware from the 40s, 50s & 60s,** 4th Ed., Florence $19.95
1810 Collector's Encyclopedia of **American Art Glass,** Shuman $29.95
4938 Collector's Encyclopedia of **Depression Glass,** 13th Ed., Florence $19.95
1961 Collector's Encyclopedia of **Fry Glassware,** Fry Glass Society $24.95
1664 Collector's Encyclopedia of **Heisey Glass,** 1925–1938, Bredehoft $24.95
3905 Collector's Encyclopedia of **Milk Glass,** Newbound $24.95
4936 Collector's Guide to **Candy Containers,** Dezso/Poirier $19.95
4564 **Crackle Glass,** Weitman $19.95
4941 **Crackle Glass,** Book II, Weitman $19.95
2275 **Czechoslovakian Glass** and Collectibles, Barta/Rose $16.95
4714 **Czechoslovakian Glass** and Collectibles, Book II, Barta/Rose $16.95
4716 **Elegant Glassware** of the Depression Era, 7th Ed., Florence $19.95
1380 Encylopedia of **Pattern Glass,** McClain $12.95
3981 Ever's Standard **Cut Glass** Value Guide $12.95
4659 **Fenton** Art Glass, 1907–1939, Whitmyer $24.95
3725 **Fostoria,** Pressed, Blown & Hand Molded Shapes, Kerr $24.95
4719 **Fostoria,** Etched, Carved & Cut Designs, Vol. II, Kerr $24.95
3883 **Fostoria Stemware,** The Crystal for America, Long & Seate $24.95
4644 **Imperial Carnival Glass,** Burns $18.95
3886 **Kitchen Glassware** of the Depression Years, 5th Ed., Florence $19.95

COLLECTOR BOOKS

Informing Today's Collector

4725 Pocket Guide to **Depression Glass,** 10th Ed., Florence $9.95
5035 Standard Encyclopedia of **Carnival Glass,** 6th Ed., Edwards/Carwile $24.95
5036 Standard **Carnival Glass** Price Guide, 11th Ed., Edwards/Carwile $9.95
4875 Standard Encyclopedia of **Opalescent Glass,** 2nd ed., Edwards $19.95
4731 **Stemware Identification,** Featuring Cordials with Values, Florence $24.95
3326 **Very Rare Glassware** of the Depression Years, 3rd Series, Florence $24.95
4732 **Very Rare Glassware** of the Depression Years, 5th Series, Florence $24.95
4656 **Westmoreland Glass,** Wilson $24.95

POTTERY

4927 **ABC Plates & Mugs,** Lindsay $24.95
4929 **American Art Pottery,** Sigafoose $24.95
4630 **American Limoges,** Limoges $24.95
1312 **Blue & White Stoneware,** McNerney $9.95
1958 So. Potteries **Blue Ridge Dinnerware,** 3rd Ed., Newbound $14.95
1959 **Blue Willow,** 2nd Ed., Gaston $14.95
4848 Ceramic **Coin Banks,** Stoddard $19.95
4851 Collectible **Cups & Saucers,** Harran $18.95
4709 Collectible **Kay Finch,** Biography, Identification & Values, Martinez/Frick $18.95
1373 Collector's Encyclopedia of **American Dinnerware,** Cunningham $24.95
4931 Collector's Encyclopedia of **Bauer Pottery,** Chipman $24.95
3815 Collector's Encyclopedia of **Blue Ridge Dinnerware,** Newbound $19.95
4932 Collector's Encyclopedia of **Blue Ridge Dinnerware,** Vol. II, Newbound $24.95
4658 Collector's Encyclopedia of **Brush-McCoy Pottery,** Huxford $24.95
2272 Collector's Encyclopedia of **California Pottery,** Chipman $24.95
3811 Collector's Encyclopedia of **Colorado Pottery,** Carlton $24.95
2133 Collector's Encyclopedia of **Cookie Jars,** Roerig $24.95
3723 Collector's Encyclopedia of **Cookie Jars,** Book II, Roerig $24.95
4939 Collector's Encyclopedia of **Cookie Jars,** Book III, Roerig $24.95
4638 Collector's Encyclopedia of **Dakota Potteries,** Dommel $24.95
5040 Collector's Encyclopedia of **Fiesta,** 8th Ed., Huxford $19.95
4718 Collector's Encyclopedia of **Figural Planters & Vases,** Newbound $19.95
3961 Collector's Encyclopedia of **Early Noritake,** Alden $24.95
1439 Collector's Encyclopedia of **Flow Blue China,** Gaston $19.95
3812 Collector's Encyclopedia of **Flow Blue China,** 2nd Ed., Gaston $24.95
3813 Collector's Encyclopedia of **Hall China,** 2nd Ed., Whitmyer $24.95
3431 Collector's Encyclopedia of **Homer Laughlin China,** Jasper $24.95
1276 Collector's Encyclopedia of **Hull Pottery,** Roberts $19.95
3962 Collector's Encyclopedia of **Lefton China,** DeLozier $19.95
4855 Collector's Encyclopedia of **Lefton China,** Book II, DeLozier $19.95
2210 Collector's Encyclopedia of **Limoges Porcelain,** 2nd Ed., Gaston $24.95
2334 Collector's Encyclopedia of **Majolica Pottery,** Katz-Marks $19.95
1358 Collector's Encyclopedia of **McCoy Pottery,** Huxford $19.95
3963 Collector's Encyclopedia of **Metlox Potteries,** Gibbs Jr. $24.95
3837 Collector's Encyclopedia of **Nippon Porcelain,** Van Patten $24.95
2089 Collector's Ency. of **Nippon Porcelain,** 2nd Series, Van Patten $24.95
1665 Collector's Ency. of **Nippon Porcelain,** 3rd Series, Van Patten $24.95
4712 Collector's Ency. of **Nippon Porcelain,** 4th Series, Van Patten $24.95
1447 Collector's Encyclopedia of **Noritake,** Van Patten $19.95
3432 Collector's Encyclopedia of **Noritake,** 2nd Series, Van Patten $24.95
1037 Collector's Encyclopedia of **Occupied Japan,** 1st Series, Florence $14.95
1038 Collector's Encyclopedia of **Occupied Japan,** 2nd Series, Florence $14.95
2088 Collector's Encyclopedia of **Occupied Japan,** 3rd Series, Florence $14.95
2019 Collector's Encyclopedia of **Occupied Japan,** 4th Series, Florence $14.95
2335 Collector's Encyclopedia of **Occupied Japan,** 5th Series, Florence $14.95
4951 Collector's Encyclopedia of **Old Ivory China,** Hillman $24.95
3964 Collector's Encyclopedia of **Pickard China,** Reed $24.95
3877 Collector's Encyclopedia of **R.S. Prussia,** 4th Series, Gaston $24.95
1034 Collector's Encyclopedia of **Roseville Pottery,** Huxford $19.95
1035 Collector's Encyclopedia of **Roseville Pottery,** 2nd Ed., Huxford $19.95
4856 Collector's Encyclopeida of **Russel Wright,** 2nd Ed., Kerr $24.95
4713 Collector's Encyclopedia of **Salt Glaze Stoneware,** Taylor/Lowrance $24.95
3314 Collector's Encyclopedia of **Van Briggle** Art Pottery, Sasicki $24.95
4563 Collector's Encyclopedia of **Wall Pockets,** Newbound $19.95
2111 Collector's Encyclopedia of **Weller Pottery,** Huxford $29.95
3876 Collector's Guide to **Lu-Ray Pastels,** Meehan $18.95
3814 Collector's Guide to **Made in Japan** Ceramics, White $18.95
4646 Collector's Guide to **Made in Japan** Ceramics, Book II, White $18.95
4565 Collector's Guide to **Rockingham,** The Enduring Ware, Brewer $14.95
2339 Collector's Guide to **Shawnee Pottery,** Vanderbilt $19.95
1425 **Cookie Jars,** Westfall $9.95
3440 **Cookie Jars,** Book II, Westfall $19.95
4924 Figural & Novelty **Salt & Pepper Shakers,** 2nd Series, Davern $24.95
2379 Lehner's Ency. of **U.S. Marks** on Pottery, Porcelain & China $24.95
4722 **McCoy Pottery,** Collector's Reference & Value Guide, Hanson/Nissen $19.95
3825 **Purinton Pottery,** Morris $24.95
4726 **Red Wing Art Pottery,** 1920s–1960s, Dollen $19.95
1670 **Red Wing Collectibles,** DePasquale $9.95
1440 **Red Wing Stoneware,** DePasquale $9.95
1632 **Salt & Pepper Shakers,** Guarnaccia $9.95
5091 **Salt & Pepper Shakers** II, Guarnaccia $18.95
2220 **Salt & Pepper Shakers** III, Guarnaccia $14.95
3443 **Salt & Pepper Shakers** IV, Guarnaccia $18.95
3738 **Shawnee Pottery,** Mangus $24.95
4629 Turn of the Century **American Dinnerware,** 1880s–1920s, Jasper $24.95
4572 **Wall Pockets** of the Past, Perkins $17.95
3327 **Watt Pottery** – Identification & Value Guide, Morris $19.95

OTHER COLLECTIBLES

4704 Antique & Collectible **Buttons,** Wisniewski $19.95
2269 Antique **Brass & Copper** Collectibles, Gaston $16.95
1880 Antique **Iron,** McNerney $9.95
3872 Antique **Tins,** Dodge $24.95
4845 Antique **Typewriters & Office Collectibles,** Rehr $19.95
1714 **Black** Collectibles, Gibbs $19.95
1128 **Bottle** Pricing Guide, 3rd Ed., Cleveland $7.95
4636 **Celluloid Collectibles,** Dunn $14.95
3718 Collectible **Aluminum,** Grist $16.95
3445 Collectible **Cats,** An Identification & Value Guide, Fyke $18.95
4560 Collectible **Cats,** An Identification & Value Guide, Book II, Fyke $19.95
4852 Collectible **Compact Disc** Price Guide 2, Cooper $17.95
2018 Collector's Encyclopedia of **Granite Ware,** Greguire $24.95
3430 Collector's Encyclopedia of **Granite Ware,** Book 2, Greguire $24.95
4705 Collector's Guide to **Antique Radios,** 4th Ed., Bunis $18.95
3880 Collector's Guide to **Cigarette Lighters,** Flanagan $17.95
4637 Collector's Guide to **Cigarette Lighers,** Book II, Flanagan $17.95
4942 Collector's Guide to **Don Winton Designs,** Ellis $19.95
3966 Collector's Guide to **Inkwells,** Identification & Values, Badders $18.95
4947 Collector's Guide to **Inkwells,** Book II, Badders $19.95
4948 Collector's Guide to **Letter Openers,** Grist $19.95
4862 Collector's Guide to **Toasters** & Accessories, Greguire $19.95
4652 Collector's Guide to **Transistor Radios,** 2nd Ed., Bunis $16.95
4653 Collector's Guide to **TV Memorabilia,** 1960s–1970s, Davis/Morgan $24.95
4864 Collector's Guide to **Wallace Nutting Pictures,** Ivankovich $18.95
1629 **Doorstops,** Identification & Values, Bertoia $9.95
4567 Figural **Napkin Rings,** Gottschalk & Whitson $18.95
4717 Figural **Nodders,** Includes Bobbin' Heads and Swayers, Irtz $19.95
3968 **Fishing Lure** Collectibles, Murphy/Edmisten $24.95
4867 **Flea Market Trader,** 11th Ed., Huxford $9.95
4944 **Flue Covers,** Collector's Value Guide, Meckley $12.95
4945 **G-Men and FBI Toys** and Collectibles, Whitworth $18.95
5043 **Garage Sale & Flea Market Annual,** 6th Ed. $19.95
3819 **General Store Collectibles,** Wilson $24.95
4643 **Great American West** Collectibles, Wilson $24.95
2215 Goldstein's **Coca-Cola** Collectibles $16.95
3884 Huxford's Collectible **Advertising,** 2nd Ed. $24.95
2216 **Kitchen Antiques,** 1790–1940, McNerney $14.95
4950 The **Lone Ranger,** Collector's Reference & Value Guide, Felbinger $18.95
2026 **Railroad** Collectibles, 4th Ed., Baker $14.95
4949 **Schroeder's Antiques Price Guide,** 16th Ed., Huxford $12.95
5007 **Silverplated Flatware,** Revised 4th Edition, Hagan $18.95
1922 Standard **Old Bottle** Price Guide, Sellari $14.95
4708 Summers' Guide to **Coca-Cola** $19.95
4952 Summers' Pocket Guide to **Coca-Cola** Identifications $9.95
3892 **Toy & Miniature Sewing Machines,** Thomas $18.95
4876 **Toy & Miniature Sewing Machines,** Book II, Thomas $24.95
3828 Value Guide to **Advertising Memorabilia,** Summers $18.95
3977 Value Guide to **Gas Station** Memorabilia, Summers & Priddy $24.95
4877 Vintage **Bar Ware,** Visakay $24.95
4935 The W.F. Cody **Buffalo Bill** Collector's Guide with Values $24.95
4879 **Wanted to Buy,** 6th Edition $9.95

This is only a partial listing of the books on antiques that are available from Collector Books. All books are well illustrated and contain current values. Most of these books are available from your local bookseller, antique dealer, or public library. If you are unable to locate certain titles in your area, you may order by mail from COLLECTOR BOOKS, P.O. Box 3009, Paducah, KY 42002-3009. Customers with Visa, Discover or MasterCard may phone in orders from 7:00–5:00 CST, Monday–Friday, Toll Free 1-800-626-5420. Add $2.00 for postage for the first book ordered and $0.30 for each additional book. Include item number, title, and price when ordering. Allow 14 to 21 days for delivery.

Schroeder's ANTIQUES Price Guide

. . . is the #1 best-selling antiques & collectibles value guide on the market today, and here's why . . .

8½ x 11, 612 Pages, $12.95

- *More than 450 advisors, well-known dealers, and top-notch collectors work together with our editors to bring you accurate information regarding pricing and identification.*

- *More than 45,000 items in almost 550 categories are listed along with hundreds of sharp original photos that illustrate not only the rare and unusual, but the common, popular collectibles as well.*

- *Each large close-up shot shows important details clearly. Every subject is represented with histories and background information, a feature not found in any of our competitors' publications.*

- *Our editors keep abreast of newly developing trends, often adding several new categories a year as the need arises.*

If it merits the interest of today's collector, you'll find it in *Schroeder's*. And you can feel confident that the information we publish is up to date and accurate. Our advisors thoroughly check each category to spot inconsistencies, listings that may not be entirely reflective of market dealings, and lines too vague to be of merit. Only the best of the lot remains for publication.

Without doubt, you'll find
SCHROEDER'S ANTIQUES PRICE GUIDE
the only one to buy for
reliable information and values.

COLLECTOR BOOKS
A Division of Schroeder Publishing Co., Inc.